MARKETING

MARKETING
A Critical Textbook

Nick Ellis, James Fitchett, Matthew Higgins, Gavin Jack, Ming Lim, Michael Saren and Mark Tadajewski

Los Angeles | London | New Delhi
Singapore | Washington DC

First published 2011

SAGE Publications Ltd
1 Oliver's Yard
55 City Road
London EC1Y 1SP

SAGE Publications Inc.
2455 Teller Road
Thousand Oaks, California 91320

SAGE Publications India Pvt Ltd
B 1/I 1 Mohan Cooperative Industrial Area
Mathura Road
New Delhi 110 044

SAGE Publications Asia-Pacific Pte Ltd
33 Pekin Street #02-01
Far East Square
Singapore 048763

Library of Congress Control Number: 2010922904

British Library Cataloguing in Publication data

A catalogue record for this book is available from
the British Library

ISBN 978-1-84860-877-1
ISBN 978-1-84860-878-8 (pbk)

Typeset by C&M Digitals (P) Ltd, Chennai, India
Printed in Great Britain by CPI Antony Rowe, Chippenham, Wiltshire
Printed on paper from sustainable resources

Contents

Author Biographies

Nick Ellis is Senior Lecturer in Critical Marketing at the University of Leicester School of Management. His research focuses on inter-organisational relationships and managerial identity construction. He has also written on relationship marketing, industrial networks, supply chain ethics, and professional services marketing. Nick's discursive approach positions him productively between the disciplines of marketing and organisation studies. His journal publications include *Industrial Marketing Management, Journal of Marketing Management, Marketing Theory* and *Journal of Strategic Marketing,* as well as *Organization Studies, Human Relations* and *Organization.* He is co-editor of the Sage Major Work *Business-to-Business Marketing,* and author of the textbook *Business-to-Business Marketing: Relationships, Networks and Strategies.*

James Fitchett is Reader in Consumption and Marketing at the University of Leicester School of Management where he delivers a course in Marketing Theory. His research interests are in critical approaches to marketing, cultural theory and consumption. His research papers cover themes including marketing discourse, consumption symbolism and commodification. He was managing editor of *the Journal of Consumer Behaviour* from 2006–9 and has published work in *the Journal of Marketing Management, European Journal of Marketing, Marketing Theory* and *Consumption, Markets and Culture.*

Matthew Higgins is Senior Lecturer in Marketing and Consumption at the University of Leicester School of Management. Matthew has been extensively involved in the management and delivery of both full time and distance learning modes of study for undergraduate and postgraduate students. Originally trained as a sociologist, Matthew's research has been concerned with the interfaces between social issues, public institutions and marketing. This has included projects on science fiction and marketing (Routledge), social marketing and child adoption (*Business Ethics: A European Review*), Fair Trade and Cause Related Marketing (*Business and Society*) and the morality of relationship marketing theory and supply chain management (*Journal of Marketing Management*).

Gavin Jack is Professor of Management at the Graduate School of Management, La Trobe University, Australia. He teaches and researches in the areas of international and diversity management, cross-cultural communication, postcolonial organisational analysis and consumer culture. His publications include a special issue of the *Academy of Management Review* on international management (2008, 33: 4), and two co-authored books: (with Alison Phipps) *Tourism and Intercultural Exchange: Why Tourism Matters* (2005, Channel View publications); and (with Robert Westwood) *International and Cross-Cultural Management Studies: A Postcolonial Reading* (2009, Palgrave Macmillan).

Ming Lim is Lecturer in Global Branding and Branding and Communications at the University of Leicester School of Management. Her research interests are in consumer culture theory, ethics, critical and literary theory, political marketing and higher education marketing. She publishes in the areas of critical business ethics and philosophy (*Business Ethics: A European Review*), the marketing of leadership in Higher Education (*Journal of Marketing Management*), literary and postmodern theory, digital marketing and on critical consumption. She is Chair of the Organising Committee for the Academy of Marketing Corporate Brand, Reputation and Corporate Identity SIG and organised the conference in 2007, 2008 and 2010.

Michael Saren is Professor of Marketing at the University of Leicester School of Management. His research covers the marketing of technology, critical marketing, consumer culture and marketing theory. He is a founding editor of the journal *Marketing Theory* and co-editor of *Rethinking Marketing* (Sage, 1999). He has been a member of the organising committee for the European Association of Consumer Research conferences in 2005, 2007 and 2010 and one of a team who ran the ESRC Seminar Series and edited a book on *Critical Marketing: Defining the Field* (Elsevier, 2007). His introductory text is *Marketing Graffiti: The View from the Street* (Butterworth Heinemann, 2006)

Mark Tadajewski is Lecturer in Critical Marketing in the School of Management at the University of Leicester. His primary research interests are the history of marketing thought, the paradigm debates in marketing, critical marketing studies and globalisation and its impact on marketing theory. His research has appeared in *Organization, Journal of Marketing Management, Journal of Macromarketing, Marketing Theory* and the *Journal of Historical Research in Marketing* among others. He is the editor of six Sage Major Works including *Critical Marketing Studies* (with P. Maclaran) and the *History of Marketing Thought* (with D.G.B. Jones), along with a number of other recently published or forthcoming books.

Roll up! Roll up! 'Companion website' this way ...

Marketing provides a range of benefits to the world but is associated with a variety of unintended and unwanted side effects on wider society at the same time. Developing a course to highlight this is, of course, no easy task. Since we believe that it is extremely important that our students leave our institutions with an ability to study marketing theory and practice from multiple perspectives, we have tried to make such course development as easy as possible.

To make interpretations of 'critical marketing' more accessible to you, the companion website contains case studies, seminar materials and video links that can help inform theory ad practice. In providing these we hope they assist students in undertaking original studies in a fascinating area of social and economic life. We hope our approach is fresh, original and thought provoking and enhances your use of the textbook. You will find all of the material on the companion website at www.sagepub.co.uk/ellis

Introduction

Today, the study of marketing has truly global appeal. The number of courses and degrees in marketing offered at schools, colleges and universities across the globe has skyrocketed over the last two decades. Such a thirst for knowledge means that bookshelves are now filled with a large number of marketing textbooks. You are likely to be already familiar with certain 'set texts' (or 'prescribed reading') on marketing theory and practice. Most of them, we dare say, aim to inform and educate you about key marketing concepts and strategies and cover a wide range of topics such as branding, marketing communications and so on.

We might evaluate these observations as an indication that the field and study of marketing is in healthy shape. In the twenty-first century more people are interested in studying marketing than ever before and all kinds of organisations appear to show a desire to employ people with marketing expertise, skills and knowledge. It might be of some surprise therefore to discover that many marketers, and this includes marketing academics and marketing professionals, express serious and fundamental reservations about the state of marketing today.

Some senior marketing professors (such as Evert Gummesson, 2009) and marketing executives are genuinely worried that marketing is not delivering all that it promises to deliver. A growing number of academic marketers take the view that much of the classic body of marketing knowledge has severe flaws and limitations and that we urgently need to rethink and re-examine the purpose, scope and contribution that marketing science can and should be making. Professionals involved with the operation and delivery of marketing programmes are anxious to secure a voice for marketers in organisations, at a time when many business commentators are questioning the actual value of the contribution that marketers can and do make. These concerns are fundamental and wide-ranging. They bring into question the very purpose of marketing: Who is marketing for? What can marketing really do? What should be the priorities for marketing scholars and students?

If this general disquiet about the current state of marketing is at all credible, and we share and discuss many of these criticisms throughout this book, then we also need to ask what type of knowledge is useful, relevant and valid for students of marketing today. Perhaps if marketing is in a kind of crisis we need to urgently examine whether new tools, different approaches, and alternative perspectives might offer a necessary and viable way forward. Our overriding objective in this book is to offer a different way for students to look at and understand marketing.

This is easy to say. Indeed you might say that it sounds like an advertising slogan. But we take the view that an alternative perspective is really important and necessary. This is not to suggest that all marketing knowledge and all marketing textbooks are wrong or misplaced. Marketing science developed very rapidly over the last 50 years and this has helped to shape the way that organisations operate and function. But we do need to evaluate this existing knowledge much more rigorously now, by placing marketing ideas in an appropriate historical and cultural context, and by assessing them in broader analytical terms. In short, we need to become critical marketers – open to new, often unfamiliar perspectives, and be prepared to ask penetrating and fundamental questions about the type of marketing knowledge that is relevant today.

This is, then, a very different kind of book. We believe that the study of marketing is immensely valuable and rewarding because it is *a way of looking at the world or worlds we live in*. We would like to think, therefore, that this book demonstrates this view in different ways, through different perspectives, different writing styles and different philosophical assumptions. We hope that this approach would thus have a significant impact upon your learning about marketing, and, perhaps, allow you to think differently about it, in ways which other books may not so readily encourage. Developing this alternative view of marketing should make you stand out from the crowd – an increasingly large crowd – when you enter the job market. You probably want to be equipped with marketing knowledge and graduate with a good degree in marketing so that you can enhance your career potential in professional marketing practice, or perhaps in academic research. We think this book could provide you with a cutting edge for both.

Accordingly, the book you hold in your hands gives you an opportunity to develop an *interdisciplinary* understanding and appreciation of the nature of marketing theory and practice. It does so by drawing on the insights and research available from multiple academic disciplines, not so much the typical resources of behavioural economics or psychology that inform the mainstream of marketing and consumer research (Reibstein et al., 2009). Instead, the book draws upon important interdisciplinary resources that can lend the subject of marketing considerable intellectual excitement and strength: sociology, philosophy, linguistics, the visual and performing arts, literature, psychology, history and so on. From this perspective, the study of marketing should not just be about giving you a toolkit of concepts and strategies to apply in the examination hall or at the workplace, it can inform your everyday life.

Let us now explain what we are trying to do by writing this book and what this means for you.

Chapters and Themes

There are 11 chapters in total. These 11 chapters can be roughly organised into four themes. Be aware, however, that:

- There are a number of ideas and concerns that continue right the way through all the chapters in the book;
- There are a number of ideas that intersect and are discussed in different ways in particular chapters throughout the book;
- In your own reading of the different chapters, you will make connections between the chapters that breach our rough template here (and this is a good thing!).

As such, the outline of these four key themes is simply intended to provide you with a provisional understanding of the structure of the book as a whole.

Theme One: Marketing History

This broad theme can be found most strongly in Chapters 1–5. These chapters discuss the political, economic and cultural forces which have shaped the field of marketing over time, both as an academic discipline as well as a practice which governs corporations and consumers. A key concern here is to give you a picture of how marketers gather information about the consumer and how he or she responds to those practices. We also introduce you at this early stage to important concepts of marketing theory which are relevant to all your studies of marketing in the future, and, indeed, to the study of the social sciences in general. Thus, you are introduced to research 'paradigms' or models such as the 'positivist', or 'critical-theoretical' paradigms, as well as the impact of postmodern thought on marketing theory.

Crucially, you should realise that some of these paradigms – like 'positivism', for instance – are shaped by 'real' world events in political history (such as the Cold War between the US and the USSR after the Second World War), the pressures of which forced universities in the United States to promote and defend a certain way of conducting research. These themes are specifically covered in Chapters 1, 2 and 3 and they encourage you, by implication, NOT to think 'of marketing as a homogenous, almost universally applicable concept, transcending cultures as well as contexts' (Cannon, 1980: 140) (we will come back to this quotation in Chapter 1). Marketing comprises a set of concepts and practices, as well as an ideology that has a very particular history and is rooted in very particular cultural contexts – those of the USA and Western Europe, and associated values of individualism, rationalism, and a belief in science and progress.

But the world has changed, and this change is wide-ranging. The ideological struggles of the post-Cold War period have left their legacy on the economy and politics but this influence is waning. Globalisation, technology, the internet, population mobility, deregulation, climate change, consumerism, and many other themes occupy the headlines now and in part shape and define our experiences today. Marketing is part of all of these developments, and the priorities of marketing science are also changed by them. And as such, marketing knowledge must embrace these issues and others like them in a full and detailed way. It is not enough to simply append these themes to the existing frameworks and models, to update them like a kind of on-going brand extension exercise. The way that conventional marketing knowledge represents the world of marketing might be basically incompatible with these new realities. Adhering to established principles, albeit slightly modified, might prevent marketers from making real and substantial progress on the subject.

This theme also covers something many students are curious about: What do marketing managers actually *do*? Chapters 4 and 5 invite you to reconsider the role of the marketing manager as something which is constructed by managers; that is, managers have particular views of the 'market' or 'markets' they work in and, over time, they develop a certain expertise which is then confirmed by the market as 'legitimate' or 'professional'. We show how certain marketing concepts, like the 'marketing mix' and 'marketing planning and control' become codified into a powerful body of knowledge which is then communicated as organisationally necessary for something called 'marketing' to take place.

Across a number of chapters you will come across the word 'discourse'. This is a complex term in the social sciences, and can mean a number of different things. In this book, the authors use it in two distinct ways. In Chapters 3 and 4, we talk about various discourses of marketing. What we are referring to here are the ways in which particular understandings or representations of marketing, and its concepts (like the marketing mix, or marketing planning) were constructed with reference to the particular values and material practices of the wider knowledge systems and institutional contexts in which they developed historically. In Chapter 6, the word discourse is mainly used in a different sense. It does not so much refer to the broader systems of thought in which marketing came to the fore. Instead, it refers to the everyday practices of representation of marketing managers and consumers. Discourse here is conceived in terms of performing speech acts – that is, each time we use language, we are creating and enacting a particular version of the world that brings into being its concepts (like that of marketing) and enables us to intervene and behave in a particular way. Chapter 5 makes use of both these understandings of discourse.

Theme Two: The Business of Marketing and Consumer Behaviour

This theme corresponds (more or less) to Chapters 6 through to 9 of the book (though 8 and 9 also intersect with the third theme). It encompasses a broad view of how markets work in practice, nationally and internationally, and how customers act in the market. Chapter 6, for example, examines how organisations do their marketing to, and with, each other. This relationship is normally characterised as 'Business-to-Business' (B2B) marketing. B2B marketing is particularly important in a globalised economy where large companies as well as small to medium-sized enterprises trade across networks, marketing channels and supply chains which span countries and continents. The well-known brand mark, Fairtrade, is an exemplary case of how supply chains come together to support a global initiative in 'ethical' trading.

Chapter 7 tackles an increasingly important area of consumer research: surveillance. We take a good look at the notion of surveillance and analyse how it has evolved through time and become accepted as a marketing practice. Seeking to know more about one's customers is now a highly institutionalised activity for companies and an indispensable tool in every marketer's armoury. We examine the practices of marketing research in the twenty-first century, the techniques which are used for measuring and tracking buyer behaviour and new product development and what this means for the 'surveillance culture' we live in. Does this mean for example, that, as consumers, our behaviours, thoughts and paths through life are mapped out, prescribed and controlled by marketers? Chapters 8 and 9 demonstrate that this is hardly the case. Instead, we highlight how people are active in the varied processes of consumption (purchasing, display, re-use, collection etc.), not just passively consuming the products and messages developed by omnipotent marketing managers.

Theme Three: Society and Identity

Chapters 5, 8 and 9 traverse themes two and three. Whilst chapters 8 and 9 examine consumers' identities on the level of the individual and explore what philosophers, linguists and novelists can show us about how the individual 'self' or 'identity' is constructed via acts of consumption (in the symbolic sense of the term), Chapter 5 looks at marketing managers' identities. In Chapter 9, for instance, we probe more deeply into some of the concepts which were introduced in earlier chapters and now begin to ask questions such as: 'what' or 'who' is the self which consumes? What can non-marketing texts (such as novels, films and other forms of 'high' and 'low' culture) reveal about our behaviour as consumers? Why and how are consumers more complex than we think?

These chapters look at some of these questions through concepts drawn from linguistics, sociology and philosophy. In the same way that earlier chapters will argue for how and why certain practices of marketing (and marketing managers) become widely accepted or taken-for-granted in our world today, the study of signs or 'semiology' in Chapter 10 argues for how and why 'signs' or 'images' or 'words' and so on (a dress on a model or a slogan in an advertising campaign, for instance) are acceptable in certain cultures and not others, or at certain times and not others.

Theme Four: Taking A Global and Ethical View of Marketing

We turn, in the ultimate chapter of the book, to a macro or global view of the world of marketing. In a time of extremely serious environmental challenges, financial crises and worsening inequalities around the world, marketers are called upon to re-evaluate and reflect upon how products, services and the chains of supply and demand you have now studied are produced, consumed, bought and sold. Questions of ethics and social responsibility dominate the news and throw new light upon the practices and beliefs of the boards of companies, their shareholders, customers, employees and suppliers.

A Critical Marketing Approach

Although the word 'ethical' is listed in the title of Theme Four above, it does in fact comprise a principal element in the continuing theme that runs throughout this 'critical' marketing textbook. The central belief that runs throughout the book is the notion that a *'critical-ethical' orientation* should be central to marketing education in the twenty-first century. We take this view to be much broader than current debates on corporate social responsibility (CSR) or business ethics: it involves an understanding of marketing as an integral part of what excites, provokes and inspires the hearts, minds, values and emotions of diverse, sometimes mutually antagonistic groups of people: political leaders, environmental activists, business people, teachers, students ... the list goes on. One of our key aims in writing this book is to remain committed to just such a 'critical-ethical' project. By 'ethical', we mean, amongst other things, demonstrating that as humans we have responsibilities for the recognition and well-being of others. Marketing is a system of ideas and practices that draws people together into a set of mutually overlapping relationships. That is to say, whilst marketing is a key social context for ethical conduct, the ethical codes and moral complexes of different cultures also impact upon how marketing is conducted and understood.

To demonstrate and share this commitment, many chapters of the book draw attention to how marketing practice and thought is infused with some of our greatest challenges: the effects of globalisation and its impact upon international markets; climate change; the 'ethics' and 'politics' of manufacturing, producing, consuming and distributing goods, commodities and services to different markets; the challenges to global corporations as well as smaller companies posed by customers' demands for fairer systems of trade which benefit developing countries and how companies and consumers confront emerging rules on data capture, collection and surveillance. Chapters 4, 6, 7, 8, 10 and 11 are particularly focused on these themes, although the book as a whole is informed by an acute awareness of the challenges of 'marketing ethics'.

Indeed, the study of marketing (or marketing education) is itself a choice which has a moral dimension to it. While 2008 may well go down in history as one of the worst years in recent world economic history. The years to come will, hopefully, be remembered as a time when all business practitioners were forced to reflect upon the choices which can still be made in a post-global financial crisis world. It is, perhaps, still too soon to draw conclusions from the lessons of the global financial crisis, but we believe that a new generation of students in marketing can add their voices to the debates around social responsibility and a moral sensitivity to emerging issues in marketing education.

This is not to say that these points or criticisms of marketing are new. There is a long history, as you shall read in Chapters 1 and 2, of criticism of marketing as a professional (and sometimes unprofessional) practice, as well as a cultural ideology. Criticism of advertising, for example, was widespread in the eighteenth and nineteenth century (McFall, 2004) and accelerated throughout the twentieth and twenty-first centuries. By contrast, marketing has also been depicted as providing consumers with access to the products and services that they need, at the right place, correct time and appropriate price points, whilst communicating product information in ways that interested and amused the customer (Alderson, 1934; Hopkins, 1927/1997). This is not to say that such scholars and commentators believed that the marketing system could not be improved or that it benefitted all equally. For example, founding members of the discipline such as the German Historical School (Jones and Monieson, 1987/2008) were most definitely interested in issues of distributive justice. This related to the idea that those participating in the distribution system, such as farmers, should receive a fair premium for their products and that the ultimate consumer should still be able to buy products at a fair, rather than extortionate, price. Similar interests in distributive justice continue to motivate the work of the 'macromarketing' and 'critical marketing' schools of thought today.

The activities of early members of the marketing community were thought to undermine consumer reason and rationality (Fromm, 1956/2005; Veblen, 1919/2005). For adherents of this viewpoint, marketing and advertising communications mislead the consumer into buying products that offered little or no additional benefit over those already found in the marketplace or occupying space in the consumer's cupboard (Veblen, 1919/2005). At a general level, marketing and salesmanship were claimed to be largely pointless activities that distracted people from pursuing more developmental and beneficial pastimes (Fromm, 1956/2005; Marcuse, 1966). These criticisms continue in new forms today, only now commentators refer not just to the development of 'marketing orientations' by people (Fromm, 1956/2005), whereby they deliberately shape their personalities, knowledge and skills in line with the requirements of the marketplace. They also note how people are being redefined on the basis of their medical and mental health (this is termed a process of 'medicalisation') by corporations with huge marketing budgets that aim to maximise their investments in expensive research and development for drugs, by further expanding the market for what are often quite harmful products, to greater and greater numbers of the population (Applbaum, 2009).

So, when we talk about this text adopting a critical marketing approach, although the label critical marketing is relatively new, dating back to the early 1980s, we believe that a critical–ethical approach has always been important to marketing academics and practitioners. To be sure, interest in distributive justice and ethics waxes and wanes depending on the economic climate and governmental and legislative interest in marketplace activities. Nevertheless such a focus constitutes a running theme throughout the history of marketing thought, from its inception as an academic discipline in the early twentieth century all the way to the present. Cementing this 'critical–ethical' perspective has been the publication of a number of recent explicitly 'critical marketing' texts (e.g. Hackley, 2009; Saren et al., 2007; Tadajewski and Brownlie, 2008; Tadajewski and Maclaran, 2009a, 2009b, 2009c), as well as calls by prominent journal editors for much more research on critical–ethical issues and marketing practice (Shultz, 2007) and special issues of academic journals on this topic (see also Brownlie et al., 1999; Firat et al., 1987).

What Will I Get Out of Studying This Book Carefully and Systematically?

You might be asking yourself this question by now. We can think of at least four things.

1   A strong understanding of how to think critically and independently about traditional concepts. Each chapter focuses on various definitions of marketing – 'marketing concepts', 'marketing knowledge', 'marketing management' and so on – and also shows how they can be questioned in terms of their assumptions and practical impact.

2   An idea about how marketing relates to other vital issues in the field of management and business studies, and, indeed, to our lives today. Every serious student of management is, rightly, concerned with 'headline issues' such as globalisation, business ethics, consumer rights, privacy and surveillance. This book provides a creative and ethical engagement with these issues through the lens of marketing. Instead of trying to master these topics independently of each other we offer what we hope is a fruitful alternative: seeing how marketing scholars describe these concepts and how they are applied in different contexts.

3   A new vocabulary and perspective drawn from different fields of study and a diversity of writing styles: business history and social theory (Chapters 2 and 3), literature and media studies (Chapter 9), linguistics (Chapter 10) just to name a few. The presentation of ideas and the ways in which they are argued are designed to offer imaginative thinking about conventional concepts. The presentation is achieved by using a number of different styles of writing that reflect the tone of these different fields of thought. We hope that in reading our text, you can avoid the 'McDonaldized' (Ritzer, 2001) experience of reading other, more conventional textbooks on marketing.

4   Putting all these together, an intellectual edge over others when going for jobs (be it in marketing, consulting, management), and especially when pursuing a research career.

How Should I Go About Studying This Book Carefully and Systematically?

You have already started off in the best way possible – by reading this introduction! Most students tend not to bother reading textbook introductions. However, they are key not only for explaining what is in the book, but also for understanding how best to approach the book's various features. When beginning to work on a new chapter, a good idea is to start by reading the introduction and the conclusion first. This strategy ought to enable you to understand where you are supposed to get to after reading the chapter, and what the final outcome actually looks like. It should provide you with a working framework for doing the reading.

When you come across a word that you do not understand in a chapter, first see whether it is defined in the glossary at the end of the book. If it is, you should spend some time reading and trying to understand the glossary definition, and perhaps do a little more research about the concept. The word you do not understand may not however be a glossary entry, in which case you will need to have a good dictionary, and possibly also a thesaurus on your bookshelf.

Finally, make sure to engage in all the learning activities set at the end of each chapter, and complete the further readings (paying particular attention to the short comments we have made about each reading). In terms of the latter task, you should make this part of a 'reading strategy' (see below) which you should devise not only for reading this book, and the module/unit for which it has been recommended, but for application across all the work you are doing.

What Should I Read?

Many students ask us for practical guidance on what kind of journals, papers, books and so on they should read in order to do well in the subject. Every chapter in this book provides information on further readings but a few other basic pointers may come in useful at this stage.

First, see your librarian as soon as you can. They are knowledgeable and helpful professionals who only want to assist you so use them often! Explain that you are a marketing student and that you would like them to show you how to use the resources on offer at your institution. Also begin by becoming familiar with the digital databases and marketing reports provided by consultancies, e-publishers and research organisations. These might include EBSCO, SWETS, Mintel reports, Euromonitor, Reuters and so on.

Second, and in this regard, there are numerous high-quality journals on marketing. They all generally cater to specific academic communities within the broad discipline of marketing – such as the *Journal of Marketing*, the *Journal of Marketing Research* – or those which reflect cultural, geographic, demographic interests (e.g. the *European Journal of Marketing*, the *Journal of International Marketing*, the *Asian Journal of Marketing* and the *Asia-Pacific Journal of Marketing*). Others appeal to researchers working within various industry sectors (e.g. *Journal of Financial Services Marketing*, *Journal of Sport Marketing* and so on). Still others focus on specific branches of scholarly research. Those of you seeking information on B2B marketing and globalisation/international business, for example, may well find *Industrial Marketing Management* and *International Marketing Review* useful. Marketing communications research can be found in the *International Journal of Advertising*.

Given the critical and ethical orientation of this textbook, we would particularly recommend that you consult the following journals when looking for reading materials:

- *Marketing Theory*
- *Journal of Macromarketing*
- *Journal of Marketing Management*
- *European Journal of Marketing*
- *Consumption, Markets and Culture*
- *Journal of Consumer Research*

- *Journal of Public Policy and Marketing*
- *Journal of Historical Research in Marketing*
- *Human Relations*
- *Journal of Management Studies*
- *Organization and Environment*

Third, try to read at least two journal articles every week. This is likely to represent quite a new experience for many of you who are perhaps much more used to memorising (rather than critically applying learning from) textbooks. At university, especially in the UK context, however, you are expected to undertake independent research and to study in a new way, questioning, investigating and exploring information from academically rigorous sources. Academic journals in virtually every field of study in modern universities represent just such a source of up-to-date research by academics and practitioners. It is vital, therefore, that you get used to reading them.

Fourth, you should (if you are not already) get into the habit of reading good quality journalism either in print or on the web. Most of the world's best media can be accessed freely or quite cheaply now thanks to the internet, so you can access the BBC, *The New York Times, The Washington Post* etc. Don't be afraid to explore influential blogs and to listen to a high-quality radio news programme. This is a necessity simply because marketing – as, indeed, all business disciplines – is a 'live' discipline: it is a dynamic, evolving field of activity and study which draws on current affairs in the worlds of business, industry, finance, innovation and strategy. Most students fail to do this simple exercise and are sometimes, therefore, woefully out of touch with how companies deal with marketing issues, such as how branding affects consumers' perceptions or how emerging technologies affect the marketing choices available to managers in every industry.

Newspapers are one of the best sources of such information. In the UK, students have access to the *Financial Times*, the *Guardian* and its supplements throughout the week. *The Economist* also represents a high-quality, broad-coverage and international publication that surveys developments in economic, political, social, cultural and environmental affairs. There are also a number of trade publications which feature the latest news on corporate strategies in advertising, PR, media, corporate communications, job postings and useful career advice. Leading titles like *BrandRepublic, B2B Marketing, PRWeek, Event, OMMA* and others are all well worth taking an occasional look at.

In-Chapter Materials and Activities

As noted earlier, the diversity of styles in which this textbook is written, as well as the complexity of much of the material, means that this book is likely to be a challenging, but hopefully rewarding read. To address these challenges, the book contains a number of pedagogical features – basically materials and activities to help you understand things better.

- **In-Text Boxes:** The title and content of these in-text boxes will differ according to the point being made. Sometimes you will be given some statistics and numbers to demonstrate or elaborate a point. In other boxes, you will have an explanation of a core concept or a short example of a corporation or a group of consumers to illustrate a theme from the text.

- **Glossary**: At the end of the book, the glossary provides brief and accessible definition of key terms used in the book. You should view these glossary definitions merely as a starting point for gaining an understanding of what they refer to, and do some more reading and research around them.
- **Further Readings**: You should ensure that you complete all the further readings, as these will help you refine your knowledge of key ideas and concepts from the chapters in more detail.
- **Learning Activities**: Found at the end of each chapter.

The *Learning Activities* are very important. They are offered to enable you to subject ideas and themes from the book to further research and enquiry. They are designed to lead you from the pages of the book, to provoke thought, and to develop your personal research and analytical skills.

The learning activities build from the aims for the chapter. These broad aims are outlined in the Introduction of each section. Each activity will require time and energy to complete satisfactorily. No doubt you would like to know how much work is involved and how long you should allow. Unfortunately, it is not possible to set a precise duration for each activity, but in general most activities can be completed in about two hours. Do remember before you begin the learning activities to remind yourself of the learning aims for the chapter so that your time and efforts are focused.

Before you get started with the learning activities at the end of this Introduction, we wish you all the very best for your studies and hope you will enjoy this textbook.

Nick Ellis
James Fitchett
Matthew Higgins
Gavin Jack
Ming Lim
Mike Saren
Mark Tadajewski

Learning Activities

Learning Activity One: How Different is 'Different'?

There are a number of influential accounts of marketing in the highly competitive textbook market. Some of the key authors in the field include Professor Philip Kotler, Dr Frances Brassington and Dr Stephen Pettitt, Professor Charles Lamb and Professor Michael Solomon. Each of these authors has produced best-selling and authoritative accounts of marketing. The authors of this textbook claim to be positioning the book as 'different' to conventional marketing textbooks. The aim of this learning activity is to establish how the textbook you are reading now is positioned relative to the competition and what marks this book out from others in this market.

You are encouraged to visit your library and to browse the table of contents and introductory chapters of books by two or more of these authors. Look carefully at the organisation of each of these books, the themes covered, the tone that the author is adopting and the overall objectives of the book. Compare and contrast the different styles. What's different about this one?

Learning Activity Two: Rebirth and the Global Financial Crisis

This book was written over a period that included the global financial crisis of 2007–2010. During this time there was a sense that a particular form of capitalism would need to change to address some of the major failings exposed by the crisis. Some people even proposed that we would be living in a 'post-capitalist' world as a consequence of the crisis. Many business leaders and academics embraced this sense of change, attempting to predict what the new business landscape would look like. The Director General of the CBI, Richard Lambert is quoted as suggesting that: 'The new world will be less about complex financial transactions … more about collaboration, partnership, and longer-term relationships with a wide group of stakeholders' (Madslien, 2009).

In this activity we want you to consider the extent to which the approach to business has changed following the financial crisis of 2007 to 2010. Ask yourself how the crisis impacted marketing practice and thought and consider Professor Don Schultz's claim that marketing and marketers were responsible for the crisis (Schultz, 2009). You are encouraged to undertake desk research (to include quality news outlets, academic journals and practitioner magazines) to establish the reasons for the financial crisis. In this regard, you may find the work of Robert Peston on the BBC News website particularly helpful. Evert Gummesson's (2009) recent study of marketing and the financial crisis should also be useful.

References

Alderson, W. (1934) 'Marketing problems under a planned economy', *Bulletin of the Taylor Society,* February: 2–3, 17 and 170.

Applbaum, K. (2009) 'Getting to yes: Corporate power and the creation of a psychopharmaceutical blockbuster', *Culture and Medical Psychiatry*, 33: 185–215.

Brownlie, D., Saren, M., Wensley, R. and Whittington, R. (eds) (1999) *Rethinking Marketing: Towards Critical Marketing Accountings*. London: Sage.

Cannon, T. (1980) 'Marketing: The state of the art (or science)', *Management Learning*, 11: 138–44.

Firat, A.F., Dholakia, N. and Bagozzi, R.P (eds) (1987) *Philosophical and Radical Thought in Marketing*. Lexington: Lexington Books.

Fromm, E. (1956/2005) *The Sane Society*. London: Routledge.

Gummesson, E. (2009) 'The global crisis and the marketing scholar', *Journal of Consumer Behaviour*, 8 (2): 119–35.

Hackley, C. (2009) *Marketing: A Critical Introduction*. London: Sage.

Hopkins, C.C. (1927/1997) *My Life in Advertising & Scientific Advertising*. New York: McGraw Hill.

Jones, D.G.B. and Monieson, D.D. (1987/2008) 'Origins of the institutional approach in marketing', in M. Tadajewski and D.G.B. Jones (eds), *The History of Marketing Thought*, Volume III, pp. 125–44. London: Sage.

Madslien, J. (2009) 'CBI say collaboration "will bring recovery"'. http:// news.bbc. co.uk/1/hi/ business/8873076.stm, accessed 23 November 2009.

Marcuse, H. (1966) *Eros and Civilization: A Philosophical Inquiry into Freud*. Boston: Beacon Press.

McFall, L. (2004) *Advertising: A Cultural Economy*. London: Sage.

Reibstein, D.J., Day, G. and Wind, J. (2009) 'Guest editorial: Is marketing academia losing its way?', *Journal of Marketing*, 73 (July): 1–3.

Ritzer, G. (2001) *Explorations in Social Theory: From Metatheorizing to Rationalization*. London: Sage.

Saren, M., Maclaran, P., Goulding, C., Elliott, R., Shankar, A. and Catterall M.S. (eds) (2007) *Critical Marketing: Defining the Field*. Amsterdam: Elsevier.

Schultz, D.E. (2009) 'Golden goose eggs', *Marketing Management*, (July/Aug), 18 (4): 6–7.

Shultz, C. J. (2007) 'The unquestioned marketing life? Let us hope not', *Journal of Macromarketing*, 27 (3): 224.

Tadajewski, M. and Brownlie, D. (eds) (2008) *Critical Marketing: Issues in Contemporary Marketing*. Chichester: Wiley.

Tadajewski, M. and Maclaran, P. (eds) (2009a) *Critical Marketing Studies*, Volume I. London: Sage.

Tadajewski, M. and Maclaran, P. (eds) (2009b) *Critical Marketing Studies*, Volume II. London: Sage.

Tadajewski, M. and Maclaran, P. (eds) (2009c) *Critical Marketing Studies*, Volume III. London: Sage.

Veblen, T. (1919/2005) *The Vested Interests and the Common Man*. New York: Cosimo.

Introducing the History of Marketing Theory and Practice

1

1.1 Introduction

The global popularity of marketing as a subject for study might suggest that those studying and teaching the subject know what it is that they are studying and how this study should be undertaken. But as we shall see in this chapter and others in this book, this has often not been the case. Marketing as a subject has proved almost impossible to pin down, and there is little consensus about what it means to study marketing. Most organisations now employ marketers. Marketing roles were traditionally found in commercial firms, but increasingly all kinds of organisations feel the need to employ marketers or to commission services from marketing consultants.

The popularity and pervasiveness of marketing is, however, a relatively recent phenomenon. Academics have only studied marketing as a discipline in its own right for just over a century, and during its short history the study of marketing has been influenced by many different academic movements, fads and priorities. This variability can be viewed as a positive state of affairs, because it means that the subject is always open to new ideas and new trends. On the other hand, it has the potential to undermine the value of marketing knowledge because there is no general consensus on what the study of marketing should be for, how these studies should be conducted, or what the outcomes should be. Before we can begin to study marketing, we need to understand something about this history and the debates and controversies that have shaped the field.

In this chapter, we shall review the origins of marketing thought, examining when the term 'marketing' was first used, its subsequent development, and provide an overview of the development of marketing thought and practice. Marketing, clearly, is probably as old as human civilisation itself (see Jones and Shaw, 2002; Minowa and Witkowski, 2009; Moore and Reid, 2008; Shaw and Jones, 2005). For our purposes, we will restrict our attention to the emergence of marketing as an academic discipline and business practice early in the twentieth century.

What confronts most students and academics alike when they begin to study the development of marketing is the overwhelmingly American emphasis of much of the literature. The key textbooks, for instance, often contain examples of American corporate activities, sometimes tweaked for other markets, sometimes not. In writing this introduction we will obviously be tied to some extent to the history of American marketing. Many of the earliest college courses were developed there, most of the principal thinkers in marketing throughout the twentieth century worked there, and as such it is natural that we talk about these people, institutions and their theoretical contributions.

But, in an effort to ensure that the material presented resonates with more than just an American audience, and to provide more balance to the history of marketing than is generally seen in introduction and advanced texts alike, we provide numerous examples of non-US marketing theory and practice.

As will be shown, not all countries adopted key marketing practices at the same time as they were discussed by US marketing scholars. Some countries like the UK, for example, turned to formal marketing education relatively late, even if the UK did have a number of companies and entrepreneurs who were naturally marketing oriented fairly early, such as the confectionery manufacturer Cadbury's (Corley, 1987; Fitzgerald, 1989). Other countries, such as Spain, underwent their own 'marketing revolution' (Keith, 1960) even later. So, in short, we would ask that you remember that the theory and practice discussed in this and the following chapter are the result of very specific political, social, technological, and economic environments in the economies discussed. We would encourage you NOT to think 'of marketing as a homogenous, almost universally applicable concept, transcending cultures as well as contexts' (Cannon, 1980: 140).

1.2 The Early Development of Marketing Thought

In his important history of marketing, Bartels (1988) proposes that the term 'marketing' was first used 'as a noun', that is, as a label for a particular practice, sometime 'between 1906 and 1911' (Bartels, 1988: 3). Nonetheless, Bartels' historical account has been challenged by scholars who assert that there were people writing about the subject before 1906 (Brussière, 2000). In appraising the Publications of the American Economic Association, Brussière found that the term marketing was actually used in 1897. Tamilia (2009), on the other hand, suggests that it was used even earlier than this in the *Quarterly Journal of Economics*.

These examples are clearly taken from the academic literature. But it was not just academics writing about the subject. For example, Shaw (1995) notes that in *Miss Parloa's New Cookbook and Marketing Guide* which was published around 1880, 'marketing' related to buying and selling activities. This was not the only book using the term at this time or previously. Shaw says that if we look at dictionaries prior to the Bartels statement the intellectual history of the term 'marketing' can be extended much further, all the way back to 1561 (Shaw, 1995: 16).

On a related point, Dixon argues that 'The *Oxford English Dictionary* traces the use of this term [marketing] to the sixteenth century; it certainly did not originate in the United States between 1906 and 1911' (Dixon, 2002: 738). Nor should we think that marketing education originated in the United States. In actual fact, the first courses were found in Germany at the turn of the twentieth century (Jones and Monieson, 1990). Having said this, the American Marketing Association and American marketing educational system has obviously been very important in terms of the development of marketing thought. As an anchor for the rest of the chapter therefore, consider the changing definitions of marketing in the Box below. These definitions illustrate how marketing as we know it has taken the shape it has.

Voices – The American Marketing Association and the Changing Definitions of Marketing

Wilkie and Moore (2006) tell us that there is one important issue that we should acknowledge in the changing definitions of marketing inasmuch as the definitions become more managerial over time. That is, less attention is paid to the influence of marketing in and on society and more attention is devoted to articulating the management function that marketing performs inside an organisation.

So, from the first definition of marketing provided in 1935, through to the 1985 and 2004 modifications, the definitions change from marketing being: 'the performance of business activities that direct the flow of goods and services from producers to consumers' (1935). [To marketing as] 'the process of planning and executing the conception, pricing, promotion, and distribution of ideas, goods and services to create exchanges that satisfy individual and organisational objectives' (1985); [to marketing as] 'an organizational function and set of processes for creating, communicating and delivering value to customers and for managing customer relationships in ways that benefit the organization and stakeholders' (Wilkie and Moore, 2006: 227).

The problem with the last definition is that attention is focused on marketing as an organisational activity – there is no mention of marketing's role extending beyond those activities most closely associated with the firm. Thus, by removing the societal emphasis that earlier scholars demonstrated in their desire to improve marketplace efficiency, distributive justice, standards of living and the distribution of products at lower prices, later definitions in effect encourage people not to think about such improvements in the marketing and distributive system as a whole, but simply focus on those aspects relevant to an individual firm. It also assumes that individual firm activities will in the aggregate be unproblematic.

As far as one of the most recent definitions is concerned, marketing activities do not actually impact on wider society. It was the excessive managerial emphasis of this definition that led to a series of heated exchanges both online and in the *Journal of Public Policy and Marketing*. Ultimately, the American Marketing Association went quickly back to their drawing board, bringing out a new, updated definition that responded to the criticism by scholars, so that the latest definition reads: 'Marketing is the activity, set of institutions, and processes for creating, communicating, delivering, and exchanging offerings that have value for customers, clients, partners, and society at large' (Lib, 2007).

1.3 The First Courses in Marketing in the Early Twentieth Century

As was mentioned above, some of the first courses in marketing appear to have been delivered in Germany. There is, unfortunately, little detailed discussion of these in the marketing literature. Studies of early courses in marketing in USA are far better documented. Dr E.D. Jones is often credited with offering the first course in marketing in 1902 at the University of Michigan (Maynard, 1941). This course was not actually called marketing at all when it was first offered, but 'The Distributive and Regulative Industries of the US' (Bartels, 1951a). The first course actually called simply 'Marketing' was delivered some nine years later by Ralph Starr Butler at the University of Wisconsin. In the intervening period, other universities had nevertheless started providing their own courses on distribution, advertising, salesmanship and related subjects.

At a general level, we can consider marketing as a form of 'applied economics' (Shaw and Jones, 2005). Its emergence is often attributed to the fact that despite the variety of academics working in the various sub-disciplines of economics in the late nineteenth and early twentieth century, there was still a great deal of concern that economic reflections on the marketplace were not used to formulate guidance for practising managers (Kemmerer et al., 1918).

Furthermore, the information that was available was often found in relatively obscure academic sources that few, if any, actually managed to access and read (Ashley, 1908). These access issues were compounded by the fact that: 'The greater part of the economic world has not yet been surveyed descriptively and realistically' (Ashley, 1908: 188). It was here that marketing scholars and consultants had the opportunity to contribute to knowledge about the functioning of the economic system. They could help practitioners understand the marketplace and help investigate consumer needs and desires which had largely been ignored by economists (Mason, 1998).

In the very beginning, early marketing academics focused their attention on 'describing, explaining, and justifying prevailing marketing practices and institutions, particularly newer ones' (Bartels, 1988). Early scholarship was partly written with the intent of modifying 'misconceptions held among the public, such as the belief that the wholesaler was parasitic and would disappear from the distributive system, [the] fear of [the] annihilation of small stores by chain organizations, and dismay at the plight of consumers before the ruthless practices of vendors' (Bartels, 1988: 29).

To effectively understand the rapidly expanding industrial economy of the US, these practically minded researchers refused to spend their time theorising in their ivory towers, preferring instead to study the practice of marketing, charting the passage of goods through the distribution system (Weld, 1941). What *is* interesting is the reference made by Bartels above to the justification of marketing activities, on both the basis of its efficiency and in terms of the utilities created.

1.4 Marketing, Efficiency and Utility Creation

When we talk about justifying marketing, what we mean is that scholars wanted to demonstrate that marketing did perform a useful and valuable role in distributing goods and services to where they were needed, at appropriate price points and in so doing, enhancing the quality of life experienced by consumers. They wanted to justify the value of marketing in this way for the reason that many people living in the early twentieth century were concerned about the rising cost of distribution. People could appreciate that there were a variety of intermediary steps involved in distributing goods from the manufacturer to the wholesalers and onto the retailer and they quite rightly asked the question: Were these middlemen adding value or just cost? Were middlemen adding value to their offerings by getting the right product to the right place at the correct time, thereby adding time and place utilities? Was advertising useful to the consumer, aiding them in making more effective decisions? Or were each of these factors just adding another layer of cost which the consumer had to subsidise? These issues were especially important as prices had been continually rising from 1896, accelerating still higher during the First World War (Usui, 2008).

These issues, especially the disjuncture between the prices paid by middlemen to farmers, and the ultimate price the consumer paid, were subsumed under the label 'the marketing problem' (Jones and Monieson, 1994) and the 'distribution cost debate' (Wilkie and Moore, 1999). Such concerns have not exactly disappeared today; although these debates about the cost of distribution were first aired in 1900 or thereabouts, with 'farmers questioning why they received only a low percentage of the consumer's food dollar; today, buyers (and farmers) ask why cereal brands are priced so high relative to ingredient costs' (Wilkie and Moore, 1999: 215). While such criticism of the efficiency of the marketing system continues, theoretically this topic raised an important question about marketing – were there any elements in distribution channels, for example, that were not adding some form of utility (Benton, 1987)?

Arch Shaw (1912), a publisher and sometime marketing academic, believed the criticism of middlemen was largely unwarranted. Middlemen, Shaw claimed, provided highly valuable services in that they stored goods, assuming an element of risk in doing so, because if conditions in the marketplace suddenly changed, they might be left with a stock of goods they could no longer sell. Bearing this in mind, Shaw suggested that middlemen performed a valuable service and consequently should be properly compensated. Fleshing this point out, Wilkie and Moore summarise the utilities added by marketing activities in the following way (try thinking about these in terms of the 4 P's of product, place, price and promotion):

> … [Marketing adds] form utility … by (1) physically supplying essential inputs to the production process and (2) providing insights from the marketplace (e.g., market research) that help decide specific attributes for goods and services. Place utility is clearly marketing's province, representing the value added by providing goods where buyers need them. Marketing adds time utility through preplanning, inventory, and promotion activities to ensure customers can obtain goods when needed. Finally, possession utility is offered through marketing transactions and enables customers to use goods for desired purposes. (Wilkie and Moore, 1999: 209)

So, if we were to frame our discussion so far in terms of concepts from the philosophy of science which take the form of a 'reflection on the nature and practices of [marketing] science' (Jones, 2007: 1243), we can say that early marketing scholarship was thoroughly grounded in empiricism. Empiricism is a theory of knowledge that refers to the idea that if we want to justify knowledge, then it must have some basis in experience. In other words, early marketing scholars went out into the marketplace to examine market institutions such as retailing environments or farming product exchanges to formulate descriptions of how these institutions functioned. From an empiricist, we would expect to hear comments like those uttered by Louis Weld on the need for the interconnection of economic theory with marketplace reality: 'I am not denouncing theoretical economics by any means…[but] valuable contributions can be made to the theory of market price by getting out into the markets with a market reporter than by cogitation in a closet' (Weld in Kemmerer et al., 1918: 267).

With this turn toward a more 'applied economics' focus (i.e. trying to use economic theory to improve marketing practice or using the knowledge gained from studying the market to critically examine economic theory such as the view of the utility maximising consumer), academics and 'marketing counsellors' began directing their attention towards the actual functioning of the marketing system. And it is around this time – the early twentieth century – that the first philosophy of science debates in marketing appeared.

1.5 German Historical School

Those thinking about a teaching and research career in marketing in the late nineteenth, early twentieth centuries were often taught by scholars who had been trained in Germany and subsequently absorbed the worldview of the German Historical School (Jones and Monieson, 1990). Academics trained in this worldview thought that the marketplace should not operate unfettered. Rather than letting the invisible hand of the market dictate production and economic relations, they thought that the government should attempt to regulate the market where necessary, with scholars providing knowledge about the problematic workings of the marketplace to government or other officials.

In terms of the philosophy of science underpinning the German Historical School, they subscribed to an inductive, 'positivist' epistemology, and hoped to develop a science of marketing (Jones, 1994; Jones and Monieson, 1990). What this means is that they studied the marketplace, examining specific cases that showed how the market worked (i.e. in relation to agricultural distribution etc) and then used this information to generalise about the operation of the marketplace (going from specific to general cases = induction).

By formulating and validating such generalisations, marketing scholars could then, through their involvement with public policy, either work to improve the operation of the market, or legislate against detrimental or inefficient practices. This latter point indicates a further issue that was important to this group: ethics and distributive justice. By distributive justice we mean 'how a community treats its members in terms of benefits and burdens [that are shared] according to some standard of fairness' (Laczniak and Murphy, 2008: 5). The German Historical School, put simply, viewed their work as contributing to ensuring that all participants in the market were treated fairly, including customers and middlemen.

Unfortunately, as Jones and Shaw (2002) reveal, those associated with this school of thought were not successful in creating the science of marketing that they wanted. Pretty soon, issues of distributive justice and ethics faded from the mainstream of marketing thought. From distributive justice and a concern for the 'marketing problem', commentators across the spectrum of marketing began to devote more attention to what was called the 'consumer problem' (Tadajewski and Brownlie, 2008).

In the context of the first two decades of the twentieth century, supply began to exceed demand, so that the focus of marketers' attention became selling products efficiently and effectively through well thought out combinations of product, price, promotion and distribution strategies (Zaltman and Burger, 1975) and in recognition of changing demand and supply relations, alongside increasing competition between firms (Hoyt, 1929/2000), it was also more important for businesses to effectively control the interactions between their salesforce and the customer. Similar views had long been held by retailing pioneers like John Wanamaker (Appel, 1938), who like later scientific sales managers, wanted to foster positive customer relations and develop long-term relationships between a company and its most desirable clientele, and controlling the sales force was one means of doing so (Graham, 2000; Strong and D'Amico, 1991).

1.6 Frederick Taylor and Scientific Sales Management

An important, but all too often neglected, contribution to marketing theory and practice was made via the work of Frederick Winslow Taylor, the father of scientific management.

Marketing scholars recognised in Taylor's work a way to make marketing, retailing and salesmanship more efficient (Cowan, 1924; Graham, 2000; La Londe and Morrison, 1967; Usui, 2008). Taylor had come to popular attention via his attempts to place production on a scientific level. By this, we mean Taylor sought to examine the way that particular activities were undertaken such as shovelling coal, in order to determine the most effective way of doing so.

Behind this strategy of determining the 'one best way' of engaging in any given activity was the issue of organisational efficiency. Connected to this, management were expected to study their workforce, drawing up detailed guidelines for workers that aimed to encourage them to work at their optimal level, 'at the highest grade of work for which his [*sic*] natural abilities fitted him' (Taylor, 1911/1998: 1). This standard was itself based on the standardisation of worker tasks into the key elements that must be undertaken, with all superfluous activities disregarded. Taylor's work was heralded as encouraging a revolution in management practice, increasing production efficiency to rates previously unheard of. The problem was, however, that increasing production in this way required a similar increase in distribution efficiency. After all, there was no point producing goods at ever increasing speed, if they could not be sold in a similarly efficient manner.

Into this breach strode a number of early marketing thinkers who sought to apply Taylor's insights to marketing practice, including such scholarly pioneers as Arch W. Shaw, Paul Converse, Charles W. Hoyt, Stuart Cowan and Percival White, as well as practitioners such as H.W. Brown of Tabor Manufacturing Company and Edward A. Filene, the famous retailer (Cowan, 1924; Filene, 1930; Hoyt, 1929/2000; La Londe and Morrison, 1967; Scully, 1996; Usui, 2008). In effect, what these individuals wanted to achieve was the transformation of the 'art' of salesmanship into a science of selling (Strong and D'Amico, 1991). This required a shift in understanding of salesperson characteristics. Where once it was thought that salespeople were innately predisposed to and skilled at selling, now marketing thinkers believed salespeople could be created through appropriate courses of training and instruction.

Hoyt, for example, in his 1913 text, *Scientific Sales Management*, outlined the various ways in which sales management could be made more efficient, and most of the ideas he enunciated revolved around the idea of standardisation (as did Taylor's system) (Hoyt, 1929/2000). In an effort to standardise sales activities, Hoyt suggested that 'If we analyze the sales job we have gone a long way toward finding out how to do it. If we break the job up into its component parts, we discover new tools to hasten the process and increase volume' (Hoyt, 1929/2000: 24). Firms also rationalised their production processes, discontinuing the manufacture of unprofitable lines, thereby enabling their salespeople to focus on the most profitable product ranges. And in line with a sales orientation (see the Box on p. 20–1) 'sales volume' was an important criterion against which to measure business practice. But it was not the sole objective: 'Given the job of keeping a factory operating profitably at capacity throughout the year, obviously sales volume is the first requirement' (Cowan, 1924: 76; cf. Strong and D'Amico, 1991: 232). Profit targets were also important (Usui, 2008).

In addition, sales management, it was claimed, could be made more effective if the routes salesmen travelled across their sales territories were planned using the optimal transportation options and if their sales 'patter' or talk was standardised. We should be clear here: this is not to suggest that each and every salesman was given one sales talk that they repeated without modifying. They were given broad outlines of what might be a good way of presenting a given product, but each 'individual salesman is expected and taught to use the words which come to him naturally' (Cowan, 1924: 84).

Sales talk standardisation was possible because although each customer had their own individual personality and thus was likely to respond to the sales pitch in slightly different ways, 'Extensive experiences show that on the average human nature is much the same, and that the difference between individuals is not nearly as great as the degree of likeness' (Cowan, 1924: 84). The function of management from this perspective was to produce sales pitches that were likely to appeal to the mass of consumers. In other words, and here we see the contribution of Taylor's ideas, management had to try to develop the 'one best sales story' for use in the field. According to Cowan (1924: 84), doing so was 'a result of research and experiment, and it involves planning a basic method of sales. The salesman, therefore, must be selected with respect to their ability to comprehend the basic method, and their ability to utilize it in personal contact with buyers'. Moreover, management needed to convince otherwise largely 'freewheeling commissioned salespeople' that they needed management's help in devising their travelling schedules and sales talks (Strong and D'Amico, 1991). One way of doing this was to suggest that salespeople might make more money if their everyday sales activities were better structured.

Although Taylor's work was criticised by some (Graham, 2000), it was influential in marketing and advertising (Scully, 1996), with many of the respondents surveyed by Paul Converse in the early 1940s acknowledging its impact on their thinking (Converse, 1945). This said, gradually there was a movement away from a limited focus on sales management activities (Strong and Hawes, 1990), that is, from a focus on supply side efficiency issues, to a greater emphasis on consumer needs, wants and desires (White, 1927). This was in part a natural shift in business practice that reflected the fact that as markets became ever larger, and producers ever more distant from their ultimate consumers, that some activity was required to allow manufacturers to maintain contact with their customer base. Marketing research consequently gained a foothold in industry. See the Box below.

The Key Characteristics of the Production, Sales and Marketing Eras (modified from Jones and Richardson, 2007: 18)

Production Era (according to Keith (1960) this ran from 1870–1930)

P1. Demand exceeds supply. There are shortages and intense hunger for goods.
P2. There is little or no competition within product markets (between firms selling the same goods to the same markets).
P3. The company, not customers, is the centre of focus for a business.
P4. Businesses produce what they can produce and focus on solving production problems.
P5. Businesses produce limited product lines.
P6. Products sell themselves. Wholesalers and retailers are unsophisticated in their selling and marketing.
P7. Profit is a by-product of being good at production.

Sales Era (according to Keith (1960) this ran from 1930 until 1950)

S1. Supply exceeds demand.
S2. There is competition within product markets.
S3. Businesses are conscious of consumers' wants, and some market research is done.

S4. Businesses must dispose of the products they produce and therefore focus on selling.

S5. Businesses produce limited product lines.

S6. Hard selling is necessary, backed by advertising.

S7. The primary goal of the firm is sales volume; profit is a by-product.

Marketing Era (according to Keith (1960) this ran from 1950 onwards, turning into an era of 'marketing control' in the late 1950s, early 1960s)

M1. Supply exceeds demand.

M2. There is intense competition within product markets.

M3. The customer is at the centre of a company's business; the purpose is to satisfy customers' needs and wants.

M4. Customers determine what products are made. Businesses focus on marketing problems.

M5. Businesses produce extensive product lines.

M6. A wide range of marketing activities is used and coordinated to satisfy customers' needs.

M7. Businesses focus on profit rather than sales volume.

Shaw (1912: 755), for one, bemoaned business people who did not study the marketplace in a careful, systematic manner despite 'investing tens, even hundreds, of thousands of dollars in a selling campaign'. Systematic understanding of buyer behaviour was vital (Kitson, 1923; Muir, 1924; Starch, 1923; Weaver, 1935): management needed to understand what products the marketplace demanded, if they were to scientifically manage their levels of production in line with likely consumption (Schell, 1930; White, 1927). Again, these ideas were not totally radical departures for business, as similar views were expressed with increased frequency from the late nineteenth century onwards (Jones and Richardson, 2007; Laird, 1951; Lockley, 1950), although this is not to say that all companies listened to their customer base, and acted upon the marketing intelligence that was available (Elder, 1932).

Even so, the attentiveness of industry, marketing academics and consultants alike to the consumer and their desires generally passes unacknowledged. Notwithstanding this, ideas associated with the marketing concept were surprisingly widespread during the 1920s and 30s and probably for quite some time before, as we discuss further in Chapter 4 (Fullerton, 1988; Hollander, 1986; Jones and Richardson, 2007). During the 1920s and 30s, however, there was a definite shift in some books from thinking about the sales manager as just involved with organising the sales force, to them taking on roles much more consistent with the modern marketing manager. As Strong and D'Amico (1991: 232) highlight in reference to a text published by J. George Frederick in 1919:

Frederick's sales manager was concerned with product quality and new product development as determined by the needs of the market. It was the sales manager's job, he wrote, to synchronize the standardization needs of production with the market's demand for a varied product line. Sales management had begun to evolve from the narrow supervisory role of the pre-1920 era to a broader one embracing the marketing concept, though not, as yet, so labelled.

In conjunction with this new role for the sales manager, we can also say that marketers were very interested in producing more expensive products, either for the business-to-business market or as 'speciality goods', in a way that reflected consumer requirements most closely (Shaw and Jones, 2005; Tadajewski, 2009b; Tadajewski and Saren, 2009). This said, the reason why it is often claimed that marketers only started to pay attention to customer needs and wants in the 1950s is due to a paper that appeared in the *Journal of Marketing* written by an executive at the Pillsbury Company.

Robert J. Keith's article was based on changes in business and customer relations that characterised the history of the company where he worked: The Pillsbury Company. He maintained that his firm was currently revolutionising the way they thought about marketing and sales management. Marketers were no longer producing whatever products they could manufacture, just because they possessed the manufacturing capacity and skill to do so, as would have been the case if they had been 'production' oriented: 'In today's economy the consumer, the man or woman who buys the product, is at the absolute dead center of the business universe. Companies revolve around the customer, not the other way around' (Keith, 1960: 35).

Importantly, Keith argued that his case study was generalisable to the rest of the 'business universe'. This is a problematic statement for a number of reasons. Firstly, General Electric is considered the first company to fully implement the marketing concept by many. So Keith's attempt to claim first mover status is slightly questionable. With respect to his claim to generalisability, we should note that Keith presented an American case study that does not reflect the nature of business practice around the world, most notably in Spain (see the Box below).

Voices – Marketing in Spain: On Not Transplanting American Marketing Methods

As we mentioned above, there is often a very pronounced American bias in much published marketing scholarship. America is the archetypical consumer society; many of the most well-known marketing journals are American and thus our knowledge about marketing and consumer research necessarily reflects this bias. We also often hear about how American marketing practices have slowly but surely spread across the globe. Keith (1960) talks about a 'marketing revolution' taking place that he implies many companies will follow, presumably in whatever country they hail from. Yet, as García Ruiz (2007) documents, there is often widespread cultural antipathy to marketing, especially in Spain.

Like some merchants in medieval times (Dixon, 2008; Strong and D'Amico, 1991), marketers in America (Farmer, 1967) or advertising practitioners in Germany (Berghoff, 2003), marketers in Spain were looked down upon. It was not a profession many wanted to be associated with; the treatment of consumers left much to be desired and until 'the late 1980s, less than ten percent of firms had implemented a marketing strategy' (García Ruiz, 2007: 367). Even before this time, those interested in marketing were aware that although American forms of marketing practice were useful, these needed to be modified to fit with the cultural context in which a company was operating. And the first marketing conference in Spain in 1963 was brought to a close by Pedro Gual Villabí, Minister and President of the National Economic Council stating that Spanish firms should 'not imitate. We talk a lot about the American or the German methods, for example. They are fine and they are interesting. However, each country has its own methods, because the behaviour of people naturally agrees with national idiosyncrasies, temperaments, their environment, all of which are very difficult to transplant. Of course, any rule or model should not be considered universal. We, the Spaniards, are very opposed to wearing foreign clothes!' (García Ruiz, 2007: 372).

A further criticism is that other writers working around the same time as Keith (1960) argued that the theoretical debates surrounding various 'business philosophies' were not new. They were further developments of arguments already found in the historical record (Borch, 1958). Academics and practitioners had even before General Electric implemented what was later called the marketing concept, discussed positioning the customer as the 'fulcrum' – to use Borch's term – of business activities; Percival White's (1927) work being a key example. But, let us move on, leaving this focus on the intellectual priority debates around the marketing concept to one side. We will come back to them in Chapter 4.

What these examples should tell us is that more often than not, when we read the original publications of some of the key thinkers in marketing or look at specific examples of marketing practice, we find their arguments demonstrate more nuance than they are given credit for; the case of Fred Borch's work on the marketing concept is a good example of this. Borch appreciated the value of a customer orientation, but he remained convinced of the value of some of the tactics associated with a sales orientation. We should not, he said, simply produce products and hope that the customer will seek them out. We should actively promote our goods. Marketing practice, on this reading, is not just about responding to customer desire, but about stimulating it.

1.7 Demand Creation and Marketing Research

Marketing, we can say then, is concerned with what has varyingly been called 'demand creation' (A.W. Shaw in Usui, 2008; Doubman, 1924), 'demand activation' (Copeland, 1958) or 'demand generation' (Shaw and Jones, 2005), with one scholar going so far as to associate marketing with propaganda and 'the conditioning of buyers or sellers to a favorable attitude' (Shaw and Jones, 2005: 247). 'Marketing students', Converse (1951: 3) attested, 'are interested in increasing or stimulating human wants, in general and for the good of individual sellers. This leads them to the study of advertising, salesmanship, and merchandising, marketing research and packaging'.

Since marketers were actively interested in selling to consumers, and have often tried to adopt the customer's viewpoint in an effort to produce those goods and services likely to appeal to their target market for quite some time, why, we might ask, was marketing practice increasingly viewed in more favourable terms in the boardrooms of large companies only really in the 1950s? It appears that this is attributable to the Second World War (Tadajewski, 2009a).

As was the case with the American Civil War (Appel, 1911) and the First World War (Usui, 2008), the Second World War led to a massive expansion of industry, based on the orders placed by the Army, Navy and other wartime bodies. One observer stated 'that the end of the war will find the United States with the greatest productive capacity that it has ever had. In the United States, new plants have been constructed and old plants converted to augment enormously the flow of commodities. New processes have been developed and have been introduced; ideas that once seemed visionary have been made realities and have increased production in an unheard of degree' (Tosdal, 1941: 75).

Since the postwar world was going to represent probably the most competitive landscape business had ever seen, the blossoming romance with the consumer turned into organisational infatuation for some. Understanding the consumers' needs, wants and desires became a priority. At the same time as the marketing concept was being further diffused throughout large companies across the United States (Moore, 1957), marketing scholars themselves remained embroiled in a debate that began roughly in the 1920s and continues until the present day (Szmigin and Foxall, 2000). This dispute centred on the idea of whether marketing was an art or a science. Science, of course, sounds slightly more academically legitimate; and 'marketing science' is likely to be more respectable and useful as a rhetorical tool in boardroom debate.

1.8 Art or Science

In view of what we now know about the attempts to turn the art of salesmanship into a science, the 'art or science' debate of the 1950s can be considered an extension of earlier concerns. This debate raged throughout the 1950s, having been stimulated by Paul Converse (1945). Some academics sidestepped the issue (Converse, 1945); others offered an implicit affirmation of the idea that marketing was a science (Alderson and Cox, 1948; Bartels, 1951a; Brown, 1948); and others still questioned whether marketing was scientific, given that certain aspects of marketing, especially the development of advertising, product innovation and planning (Cannon, 1980) required creative flair and artistic sensibilities (Stainton, 1952).

Bartels, for one, was not convinced that marketing had achieved scientific status. He said that since the discipline was still a comparative infant in relation to other academic subjects, that we were being over-optimistic to assume that marketing was a science, as yet. When he reviewed the literature, his caution was confirmed. There was a conspicuous lack of the scientific devices that we would have expected were marketing a science (i.e. no real marketing theories, principles and law-like generalisations that an accredited science should have possessed). This said, he did see some scholars using the scientific method (they developed hypotheses which they then either supported or refuted through empirical research) (Bartels, 1951: b). Even so, other scholars, after examining the marketing literature, saw little change in scientific style from the earliest days in marketing thought, claiming that marketing scholarship remained wedded to a 'thoroughgoing empiricism' (Buzzell, 1964: 33). Research was still largely descriptive and qualitative.

Here we have broached a key issue. Buzzell (1964), for example, is critical of the use of qualitative methods in marketing. This is not simply a comment from nowhere. It was a debate that ran far deeper in the marketing community than the vague gesture above can do justice and was marked by often quite bitter exchanges between two groups of scholars. On the one hand there were those who subscribed to 'positivism' versus those inclined toward interpretive approaches, using psychological, psychoanalytical and anthropological thought to understand consumer behaviour.

1.9 Positivism and Motivation Research

Generally speaking, 'positivist' research is interested in the prediction or explanation of consumer behaviour, often using large scale survey research and quantitative methods to produce generalisations about what kinds of behaviour a given population of people will engage in. By contrast, for 'motivation research' and 'interpretive research', a common aim is 'understanding' 'why' people engage in certain forms of consumer behaviour (Hudson and Ozanne, 1988; Tadajewski, 2006). A key figure in the debate between the proponents of motivation research and the 'positivists' was Ernest Dichter who was one of a number of influential scholars and practitioners who migrated to the United States from Europe just prior to, and during the second World War, who revolutionised aspects of academia and business practice (see the Box below).

Food for Thought – Marketing and Consumer Research in Europe

As noted previously, historical evidence indicates that there were courses in business and marketing in Germany before the United States (Jones and Monieson, 1990). Extending this line of thought Fullerton (1994, 2009) has examined marketing and consumer research practice, as well as the theoretical underpinnings of research in Europe, and argued that whilst European scholars like Wilhelm Vershoften and H.F.J. Kropff did appreciate the important contributions made by American scholars and practitioners, the work of people studying consumer behaviour in Germany was often equally advanced, if not more so in some cases.

Most notably, Fullerton pointed to the work conducted by Paul Lazarsfeld at the Office of Economic-Psychological Research at the University of Vienna (1927–1934), along with that undertaken under the auspices of the Society for Consumer Research affiliated with Nuernberg University. The first of these was heavily influenced by a variety of streams of theoretical thought including 'social psychology, Marxism, Freud, behaviorism, introspection, statistics, and psycholinguistics' (Fullerton, 2009: 97). Paul Lazarsfeld, arguably one of the most influential marketing and communication scholars of his generation, was one of the pioneers of consumer research. He was convinced that through careful, detailed interviewing that the reasons that lay behind any given purchase could be established. He later moved to the United States when the political climate in Austria turned particularly ugly, and with Ernest Dichter, Herta Herzog and others, played a key role in further diffusing interpretive and qualitative approaches in marketing and consumer research.

Unfortunately, the Second World War brought much of the advanced marketing and consumer research taking place in Germany and Austria to a resounding halt. Nevertheless, according to Berghoff (2003), some commentators working in Germany during the run up to the Second World War believed that Third Reich policies were going to have a beneficial effect on the way Germans viewed advertising practice. On the one hand, working in advertising was generally frowned upon, being seen as an undesirable job. The Third Reich was, on the other hand, well known to be very interested in the role of advertising in mobilising political support for its policies (the work of Freud's nephew, the pioneering public relations guru, Edward Bernays, was of great interest to the Nazi propagandist, Joseph Goebbels).

(Cont'd)

The German Advertising Association, as a case in point, 'put a portrait of Hitler on the cover of its official organ and saluted the man who 'is Germany's greatest advertiser, selfless in duty and whom we are all beholden follow. From now on advertising must accord with his vision' (in Berghoff, 2003: 131). At the same time, as a stern political regime, it was willing to legislate against and prosecute inappropriate forms of advertising (e.g. misleading advertising) and this, observers at the time thought, would lead to improvements in industry practice, and consequently improvements in the public perception of advertising. As Berghoff appreciates, there was some degree of validity to these views. The German authorities did clamp down on certain advertising practices. Yet, they also prohibited talented advertising practitioners from working out of racism and myopia simply because they were Jewish or otherwise seen as undesirable from the point of view of the authorities.

However, advertising practitioners are nothing if not creative and opportunistic. In Germany advertisers quickly took creative inspiration from the Nazi authorities: 'there was an onslaught of swastikas and Hitler portraits being used in advertisements. Exploitation and tastelessness knew no bounds. Aprons and scrub brushes adorned with swastikas flooded the market, as well as playing cards ornamented with the heads of top Nazis. Butchers decorated their front windows with busts of the Führer carved from pig lard, and bakers cut swastikas into their dough. The catchphrase, 'It is the Führer's desire', was used for virtually every product. Sales representatives donned Stormtrooper uniforms in order to impress their clients' (Berghoff, 2003: 138–9). The Nazis were not especially impressed by advertisers jumping on this bandwagon: 'for it trivialised National Socialism's central symbols and even made them look silly' (Berghoff, 2003: 139). They therefore made it illegal to use the logos and symbols associated with the party without proper consent. Recalling the comments above, then, consumer research in Germany was theoretically and practically sophisticated and it should come as no surprise that 'Advancing the theoretical tools for this [German] propaganda [in the years before the second World War] were economists from the Nuremberg Institute for Economic Research and Nuremberg's Society for Consumer Research' (Berghoff, 2003: 142).

In his work, Dichter essentially translated psychological theory and concepts into marketing and consumer research. By contrast to those scholars who used experimental, usually statistical forms of research, Dichter claimed such methods were outdated and could not give an accurate picture of consumption behaviour. By asking consumers direct questions, he pointed out that you are likely to receive socially desirable responses from them (i.e. if a consumer enjoys looking at nude pictures in a magazine which they frequently buy, they might still tell the interviewer that they buy it because of the informative stories (Dichter, 1979)).

Sketching the ontology, epistemology, axiology and view of human nature that the motivation researchers subscribed to, we can think of it in the following terms:

- Regarding the nature of reality (ontological assumptions) held by the motivation researchers, they saw consumer reality, that is, the consumer society and our place in it, as essentially socially constructed. There would be multiple factors that impact on how we act and which shape our consumption choices, but as individuals we can still exhibit a degree of agency. In other words, the society in which we live might set certain boundaries and the motivation researchers may have tools that can unpick our deepest desires, but we can refuse to be constrained or influenced by them. The consumer, to use the language deployed in Chapter 3, is still sovereign in the market.

- Regarding axiology, that is, the overriding goals that underpinned the production of motivation research, they were interested in 'understanding' consumer behaviour. Understanding, they said, was a necessary precondition for explaining and predicting how consumers will act, if indeed this was possible with any degree of certainty (Krugman, 1956–7).
- Epistemologically, the motivation researchers adopted a largely ideographic approach. This means that they believed 'that one can only understand the social world by obtaining first-hand knowledge of the subject under investigation. It thus places considerable stress upon getting close to one's subject and exploring its detailed background and life history' (Burrell and Morgan, 1979/1991: 6). Unlike conventional interpretive research (e.g. Thompson et al., 1989), the motivation researchers did not trust the responses provided by those they questioned. People, they thought, rationalise their consumption and buying behaviours. Researchers therefore needed to use indirect methods of accessing consumer subjectivity.
- The above point with respect to epistemology links with the overriding goal of motivation research: it seeks understanding, hence is ideographic (Burrell and Morgan, 1979/1991). Motivation research is concerned with understanding consumer subjectivity, that is, how a consumer (as part of a wider sample of people) perceives specific consumption behaviours (e.g. smoking). Motivation researchers want to look at the world through the consumer's eyes, as far as this is possible.
- The view of human nature that motivation researchers supported is already hinted at above. They are interested in consumer subjectivity and agency (how we understand the world, how we act in it) and thus require consumers to be 'co-participants' in any research being undertaken (the researcher is not in charge of the research – they have to listen and explore the topic with their research partner – the individual consumer). This does not mean that motivation researchers tell the 'co-participants' about the subject they are interested in exploring; there is a good reason for this, as they want to minimise any potential bias.

1.9.1 The Decline of Motivation Research

By the early 1960s, motivation research was – at least in academia – in decline. In business practice, it continued to provide its key advocates with a lucrative income. Within the business school though, it was never an especially popular subject, having had its scientific credentials examined by a variety of commentators in prominent journal publications and been criticised. But it did not disappear completely. Rather it was translated into psychographics. Admittedly that is putting it a little simply. Marketing scholars raided motivation research for its methodological tool box (qualitative methods) as well as for various strains of psychological theory, which were then used to improve market segmentation techniques (general personality traits and demographic information was used). This shift from the use of interpretive research and qualitative methods is, we should add, a theoretical microcosm of much wider changes in business education and research which had shifted in response to the growing calls for more academic rigour that were made throughout the 1950s and accelerated into the 1960s. But these are issues that we will explore in Chapter 2.

1.10 Conclusion

This chapter has introduced the development of marketing as an academic discipline and business practice. Originally marketing was studied for a variety of reasons. One of the most important is that business people were increasingly aware that as their business enterprises expanded, and their production facilities became capable of producing ever larger quantities of goods, that they needed to find some way of selling these goods more efficiently. They did this by expanding the markets they served, creating demand where previously there was none. This is why marketing is often associated with demand stimulation. In equal measure marketing scholars and practitioners legitimised their activities on the basis of satisfying customer needs (i.e. the marketing concept). Part of the legitimation strategy used by marketers was their attempt to demonstrate how their marketing activities added value; they did this by demonstrating that distribution costs were reasonable and that middlemen, including distributors, agents and retailers among others, deserved to be compensated for their activities (Shaw and Jones, 2005).

Early in the history of marketing, there were a variety of different strands of scholarship and multiple schools of marketing thought (see Shaw and Jones, 2005). A few writers and practitioners were heavily influenced by the work of Frederick Winslow Taylor and his writings on scientific management. These were used to make salesforce management more efficient. Others aligned themselves with issues of social and distributive justice as a function of their scholarly training in Germany and interest in the work of the German Historical School. From this resulted a debate between neo-classical economics-influenced marketing scholars and the German Historical School which forms the intellectual foundation for the first 'paradigm debate' (see Jones and Monieson, 1990). This was followed by the vigorous debate on the idea of whether marketing was an art or science. Developing out of these discussions were similar arguments between the 'positivist' marketing scholars and those influenced by more interpretive, qualitative studies. These issues would continue to exercise scholars in the period from the late 1980s until the present and we turn to these in the next chapter.

1.11 Learning Activities

The history of marketing is shown in this chapter to be subject to claims and counter claims. Despite the questions that arise from this, the critical point is that the idea of marketing is neither stable, modern nor constant. Both of the activities below will enable you to explore key themes within the chapter in far greater detail and assist you in framing the debate and situating these arguments into a clearer context. Before you begin the learning activities remind yourself of the learning aims for the chapter, so that your time and efforts are focused.

Learning Activity One: An American Affair in Germany

The chapter locates the origins of contemporary marketing with the German Historical School. How does the approach taken by the German Historical School differ from that of managerial marketing scholars and practitioners? You may want to begin trying to answer this question by reading Desmond and Crane (2002).

Learning Activity Two: Taylorism and Customer Orientation

If you were a salesperson working under the Taylorist influenced system of scientific salesmanship, would the fact that your employer encouraged 'sales contests' whereby salespeople competed to secure the maximum number of customers have encouraged you to be customer oriented or not? To begin thinking about this question read Strong and D'Amico (1991).

Further Reading

La Londe, B.J. and Morrison, E.J. (1967) 'Marketing management concepts yesterday and today', *Journal of Marketing*, 31(1): 9–13.

La Londe and Morrison introduce early figures in the history of marketing thought, and question taken-for-granted ideas about when the practice of marketing management first appeared.

Benton, R. (1987) 'The practical domain of marketing: The notion of a 'free' enterprise economy as a guise for institutionalized marketing power', *American Journal of Economics and Sociology*, 46 (4): 415–30.

Benton asks us to question the idea that companies are interested in responding to the consumer, suggesting instead that perhaps key marketing ideas serve as ideological blinkers that redirect attention away from unequal power relations in the marketplace.

Tadajewski, M. (2010) 'Reading "the marketing revolution" through the prism of the FBI', *Journal of Marketing Management*, 26(1–2): 90–107.

Tadajewski examines the argument made by Keith in his seminal 1960 paper and argues that Pillsbury's development of a marketing orientation is not quite as clear cut as Keith maintains. Instead, Pillsbury were involved in anti-competitive business practices that are not consistent with a marketing and customer focus.

Sage Online Titles

Shaw, E.H. and Jones, D.G.B. (2005) 'A history of schools of marketing thought', *Marketing Theory*, 5 (3): 239–81.

In this paper Shaw and Jones introduce the major schools of marketing thought: marketing functions, commodity, institutional, interregional, marketing management, marketing systems, consumer behaviour, macromarketing, exchange, and marketing history schools respectively.

Wilkie, W.L. and Moore, E.S. (2006) 'Macromarketing as a pillar of marketing thought', *Journal of Macromarketing*, 26 (2): 224–32.

Wilkie and Moore examine the history of marketing thought and find that earlier marketing scholars adopted a far more macromarketing perspective than is often recognised by mainstream marketing commentators. They were interested in distributive justice, ethics and the impact of marketing on society and society on marketing.

Jones, D.G.B. and Richardson, A. (2007) 'The myth of the marketing revolution', *Journal of Macromarketing*, 27 (1): 15–24.

Critically examining the argument made by Keith (1960) that marketing suddenly focused on consumer needs, wants and desires in the 1950s, Jones and Richardson assert that Canadian marketing practitioners have long registered the importance of the customer when making production decisions.

Monieson, D.D. (1988) 'Intellectualization in macromarketing: A world disenchanted', *Journal of Macromarketing*, 8(Fall): 4–10.

Monieson argues that over the history of marketing thought, marketing has become increasingly 'intellectualized'. Put simply, issues of ethics and social responsibility have been jettisoned from their central role in marketing theory and practice. As marketing is a human science, such values should be the foundation, along with distributive justice, of the discipline, Monieson says.

Tadajewski, M. (2006) 'Remembering motivation research: toward an alternative genealogy of interpretive consumer research', *Marketing Theory*, 6 (4): 429–65.

Tadajewski scrutinises the 'received wisdom' found in the history of marketing thought that interpretive consumer research first appears in the 1980s. By contrast, he asserts that such ways of thinking about and conceptualising the consumer were found much earlier in the development of marketing theory and practice in the form of 'motivation research'.

1.13 References

Alderson, W. and Cox, R. (1948) 'Towards a theory of marketing', *Journal of Marketing*, 13 (2): 137–52.

Appel, J.H. (1911) *Golden Book of the Wanamaker Stores*, Vol. 1. Philadelphia: John Wanamaker.

Appel, J.H. (1938) 'Reminiscences in retailing', *Bulletin of the Business Historical Society*, 12 (6): 81–90.

Ashley, W.J. (1908) 'The enlargement of economics', *The Economic Journal*, 18(70): 181–204.

Bartels, R. (1951a) 'Influences on the development of marketing thought, 1900–1923', *Journal of Marketing*, 16 (1): 1–17.

Bartels, R. (1951b) 'Can marketing be a science?', *Journal of Marketing*, 51(January): 319–28.

Bartels, R. (1988) *The History of Marketing Thought*, 3rd Edn. Ohio: Publishing Horizons.

Benton, R. (1987) 'The practical domain of marketing: The notion of a "Free" enterprise economy as a guise for institutionalized marketing power', *American Journal of Economics and Sociology*, 46 (4): 415–30.

Berghoff, H. (2003) '"Times change and we change with them": The German advertising industry in the Third Reich – between professional self-interest and political repression', *Business History*, 46: 128–47.

Borch, F.J. (1958) 'The marketing philosophy as a way of business life', in E.J. Kelley and W. Lazer (eds) *Managerial Marketing: Perspectives and Viewpoints A Source Book*, pp. 18–24. Homewood: Richard D. Irwin.

Brown, L.O. (1948) 'Towards a profession of marketing', *Journal of Marketing*, July: 27–31.

Brussière, D. (2000) 'Evidence of a marketing periodical literature within the American Economic Association, 1895–1936', *Journal of Macromarketing*, 20 (2): 137–43.

Burrell, G. and Morgan, G. (1979/1991) *Sociological Paradigms and Organisational Analysis*. Aldershot: Ashgate.

Buzzell, R.D. (1964) 'Is marketing a science?', *Harvard Business Review*, 41 (1): 32–40.

Cannon, T. (1980) 'Marketing: The state of the art (or science)', *Management Learning* (formerly *Management Education and Development*), 11: 138–44.

Converse, P.D. (1945) 'The development of the science of marketing: An exploratory study', *Journal of Marketing*, 10(July): 1–34.

Converse, P.D. (1951) 'Development of marketing theory: Fifty years of progress', in H.G. Wales (ed.), *Changing Perspectives in Marketing*, pp. 1–31. Urbana: University of Illinois Press.

Copeland, M.T. (1958) *And Mark an Era: The Story of the Harvard Business School*. Boston: Little, Brown and Company.

Corley, T.A.B. (1987) 'Consumer marketing in Britain 1914–60', *Business History*, 29 (4): 65–83.

Cowan, S. (1924) 'Tendencies in sales management', *Bulletin of the Taylor Society*, (April): 72–85.

Desmond, J. and Crane, A. (2002) 'Morality and the consequences of marketing action', *Journal of Business Research*, 57 (11): 1222–30.

Dichter, E. (1979) *Getting Motivated by Ernest Dichter: The Secret Behind Individual Motivation by the Man Who Was Not Afraid to Ask 'Why?'*. New York: Pergamon Press.

Dixon, D.F. (2002) 'Emerging macromarketing concepts: From Socrates to Alfred Marshall', *Journal of Business Research*, 55: 737–45.

Dixon, D.F. (2008) 'Consumer sovereignty, democracy and the marketing concept: A macromarketing perspective', in M. Tadajewski and D. Brownlie (eds), *Critical Marketing: Issues in Contemporary Marketing*, pp. 67–84. Chichester: Wiley.

Doubman, J.R. (1924) 'The modern sales manager and his developing technique', *The Annals of the American Academy of Political and Social Science*, 115: 174–82.

Elder, R.F. (1932) 'Product design for the market', *Mechanical Engineering*, (August): 543–6.

Farmer, R.N. (1967) 'Would you want your daughter to marry a marketing man?', *Journal of Marketing*, 31 (3): 1–3.

Filene, E.A. (1930) 'The new capitalism', *The Annals of the American Academy of Political and Social Science*, 149: 3–11.

Fitzgerald, R. (1989) 'Rowntree and market strategy, 1897–1939', *Business and Economic History*, 18: 45–58.

Fullerton, R.A. (1988) 'How modern is modern marketing? Marketing's evolution and the myth of the "production era"', *Journal of Marketing*, 52(January): 108–25.

Fullerton, R.A. (1994) '"And how does it look in America?": H.F.J. Kropff's historic report on US Marketing', *Journal of Macromarketing*, (Spring): 54–61.

Fullerton, R.A. (2009) 'When the owl of Minerva flew at dusk: Marketing in greater Germany, 1918–1939', *European Business Review*, 21 (1): 92–104.

García Ruiz, J.L. (2007) 'Cultural resistance and the gradual emergence of modern marketing and retailing practices in (Spain), 1950–1975', *Business History*, 49 (3): 367–84.

Graham, L. (2000) 'Lilian Gilbreth and the mental revolution at Macy's, 1925–1928', *Journal of Management History*, 6 (7): 285–305.

Hollander, S.C. (1986) 'The marketing concept: A déjà vu', in G. Fisk (ed.), *Marketing Management as a Social Process*, pp. 3–29. New York: Praeger.

Hoyt, C.W. (1929/2000) *Scientific Sales Management Today*. Bristol: Thoemmes Press.

Hudson, L.A. and Ozanne, J.L. (1988) 'Alternative ways of seeking knowledge in consumer research', *Journal of Consumer Research*, 14(March): 508–21.

Jones, C. (2007) 'Philosophy of science' in S. Clegg and J. Bailey (eds), *International Encyclopedia of Organization Studies*, pp. 1243–6. London: Sage.

Jones, D.G.B. (1994) 'Biography and the history of marketing thought: Henry Charles Taylor and Edward David Jones', in R.A. Fullerton (ed.), *Explorations in the History of Marketing*, pp. 67–85. Greenwich: JAI Press.

Jones, D.G.B. and Monieson, D.D. (1990) 'Early development of the philosophy of marketing thought', *Journal of Marketing*, 54(January): 102–13.

Jones, D.G.B. and Monieson, D.D. (1994/2008) 'Origins of the institutional approach in marketing', in M. Tadajewski and D.G.B. Jones (eds), *The History of Marketing Thought*, Volume III, pp. 125–44. London: Sage.

Jones, D.G.B. and Richardson, A.J. (2007) 'The myth of the marketing revolution', *Journal of Macromarketing*, 27 (1): 15–24.

Jones, D.G.B. and Shaw, E. (2002) 'A history of marketing thought', in B. Weitz and R. Wensley (eds), *Handbook of Marketing*, pp. 39–65. London: Sage.

Keith, R.J. (1960) 'The marketing revolution', *Journal of Marketing*, 24 (3): 35–8.

Kemmerer, E.W., MacGibbon, D.A., Bilgram, H., Weld, L.D.H., Anderson, B.M. and Fisher, I. (1918) 'Money and prices – discussion', *The American Economic Review*, 8 (1): 259–70.

Kitson, H.D. (1923) 'Understanding the consumer's mind', *The Annals of the American Academy of Political and Social Science*, 110: 131–8.

Krugman, H.E. (1956–7) 'A historical note on motivation research', *Public Opinion Quarterly*, 20 (4): 719–23.

La Londe, B.J. and Morrison, E.J. (1967) 'Marketing management concepts yesterday and today', *Journal of Marketing*, 31 (1): 9–13.

Laczniak, G.R. and Murphy, P.E. (2008) 'Distributive justice: Pressing questions, emerging directions, and the promise of Rawlsian analysis', *Journal of Macromarketing*, 28 (1): 5–11.

Laird, D.A. (1951) 'The new salesmanship', *Management Review*, (September): 560–2.

Lib, A. (2007) 'Definition of marketing', *ELMAR: Electronic Marketing*, 24 December.

Lockley, L.C. (1950) 'Notes on the history of marketing research', *Journal of Marketing*, 14 (5): 733–6.

Mason, R.S. (1998) 'Breakfast in Detroit: Economics, marketing, and consumer theory, 1930 to 1950', *Journal of Macromarketing*, 18 (2): 145–52.

Maynard, H.H. (1941) 'Early teachers of marketing', *Journal of Marketing*, 7 (2): 158–9.

Minowa, Y. and Witkowski, T. (2009) 'State promotion of consumerism in Safavid Iran: Shah Abbas I and Royal Silk Textiles', *Journal of Historical Research in Marketing*, 1 (2): 295–317.

Moore, D.G. (1957) 'Marketing orientation and emerging patterns of management and organization', in F.M. Bass (ed.), *The Frontiers of Marketing Thought and Science*, pp. 102–9. Chicago: American Marketing Association.

Moore, K. and Reid, S. (2008) 'The birth of brand: 4000 years of branding', *Business History*, 50 (4): 419–32.

Muir, M. (1924) 'Breaking down sales resistance in industrial selling. A survey of the buying habits of industry', *The Annals of the American Academy of Political and Social Science*, 115: 83–94.

Schell, E.H. (1930) 'The future of production', *The Annals of the American Academy of Political and Social Science*, 149: 28–35.

Scully, J.I. (1996) 'Machines made of words: The influence of engineering metaphor on marketing practice, 1900 to 1929', *Journal of Macromarketing*, (Fall): 70–83.

Shaw, A.W. (1912) 'Some problems in market distribution', *Quarterly Journal of Economics*, 26 (4): 703–24.

Shaw, E.H. (1995) 'The first dialogue on macromarketing', *Journal of Macromarketing*, 15 (1): 7–20.

Shaw, E.H. and Jones, D.G.B. (2005) 'A history of schools of marketing thought', *Marketing Theory*, 5 (3): 239–81.

Stainton, R.S. (1952) 'Science in marketing', *Journal of Marketing*, 17 (1): 64–6.

Starch, D. (1923) 'Research methods in advertising', *The Annals of the American Academy of Political and Social Science*, 110: 139–43.

Strong, J.T. and D'Amico, M.F. (1991) 'American sales management practice and thought: Developments to World War II'. Available at: http://faculty.quinnipiac.edu/charm/CHARM%20proceedings/CHARM%20article%20archive%20pdf%20format/Volume%205%201991/227%20strong%20d%27Amico.pdf

Strong, J.T. and Hawes, J.M. (1990) 'Harry R. Tosdal', *Journal of Personal Selling & Sales Management*, 10(Spring): 73–6.

Szmigin, I. and Foxall, G. (2000) 'Interpretive consumer research: How far have we come?', *Qualitative Market Research: An International Journal*, 3 (4): 187–97.

Tadajewski, M. (2006) 'Remembering motivation research: Toward an alternative genealogy of interpretive consumer research', *Marketing Theory*, 6 (4): 429–66.

Tadajewski, M. (2009a) 'Eventalizing the marketing concept', *Journal of Marketing Management*, 25 (1–2): 191–217.

Tadajewski, M. (2009b) 'Competition, cooperation and open price associations: Relationship marketing and Arthur Jerome Eddy (1859–1920)', *Journal of Historical Research in Marketing*, 1 (1): 122–43.

Tadajewski, M. and Brownlie, D. (2008) 'Critical marketing: A limit attitude', in M. Tadajewski and D. Brownlie (eds), *Critical Marketing: Issues in Contemporary Marketing*, pp. 1–28. Chichester: Wiley.

Tadajewski, M. and Saren, M. (2009) 'Rethinking the emergence of relationship marketing', *Journal of Macromarketing*, 29 (2): 93–206.

Tamilia, R. (2009) 'An overview of the history of marketing thought', *Journal of Historical Research in Marketing*, 1 (2): 346–60.

Taylor, F.W. (1911/1998) *The Principles of Scientific Management*. Mineola: Dover Publications.

Thompson, C.J., Locander, W.B. and Pollio, H.R. (1989) 'Putting consumer experience back in consumer research', *Journal of Consumer Research*, 16 (2): 133–47.

Tosdal, H.R. (1941) 'Significant trends in sales management', *Journal of Marketing*, 5 (3): 215–18.

Usui, K. (2008) *The Development of Marketing Management: The Case of the USA, c.1910–1940*. Aldershot: Ashgate.

Weaver, H.G. (1935) 'Consumer research and consumer education', *The Annals of the American Academy of Political and Social Science*, 182: 93–100.

Weld, L.D.H. (1941) 'Early experience in teaching courses in marketing', *Journal of Marketing*, 5 (4): 380–381.

White, P. (1927) *Scientific Marketing Management: Its Principles and Methods*. New York: Harper.

Wilkie, W.L. and Moore, E.S. (1999) 'Marketing's contributions to society', *Journal of Marketing*, 63(Special Issue): 198–218.

Wilkie, W.L. and Moore, E.S. (2006) 'Macromarketing as a pillar of marketing thought', *Journal of Macromarketing*, 26 (2): 224–32.

Zaltman, G. and Burger, P.C. (1975) *Marketing Research: Fundamentals and Dynamics*. Hinsdale: The Dryden Press.

Marketing 'Science' and the Paradigm Debates

2

2.1 Introduction

The field of marketing is characterised by many different, often competing, approaches and techniques. Marketers, it seems, have never really managed to come to any lasting agreement about what the study of marketing should look like or what approaches are best able to advance the discipline in a consistent way. There are many reasons for this and one of the most important features of the history of marketing thought has been the desire for marketers to appear credible and useful. It seemed to many writers that in order for marketing to become a serious and reputable subject, it needed to be conducted as a science as noted in Section 1.8 of the previous chapter. This view became incredibly powerful and for a period it looked like the marketing discipline had finally found a central guiding principle and philosophy. In order to establish marketing as a science, however, scholars needed some criteria against which to measure it. This chapter first reviews scholarly debates on the nature of such criteria, linking them with the 'paradigm wars' that have periodically erupted.

In time, the belief that scientific principles would advance marketing theory did itself become subject to critique and disagreement. Some scholars questioned whether we could, in positivistic fashion, predict and control consumer behaviour. The second interest of this chapter is to introduce to you some of the many different perspectives which have emerged in the marketing field and considers some of the debates that have taken place as a result. Specific focus is placed on the questioning of the managerial agenda of marketing theory and practice that was critiqued by a small group of consumer researchers in the late 1960s, early 1970s and who went on to found the Association for Consumer Research.

Having established this institutional structure, along with a publication outlet that was interested in publishing consumer research studies that were not necessarily produced with a view to making managerial practice more efficient (the *Journal of Consumer Research*), consumer research took what was called an 'interpretive turn'. We discuss how the insights of qualitative, interpretive studies appear back on the agenda after decades of comparative marginalisation. With this subsequent pluralisation of marketing theory, we trace the emergence and development of a number of different paradigms, bringing the historical study of marketing theory all the way up to the latest paradigmatic developments such as the use of poststructuralist, postmodernist, feminist and critical marketing perspectives.

2.1.1 Marketing 'Science' and Analysis, Planning, Implementation and Control

In his review of the history of consumer behaviour, Kassarjian maintains that 'by the end of World War II, business schools in general and marketing departments in particular were in a very weak position ... Academic research was impressionistic ... Good research might consist of a case study or perhaps detailed interviewing with a couple of middlemen' (Kassarjian, 1989: 123). This would change as a result of two important reports that were published by the Ford and Carnegie Foundations respectively which criticised the state of business education, especially the lack of engagement by business academics with mathematically oriented, behavioural science research.

Both the Ford and Carnegie reports were influential in stimulating a whole range of changes in business education: management educators were pushed to earn PhD degrees and to 'upgrade' (Bartels, 1988) their research skills, mainly in terms of improving their ability to manipulate complex mathematics. And the funding provided by the Ford Foundation 'served to usher in a new age for marketing' (Tadajewski, 2006: 179). This Foundation financially supported a range of textbooks, seminars and training programmes that diffused their scientific vision for business research. Research had to be objective, scientific and rigorous. Academic journals soon reflected this emphasis, most notably the newly founded *Journal of Marketing Research*. Ideally, says Kernan (1995), a published research paper had to contain some element of mathematical symbolism or involve 'laboratory research, experimental design, computer simulation, operations research, mathematical models, and high powered statistics' (Kassarjian, 1989: 124).

Many of the leading marketing thinkers to the present day were either directly involved in the Ford Foundation mathematical seminars, or have been taught by scholars that were. Practitioners were equally interested in these new mathematical and methodological tool-kits in anticipation that they could enhance managerial decision making (Kotler, 1961). To give us some insight into the importance of these seminars we should note that one of the key figures in the history of marketing thought, Philip Kotler, was part of a large cohort of marketing academics and teachers trained in advanced behavioural science techniques by the Ford Foundation sponsored seminars in advanced mathematics that were held at the Harvard Business School (and elsewhere) in the late 1950s. The success of these ideas can be illustrated by the fact that later thinkers call marketing a 'behavioural science'.

In fact, Kotler's seminal textbook, *Marketing Management: Analysis, Planning, and Control* that was published in 1967 and continues to be used worldwide today was, in a first draft, a very quantitatively oriented text. It contained little of the graphics and pictures that we associate with the latest editions today. As he relates this story:

> In examining the existing marketing textbooks, I felt that they lacked the tight analytical quality of the economics textbooks. They contained many lists (such as the advantages and disadvantages of wholesalers, etc.) and hardly any theory. Little was reported in the way of research findings and methodologies from the social, economic, and quantitative sciences. As a result, I decided around 1964 to write my own marketing textbook. The original draft was highly quantitative and my publisher advised me to 'tone down the math' and 'beef up the prose and stories.' The result was *Marketing Management* published in 1967. (Kotler in Bartels, 1988/2008: 108)

Kotler's text and its structured way of approaching marketing planning and implementation obviously chimed with the business climate. As was discussed in Chapter 1, the Second World War had led to massive increases in the production infrastructure of the United States, which had largely escaped the ravages of the conflict that decimated the production and distribution structures of Europe. Planning for production and marketing thus took on a whole new meaning: with large industrial production facilities, massive untapped and under-supported markets in Europe with all their attendant cultural differences, marketing had to take a more scientific, more systematic approach, utilising a range of key concepts that were popularised in the 1950s (see the Box below).

Key Concepts in Marketing Management

1 Product Differentiation and the Segmentation of Markets (Smith, 1956).
2 The Product Life Cycle (Wasson, 1960).
3 The Marketing Mix (Borden, 1964).
4 A Customer Orientation (Keith, 1960).

Source: Adapted from Shaw and Jones (2005: 257).

Kotler obviously did much to place marketing theory and practice on the intellectual map and in boardroom discussion, but we should not assume that the analysis, planning and control model that he put forward was a discontinuous innovation – something so radical that it had never been considered before. Historically, its lineage can be traced back to Frederick Taylor and the spin given to scientific management by those interested in scientific sales management. Stuart Cowan, writing in 1924, for instance, stressed the impact of competition on companies as encouraging, if not demanding, managerial planning and systematic research into the needs and wants of the marketplace. In a refrain similar to Kotler, Cowan stated:

> Broadly, the selling problem involves such questions as these: what to make; what type of product and at what price; what features are desired by the public; what service will make a strong appeal to the public or to the trade; what volume can be sold; will the profits be satisfactory; will the business be permanent. More narrowly, the selling problem is to work for a set quota at a definite cost, to earn a predetermined profit. Let us divide that work into four functions:
>
> 1 Analysis and research.
> 2 Planning, including preparation and scheduling.
> 3 Actual selling and advertising campaigns.
> 4 Control; through records, supervision, investigations and other methods. (Cowan, 1924: 77)

While Kotler's form of managerial marketing has become probably the best-known element of marketing theory and practice, it was only one stream of scholarship that looked at marketing in a very particular way, a way that not all agreed with.

Critics railed against the growing irrelevance of 'marketing science', which was perceived to be ignoring the impact of marketing on society, focusing instead on issues related to managerial and firm competitiveness exclusively. Many interested observers called for marketing intellectuals to devote attention to issues central in contemporary public policy debates or to study the impact of marketing on society and vice versa – i.e. to take a 'macromarketing' perspective (Shapiro, 2006). For Kassarjian (1994/2008: 307) the critics of managerial, mainstream marketing were generally younger members of the academic community who hadn't yet lost their idealistic desire to try to transform the marketing system for the better, severing the close relationship between marketing and the 'military-industrial-complex' (i.e. big business).

Such distancing was achieved in a number of ways. One way in which scholars tried to link marketing theory and research with wider societal concerns was to broaden the domain of marketing, to include not just business exchanges (i.e. the selling of soap and toothpaste), but to stress that many organisations engaged in marketing. Having established this idea, it was a short step to claiming that marketing techniques and tools could be used not only to sell toothpaste and armaments, but also to encourage people to attend church more frequently or donate blood. On the basis of this broadening of marketing activities, non-profit and other interested parties were further possible beneficiaries of marketing know-how.

But what did marketers actually mean when they referred to the 'science of marketing'? How did they know, or judge, what was scientific and what was not? Vigorous debate would emerge over this question amongst marketing scholars.

2.2 The Criteria for a Marketing Science

What is interesting about marketing thought after the critique of the Ford and Carnegie reports is that we get a split in the way marketing tries to present itself (Hackley, 2009). Some academics argued that marketing is a science that is essentially value-neutral. At the same time though, there were those who made quite explicit value judgments about what is or is not an appropriate consumption and behavioural choice (i.e. the social and societal marketers). For those in the former group, effort needed to be made to work out how we could assess whether marketing was a science.

Buzzell (1964), for instance, proposed a set of general criteria that a science of marketing should emulate. These included: the development of a classified and systematic body of knowledge coalescing around one or a number of central theories and principles, ideally expressible in quantitative terms which enable the prediction and control of marketing phenomena. The criteria proposed by Buzzell were, even so, problematic according to some. Hunt, most notably, said they were far too strict. As a substitute, he offered a position that is subscribed to by a large number of people in marketing and commonly called the 'positivist' paradigm. Hunt asserted that the label 'science' presupposes *'the existence of underlying uniformities or regularities among the phenomena that comprise its subject matter. The discovery of these underlying uniformities yields empirical regularities, law-like generalizations (propositions) and laws'* (Hunt, 1976: 26; emphasis in original). This position represents what is the 'orthodox approach' to the production of knowledge in marketing (Easton, 2002).

The premises underpinning research conducted according to the tenets of this paradigm are that, ontologically speaking, the world assumes a concrete existence that remains independent of perception (the world exists whether or not we are studying it). Epistemologically, 'positivist' research takes a reductionist orientation in that it is assumed that the focus of attention, no matter what the domain of study, can be broken down into its various constituent parts and made subject to analysis.

When taking a positivist approach, marketing 'scientists' engage in a process of hypothesis development (after appropriate literature reviews, etc) which they then test in the marketplace in order to either refute the hypothesis (which they then modify) or which is tentatively assumed to be empirically supported (Hunt, 1976). Analysis then, with any luck, yields the law-like generalisations mentioned by Hunt (Hudson and Ozanne, 1988).

Research grounded in this paradigm aims to produce practically useful knowledge geared to the requirements of the marketing organisation – it takes a so-called 'channel captain' perspective, because of the managerial focus of this paradigm (Arndt, 1985). The problem is, however, that marketing has not actually been that successful in developing empirical generalisations (Gummerson, 2005). And as with any position, not all agree with it. Nonetheless, any extended critique of this paradigm was slow to appear. We can say that this delay was due to pragmatism, in that 'positivism' was the paradigmatic position subscribed to by the majority of scholars, including the gatekeepers of important journals. It therefore made it difficult to publish in certain academic publications if your paradigm differed from that of the gatekeepers. Criticism of the then present state of marketing as an academic discipline did, even so, appear. Some scholars distanced their intellectual activities from the prevailing managerial trends in marketing, working with public policy practitioners in trying to make the marketing system operate more effectively for all groups in society.

Intellectually, the Association for Consumer Research (ACR) is probably the most important institution promoting alternative ways of understanding consumption behaviour. Formed in 1969, the ACR:

> … was not meant to be an arm of the business establishment and it was not intended to be an offspring of marketing. It was intended to function as a legitimate interdisciplinary field during difficult social times. Consumer research could be used for the good or evils of trade. We wanted to believe that it could be applied to the protection of consumers as well as to their exploitation … From the local court house to the nation's capital, marketing and consumer researchers were plying their trade … Articles on deceptive advertising, on counter and corrective advertising, on research on labelling, on nutritional information, and on information overload abounded. The outcasts were those who worked for or defended the military-industrial complex and those who asked, What are the managerial implications.(Kassarjian, 1994/2008: 307)

Questions began to be asked about whether marketing should affiliate itself with the practical requirements of marketing managers or whether it should ask similar questions to those posed by the German Historical School about social and distributive justice. Along with this disciplinary introspection, marketing theorists sought to examine the tenets of the 'positivist' paradigm: were its assumptions valid? Could we ever produce research that was 'objective'? 'True' and so on?

2.2.1 A 'Spirited Debate'

Registering the *apparent* epistemological dominance of 'positivism' in marketing theory and the impact that this epistemological stance has had on the production of knowledge, there was a 'spirited debate' (Hunt, 1991) between proponents of a diverse range of philosophical viewpoints. A key motivator behind the promotion of alternative views of scientific activity was the lack of engagement that marketing scholars had had with the history and philosophy of science. To make a long story much shorter, when marketing scholars did read the latest works in the history and philosophy of science, they found that the image of science that some commentators had encouraged marketers to pursue was unattainable.

The critics of 'positivist' approaches in marketing questioned the idea that there was one way of seeking knowledge, one scientific method that would provide insight into any given topic of interest. A key issue was the idea that scientific knowledge had to be tested against empirical evidence. This might sound quite reasonable. Scientists should, you might think, have to develop hypotheses and then investigate whether these were corroborated by evidence or refuted. However, to assume that this is necessarily the best way of seeking knowledge is to have already made a particular choice about the paradigm – philosophical worldview – you most highly value or find compelling. Scientific practice is a human activity and as such human values will influence how we practise and understand science. They will affect whether or not we consider a particular judgment truthful or appropriate or not. Thus a 'critical relativism' argues against 'positivism' and its associated language of law-like generalisations that

> ...disciplinary knowledge claims are viewed as contingent upon the particular beliefs, values, standards, methods, and cognitive aims of its practitioners. Moreover, critical relativism recognizes that knowledge production in the social sciences is impacted by the broader cultural milieu in which it is embedded. (Anderson, 1986: 156)

Science, in short, is shot through with human values. This is no bad thing, as Karl Popper appreciated. What we must demonstrate clearly for those trying to evaluate a claim to knowledge is 'a theory's mode of production, the criteria against which it is judged, the ideological and value commitments that inform its construction, and the metaphysical beliefs that underwrite its research program' (Anderson, 1986: 156). To be a relativist in marketing thus indicates a subscription to epistemological pluralism for Anderson.

This recognition that there are many different ways of seeking knowledge, which are often adopted by academic disciplines to varying extents, and consequently used to formulate alternative ways of comprehending human behaviour, suggests that marketing and consumer research should embrace multiple paradigmatic positions along with 'theoretical eclecticism' (Olson, 1982). Alternative research programmes are therefore best thought of as different, but not as wholly 'incommensurable' ways of exploring and analysing the phenomena of interest (Anderson, 1986).

2.3 Incommensurable Paradigms

For the historian and philosopher of science, Thomas Kuhn (1970), two paradigms are incommensurable when there is no 'neutral algorithm of theory-choice, no systematic decision procedure which, properly applied, must lead each individual in the group to the same decision' (Kuhn, 1970: 200). Essentially he was arguing that you cannot compare the theories produced by two different paradigms on a like-for-like basis, without any loss of detail. Later, he retracted his incommensurability thesis by noting that there were various values that could be used to compare such theories. However, his view is still perceived by some to be relativistic (Nola and Sankey, 2007) in that there is no ultimate arbiter who can define unequivocally which perspective is correct, to the satisfaction of all researchers. In terms of marketing theory, therefore, each paradigm that we examine below (interpretive, critical marketing, poststructural and feminist) is held to possess specific advantages and liabilities and these will be recognised by the members of alternative paradigmatic communities, if only grudgingly.

In terms of marketing research, Anderson suggests that scholars will have specific perspectives which they prefer; some will be inclined toward 'positivism' and its associated methods; others will prefer interpretive approaches and their methodological tool-kits. Since researchers adopt different paradigmatic perspectives, which are underpinned by a diverse range of assumptions, there is likely to be some disagreement about which approach reflects the most appropriate philosophical and methodological course for the production of marketing theory. This leads Anderson to talk about a 'weak form' of incommensurability. Naturally enough, we still understand the work produced by other scholars working in different paradigms (provided we put in the hard work to do so obviously) but we will still disagree about 'the appropriate program for researching a particular topic' (Anderson, 1986: 158).

In response, Anderson proposed rethinking marketing 'science'. Basically he argues that no one perspective is likely to hold all of the answers, nor will all marketing researchers evaluate the same piece of research in an identical way, appreciating the value of the findings equally (i.e. those who appreciate large survey studies are not likely to be convinced by the seven or so 'phenomenological interviews' characteristic of interpretive research). As such, Anderson advocated paradigmatic tolerance. He thought we should turn multiple perspectives on to marketing and consumer behaviour, rather than limit ourselves to one approach.

2.3.1 Truth, Objectivity and Nonsense

Given the political nature of knowledge production, a rapid and sustained critique of Anderson's 'critical relativism' was to be expected. Hunt was especially critical because on his reading, 'truth' is presented by relativists as an inappropriate goal for marketing 'science' (Hunt, 1990). Instead, Hunt argues for retaining truth as a central feature of a 'scientific realist' approach to marketing.

For Hunt, scientific realism maintains the goal of objectivity in science and assumes that reality exists independently of subjective perception (Hunt, 1984). 'To assume otherwise', Hunt asserts, 'makes a nonsense out of science' (1990: 9) for reasons that will become clear in a moment. Hunt sees the role of science and the research process to be directed towards the improvement of our 'perceptual processes', so that we are able to distinguish 'illusion from reality' (Hunt, 1990: 9). We differentiate illusion from reality via empirical research, testing our hypotheses using empirical evidence. This, in turn, allows us to determine whether our perceptions can be corroborated and therefore considered truthful. By contrast, for the critical relativist, the ideal of attaining 'truth' is not essential for continued scientific progress. For Anderson, a more productive way of approaching our research is to adopt a 'benign agnosticism' regarding the ontology of social science, that is, to refrain from asking the question will we know what reality really is through our research (Anderson, 1988).

Whilst the early conflict seen between scientific realism and critical relativism has ebbed slightly, the later stages of the debate between the realists and relativists has continued, albeit with contributors successively refining and responding to the misinterpretation of relativism by the realists (Hunt, 1992; Peter, 1992), the misuse of the label 'positivism' (Hudson and Ozanne, 1988; Hunt, 1991), while others have worked on developing the empirical basis of alternative paradigms, notably the interpretive paradigm (Arnould and Thompson, 2005).

2.4 The (Re)emergence of the Interpretive Paradigm

In our earlier reference to motivation research in Chapter 1, it was argued that this approach was largely ideographic and interpretive in stance. Our perspective in this book differs from that generally found in histories of consumer research. Until recently, for instance, it was generally said that the mid-1980s represent the major turning point during which consumer researchers, in particular, were willing to challenge the 'positivist' paradigm and begin exploring alternative avenues for the production of marketing knowledge (Shankar and Patterson, 2001). Having examined the contributions of the motivation researchers, we know that this view is somewhat of an overstatement. Still, we can say that the popularisation of interpretive research in the late 1980s, early 1990s, was a result of the work by the 'Consumer Behavior Odyssey', who studied the multitude of ways in which people are involved with consumption using what was called a 'naturalistic' research strategy (Belk et al., 1989). This work was a major catalyst for the 'interpretive turn'.

We can explain the difference between the 'positivist' paradigm referred to above and those who subscribe to the variety of interpretive, constructionist and humanistic forms of marketing research in the following manner. Proponents of the 'subjective world' (Arndt, 1985) or 'interpretive' paradigm hold that the social world exhibits a 'precarious ontological status' (Burrell and Morgan, 1979/1992). In questioning the ontological status of social reality, the emphasis in interpretive research is on the de-emphasis of an external concrete social world. Much like the critical relativists above, there is less concern with touching base with some external 'real' world and more interest in investigating the social world at the level of subjective experience. We can say, therefore, that social reality for interpretive researchers is essentially inter-subjectively composed and the product of historical development and socialisation (Solomon, 1983). As an example of an interpretive approach, let us turn briefly to a 'symbolic interactionist' examination of product use (see the box below).

Symbolic Interactionism and Product Use Behaviour

In his important contribution to the literature, Michael Solomon sketched out the difference between the way marketing theory traditionally thinks about why people use particular products and how a symbolic interactionist perspective reflects on product use. Symbolic interactionism, Solomon suggests, 'focuses on the processes by which individuals understand their world' (Solomon, 1983: 320). Distilling the key insights of the work of thinkers like George Herbert Mead, Solomon argues that the way we think about who we are (our self-concept) is partially constituted by the reactions of others to the way we present ourselves to them. Our own self-concept, in other words, orients the way we act

(Cont'd)

in the world and is actively interpreted by those we come into contact with. By presenting a particular self image to a particular individual or social group, these individuals will evaluate us and pass judgment on our presentation of self. This, in turn, impacts on the way we think about ourselves, perhaps leading us to modify the way we present ourselves in future.

Products, Solomon says, are an important element of the way we define ourselves but also function as a means of negotiating certain roles. They can, Solomon asserts, help us satisfy some innate need. They can also be valuable in terms of the type of 'impression management' discussed by Goffman (1959/1990: 29). Thus we use products like expensive cars and jewellery to present a certain idealised image of how we want to be seen by others (Solomon, 1983). Solomon, however, contrasts this form of impression management with those situations where products actually direct appropriate behaviours, rather than simply being a form of symbolic communication.

Solomon draws upon 'a simple but pervasive example' that of 'adolescent boys' use of such "macho" products as cars, clothing, and cologne to bolster developing and fragile masculine self-concepts' (1983: 325). He also makes reference to other fragile senses of self that illustrate how products and their associated meanings buttress a weaker sense of self. For example, he draws from research conducted on MBA students. Those students less likely to succeed often consumed the appropriate mix of products used by successful business people, while at the same time avoiding 'long hair or facial hair' (Solomon, 1983: 326).

Overall, then, products can be used to satisfy particular needs, as part of impression management, and equally as a way of directing consumer behaviour when the individual concerned might not be fully sure about how they should act in a new situation (e.g. when getting a new job and so forth). Consider your own consumer behaviour when arriving at university: did you change the way you supported your sense of self with particular products? Were you conscious of presenting a certain image to your new colleagues? Did you change your consumption behaviour as a result of comments by others? Do you agree with Goffman (1959/1990) and Ligas and Cotte (1999: 610) who claim that 'the self is itself multifaceted'. In other words, do you have different ways you present yourself to others: are you like the 'youth who is demure enough before his parents and teachers, [but] swears and swaggers like a pirate among his "tough" youth friends' (Goffman, 1959/1990: 57)?

Researchers subscribing to the interpretive paradigm do not believe that the most effective way of understanding the social and cultural world is by generating a priori a list of hypotheses (i.e. determining a list of hypotheses that might be consistent with reality). Instead, some very general ideas about the consumption phenomena to be studied are sketched out and investigated further through detailed study of the phenomena as it is either engaged in by the interviewee or as they recollect it. In exploring consumer behaviour, interpretive consumer researchers often (but not exclusively) use qualitative methods, such as interviews and ethnography.

For instance, in discussing a fairly typical form of interpretive research, Elliott and Jankel-Elliott make the case that simply asking consumers about their media consumption (i.e. watching TV) is not likely to tell us the whole story about this consumption behaviour. Elliott and Jankel-Elliott claim that when they studied consumer behaviour using ethnography, it enabled them 'to access what people actually do rather than what they say they do. For example, people watched many more hours of TV than they said, spent far more hours gaming than they claimed, and used the mobile phone in surprising ways, including when in the toilet' (Elliott and Jankel-Elliott,

2003: 220). In the case of this study it was important that the consumer researcher was able to get beyond the representation of the consumer's behaviour which may have been influenced by social desirability bias; in other words, where 'respondents … provide socially desirable answers' (Fisher and Katz, 2000: 105); or, in other words still, where they may be inclined to tell white lies.

This type of interpretive research thus tries to compare what respondents say they do, with what they actually do. Obviously, interpretive research has value for the marketing practitioner. Nevertheless, recently the growth in new methods and ways of understanding the marketplace has been accompanied by a belief that not all marketing and consumer research necessarily needs to have any managerial relevance. After all, there are other stakeholders who could be the recipients of marketing know-how. As Kassarjian (1994/2008) points out, just as marketing research can be used to manipulate consumers, through being used to develop more effective communications campaigns, it could also be used to improve consumer decision-making skills, making consumers more 'reflexive' when it comes to taking marketplace decisions. Consumers can, through the provision of appropriate information, thereby become 'reflexively defiant consumers' (Ozanne and Murray, 1995) who not only seek out additional information to make informed choices with respect to the goods they purchase, they also question the existing structure of consumption, asking questions about whether it truly satisfies their needs, wants and requirements (see also Chapter 8).

Here consumers begin to question the rhetoric of marketers, realising perhaps that buying and consuming ever greater quantities of products and services does not actually make them any happier as a result. This type of research takes us into the domain of critical marketing studies. When discussing critical marketing studies in the following section, we are talking primarily about a Critical Theory influenced version of critical marketing studies. In line with recent work, we use the plural critical marketing 'studies' instead of critical marketing 'theory' to indicate that there is no single paradigm uniting critical marketing academics (Tadajewski and Maclaran, 2009).

2.5 Critical Marketing Studies

For marketing and consumer research, the 'positivist' and the interpretive paradigms are the two main perspectives used in the production of marketing and consumer theory. Still, research based on alternative theoretical traditions grounded, for example, in critical social theory has a quite long history in marketing (Tadajewski, 2010).

In general terms, research that draws on Critical Theory assumes that social reality is socially manufactured, but asserts that there are certain structural factors such as the way we are schooled and socialised that ensure we look at the world in certain ways and not others. In this regard, Critical Theorists and critical marketers make frequent reference to the role of 'culture industries' in the processes of enculturation. These are all institutions and industries that are involved in some way with the production of popular culture. Marketing and advertising are prominent within the culture industries. Critics point to the role of advertising, which presents a perfect world only achievable through consumption, the prominence of product-placement in film and its role in the creative process, and the production of ideal-images associated with cosmetics. The list of issues could go on. Individually and collectively, these work to produce particular ways of seeing and relating to the world as natural (i.e. through consumption I gain happiness).

In the context of this paradigm, criticism functions to raise consciousness and encourage the transformation of the social world, particularly the one-dimensionality that cultural critics saw accompanying the industrial transformation of the United States. Looking at marketing through the prism provided by this paradigm, we can say that Critical Theorists view marketing as playing a major role in encouraging people to evaluate their lives on the basis of the level of material consumption that they have attained. Increased consumption, Critical Theorists bemoan, has become the proxy for 'social progress', which orients the way an individual lives their life (Kline and Leiss, 1978).

Thus people work harder to maintain their positional status in society and their inter-personal relations with other human beings suffer as a result (Bauman, 2007). We work harder for products because they provide a sense of self. This, interpretive researchers would have little problem with (Belk, 1988); for the critical marketing commentator, by contrast, the self that is created through the consumption of goods is not necessarily an individual creation – we do not build up our own individual personalities through consumer durables. At best we can only say we are producing self-images that are 'pseudo-individualistic'. To make sense of this consider that a) We buy mass produced goods; b) Other people buy the same mass produced goods. So how can we possibly be individuals? How can lots of people, all consuming a certain product – say, a pair of Levi jeans – really differentiate themselves from the masses? They cannot, critical scholars would claim. From the perspective of this paradigm, therefore, the culture industries modify the way we think about consumption, indeed about the very nature of selfhood, in ways that serve their interests, not those of the individual consumer. Mass production requires mass consumption. Since consumers do not like to feel manipulated, they must believe that products speak to them individually.

This view of the consumer as a 'victim' of wider social and political structures has become less and less persuasive to some marketing scholars, slipping further out of favour as postmodernism came to prominence (Gabriel and Lang, 1995). Connected with the economic policies of the Reagan and Thatcher governments, rising affluence and what King (1985) calls 'new individualism', consumption is now celebrated as an active pursuit, with the consumer selecting the lifestyle that suits their requirements, rather than having their consumption choices dictated to them via powerful forms of persuasion (as also noted in Chapter 9). As King puts it,

> In the UK, as in the US and most of Europe, research shows that there have been huge changes in people's interests, tastes and aspirations. They have moved from fixed and inherited values to individual and discovered values. Their horizons have widened in many ways, but especially in a desire for self-expression and self-determination. People want to own their own homes, to decorate and furnish them in their own particular style. The same goes for their cars and clothes and cooking. They want to explore and experiment, to be individuals. (King, 1985: 5)

This about-turn in the way that consumption can be thought about is nothing short of extraordinary when juxtaposed against the writings of the Critical Theorists and other critical observers. By contrast to Vance Packard (1960) who viewed the consumer as the object of manipulation by powerful motivation researchers or James Vicary who convinced the public that they could be manipulated by messages operating below the level of consciousness (i.e. via subliminal advertising), the literature is now dominated by accounts that emphasise consumer advertising literacy and by depictions of consumer agency that lay emphasis on the ease of identity changes (Brown, 1998). Consumers are no longer the marionettes of marketers, but actively construct their own stylised ways of living (Gabriel and Lang, 1995; King, 1985).

2.6 Postmodernism

In the late 1980s and early 1990s, postmodernism began to be discussed in marketing. According to some, in a postmodern world, we no longer derive our identity from the jobs we do or the class into which we were born. People derive personal satisfaction from their consumption behaviours. We might work, but we define ourselves in the realm of consumption (Brown, 1995).

Consistent with this, individuals are apparently able to create their own identities through their consumption behaviours and receive their emotional and spiritual sustenance 'by accessing the world of consumerism and becoming a product of the global consumer culture' (Venkatesh, 1994: 23). As Venkatesh also notes, these consumption options are not available to everyone. Not everyone can literally buy the consumption goods that they crave (see Chapter 11).

In spite of this, it is generally conceded that people use the products of marketers' imaginations – marketing communications, products themselves, brand images – to project an image of themselves, as they would like other people to see them. People in Hong Kong, for example, are privileged to live in a city 'described as a 'global cultural supermarket' where consumers fashion their identities by accessing a transnational and global network of images, ideas, and practices' (Cayla and Eckhardt, 2008: 223). And in Shanghai people have adopted the fashion for plastic surgery with verve, literally reproducing themselves in a manner consistent with Western images of beauty (Lindridge and Wang, 2008).

Taking a more philosophical look at postmodernism we can say that it is widely viewed as a departure from the philosophical certainty of the Enlightenment (i.e. that the scientific method will enable us to attain truth, sweeping away religious (or whatever) forms of mysticism). By contrast, postmodern perspectives on marketing adhere to the view that there is no one correct, universal scientific method (Brown, 1995). More radical than this claim is the proposal by postmodernists that as all concepts, scientific investigations and claims to truth are grounded in our everyday language, then it is no longer possible for scientific investigation to reveal the true, ontological nature of the world (Brown, 1995). There is no objective truth, no ontological structure to be tapped through the use of any method or paradigm. There can be no reliable statements about the nature of reality. Postmodern marketing research thus assumes a relativistic ontological *and* epistemological stance (Shankar and Patterson, 2001) (see Table 2.1).

The dismissal of any belief in scientific objectivity, leads advocates of postmodernism to rule out

> … the possibility of presuppositionless representation, instead arguing that every knowledge is contextualized by its historical and cultural nature … Social science becomes an accounting of social experience from … multiple perspectives of discourse/practice, rather than a larger cumulative enterprise committed to the inference of general principles of social structure and organisation. Thus, like poststructuralism, postmodernism rejects the project of a universal social science, falling back on the particular modes of knowledge defined by the multiplicity of people's subject positions. (Agger, 1991: 117)

Let us put these epistemological issues aside as scholars associated with other paradigmatic positions have focused most of their attention on the way postmodern commentators conceptualise the consumer. The problem here relates primarily to the idea that the postmodern consumer shifts their identity and lifestyle choices, as frequently as they change their clothes.

Table 2.1   Postmodern conditions and main themes

Hyperreality	Fragmentation	Reversal of Production and Consumption	Decentred Subject	Juxtaposition of Opposites
Reality as part of the symbolic world and constructed rather than given.

The emergence of symbolic and spectacle as the basis of reality.

The idea that marketing is constantly involved in the creation of more real than real consumption experiences (see, for example, the Venetian Hotel in Las Vegas).

The blurring of the distinction between real and non-real (e.g. Walt Disney World). | Consumption experiences are multiple, disjointed.

Human subject has a divided self.

Terms such as 'authentic-self' and 'centered connections' are questionable.

Lack of commitment to any (central) theme.

Abandonment of history, origin and context.

Marketing is an activity that fragments consumption signs and environments and reconfigures them through style and fashion. | Postmodernism is basically a culture of consumption, while modernism represents a culture of production.

Abandonment of the notion that production creates value while consumption destroys it.

Sign value replaces exchange value as the basis of consumption.

Consumers are active creators and producers of symbols and signs of consumption, as are marketers.

Consumers are objects in the marketing process, while products become active agents. | The following modernist notions of the subject are called into question:

1 Human subject is a self-knowing autonomous agent
2 Human subject is a cognitive subject
3 Human subject is a unified subject.

Postmodernist notions of the subject:

1 Human subject is historically and culturally constructed
2 Authentic self is displaced by a made-up self. | Fragmentation rather than unification is the basis of consumption. |

Source: Adapted from Firat, A.F. and Venkatesh, A. (1995) 'Liberatory postmodernism and the reenchantment of consumption', *Journal of Consumer Research*, 22 (December): 239–67. Reprinted with permission. © 1995 by the Association for Consumer Research.

In a discussion of the 'protean' individual (based on Proteus, the mythical sea God who could change shape at will), Lifton (1993) outlines what he means by the protean nature of self development. He says that we do change our lifestyles, partners and so on, more frequently than in the past. In a discussion that questions the idea that we can ever have an essential self, that is, one way of being that represents our real identity, Brown argues that from a postmodern perspective we have little hope of developing a 'unified personality':

> ... the luxury of 'finding oneself' has been undermined by assertions that the unified personality, or even the 'split subject' identified by Freud, is little more than a *mélange* of roles or personae which are adopted, employed and abandoned in rapid succession. The 'wife and mother' of the breakfast table, may give way to the 'career woman' during the working day, the 'sports enthusiast' of the evening or the 'fashion victim', 'DIY enthusiast' or 'culture vulture' of the weekend. The 'empty self' is thus refilled, decanted and replenished with whatever persona the occasion demands. (Brown, 1995: 80)

Tadajewski and Brownlie (2008) take a slightly different perspective. They point out that most people in this world do not possess the degree of affluence that postmodern lifestyles require. This is not to say that consumers in developed and developing nations do not use products to define who they are or in constructing a sense of self that is understandable to others, since as Cahn (2008) illustrates with respect to middle class Mexicans, Hansen (1999) in relation to Zambian consumers, Askegaard (2006) with respect to people living in Nepal, and a variety of other writers on Thai (Mills, 1997) and Asian consumers (Cayla and Eckhard, 2008; Lindridge and Wang, 2008), there are many that do this or are interested in building a self image using particular commodities. But what Tadajewski and Brownlie suggest is that people in 'developed' and 'developing' countries cannot all engage in the types of 'liberatory' consumption (Firat and Venkatesh, 1995) discussed by postmodern marketing scholars. Few consumers have the financial resources to become the kind of 'optimistic theoretical construction' that Thompson and Hirschman (1995) perceive the postmodern consumer to be, even if they actually wanted to (see box below).

Liberatory Consumption and the Postmodern Consumer

Critical marketers and sociologists of consumption have devoted attention recently to critically questioning some of the key ideas that underpin postmodern discourse, especially this notion of liberatory consumption. What is far too infrequently noted, critical marketers claim, is that while a 'consumer mentality' (Asgary and Walle, 2002: 62) is indeed spreading across the globe, that the ability of people to adopt a consumer lifestyle still remains the privilege of a comparatively small number of people in the world.

Although it is often easy to forget it, the cheap consumer goods that we can purchase are often made in locations where labour is cheap, where people are made to work very long hours, and where the legal protection of worker rights is minimal. In other words, our glittering consumer society is founded on 'the systemic exploitation of subaltern groups and nation states at the periphery of the global system ... This is a *fundamental prerequisite* for the *consumer revolution to take place in the richer countries*' (Varman and Vikas, 2007: 123; emphases in original).

For example, in their research conducted in the North Indian city of Kanpur, Varman and Vikas (2007) document the 'wretched living conditions of subaltern consumers' and their inability to engage in the types of consumption that many of us take for granted.

(Cont'd)

These people are far removed from the liberatory consumption behaviours discussed by postmodernists. Those labouring in the factories that produce branded products at low prices, earning themselves low wages in turn,

> ...struggle to make their two ends meet [*sic*] and they live in shanty houses sur-rounded by extremely unhygienic conditions. These houses are also overcrowd-ed with little personal space for their inhabitants. Food consumption just about meets the bare minimum requirement that is necessary for the biological survival of this group of consumers. These wretched living conditions lead to frequent outbreak[s] of diseases, which further worsen the lives of these consumers. Our data show that most of these subaltern consumers barely possess a set or two of clothing, which are just about adequate to cover their bodies. Low levels of access in the areas of food, clothing and shelter, provide a powerful, albeit tragic, description of unfreedom for this subaltern consumer group.' (Varman and Vikas, 2007: 126)

Why do you think that even when people are told about the sometimes horrendous production conditions in which certain branded products are made, do people con-tinue to buy such goods? Do you know of any companies whose labour policies have been condemned, but who are well known marketing companies? Do you or would you ever purchase goods made in conditions like those mentioned above? Be honest! When thinking about this issue, you might want to begin by reading Salzer-Mörling, and Strannegård (2007).

Perhaps it is no wonder that some are now suggesting that the distance of the postmodern perspective from the concerns of many in the developing and developed world alike renders it 'almost farcical' (Scott, 1993). So, although postmodernism may represent 'a slogan of dissent against intellectual domination, or otherwise', commentators seem to be working towards the perspective that its apparent inat-tention to power relations and the inequalities that structure the social world render its usefulness in understanding marketing and consumption behaviour limited (O'Shaughnessy and O'Shaughnessy, 2002: 131).

2.7 Poststructuralism and Feminism

Let us now turn to study the contribution that poststructural analysis offers to marketing and consumer research. Since we have already discussed postmodernism, it might be worth distinguishing postmodernism from poststructuralism, especially given the critique levelled at the former in the paragraph above.

Elliott and Ritson (1997) argue that poststructuralism can be distinguished from postmodernism by virtue of its ontological commitments, viewing social reality as 'historically, socially and culturally specific yet [at the same time] ... not deny[ing] the importance of the material as well as the symbolic' (Elliott and Ritson, 1997: 190). What this means in terms of the consumer is that the definition of the self that we often take for granted is essentially a category constructed by various impersonal forces including 'cultural institutions, economic interests, power relationships, gender relationships, [and] class divisions' (Thompson and Hirschman, 1995: 139). For example, the way that we view our selves, the satisfaction we derive from our body and lifestyle is mediated by advertising, discussions of health and healthy living by authoritative scientific bodies and the medical profession, as well as our interpersonal relations which shape the values we attribute to particular bodily shapes (Thompson and Hirschman, 1995).

Marketing theory is in much the same way shaped by power relations and gender relations, as Fischer and Bristor (1994) highlight most vividly. Before discussing the key feminist perspectives in marketing, we should begin by thinking about what we mean by 'feminism'. Feminism is a label used to refer to the various political goals and philosophical outlooks associated with the women's movement and its attempts to improve the position of women in society. Broadly speaking feminism takes the view that women are disadvantaged by their sex/gender and subjugated by men, and the goal of the women's movement is to change this state of affairs.

There are many review articles that compare and contrast the similarities, differences and points of criticism between these perspectives (we highly recommend Calás and Smircich, 2009). We can summarise some of the most salient points from these reviews as follows:

- Liberal feminists assume that men and women are both capable of rational thought and behaviour, and need to be given the same opportunities to express and develop them. The goal of the women's movement should be the pursuit of liberal principles, most notably equality, through social institutions like the law.
- Unlike liberal feminists, radical feminists believe that men and women are fundamentally and irreconcilably different. These differences are seen to reside either in biology and/or in experiences. The goal of the women's movement should be to encourage society not only to recognise these differences, but to value women's bodies and experiences as much as men's, and to create alternative forms of knowledge and organisation based on women's knowledge and, in some cases, solely for women. Sometimes this is called standpoint theory.
- Poststructuralist feminism would take a different stance to both of the above. Poststructuralists do not believe in the fixed identities and rational logic of liberal feminists, or in the essential differences between men and women. They also refuse to subscribe to the notion of gender based on 'sexed' bodies (i.e. that gender is based solely on our endowment with particular genitalia), as in the case of liberal feminists and some radical feminists. Instead they view identity and experience as historically and linguistically constructed phenomena, which are unstable, changing and ambiguous.
- Black feminists and lesbian feminists share a common criticism of liberal feminists, namely that liberal feminists serve the interests of white, middle-class, straight women, and do not speak to the issues that black and lesbian women face. The idea of a universal category of women, which radical feminists speak of, also falls foul of the same criticism. As a group, women exhibit numerous differences which, when taken together (e.g. black/lesbian/working class) create different sorts of experiences.
- Marxist/socialist feminists would also critique liberal feminist ideals, as well as the assumption that gender is contained in our sexed bodies. Instead they

would emphasise that gender is a product of capitalist relations of production, and an historical outcome of the development of capitalism. As such, gender lies in historical and societal relations, not in biology.

When talking about feminist theory, then, we need to be careful to specify which version we are using. But how has feminist thinking been used in marketing theory and consumer research?

Multiple studies in the early 1990s paved the way for feminist analysis. Beginning with consumer research, two important pieces stand out. The first is Hirschman's (1993) analysis of the articles published in the 1980 and 1990 volumes of the *Journal of Consumer Research*. The *JCR* is the leading journal in consumer research and is published out of the USA. Deploying feminist principles to analyse the 37 articles published in both these volumes, Hirschman found not only the prevalence of a masculine ideology, but also the fact that there was little change in the presence of this ideology in the pages of *JCR* from 1980 to 1990.

Hirschman explains that a masculine ideology is one based on a system of dualisms where what is masculine gains meaning from its difference to what is considered feminine. These dualisms include the following where the first term is stereotypically associated with masculinity and the second with femininity: rationality/emotionality; objectivity/subjectivity; quantitative/qualitative; hard/soft; personal detachment/ personal involvement; universalistic/particularistic; independent/dependent; public/ private; dominance/submission; active/passive. As poststructuralist feminists would point out, there is no equality between these pairs of words – the first/masculine term tends to take precedence in both culture and in theory. Hirschman's analysis shows that in the articles, there is a bias towards a masculine ideology and this takes form in the privileged use of quantitative methods in consumer research; the deployment of information processing and machine metaphors to conceptualise consumer behaviour; the assumption that behaviour is driven by goals of rational, utility maximisation; the use of detached methods; the assumption of a capitalist point of view; and the use of sex-role stereotyping.

Bristor and Fischer's (1993) discussion of feminist concerns with theory and knowledge in consumer research reinforces Hirschman's analysis. They describe the masculine ideology of theoretical discourse in consumer research as evident in the following ways. First, in the pursuit of objectivity amongst consumer researchers, they note that objectivity is a construct historically associated with masculinity – whilst men are stereotypically associated with objectivity, women are associated with subjectivity. According to Bristor and Fischer, this association has made it difficult for women's subjective knowledges (here we assume a radical feminist or a women's voice standpoint) to be heard and validated in consumer research. Women are positioned as objects rather than subjects of knowledge, a position clearly encoded in the historically embedded assumption in marketing that consumers are female. In order to become subjects of knowledge, Bristor and Fischer continue, they have been required to take up this male perspective, and in the process to suppress their own, women's knowledge. Of course, a poststructuralist feminist would not accept such a premise, since they would likely view the whole idea of objectivity as an impossible goal. Instead they would argue that all of us are socialised into particular gendered positions through the discourses (i.e. the systems of representation and institutional practices) we come to inhabit, and these discourses simultaneously privilege some of us and disadvantage others. Bristor and Fischer conclude:

Knowledge claims about women in consumer research largely have been generated within the dominant patriarchal discourse and reflect the taken-for-granted status of women as objects of investigation. These knowledge claims thus appear to convey 'knowledge about' rather than 'knowledge of' female consumers. (Bristor and Fischer, 1993: 524)

2.8 Conclusion

This chapter has covered a great deal of ground. As you can see, marketing thought is historically and theoretically rich. There are some approaches that have been widely utilised, some that have received slightly less attention, as well as a number of emerging theoretical approaches that look like they will stimulate marketing in the future.

To restate the topics we have covered. We began with reference to the Ford and Carnegie reports. Attention then turned to Kotler's endorsement of analysis, planning, implementation and control in marketing, along with the promotion of marketing 'science'. Moving on, the recent paradigm debates were examined. The political nature of knowledge production was highlighted. The emergence of some of the newer paradigms to marketing was discussed, with attention devoted to the re-emergence of interpretive research. Less popular amongst the marketing community but of equal importance theoretically were the critical, postmodernist, post-structuralist and feminist perspectives. Whilst each of these remains at the periphery of marketing thought, all provide some insight into marketing and consumption phenomena.

2.9 Learning Activities

This chapter has provided an extensive and expansive discussion of histories of marketing and the role of paradigm debates in its development. Both of the activities below are designed to encourage you to apply the complex ideas within the chapter to a context with which you are familiar. Before you begin the learning activities remind yourself of the learning aims for the chapter, so that your time and efforts are focused.

Learning Activity One: I Shop Therefore I Am?

Imagine that you are joining a social networking website. One part of the registration process requires you to provide a summary that accurately describes who you are. You only have 75 words to do this. What would you write? According to postmodern marketing scholars, many people define themselves through their consumption habits, rather than through their work activities (i.e. as a teacher, plumber, doctor etc). To what extent do you agree with this idea?

Before you try to answer this question, read Rothstein, 2005.

Learning Activity Two: Paradigms Being Put to Work

A key learning outcome of this chapter is for you to appreciate the differing assumptions and approaches associated with the different paradigms. To further assist you,

you will find a task below which directs you to undertake a little further reading to enable you to comprehend, compare and contrast the debates that you have encountered in this chapter.

You have been tasked with producing a short report for a marketing manager. The marketing manager is concerned that discussions in the classroom of marketing histories and paradigms are a distraction from the real work of marketers. The manager has asked you to summarise the paradigm debates and explain to her why they are relevant to her in her day-to-day activities. You may wish to read Cova (1996) and Firat and Shultz (1997) before producing your short report.

2.10 Further Reading

Arndt, J. (1985) 'On making marketing science more scientific: Role of orientations, paradigms, metaphors, and problem solving', *Journal of Marketing*, 49(3): 11–23.

In this paper Arndt examines the development of marketing theory and highlights how multiple perspectives are likely to be useful in overcoming what he calls the one dimensionality of marketing thought at present, which remains wedded to the 'logical empiricist' paradigm.

Hudson, L.A. and Ozanne, J.L. (1988) 'Alternative ways of seeking knowledge in consumer research', *Journal of Consumer Research*, 14 (4): 508–21.

Hudson and Ozanne extend an element of Arndt's discussion by focusing in detail on two of the paradigms Arndt discusses. They explain the philosophical assumptions that undergird the 'positivist' (or logical empiricist) and interpretive paradigms.

Brown, S. (1994) 'Marketing as multiplex: Screening postmodernism', *European Journal of Marketing*, 28 (8/9): 27–51.

Brown is a prominent commentator on marketing theory who uses examples from postmodern theory to encourage us to examine the limitations of the way we reflect (or do not reflect) on marketing theory and practice.

Sage Online Titles

Fox, K.F.A., Skorobogatykh, I.I. and Saginova, O.V. (2005) 'The Soviet evolution of marketing thought, 1961–1991: From Marx to marketing', *Marketing Theory*, 5 (3): 283–307.

The former Soviet Union has had a complex relationship with marketing. This paper introduces key figures involved with marketing in Russia.

Firat, A.F. and Dholakia, N. (2006) 'Theoretical and philosophical implications of postmodern debates: Some challenges to modern marketing', *Marketing Theory*, 6 (2): 123–62.

Postmodern ideas have permeated marketing theory and offered new and radical insights in both theory and practice. This paper introduces key postmodern ideas, juxtaposing these against 'modern' marketing theory and practice via a series of case studies.

Bristor, J. and Fischer, E. (1995) 'Exploring simultaneous oppressions: Toward the development of consumer research in the interest of diverse women', *American Behavioral Scientist*, 38 (4): 526–36.

This paper is a reflection by the authors on a piece of previous research that appeared in the *Journal of Consumer Research*. They make the case that their original feminist analysis oversimplified the pressures facing different female groups, affected in diverse ways by issues of sexuality, race, poverty and so forth.

Gabriel, Y. and Lang, T. (2008) 'New faces and new masks of today's consumer', *Journal of Consumer Culture*, 8(3): 321–40.

Gabriel and Lang examine how the domain of production has impacted on the domain of consumption and explain the reasoning behind how consumption became such a powerful influence in our everyday lives.

Honneth, A. (2004) 'Organized self-realization: Some paradoxes of individualization', *European Journal of Social Theory*, 7(4): 463–78.

Honneth is a contemporary Critical Theorist who discusses issues related to emancipation and proposes that certain social changes are not necessarily representative of new forms of freedom as they might otherwise appear at first glance.

2.11 References

Agger, B. (1991) 'Critical theory, poststructuralism, postmodernism: Their sociological relevance', *Annual Review of Psychology*, 17: 105–31.

Anderson, P.F. (1986) 'On method in consumer research: A critical relativist perspective', *Journal of Consumer Research*, 13 (2): 155–73.

Anderson, P.F. (1988) 'Relativism revidivus: In defence of critical relativism', *Journal of Consumer Research*, 15 (3): 403–6.

Arndt, J. (1985) 'On making marketing science more scientific: Role of orientations, paradigms, metaphors, and problem solving', *Journal of Marketing*, 49 (3): 11–23.

Arnould, E.J. and Thompson, C.J. (2005) 'Consumer Culture Theory (CCT): Twenty years of research', *Journal of Consumer Research*, 31 (4): 868–82.

Asgary, A. and Walle, A.H. (2002) 'The cultural impact of globalisation: Economic activity and social change', *Cross Cultural Management*, 9 (3): 58–75.

Askegaard, S. (2006) 'Brands as global ideoscape', in J.E. Schroeder and M. Salzer-Mörling (eds), *Brand Culture*, pp. 91–102. London: Routledge.

Bartels, R. (1988) *The History of Marketing Thought*, 3rd Edn. Columbus: Publishing Horizons.

Bauman, Z. (2007) 'Collateral casualties of consumerism', *Journal of Consumer Culture*, 7 (1): 25–56.

Belk, R.W. (1988) 'Possessions and the extended self', *Journal of Consumer Research*, 15 (2): 139–68.

Belk, R.W., Wallendorf, M. and Sherry, J. (1989) 'The sacred and the profane in consumer behavior: Theodicy in the Odyssey', *Journal of Consumer Research*, 16 (1): 1–38.

Borden, N.H. (1964) 'The concept of the marketing mix', *Journal of Advertising Research*, 4(June): 2–7.

Bristor, J.M. and Fischer, E. (1993) 'Feminist thought: Implications for consumer research', *Journal of Consumer Research*, 19 (4): 518–36.

Brown, S. (1995) *Postmodern Marketing*. London: Routledge.

Brown, S. (1998) *Postmodern Marketing Two*. London: International Thomson Business Press.

Brown, S. (2006) 'Recycling postmodern marketing', *Marketing Review*, 6 (3): 211–30.

Burrell, G. and Morgan, G. (1979/1992) *Sociological Paradigms and Organisational Analysis*. Aldershot: Ashgate.

Buzzell, R.D. (1964) 'Is marketing a science?', *Harvard Business Review*, 41 (1): 32–40.

Cahn, P.S. (2008) 'Consuming class: multilevel marketers in neoliberal Mexico', *Cultural Anthropology*, 23 (3): 429–52.

Calás, M.B. and Smircich, L. (2009) 'Feminist perspectives in organizational research: What is and what is yet to be', in D. Buchanan and A. Bryman (eds), *The Sage Handbook of Organizational Research Methods*, pp. 246–69. London: Sage.

Cayla, J. and Eckhardt, G.M. (2008) 'Asian brands and the shaping of a transnational imagined community', *Journal of Consumer Research*, 35(August): 216–30.

Cova, B. (1996) 'Community and consumption: Toward the definition of the 'linking value' of products or services', *European Journal of Marketing*, 31 (3/4): 297–316.

Cowan, S. (1924) 'Tendencies in sales management', *Bulletin of the Taylor Society*, (April): 72–85.

Easton, G. (2002) 'Marketing: A critical realist approach', *Journal of Business Research*, 55 (2): 103–9.

Elliott, R. and Jankel-Elliott, N. (2003) 'Using ethnography in strategic consumer research', *Qualitative Market Research: An International Journal*, 6 (4): 215–23.

Elliott, R. and Ritson, M. (1997) 'Post-structuralism and the dialectics of advertising', in S. Brown and D. Turley (eds), *Consumer Research: Postcards from the Edge*, pp. 190–219. London: Routledge.

Firat, A.F. and Venkatesh, A. (1995) 'Liberatory postmodernism and the reenchantment of consumption', *Journal of Consumer Research*, 22 (3): 239–67.

Firat, A.F. and Shultz, C.J. (1997) 'From segmentation to fragmentation: markets and marketing strategy in the post modern era', *European Journal of Marketing*, 31 (3/4): 183–207.

Fischer, E. and Bristor, J. (1994) ' A feminist poststructuralist analysis of the rhetoric of marketing relationships', *International Journal of Research in Marketing*, 11 (4): 17–31.

Fisher, R.J. and Katz, J.E. (2000) 'Social-desirability bias and the validity of self-reported values', *Psychology and Marketing*, 17 (2): 105–20.

Gabriel, Y. and Lang, T. (1995) *The Unmanageable Consumer: Contemporary Consumption and its Fragmentations*. London: Sage.

Goffman, E. (1959/1990) *The Presentation of Self in Everyday Life*. London: Penguin.

Gummesson, E. (2005) 'Qualitative research in marketing: roadmap for a wilderness of complexity and unpredictability', *European Journal of Marketing*, 39 (3/4): 309–27.

Hackley, C. (2009) 'Parallel universes and disciplinary space: The bifurcation of managerialism and social science in marketing studies', *Journal of Marketing Management*, 25 (7–8): 643–60.

Hansen, K.T. (1999) ' Second-hand clothing encounters in Zambia: Global discourses, Western commodities, and local histories, *Africa*, 69 (3): 343–65.

Hirschman, E.C. (1993) 'Ideology in consumer research, 1980 and 1990: A Marxist and Feminist critique', *Journal of Consumer Research*, 19: 537–55.

Hudson, L.A. and Ozanne, J.L. (1988) 'Alternative ways of seeking knowledge in consumer research', *Journal of Consumer Research*, 14 (4): 508–21.

Hunt, S.D. (1976) 'The nature and scope of marketing', *Journal of Marketing*, 40 (3): 17–26.

Hunt, S.D. (1984) 'Should marketing adopt relativism?', in M. Ryan and P.F. Anderson (eds), *Marketing Theory: Philosophy and Sociology of Science Perspectives*, pp. 30–4. Chicago: American Marketing Association.

Hunt, S.D. (1990) 'Truth in marketing theory and research', *Journal of Marketing*, 54 (3): 1–15.

Hunt, S.D. (1991) 'Positivism and paradigm dominance in consumer research', *Journal of Consumer Research*, 18 (June): 32–44.

Hunt, S.D. (1992) 'For reason and realism in marketing', *Journal of Marketing*, 56 (2): 89–102.

Kassarjian, H.H. (1989) 'Review of philosophical and radical thought in marketing', *Journal of Marketing*, 53 (1): 123–6.

Kassarjian, H.H. (1994/2008) 'Scholarly traditions and European roots of American consumer research', in M. Tadajewski and D.G.B. Jones, *The History of Marketing Thought*, Volume III, pp. 301–12. London: Sage.

Keith, R.J. (1960) 'The marketing revolution', *Journal of Marketing*, 24 (3) 35–8.

Kernan, J.B. (1995) 'Declaring a discipline: Reflections on ACR's Silver Anniversary', *Advances in Consumer Research*, 22 (1): 553–60.

King, S. (1985) 'Has marketing failed, or was it never really tried?', *Journal of Marketing Management*, 1: 1–19.

Kline, S. and Leiss, W. (1978) 'Advertising, needs and commodity fetishism', *Canadian Journal of Political and Social Theory*, 2 (1): 5–30.

Kotler, P. (1961) 'Usefulness of higher math just dawning on untrained managers', *Business and Society*, (Spring): 18–22.

Kotler, P. (1967) *Marketing Management: Analysis, Planning, and Control*. Englewood Cliffs: Prentice Hall.

Kuhn, T.S. (1970) *The Structure of Scientific Revolutions*, 2nd Edn. Chicago: University of Chicago Press.

Lifton, K.J. (1993) *The Protean Self: Human Resilience in an Age of Fragmentation*. Chicago: University of Chicago Press.

Ligas, M. and Cotte, J. (1999) 'The process of negotiating brand meaning: A symbolic interactionist perspective', *Advances in Consumer Research*, 26: 609–14.

Lindridge, A.M. and Wang, C. (2008) 'Saving "face" in China: Modernization, parental pressure, and plastic surgery', *Journal of Consumer Behaviour*, 7(December): 496–508.

Mills, M.B. (1997) 'Contesting the margins of modernity: Women, migration, and consumption in Thailand', *American Ethnologist*, 24 (1): 37–61.

Nola, R. and Sankey, H. (2007) *Theories of Scientific Method*. Stocksfield: Acumen.

O'Shaughnessy, J. and O'Shaughnessy, N.J. (2002) 'Postmodernism and marketing: Separating the wheat from the chaff', *Journal of Macromarketing*, 22 (1): 109–35.

Olson, J.C. (1982) 'Presidential Address – 1981: Toward a science of consumer behavior', in A. Mitchell (ed.), *Advances in Consumer Research* 9, pp. v-x. Provo, UT: Association for Consumer Research.

Ozanne, J.L. and Murray, J.B. (1995) 'Uniting critical theory and public policy to create the reflexively defiant consumer', *American Behavioral Scientist*, 38 (4): 516–25.

Packard, V. (1960) *The Hidden Persuaders*. Harmondsworth: Penguin.

Peter, J.P. (1992) 'Realism or relativism for marketing theory and research: A comment on Hunt's "Scientific Realism"', *Journal of Marketing*, 56 (3): 72–9.

Rothstein F.A. (2005) 'Challenging consumption theory production and consumption in Central Mexico', *Critique of Anthropology*, 25 (3): 279–306.

Salzer-Mörlang, M. and Strannegård, L. (2007) 'Ain't misbehaving – consumption in a moralized brandscape', *Marketing Theory*, 7 (4): 407–25.

Scott, L. (1993) 'Spectacular vernacular: Literacy and commerical culture in the postmodern age', *International Journal of Research in Marketing*, 10 (3): 251–75.

Shankar, A. and Patterson, M. (2001) 'Interpreting the past, writing the future', *Journal of Marketing Management*, 17 (5/6): 481–501.

Shapiro, S.J. (2006) 'Macromarketing: Origins, development, current status and possible future direction', *European Business Review*, 18 (4): 307–21.

Shaw, E.H. and Jones, D.G.B. (2005) 'A history of schools of marketing thought', *Marketing Theory*, 5 (3): 239–81.

Smith, W.R. (1956) 'Product differentiation and market segmentation as alternative marketing strategies', *Journal of Marketing*, 21(July): 3–8.

Solomon, M.R. (1983) 'The role of products as social stimuli: A symbolic interactionist perspective', *Journal of Consumer Research*, 10(December): 319–29.

Tadajewski, M. (2006) 'The ordering of marketing theory: The Influence of McCarthyism and the Cold War', *Marketing Theory*, 6 (2): 163–200.

Tadajewski, M. (2010) 'Toward a history of critical marketing studies', *Journal of Marketing Management*.

Tadajewski, M. and Brownlie, D. (eds) (2008) 'Marketing: A limit attitude', in M. Tadajewski and D. Brownlie (eds), *Critical Marketing: Issues in Contemporary Marketing*, pp. 1–28. Chichester: Wiley.

Tadajewski, M. and Maclaran, P. (2009) 'Critical marketing studies: Introduction and overview', in M. Tadajewski, and P. Maclaran (eds), *Critical Marketing Studies*, Volume I, pp. xvii-xlvi. London: Sage.

Thompson, C.J. and Hirschman, E.C. (1995) 'Understanding the socialized body: A poststructuralist analysis of consumers' self-conceptions, body images, and self-care practices', *Journal of Consumer Research*, 22(September): 139–153.

Varman, R. and Vikas, R.M. (2007) 'Freedom and consumption: Toward conceptualizing systemic constraints for subaltern consumers in a capitalist society', *Consumption, Markets and Culture*, 10 (2): 117–31.

Venkatesh, A. (1994) 'Business beyond modernity: Some emerging themes', *Organization*, 1 (1): 19–23.

Wasson, C. (1960) 'What is "new" about a new product?', *Journal of Marketing*, 24(July): 52–56.

What's the Story? Analysing Marketing Discourse

3

3.1 Introduction

The last two chapters have described in some detail how the field of marketing has changed and developed over its relatively short history. The variety and range of approaches which have been used by marketing writers to approach the subject is considerable. Part of the problem is that different types of marketers have used and continue to use different types of language, terminology, and methods of explanation to describe their discipline. This variation means that it is not always easy to compare and evaluate one approach against another because they do not conform to a common set of values or expectations. For marketing writers it seems that the way one chooses to describe the subject has a considerable effect on what is actually seen. When marketers start from one perspective or worldview they end up with particular types of outcomes and conclusions, and these are often very different from the kinds of outcomes that are produced from other starting points. One way to deal with this variation is to see the subject of marketing as a set of different types of discourse, narrative or story. From certain perspectives at least it is not of central concern whether these stories are 'true' or 'false' – after all, it seems that this is almost impossible to judge with any certainty – but whether they are meaningful or not, and to whom. This chapter seeks to identify and explain some of the most popular 'stories' that have been written by marketers to describe their field. It does so by introducing you to discourse approaches to analysis, which it then applies to particular examples of marketing theory.

According to one story, marketing and marketing practices are perceived in generally negative terms by most members of the public. If you search the internet or scan the print media you will not be surprised to find that many high-profile discussions about marketing tend to concentrate on socially questionable and ethically dubious situations and events (see Box below). Perhaps marketing is a little like party politics in this respect. Comedians for instance often satirise marketing and advertising in the same way that they lampoon politicians and political practices. Marketing roles, or representations of people involved with marketing related activities, are often correspondingly shown in less than flattering terms. It is rare to say the least to see marketing managers, advertising executives and sales professionals depicted as caring, compassionate and responsible individuals. Far more common are depictions in which marketers are shown as arch-deceivers and manipulators of events.

Marketing professionals, scholars and students are more likely to hold a different view of marketing, and to tell a different story. In contrast to this negative view these 'pro-marketing' groups are often keen to point out that marketing is (or at least can be) a constructive and progressive force for good. Marketing, after all, helps organisations to develop new and interesting products and services. It provides consumers with all kinds of information and knowledge about brands, and it collects important marketing research data from consumers and delivers them to organisations so that they can tune their practices towards buyers. Marketing, in the positive view, is an essential agent that helps to keep markets competitive, which means that in the end prices are kept low, while consumer choice is increased. Marketing approaches, these pro-marketers may even argue, can be employed to achieve all kinds of positive social outcomes.

Food for Thought – The Role of Marketing in the Tobacco Industry

Many groups argue that marketing techniques used by the large tobacco companies have been partly responsible for encouraging smoking and that this has caused harm to health. In October 2008 the US Supreme Court began hearing arguments over whether tobacco firms can be sued under state law for deceptive advertising of light cigarettes. In the same month the UK became the first EU country to require pictorial warnings on all tobacco products. The view that marketing professionals working for tobacco companies have known about the health implications of smoking for many decades but chose to continue to market tobacco as a sophisticated, fashionable and desirable product reinforces the negative view of marketing as an activity that is socially undesirable and morally dubious. At the same time there is general acceptance that marketing practices can and have been equally well deployed to discourage smoking (see for example, Andrews et al., 2004; Hastings et al., 2004). The use of pictorial and text warnings on tobacco products is itself a marketing initiative, as are the public health campaigns that use television advertising, often targeted at the young, to discourage smoking. The case of tobacco marketing illustrates how we can see that there are at least two sides to every story, and our views about marketing depend very much on which of these stories we prefer and accept, and which we dismiss and ignore. The 2005 movie *Thank You for Smoking* directed by Jason Reitman depicts yet another take on this controversial issue. In the movie the hero of the story is Nick Naylor, a Public Relations professional and lobbyist employed by tobacco companies to defend the cigarette industry in the most difficult situations. The basic argument Naylor uses is that companies should be free to produce whatever products they want even if these are potentially damaging to health and consumers should not be prevented from buying these products if they freely choose to do so. Being a free and responsible consumer means that we must be able to be free to choose things that others (governments for example) think that we shouldn't.

Our purpose in this chapter is not to review and resolve questions about the ethical and moral status of marketing. This is a theme that will be picked up on and developed further in Chapter 11. Rather, this debate reveals something about the ways that different groups in society talk about and represent marketing and marketing practices. Both advocates and critics of marketing clearly agree that marketing is important, but draw upon very different accounts and descriptions to present their arguments. In some of these accounts marketers are depicted as agents for good, while in others they are shallow and manipulative. In some accounts consumers are described almost as victims of these crafty marketing characters (e.g. Gabriel and Lang, 2006), whereas in others the consumer is a powerful, discriminating agent, with ever increasing standards and expectations, and difficult to please (also discussed in Chapter 8).

Some marketing academics have started to become more and more interested in these different ways of talking about and representing marketing. They point out that although it would be very useful to know what marketing is and is not, and what works and what doesn't, the answers to these types of questions depend very much on how one represents marketing in the first place. This research tradition tends to treat marketing and marketing practices as kinds of *discourse*, which in simple terms means taking a keen interest in the different ways that people talk about and think about marketing (Brownlie and Saren, 1997; Elliott, 1996; Morgan, 1992). This interest in discourse is not unique to marketing. Over the last quarter-century or so, scholars from across the social sciences and beyond have turned their attention to analysing discourse and ways of speaking, writing and storytelling. This broad intellectual movement has now developed a large and coherent set of ideas, theories and concepts which we can use to analyse, interpret and critique all kinds of social phenomena – including marketing.

3.2 Discourse and 'Grand' Narratives

Discourse approaches begin with the axiom that any body of knowledge can be thought of as a set of interrelated stories which seek to explain and describe a set of activities, ideas and practices. The natural sciences for instance, can be understood as providing all kinds of stories – or narratives – to explain aspects of the physical world. Theories such as the 'big-bang' for example provide a scientific account for the origins of the universe which explains how everything began, how it subsequently developed and then how it might eventually end up. In a similar way most of the world's religions provide narratives about the creation of the world. Grand narratives can be thought of as a story about – or 'inside' other stories. Try to avoid thinking that these aspects of discourse are in some way 'hidden' or deeply embedded underneath the everyday talk of daily life. Evidence of these narratives is all around us. Marketers and advertisers, for example, draw on grand narratives all the time to get their message across. As the 2005 television commercial for Guinness – *noitulovE* ('Evolution' backwards) – shows, all narratives can be used without reverence in consumer culture. You should be able to locate a copy of this commercial on the internet. What is interesting about this ad from a discourse perspective is that it is both funny and serious at the same time. The ad works by visualising the 'grand' narrative of evolutionism and blending it with a particularly 'local' brand story.

Our propensity to make up 'big stories' to account for the world around us is not only evident in the realms of science and religion. We can analyse accounts provided by social scientists and historians in a similar way by identifying the important underlying stories that help to explain and give meaning to theories and models. Marxism, for example, can be interpreted as a kind of story which tells how the material conditions of life produce particular social conditions. These social conditions create different groups in society which are unequal in terms of power and control. This in turn produces a cycle of revolutions that can be seen throughout history in which different groups struggle against one another. This narrative explains how those in power try to maintain the status quo, and how those who are disempowered seek to overthrow and challenge this authority. We can use this story to explain how human societies have moved from feudalism to capitalism for example, and then go on to imagine how capitalism itself will be overthrown and replaced by alternative social relations.

The idea that human civilisation and progress can be understood as a series of successive empires that rise, decline and fall is an alternative 'grand-narrative' of history. A popular, even 'common-sense' version of this story tells how the beginning of the 'age of enlightenment' sometime in the 1700s led to the underlying belief that rational thought and the pursuit of science would lead to all kinds of economic, political, moral and social progress. We can use this story to explain many contemporary events. The idea that democracy is the most advanced, just and beneficial form of government, or the idea that the free-market is the most efficient and well-developed form of economic organisation can be seen as deriving its meaning from this kind of story or grand-narrative.

To bring some of these theoretical ideas into marketing we need to be prepared to treat the discipline of marketing as a kind of discourse. This means that we are not only interested in finding out what marketing is (or is not), but also in the types of language that are used to talk about marketing in the first place. Using this approach we can see that marketing, like all social practices, can be thought of as a collection of narratives or stories which we deploy to make sense of the world around us (see also Chapter 2). Probably one of the most important points to remember about discourse-based analysis is that many different discourses can be applied to the same issue or practice at any one time. Sometimes two or more discourses can be seen to compete against one another whereas at other times one particular discourse seems to 'dominate' over others which remain marginal or peripheral.

3.2.1 'Free' Markets or State Intervention?

If we think of political-economic movements in discourse terms for example, we might observe how capitalist, or free market discourse 'competes' with socialist or regulated market discourses. For those advocating free-market principles (we might say those that place more faith in the free-market discourse or story) 'big-government' is often represented as a source of inefficiency, and something that distorts free market competition. Regulation, taxation and government 'interference' is depicted as a necessary evil that needs to be curtailed, controlled and reduced where ever possible. For those advocating more government involvement in the economy (we might say those who place more credibility in a discourse of greater state involvement), government intervention is necessary to curtail the dangers and risks that come with 'unbridled capitalism'.

The 'big' discourses – or what some cultural theorists call 'Grand Narratives' (Lyotard, 1979) – have a considerable impact on how we view and make sense of the world. For example, free market discourses tend to place a much greater emphasis on the rights of the individual to make active and personal choices (as a consumer) rather than having choices made for them by government for example. The alternative discourse is less supportive of the idea that the individual consumer is always best placed to make decisions and argues that government and other regulatory authorities must intervene to represent a collective interest over and above the interests of particular groups. Debates over whether the advertising industry should be regulated (i.e. censored) by laws, or whether it should be managed by industry self-regulation draw upon these competing discourses, as do arguments about the appropriate extent of private commercial involvement in public services, right down to the role of government in stipulating opening times for certain types of commercial businesses.

Although discourse analysis requires us to treat social practices as narratives, or stories, we need to be careful not to make the common mistake of assuming that this means that analysis of these practices should be thought of as being in some way trivial or inconsequential. Discourse analysis shows that while narratives are both representational and culturally determined they nevertheless have very real consequences. The interplay between various competing discourses can account for all kinds of political, economic and cultural tensions and power struggles. Just because discourse analysis leads us to treat all kinds of social practices as stories, or fictions of one sort or another, does not mean that we should downgrade our expectations of what these stories can do to the way we see and act in the world. For instance, we have already seen in our reference to the tobacco industry how the way society and government views and interprets marketing discourse affects the legal status and liability for some marketers.

3.2.2 Who 'Writes' the Stories that Shape our Views of the World?

For some groups and at certain periods we find that particular stories, narratives or discourses become more popular and more resonant than others. Many forms of discourse analysis reveal how narratives which dominate at any one time tend to be those that favour elites. We can say that one of the things that powerful and dominant groups do is 'author' dominant and powerful discourses and this further legitimises and justifies the status quo. Discourse analysts for instance often look at historical accounts to see how the rich and the powerful record past events in such a way to reinforce the current state of affairs. A case in point is the Victorian period in Britain, during which many historical narratives gained widespread dominance (some of which remain today) accounting for the rise of the British Empire. Accounts of the English and Scottish enlightenment, or 'Golden Age' revealed how from the fifteenth century onwards England, then Britain, had become world leaders in terms of military, artistic, scientific, philosophical, political and economic achievements. Whether these historical stories are true or false is of course for historians to debate and critique, but what is clear is that these types of stories provided support and justification for the idea of British supremacy during the Victorian era. For the middle and upper classes in nineteenth century Britain these discourses showed Britain to be the most advanced, civilised, and developed society in the world. This in turn played an important part in the justification of British imperialism and power. It is perhaps no surprise to recognise that the authors of much of this historical narrative were often from and supported by those groups in society who stood to gain most from this worldview. Those groups that were socially and politically excluded in Victorian Britain are also excluded from the dominant discourses of the era. In simple terms we might say that dominant views on what and when constitute a golden era in history depends very much on who holds the gold in the present (see the discussion of ideology in Chapter 4).

Although some discourses may seem to be extremely resonant at particular times, even to the point where we effectively treat them as real and actual accounts of the world, we should always bear in mind that no discourse or narrative is ever permanent. Some discourses may be extremely durable and long-standing, but even these discourses will one day recede in terms of importance, only to be replaced by others. When we view the Apple 1984 ad for example we are able to read into the story all kinds of associations to major political ideas about free-market capitalism versus totalitarianism. The ad evokes all kinds of narratives, from David-and-Goliath type struggles, through to ideas about creativity and individuality. At the time when the ad aired, these meanings were especially significant to an American audience, but we might expect these themes to be less resonant today.

3.3 Marketing Discourse

Marketing, like other disciplines, relies on one or more big stories as a background and underpinning of its theories, models and methods of interpretation (see Food for Thought below). Marketing relies on a fairly small set of relatively unsophisticated narratives to make sense of its practices and to construct marketing theory. By examining these narratives we can determine something about the character and function of marketing ideas more generally. We have already alluded to a number of different marketing discourses in this chapter. These different marketing narratives, concerning moral questions, arguments about freedom and the role of the state, and ideas about progress, represent marketing in different ways and for different reasons. One of the issues we are interested in identifying is which marketing discourses are most prominent, and which are most marginalised. We are also looking for the grand narratives that underpin these marketing discourses because by revealing these narratives we can gain insights into the dominant cultural values that reproduce marketing as we experience it today.

Food for Thought – The Language of the Life Cycle

The Product Life Cycle, or PLC, is one of the most popular and widely known ideas in marketing. Whether or not we think that the PLC is a useful idea or not, most of us can interpret and understand the basic metaphor (or simile to be more precise) which is being evoked. The PLC works by establishing a comparison between the presumed characteristics of a product and those of particular life stages. Thus we can talk about products being conceived, born, entering maturity, decline and even dying. Of course this does not mean that we believe that products are literally 'alive', but rather that we can use comparative language to make sense of marketing phenomenon. If we take this observation one stage further we can see that the way we use language, including the kinds of terminology that the community of marketing professionals and academics chooses to adopt, does not simply represent the world of marketing but actually go some way to constructing that worldview. For example the assumptions of life-cycle thinking may encourage managers to grow or cull products accordingly. When we use the language of the PLC we are concurrently re-embedding these metaphors and ideas in our understanding of marketing management.

Narratives in marketing share many of the features of narratives in other disciplines and subject areas. Moral dimensions and ideas about progress and change can all be found in marketing narratives. Probably one of the most influential stories in marketing relates to the issue of exchange. Textbook writers in the 1960s and 1970s seemed more disposed to include summaries of this story at the beginning of their books. That they tend not to be included in more current editions does not mean that this narrative is no longer present, but rather that we have come to implicitly accept the story which is then incorporated into other accounts. McCarthy's (1960) introduction in one of the first modern marketing textbooks, *Basic Marketing: A Managerial Approach*, opens with the following:

> Going back to the beginning of man's history, we find that he barely eked out an
> existence. He lived by picking wild berries and fruit, and catching fish and animals for

food. He used animal skins for clothing, and slept in a cave or some crudely improved structure. This kind of life can be described as subsistence living. (McCarthy, 1960: 21)

This rather humble beginning provides the starting point for a series of developments in which human beings gradually see the benefit of grouping together first into families and then into small communities. They learn how to domesticate animals, produce small surplus amounts of crops which then frees up some people's time to focus on activities not directly concerned with food production such as basic clothing manufacturing and leatherwork. Over time, some communities developed specialised talents for particular types of production and recognised the mutual advantages in exchanging goods between themselves. McCarthy tells us:

> One community might be efficient in all its crafts. But if another village had made great strides in the development of one special craft, it was mutually profitable for them to trade. That was the beginning of marketing. (McCarthy, 1960: 21)

This grand narrative of marketing is similar in many ways to other historical accounts of economic development. It is not that far removed from some Marxist ideas about economic development. Underlying this narrative is the idea of progress, that is, the notion that over successive years and generations societies undergo change for the better. It enables us, for instance, to construct ideas of the developing world versus the developed world, and to see some economies as more advanced and even more superior to others in some way.

3.3.1 Marketing and Progress

What is the role of marketing in this account? The first thing we observe is that marketing is depicted as a kind of progressive force. In the most basic and primitive forms of society there was no marketing, and as societies evolve and develop, marketing becomes more important and necessary. Another observation we might make from looking at this story is that a certain type of market, the 'free-market' is assumed to be the most advanced and progressive form of social and economic development. McCarthy writes:

> It seems like the American emphasis on competition – as contrasted with the European willingness to accept cartels, trusts and trade agreements – may have encouraged this more rapid evolution of the marketing structure .... Americans, along with the peoples of Canada, and some Western European Countries, are very well off compared to most of the people in South America, Africa and Asia, who have not yet risen above the subsistence level. As they do, their economies will probably go through the stages described previously. (McCarthy, 1960: 21)

Given the discussion above, it will probably come as no surprise to find that McCarthy was an associate professor of marketing management at the University of Notre Dame in the United States when this book was published. That the majority of modern marketing management textbooks are either written by US authors, or are heavily reliant on this particular way of telling the 'story' of marketing tells us that the US continues to provide the main inspiration for most marketing discourses which dominate today.

Philip Kotler, perhaps the most influential and widely read writer on marketing and senior professor at Northwestern University in the US, presents a similar narrative at the beginning of his textbook on *Marketing Management*:

> Marketing emerges when people decide to satisfy needs and wants through exchange
> ... Exchange [being] one of four ways that people can obtain products they want.
> (Kotler, 1991: 6)

The other three 'non-marketing' methods of satisfying needs identified by Kotler (1991) are self-production (which is similar to the kinds of subsistence arrangements described by McCarthy), coercion or forced exchange (i.e. through the use and fear of violence, force and threat), and begging. It is not difficult to see the way that Kotler's narrative about the history of marketing makes marketing appear somewhat more preferential, more civilised and more advanced than the alternative, non-marketing reality. Another way of reading Kotler's account would be to say that societies and individuals have a choice between marketing on the one hand, or poverty, crime and subservience on the other. And in such terms it is not unreasonable to see why most us would prefer marketing, free markets and competition. If this progressive view of marketing is only one possible marketing discourse then what, we might ask, do other less prominent discourses consist of?

3.3.2 Progress and Civilization

Underpinning the above accounts from Kotler and McCarthy is the notion that social progress and economic progress are closely linked. As economic circumstances become more complex, so too do social circumstances. Furthermore we can identify what some theorists term *Homo economicus*, or Economic man, as an underlying idea in this dominant marketing discourse. In this account human beings are assumed to be rational and self-interested, who both desire wealth, and at the same time seek to avoid unnecessary labour. As one would expect there are many possible alternative narratives to this particular account. Rather than seeing marketing as a kind of progressive force it could be argued that some aspects of marketing represent a step back. As people and societies become more market orientated and marketing becomes more central to everyday life, they also become more fragmented and more unstable. From an anthropological perspective consumer society can be viewed as equally 'barbaric' (Mestrovic, 1993; Veblen, 1899) as earlier social systems, if not more so.

At this point we should perhaps re-iterate a point made earlier about making judgments about the truth or veracity of particular narratives. The purpose of undertaking discourse analysis of marketing, or anything else for that matter, is not necessarily to show that one type of account is right, wrong or better than any other. All accounts, at least from this perspective can be understood as stories that produce particular types of *truth effects* (Brownlie and Saren, 1997). One of the advantages of this approach is that it does provide you with a way to 'get inside' a particular line or reasoning and this helps us to further understand why certain theories and ideas work and become popular in a discipline. It is also true that some theorists use a discourse approach to critique and expose some of the taken for granted ideas that underpin the marketing field. The next two sections explore two such ideas regarding marketing management (3.4) and consumer sovereignty (3.5).

3.4 Discourses of Marketing Management

In Chapter 5 of this book we outline the various views of 'marketing management' (MM) from the traditional, to the strategic, to the relational. As it progresses, the chapter begins to critically evaluate the rhetorical claims of conventional MM by considering the social construction of markets by marketing practice, taking a particular focus on language and discourse. All of this discussion is predicated on an underlying grand narrative of marketing management. The assumption underpinning the Marketing Management narrative is that although markets could conceivably exist without managers, for marketing to occur requires some activity of management. In other words, markets could operate 'by themselves' without management intervention, but market-*ing* activity implies some active managerial process.

3.4.1 The Marketing Mix

Perhaps one of the most influential and popular products of this management narrative is the Marketing Mix framework – or the 4Ps. If you have studied marketing before, or have studied some marketing as part of a general management programme, you are likely to have come across the 4Ps and the marketing mix model. The model identifies four general categories or classes of functions, each of which describes an aspect of marketing management. The model is often discussed as the marketer's tool box because it can be thought of as containing all of the generic resources which any marketer, regardless of market, product, service or industry, will need to design and inform any particular marketing strategy.

Borden (1964) is often cited as one of the main writers to promote the concept of the Marketing Mix. He states that he took the idea for the Mix from the opening sections of a book by James Culliton (1948a), titled *The Management of Marketing Costs*. Culliton's main objective was to counter the argument that expenditures on marketing (advertising, sales efforts, merchandising, etc) imposed an unnecessary and undesirable burden on organisations, customers and society as a whole. He set out to identify all the different types (or ingredients) of marketing costs in an attempt to rationally account for their contribution to and value to organisations. After developing an extensive list, Culliton turns his focus onto the management of marketing, in which he famously described the manager as a 'mixer of ingredients'. This metaphor gradually gained popularity and eventually evolved into what is probably now the most prevalent idea in marketing management. Incidentally, Culliton did not only use the idea of the 'mixer of ingredients' to describe marketing managers. In other articles (Culliton, 1948b) he likened the marketing manager to a conductor of an orchestra. Who knows, had Borden and others chosen to use this analogy, rather than that of the mix, we might be talking about the marketing 'symphony' today.

Over time Borden's popularisation of Culliton's story about the manager as a mixer of marketing variables evolved into something much more than a simple illustrative story that could be used to defend and justify marketing expenditures. McCarthy, who we talked about earlier in this chapter, was responsible for later simplifying the list as the 'Four Ps'. The eleventh edition of Kotler and Armstrong's (2006: 50) *Principles of Marketing* describes the Marketing Mix as 'one of the major concepts in modern marketing' and dedicates 10 of the 20 chapters in the book to Marketing Mix variables. Kotler's emphasis on the Mix is mirrored in other marketing texts. For example, David Jobber's (2009) *Principles and Practice of Marketing* uses the 4Ps to organise the text and Solomon et al. (2008) present the Mix as a core concept or 'tool box'. We might say that the narrative of the marketing mix has become so prevalent and permanent that it is hard to imagine what marketing theory would look like without it. Although many writers have questioned the value of the mix for over a quarter of a century (for example, Grönroos (1994), Kent (1986), Vargo and Lusch (2004), van Watershoot and Van den Bulte (1992)) it nevertheless remains important to the discipline of marketing. One reason for this is that it provides marketing professionals, students and teachers with an easy to understand, convenient and widely applicable narrative that explains what marketing is, and how marketing strategy can be formulated.

3.4.2 Market Populism

Nowadays some US writers have moved away from the original marketing *management* approach like the one illustrated by McCarthy and Kotler (see Chapter 5), towards the ideal of the 'common man', or what Frank (2000) has termed 'market populism'. This promotes the notion of markets as media of consent as much as a means of exchange: 'By their very nature markets confer democratic legitimacy, markets bring down the pompous and the snooty, markets look out for the interests of the little guy, markets give us what we want' (Frank, cited in Turner, 2004: 196). With the decline or absence of traditional hierarchical or class-based legitimacy such as that afforded to law or medicine, the 'new' professions of the late twentieth century such as marketing, advertising and other knowledge-based occupations had to establish their own reputations and to compete with anyone who wished to enter the market for these services.

3.4.3 Is Marketing Manageable?

Probably the most significant and lasting legacy of the MM narrative is the idea that marketing and markets are ultimately manageable – and that a group of professionals equipped with a set of skills, techniques (and stories) are able to perform this marketing management task for organisations. As we have seen, this 'grand narrative' of marketing has existed for a long time, at least since the 1950s. Marketing advocates have drawn upon aspects of this narrative to justify what are essentially political claims for power and authority in organisational decision making. The question we might want to ask is whether this narrative remains credible and believable today. There is at least some anecdotal evidence to suggest that although many marketers continue to buy into the MM narrative many others do not, including many senior managers, some customers and most social commentators. This might explain why marketers choose to represent marketing in a positive way, whereas many other groups prefer to promote more critical and negative narratives.

Attempts to Re-write the Marketing Discourse

In 2004 Vargo and Lusch published an article in the *Journal of Marketing* in which they argued that new perspectives are converging to form a new dominant logic for marketing, one in which service provision, rather than goods, is fundamental to economic exchange. This new 'logic', the authors suggest, is causing marketing scholars, practitioners, and educators to shift their perspective. The article has been quite influential in marketing. We can interpret this paper as an attempt to re-write marketing discourse, to make it more relevant and more in tune with contemporary circumstances. Another influential article that shares some common themes with Vargo and Lusch's evolving dominant logic is a 1998 paper from the *Harvard Business Review* by Pine and Gilmore, titled 'Welcome to the experience economy'. In this paper the authors explicitly draw upon an historical narrative of progress (not unlike the one presented by McCarthy in 1960) to explain the rise in the service sector.

Both articles are very readable. What do you think are the underlying 'grand narratives' in these two articles? How are they similar, and how do they differ from existing popular narratives in marketing? Do you think that these articles are written within the conventions of the marketing management discourse?

The discourse approach discussed in this chapter would suggest that all of those people who have an interest in marketing need to look at the narratives they employ to describe and give meaning to ideas of marketing, both to themselves and to other non-marketers, and evaluate their credibility and believability. Such an analysis might be expected to show how existing narratives need to be adapted, edited and updated to respond to more recent challenges and issues. More radically we could even propose that totally new narratives are needed to replace the MM discourse entirely, although what these alternative narratives would be is open to considerable debate.

3.5 Discourses of the Sovereign Consumer

A core value underpinning the marketing concept is the belief in choice: the right of consumers to be free to choose from a selection of options of what they buy, from where and from whom. The discourse often employed in marketing to emphasise the primary role of the customer as the market decision-maker is encapsulated by the phrase 'the customer is king'. Here we explore the narrative of consumer sovereignty, the problems with it, and its impact on marketing theory. If consumer sovereignty is a myth, then – as the Italians say – 'Se non e vero e ben trovato' (If it's not true, it's a good story).

The regal metaphor of the sovereign consumer is deeply rooted in ideas of exchange, customer service and free market choice. The notion of customers having a royal fiat in the marketplace confers them with power through apparently offering them control in terms of the options and choices available for them to choose from. As early as Shakespeare's Merchant of Venice, Antonio is described as a 'royal merchant'. Adam Smith (1776/1961) described the consumer as 'sovereign' in the marketplace.

3.5.1 Choice

The assumption is that more choice is always better, and that the consumer will see this as such. A customer can choose from a range of product features, augmented product offers, warranties, channels of delivery, and so forth. It is presumed that more choice will enable customer needs to be matched more accurately, leading to enhanced customer satisfaction. Since the nineteenth century the ideal of economic competition, a 'perfect' market, where consumer choice decides which companies survive and which fail, has dominated Western economic thinking. This thinking presumes that firms are thereby driven to innovate and establish cost effective ways to deliver high quality goods and services at lower prices for the benefit of all (Sirgy and Su, 2000). Free economies are thus structured to encourage competitive behaviour through consumer choice, and to discourage the associated practices of anti-competitive behaviour which have been engaged in by companies such as Microsoft (Sirgy and Su, 2000). This model of a rational decision-making consumer freely pursuing their choices in the marketplace has been central to the marketing concept, where 'the customer is King', and firms that meet needs and wants profitably are deemed to be on the only true route to corporate success. The assumption of consumer sovereignty underpins the notion of consumer freedom, and provides a means for consumers to exercise ultimate control over the marketplace (see Box below).

Desmond (1998) traces the origins of the marketing discipline's underlying values from the early twentieth century when the first marketing scholars were educated in both the tradition of German historicism and the social dynamics of the free market. He demonstrates that the view of marketing as satisfying human needs through exchange is not 'value-free', it inherently contains what are labelled as 'utilitarian' values which underpin the concept of the 'free' market and indeed freedom itself. As Bauman notes (of Western society): 'In our society, individual freedom is constituted as, first and foremost, freedom of the consumer' (1988: 23). Far from today's customer being 'king' however, Horkheimer (1967) argues that marketing's powerful control apparatus ('technologies of governance') means that 'the majesty of the customer hardly plays any part any longer for the individual in relation to the advertising apparatus, the standardization of commodities and other economic realities' (1967: 345).

Retailer Narratives of Consumer Choice

Discourse analysis often reveals underlying binary oppositions that seem to structure the meaning of particular narratives. These oppositions help to define the logic of particular arguments and debates. Oppositional relationships such as free market/regulated market, consumer/producer, rational choice/irrational choice, empowered/disempowered, product/service, and so on underpin many aspects of marketing discourse. Binary oppositions are rarely value neutral. In many aspects of marketing discourse the opposition between extensive choice versus limited (or no) choice is prominent, with the former normally assumed to be preferable to the latter. Marketers rarely argue that limiting choice is in the consumer interest, and the idea of variety underpins many themes important to marketing discourse from discussions about the importance of competition, through to theories of branding and segmentation. Discourse analysis reminds us that these oppositions are, however arbitrary. Nevertheless, they are often employed strategically, even though they may feel and sound quite natural most of the time. We can contrast the merchandising and marketing strategies of grocery retailers to illustrate this aspect of discourse.

Many large retailers such as TESCO promote choice as a key benefit of their market-offering and stock an extensive range of brands and product sizes in each and every product category for consumers to choose from. The implication of this narrative is that common sense would suggest that more choice is always preferable to limited choice. Discount supermarkets such as ALDI, however, draw upon the same choice/no choice opposition, but reverse its values to produce an alternative strategic offer. Discounters typically offer only one product in each category as well as a more limited product range overall. Whereas a consumer can choose between dozens of different Ketchup options in TESCO for example (organic, own brand, low-salt, different sizes), an ALDI shopper has only one choice, in a standard size. The narrative to justify this strategy of no-choice is based on the idea that while consumers only purchase one product (one bottle of ketchup) they effectively have to pay for all of the other options being available.

Extensive product ranges require more complex distribution systems, larger stores, more expensive mechanising formats, and incur other costs that ultimately are often passed on to the consumer. By offering limited choice discounters argue that they can provide better quality products at lower prices. They also argue that less choice also means less time in the store, and less pressure on the consumer to 'trade up' to more expensive brands. We can see how the choice (good)/ no choice (bad) opposition can be easily reversed.

3.5.2 Are Choices Always Rational?

One problem with the narrative of consumer choice is that it presumes a sovereign consumer who makes rational choices. Yet it has long been recognised that one of the cultural contradictions of capitalism is that rationalised production processes exist alongside irrational, hedonistic consumption, with people putting some of their own creative energies into consumption (see Chapter 2). Hirschman and Holbrook (1982) demonstrate that people frequently buy for feelings, fantasies and fun; rather than functionality or 'rational' utility. This means that they do not necessarily make their market choice in order to get the best quality at the best prices, as a rational consumer decision-making theory presumes, but that their purchase may be dictated more by the mood at the time of purchase, decision or information gathering. This better explains the phenomenon of consumers' impulse buying and also why many advertisers draw on the hedonic, creative instincts of the consumer e.g. Honda's advertising slogan 'The Power of Dreams'. The way in which many companies, such as Coca-Cola, Starbucks and Budweiser, now build strong stories that weave cultural myths around their goods and services, are described by Holt (2004) as competing in 'myth markets', rather than product markets.

Mythical narratives communicate at an emotional level in powerful and sometimes unconscious ways. In his analysis of French advertising, social theorist Roland Barthes (Barthes, 1972 – but written in the 1950s) presented a series of short essays to show how everyday artefacts and ideas operate as stories for contemporary society. In one of the essays titled 'Soap-powders and detergents' Barthes shows how advertisers take these everyday products and wrap them into meaningful mythical narratives in which dirt is banished and purged, clothing is purified, and cleaned whiter-than-white. So, in practice many marketing activities do not in fact appeal to the rational side of consumer choice on which the consumer sovereignty narrative is based. Rather, it is these marketing activities which seek to tell stories that create alluring and resonant myths around their brand image.

3.5.3 Are Choices Always Good?

A further problem with the consumer choice narrative is that not all choice is good. Some argue that people find help in trying to solve whatever personal problems they may face – whether it is loss of community, lack of self-esteem, unhappiness or boredom – by adopting a particular consumer lifestyle through the products and services associated with it. On the other hand, others argue that the potential for problem-solving through consumption is in fact quite limited by the 'structuring influence of the marketplace' (also noted in Chapters 8 and 9). Although consumers can pursue personal goals through the market they are in fact 'enacting and personalising' from a limited choice of 'cultural scripts' or lifestyles, many of which are set by marketers through the products available, via advertising and the wider 'cultural industries' of movies, music and celebrities (Arnould and Thompson, 2005). Phenomena such as Marx's 'commodity fetishism' (described in greater depth in Chapter 8) explain how the real social relations, which lie behind the marketing process, are hidden from consumers, who are nevertheless constrained and conditioned by them.

Sometimes having too much choice may actually be disempowering, because so much specialised knowledge is often required that consumers have neither the time nor the inclination to acquire all the necessary skills to make informed decisions about price–quality relationships (Sirgy and Su, 2000). Abundance of choice can also lead to greater temptation to indulge in over-consumption with a concomitant need for greater self-control. Feelings of regret and even self-disgust may be strong whenever consumers do not exercise sufficient self-control, and experience a bad outcome from their excessive consumption such as a hangover or indigestion. Consumer studies have shown that these 'addictive' consumers oscillate between their particular poison and its antidote; between indulgence and abstinence; between self-loathing and virtuous self-control (O'Donohoe, 2002). The addictive shopper obtains an experiential 'high' through purchasing, and is unable to restrict his or her purchasing behaviour, although the addict may actually feel in control temporarily during shopping activity (Eccles et al., 1999). At its extreme, addictive consumption takes a pathological form, witness the increasing prevalence of eating disorders, and alcohol and drug abuse.

Too much choice can also necessitate a huge amount of information gathering, as consumers evaluate the many and various options on offer. Davies and Elliott (2006) show how increased consumer choice for women in the 1950s and 1960s, including the widespread development of self-service supermarkets, lead to a significant change in the management of households as exemplified by the introduction of branded convenience and frozen foods, the increased importance of symbolic brands and changing shopping practices. Many women respondents describe how increased choice and responsibility was often experienced as challenging or confusing. The 'tyranny of choice', means that not only can consumers not choose efficiently anymore, but they also suffer confusion. When consumers experience retail confusion due to information overload, they may also experience panic and frustration. Furthermore, the more choice that is offered, the more opportunity there is for feelings of regret and self-doubt that other options in a choice set have had to be rejected when a final selection has been made. Post-purchase (or cognitive) dissonance is a well-recognised phenomenon that can occur when a decision, which has involved two or more close alternatives, results in making a consumer feel insecure, rather than satisfied.

Speaking up for the 'Bottom of the Pyramid'

In *The Fortune at the Bottom of the Pyramid*, Prahalad argues that 'The purpose of this book is to change that familiar image on TV. It is to illustrate that the typical pictures of poverty mask the fact that the very poor represent resilient entrepreneurs and value-conscious consumers' (2005: 3). In Chapter 1 'The market at the bottom of the pyramid' he introduces the central idea that the poor represent a 'latent market' for goods and services and they cannot participate in the benefits of globalisation without the active engagement of multinational enterprises which can provide them with the means of access to products and services that reach the quality standards expected in the 'rich world'. Globalisation can provide the world's poor with a much greater range and variety of opportunities than can be found in their isolated local areas or 'micro-economies'. Prahalad sees this as an 'untapped opportunity for value creation' and he considers that the markets at the bottom of the pyramid have remained 'invisible' for far too long. The explanation which he provides as to why businesses and marketers have not recognised these opportunities is because of what he calls 'the Power of Dominant Logic'. This is explained as the way in which we see the world as coloured by the accepted ideology and established management practices. All the agencies concerned with poverty alleviation have been influenced by the dominant logic which regards the market at the bottom of the pyramid as inherently exploitative of the poor compared to their enormous confidence in governments and aid agencies to help the poor. 'If we stop thinking of the poor as victims or as a burden and start recognizing them as resilient and creative entrepreneurs and value-conscious consumers, a whole new world of opportunity will open up. Four billion poor can be the engine of the next round of global trade and prosperity' (2005: 5).

Think about the grand narratives on which this argument of Prahalad is based. What are they? Do you agree with them? How does Prahalad utilise the concept of 'Dominant Logic' to support his views about the benefits of marketing to the poor? Compare his use of the term with the way in which Vargo and Lusch (p. 76) employ the 'Dominant Logic' of marketing. How does their use differ or is it the same?

3.6 Two Grand Narratives in Search of a Subject

By comparing the two dominant narratives in marketing (marketing management discourse and consumer sovereignty discourse), we can see that there is a paradox at the very heart of the marketing discipline which is predicated on two partially conflicting consumer and managerial narratives. One story valorises the consumer as sovereign and their needs as the paramount driver of the marketing system. The other narrative constructs management models and structures for marketing operations in order to control and influence consumer behaviour and demand. This is illustrated in marketing writings and journals which students of the subject study by the almost independent development of the sub-fields of consumer research and marketing management. These two areas rarely utilise the same theories and models, have little in common and bear all the characteristics of two separate subjects of study (Brownlie and Saren, 1997).

Much of our discussion of the consumer sovereignty narrative centred on the question of consumer choice and control. However it is inherent from the assumptions within the marketing management narrative that it is marketing managers who purport to create the choice context and control through the 'management of freedom' (Hodgson, 2001). Nowhere is this control more apparent than in the enormous amount of recent attention in marketing practice and the relationship of marketing literature to customer retention, loyalty programmes and consumer 'lifetime value' – i.e. not value for the customer themselves, but for the firm. Hirschman (1993) goes one step further in her discussion of the language employed in many marketing texts which, she argues, are littered with metaphors of war, combat and captivity (remember the feminist analyses of marketing in Chapter 2 which described these metaphors as key aspects of a 'masculine ideology' in marketing). Market segments are 'targeted' for 'penetration'. Market share must be 'fought for' and 'won'. Customers must be 'locked-in' lest they 'defect' to the opposition. Thus, consumers are worked upon until they are captive, although unaware of this captivity (Du Gay, 2001). If consumers exercise choice only as captives, then the customer is not king, not an autonomous subject, but merely a 'royal' subject, who is subject to the lordship of marketing ideology. And even further, the marketing narrative of consumer sovereignty has extended to become part of the broader metanarrative of consumer culture that is dominating Western economies and societies, whereby 'patients, parents, passengers and pupils are re-imagined as consumers' (Du Gay, 2001).

3.7 Conclusion

We have shown in this chapter how our expectations of marketing and marketing theory are dependent on the broader stories and narratives that we choose to embrace at any one particular time and place. The introduction of discourse-based views into marketing science has meant that the 'dominant' management-based narrative that emerged from the 1950s onwards has been subject to extensive critique over the last decade or so and that other, competing narratives have emerged to challenge, and sometimes complement it. None of these alternative discourses has yet been able to replace managerialism as the dominant narrative which has led some theorists to argue that marketing science is now more fragmented and disparate than in the past. Various 'local' marketing discourses now co-exist as a set of otherwise 'disinterested' communities' and this can either be seen as a sign of academic maturity or weakness (depending on the narrative being applied).

What this probably shows us more than anything else is that marketers, like social scientists more generally, have become much more sceptical about the status of a single dominant grand narrative or set of truths. In its place we are left with the difficult task of negotiating between different discourses, often without being able to draw on a common set of values or practices by which we might hope to be able to subject these competing narratives to any kind of meaningful test of credibility. In a world of text and narrative many of us would still like to know what is fact and what is fiction, and this is especially relevant for practising marketers seeking to maintain and enhance the status of the marketing profession.

3.8 Learning Activities

Within this chapter the ideas of choice and freedom associated with the discourse of consumer sovereignty compete against the logic of control within the marketing management discourse. Both of the activities below seek to build upon this imagery of wrestling discourses and are designed to enable you to explore these tensions through real-world examples. Before you begin the learning activities remind yourself of the learning aims for the chapter so that your time and efforts are focused.

Learning Activity One: An Apple for Orwell?

There is an interesting marketing tradition in the USA involving the commercial breaks that punctuate the live broadcast of the annual Football Super Bowl final. These advertising slots are extremely valuable because advertisers know that millions of Americans will tune in to see the game and therefore the commercial breaks. Advertisers often pay millions of dollars for a slot and use them to launch new, previously unseen advertisements. Probably the most famous Super Bowl ad of all time is that for Macintosh personal computers, which aired on 22 January 1984 during Super Bowl XVIII. The ad is a wonderful piece of cinema.

a Find a copy of the ad on the internet and view the ad.
b What is the story being told in the ad?
c What are the 'big stories' that the ad taps into to communicate meaning to viewers? Think about the structure of the market for personal computers in the mid-1980s, as well as the global political circumstances of the time.
d Do you think the ad would work today, if so, who would be represented by 'Big Brother'?

Learning Activity Two: Everything Under One Roof

Some critics point out that the trend towards large multinational supermarket groups has actually led to negative consequences for some people. When large supermarkets move into an area many of the local businesses and retailers are unable to compete and may end up going out of business. In some cases this creates 'food deserts' which are areas of deprivation where people do not have easy access to healthy and affordable food (Blanchard and Matthews, 2008). Revenues and profits that would have once have stayed within the local community, paid to local people in wages, and to local suppliers and so on, now get channelled into the profits of large corporations. Some argue that large retailers have sought to undermine status and power of workers in order to maximise profits and that the global nature of supermarket operations mean that many products are transported over vast distances and are therefore responsible for all kinds of global environmental and social crises. This leads some commentators to argue that this type of retail format is unsustainable, wasteful and damaging.

a Develop a counter argument to this critical position and write a short statement outlining your argument.
b What are the main discourses that you are drawing on to develop your argument?
c What problems might you encounter if you were required to judge which argument (for or against) is the most legitimate?

3.9 Further Reading

Hackley, C. (2003) 'We are all customers now … rhetorical strategy and ideological control in marketing management texts', *Journal of Management Studies*, 40 (5): 1325–52.

This paper employs a form of discourse analysis to investigate the genre of marketing management textbooks. One feature of textbooks is that they make numerous seemingly profound statements, but on closer scrutiny many of the claims and arguments made are actually quite banal, common sense and unimaginative. Why are most marketing management textbooks (and most management textbooks for that matter) written in a very particular style and format?

O'Shaughnessy, J. and O'Shaughnessy, N.J. (2002) 'Marketing, the consumer society and hedonism', *European Journal of Marketing*, 36 (5/6): 524–47.

This paper puts forward an argument to counter the claim that marketing is basically responsible for fuelling endless consumer desire and a culture of hedonism that can never be realistically fulfilled. Is marketing guilty of creating and promoting materialism? Whatever answer you come to, the paper provides a detailed account of the different narratives that structure moral and ethical questions concerning the impact of marketing on our everyday lives.

O'Malley, L. and Prothero, A. (2004) 'Beyond the frills of relationship marketing', *Journal of Business Research*, 57: 1286–94.

In this paper the authors examine the gap between the rhetoric and language of Relationship Marketing ideas and their actual consequences on consumers and the reputation of marketing. Paradoxically marketing strategies that make rhetorical promises about trust may actually have the unintended consequence of making consumers more distrustful of organisations. The paper shows quite nicely how some marketing narratives can become popular and influential even when reality and experience is quite different. How believable is marketing discourse?

Caruana, R, Crane, A. and Fitchett, J.A. (2008) 'Paradoxes of consumer independence: a critical discourse analysis of the independent traveller', *Marketing Theory*, 8: 253–72.

Many tourists have grown weary of mass-tourism and packaged holidays. They want to find the authentic, to get away from 'the crowd' (of people like themselves), get outside of commercialised and fake cultural experiences, and to find places off the beaten track. This is a good example of a particular type of discourse, one involving notions of freedom, anti-commercialism, and the search for the authentic. But where does this discourse come from in the first place, and how do consumers achieve these aspirations? Independent Travel Guides are now extremely popular for many tourists. Anyone can go into a high street bookshop and buy the independent travel guide for any city, country or region in the world. These guides promise to tell you how to get away from the tourist crowd so that you can find the real place you are visiting. If you have used one of these products what did you find when you arrived at the advised destinations? Was it more authentic? Were the people more 'real'? Or did most of them have a travel guide just like you?

Kelly-Holmes, H. (1998) 'The discourse of western marketing professionals in central and eastern Europe: Their role in the creation of a context for marketing and advertising messages', *Discourse and Society*, 9(3): 339–62.

This paper shows how it is through Western media and marketing professionals that new, 'capitalist' and market discourses have been brought to the former centrally planned economies of central and eastern Europe.

Zwick, D., Bonsu, S.K. and Darmody, A. (2008) 'Putting consumers to work: 'Co-creation' and new marketing govern-mentality', *Journal of Consumer Culture*, 8 (2): 163–96.

The idea of co-creation of value is becoming increasingly popular in marketing. The basic idea is that firms need to recognise that they do not create value which they then deliver/sell to individuals to consume. Instead firms and consumers create value together, in a partnership. The consumer is a 'co-producer' not a passive receiver of value. On the surface this sounds like a progressive and empowering idea for consumers. This paper suggests that co-creation represents a political form of power aimed at generating particular forms of consumer life at once free and controllable, creative and docile. The authors argue that the discourse of value co-creation stands for a notion of modern corporate power that is no longer aimed at disciplining consumers and shaping actions according to a given norm, but at working with and through the freedom of the consumer.

3.10 References

Andrews, J.C., Netemeyer, R.G., Burton, S., Moberg, D.P. and Christiansen, A. (2004) 'Understanding adolescent intentions to smoke', *Journal of Marketing*, 68 (3): 110–23.

Arnould, E. and Thompson, C.J. (2005) 'Consumer culture theory: Twenty years of research', *Journal of Consumer Research*, 31 (March): 868–83.

Barthes, R. (1972/1957) *Mythologies* (A. Lavers, Trans.). New York: Hill & Wang.

Bauman, Z. (1988) *Freedom*. Milton Keynes: Open University Press.

Blanchard, T.C. and Matthews, T.L. (2008) 'Retail concentration, food deserts, and food-disadvantaged communities in rural America', in C. Hinrichs, and T.A. Lyson, (eds), *Remaking the North American Food System*, pp. 201–15. Lincoln, NE: University of Nebraska Press.

Borden, N. (1964) 'The concept of the marketing mix', *Journal of Advertising Research*, (June): 2–7.

Brownlie, D. and Saren, M. (1997) 'Beyond the one-dimensional marketing manager: The discourse of theory, practice and relevance', *International Journal of Research in Marketing*, 14: 147–61.

Culliton, J. (1948a) *The Management of Marketing Costs*. Boston, MA: Graduate School of Business Administration, Harvard University.

Culliton, J.W. (1948b) 'The management challenge of marketing costs', *Harvard Business Review*, 26 (1): 74–88.

Davies, A.J. and Elliott, R. (2006) 'Evolution of the empowered consumer', *European Journal of Marketing*, 40 (9/10): 1106–21.

Desmond, J. (1998) 'Marketing and moral indifference', in M. Parker (ed.), *Ethics and Organisations*, pp. 173–96. London: Sage.

Du Gay, P. (2001) 'Servicing as cultural economy' in A. Study et al (eds), *Customer Service: Empowerment and Entrapment*, pp. 200–4. Basingstoke: Palgrave.

Eccles, S., Hamilton, E. and Elliott, R. (1999) 'Voices of control: Researching the lived experiences of addictive consumers', *Proceedings of the International Conference on Critical Management Studies*, July, UMIST.

Elliott, R. (1996) 'Discourse analysis: exploring action, function and conflict in social texts', *Marketing Intelligence & Planning*, 14 (6): 65–9.

Frank, T. (2000) *One Market Under God: Extreme Capitalism, Market Populism and the End of Economic Democracy*. London: Anchor Books.

Gabriel, Y. and Lang, T. (2006) *The Unmanageable Consumer: Contemporary Consumption and its Fragmentations*. London: Sage.

Grönroos, C. (1994) 'From marketing mix to relationship marketing: Towards a paradigm shift in marketing', *Management Decision*, 32 (2): 4–20.

Hastings, G., Stead, M. and Webb, J. (2004) 'Fear appeals in social marketing: Strategic and ethical reasons for concern', *Psychology and Marketing*, 21 (11): 961–86.

Hirschman, E. C. (1993) 'Ideology in consumer research, 1980 and 1990: A Marxist and Feminist critique', *Journal of Consumer Research*, 19 (March): 537–55.

Hirschman, E. C. and Holbrook, M. B. (1982) 'Hedonic consumption: emerging concepts, methods and propositions', *Journal of Marketing,* 46 (Summer): 92–101.

Hodgson, D. (2001) 'Empowering customers through education or governing without government?' in A. Sturdy, I. Grugulis and H. Willmott (eds), *Customer Service: Empowerment and Entrapment*, pp. 117–34. Basingstoke: Palgrave.

Holt, D. (2004) *How Brands Become: The Principles of Cultural Branding.* Boston, MA: Harvard Business School Press.

Horkheimer, M. (1967) *Towards a Critique of Instrumental Reason.* Frankfurt am Meine: Europäische Verlagsanstalt.

Jobber, D. (2009) *Principles and Practice of Marketing,* 6th edn. Maidenhead: McGraw-Hill.

Kent, R.A. (1986) 'Faith in the 4Ps: an alternative', *Journal of Marketing Management,* 2 (2): 145–54.

Kotler, P. (1991) *Marketing Management: Analysis, Planning, Implementation and Control,* 7th edn. NJ: Prentice-Hall.

Kotler, P. and Armstrong, G. (2006) *Principles of Marketing.* London: Prentice-Hall.

Lyotard, J.F. (1979/1984) *The Postmodern Condition: A Report on Knowledge.* Manchester: Manchester University Press.

McCarthy, J.E. (1960) *Basic Marketing: A Managerial Approach.* Homewood, IL: Richard D. Irwin.

Mestrovic, S.G. (1993) *The Barbarian Temperament: Toward a Postmodern Critical Theory.* London: Routledge.

Morgan, G. (1992) 'Marketing discourse and practice: towards a critical analysis', in M. Alvesson and H. Willmott (eds), *Critical Management Studies.* London: Sage.

O'Donohoe, S. (2002) 'Living with ambivalence: Attitudes to advertising in postmodern times', *Marketing Theory,* 1 (1): 91–108.

Pine, J. and Gilmore, J. (1998) 'Welcome to the Experience Economy', *Harvard Business Review,* (July–August): 97–105.

Prahalad, C. K. (2005) *The Fortune at the Bottom of the Pyramid.* Wharton, PA: Wharton School Publishing.

Smith, A. (1776/1961) *An Inquiry into the Nature and causes of the Wealth of Nations.* London: Methuen.

Sirgy, M. J. and Su, C. (2000) 'The ethics of consumer sovereignty in an age of high tech', *Journal of Business Ethics,* 28: 1–14.

Solomon, M.R., Marshall, G.W. and Stuart, E.W. (2008) *Marketing: Real People, Real Choices.* Upper Saddle River, NJ: Pearson Prentice-Hall.

Turner, C. (2004) *Planet Simpson.* London: Ebury press.

Van Waterschoot, W. and Van Den Bulte, C. (1992) 'The 4P classification of the marketing mix revisited', *Journal of Marketing,* 56 (4): 83–4.

Vargo, S.L. and Lusch, R.F. (2004) 'Evolving to a new Dominant Logic for marketing', *Journal of Marketing,* 68 (1): 1–17.

Veblen, T. (1899) *The Theory of the Leisure Class: An Economic Study of Institutions.* New York: Random House.

Interrogating the Ideological Function of Marketing

4.1 Introduction

The last chapter sought to identify and describe aspects of the marketing discourse. Of course not all marketing discourses are treated equally or are valued in the same way. Some narratives are more persuasive and popular than others and this often reflects wider beliefs that are prevalent at the time. One of the features of this discourse approach is that it reveals that narratives do not simply provide an account of the world. Marketing discourse, like all stories, not only tries to describe reality but in doing so also makes an implicit judgment about how we should see the world. Marketers clearly have an interest in promoting the idea that marketing is a good, necessary or desirable practice for firms, customers and perhaps even society more generally. This justification is important and necessary for all marketers irrespective of the particular approach or viewpoint they choose to adopt. To investigate this theme further it will be helpful for us to identify and define the characteristics of the marketing ideology. An ideological analysis of marketing will help to provide some kind of common ground for the different and divergent approaches that characterise the field, as well as showing some of the ways that marketers justify and defend marketing functions and practices.

This chapter aims to critically discuss the importance of the *idea* of marketing for the firm. One of the most important notions for marketers today is the *Marketing Concept*. Many of the features that define the modern marketing concept have existed for some time, including the idea that understanding consumer needs should be a priority for all businesses. Over the last century these ideas became more influential and by the 1960s a relatively coherent marketing concept had been developed and described by marketing writers.

4.2 Marketing as Practice, Knowledge and Idea

In the conclusion of his research note on marketing ideology Gilles Marion (2006: 260) summarised his argument as follows: 'To create and develop markets, firms need marketing and marketing related professionals'. To practise marketing these people need principles and tools, as well as good reasons to be committed to their job. To play the legitimate role of the marketer these people need to justify a particular way of looking at the world, not only to themselves but to others. In this sense, marketing can be quite easily understood as a belief system, which we will critically explore in this chapter on marketing ideology.

Ideology is a complex term that can be discussed in a number of ways. In some contexts ideology is used to explain utopian and idealistic intentions. One might say that certain political movements such as socialism, communism or democracy, for example, are motivated by a certain ideology. In this case ideology describes a set of ideal goals (such as egalitarianism, collectivism, individualism and representativeness) and those supporting these ideological positions can be presumed to believe that these ideal goals, if achieved in reality, would produce a better, more just social system than the one currently experienced.

It might seem unusual to talk about marketing as an ideology. Certainly, there have been some groups who have talked about marketing activities in just such a manner. Erich Fromm, along with many other influential writers on culture and economy (such as Horkheimer who was introduced in Chapter 3), were keenly interested in the ideological nature of markets, marketing consumption and capitalism. Although Fromm was still optimistic that people can demonstrate a considerable degree of autonomy within a capitalist marketplace he nonetheless leaves the reader in no doubt how he views marketing activities. In particular, he describes how marketing and sales promotion can 'smother and kill the critical capacities of the customer like an opiate or outright hypnosis' (Fromm, 1942/2001: 111). In a somewhat idealistic comparison to advertising of the late nineteenth, early twentieth century Fromm argues that salesmanship and advertising once attempted to communicate to customers in essentially rational ways. As he puts it:

> The sales-talk of the old-fashioned businessman was essentially rational. He knew his merchandise, he knew the needs of the customer, and on the basis of this knowledge he tried to sell. To be sure, his sales talk was not entirely objective and he used persuasion as much as he could; yet, in order to be efficient, it had to be a rather rational and sensible kind of talk. A vast sector of modern advertising is different; it does not appeal to reason but to emotion; like any other kind of hypnoid suggestion, it tries to impress its objects emotionally and then make them submit intellectually. (Fromm, 1942/2001: 110)

This is strong stuff. Marketing and advertising, for Fromm, appear to function as a system of communication, transmitting messages to consumers about the 'good society' and the virtues of 'consumerism' for the purpose of controlling them – that is, moving them through a sequential process of cognitive (stimulating thought), affective (changing attitudes and beliefs via emotion) and conative (providing motives to buy) realms. Adorno, another important theorist on culture and markets, argued that individuals can demonstrate their autonomy from the effects of the 'culture industries'. They can do this in the sense that some are 'autonomous, independent individuals who judge and decide consciously for themselves' (Adorno, 1989: 135). In the context of our interest in marketing, there are individuals who do consciously examine the structuring of consumption options that they are presented with and decide to eschew consumption, denying the label 'consumer' applies to them (Dobscha and Ozanne, 2001) (a topic further explored in Chapter 8).

Few, it is safe to suggest, would deny that marketing efforts and activities have an impact, even a major impact on most people's daily life (e.g. Schor, 2007), and many marketers would be less than comfortable with the above depiction of the ideological function of marketing and advertising. Most marketers would probably argue they have much more modest aims. They are more concerned with the day-to-day work of building brands, designing communications plans, or developing and launching new products than they are with trying to seek social change to achieve some ideal, utopian future. Just how 'ideological' marketing is or is not, and what implications these possible ideological effects may or may not have, remains a subject of on going controversy and debate.

4.3 Ideology

In the most basic terms, an ideology can be thought of simply as a coherent collection of particular ideas. The ideas that form any specific ideology are often difficult or impossible to prove as either true or false by reference to external knowledge, but rather gain their consistency from an internal logic. When viewed from alternative ideological positions certain ideas that are very important to a given ideology may appear erroneous or even nonsensical. But from within their own ideological frame of reference, these ideas can take on particular significance.

One of the core principles of marketing ideology is the idea that consumer needs and desires are very important, not only for consumers themselves, but also for organisations and society as a whole. These ideas are central to what is probably the most developed argument in marketing ideology – the 'marketing concept'. We will move on to discuss this in some depth in a moment. For now, the idea that consumers are an axis for marketing activities is directly related to ideas about consumer sovereignty and consumer rights and responsibilities. These, in turn, feed into other ideas about service provision, brand loyalty and other marketing debates. The idea of consumer sovereignty, i.e. the freedom to choose whatever lifestyle and consumption options we desire, within certain bounds (Alderson, 1957) is a core marketing mantra. The notion that the customer is 'king' or 'queen' is appealing and relevant to many marketers and others who subscribe to marketing ideology (as we noted in Chapter 3). But from other ideological positions this idea can quickly lose credibility and value. Critics of consumer society for example will often describe the consumer as someone who is in some way 'enslaved' by the needs of organisations (more generally this is framed in terms of an uncritical acceptance to capitalist values (e.g. Fromm, 1976/2007), or that consumer values have eroded and undermined democratic freedoms (cf. Schudson, 2007).

Another key aspect of ideology is that the ideas do not come together in a purely arbitrary or descriptive way. The collection of ideas that make up any ideology are often transformative in that they can be used to shape the way we evaluate everyday experiences, as well as creating a powerful means of persuasion that guides actions and behaviour. In this regard ideology is often thought of as a form of normative practice. Rather than simply explaining a given phenomenon, ideologies have the effect of confirming how things *should* be and which are good or right, and which are bad and wrong. Many marketers, for example, might be expected to take the view that market research is an essential element of any planning process because it helps organisations to understand the needs and wants of consumers (see Chapter 7). A marketing professional who dismissed the need for research on the grounds that he or she could determine the needs of consumers based on their own personal experiences might be viewed negatively and with suspicion. Ideologies affirm what is acceptable and unacceptable, often via norms and 'common-sense'.

4.4 Marketing Ideology

To understand marketing ideology we need to first distinguish between different layers of marketing (Marion, 2006). If most of us were asked to provide a quick and simple definition of marketing we would most likely draw upon a number of functional or managerial *practices* which are generally supposed to fall into the broad category of marketing management. In our definition we might, for instance, draw upon *knowledge* related to brand building, or sales growth, or market share, or advertising, or segmentation. While all of these practices and knowledge are undoubtedly involved in marketing, and for many go a long way to explain what marketing is, they do not really help us to get closer to an appreciation of marketing ideology. To understand marketing in ideological terms, we need to put aside a functional or task-orientated perspective for a moment. Instead, try to think about marketing as a collection of coherent, and relatively powerful and persuasive ideas which above all else affirm a set of values about how organisations and individuals *should* conduct themselves, as well as what they can expect as *right* and *proper* conduct from others.

Do We Need to Get Better at Marketing Marketing?

Some writers express concerns about the perceived value and status of marketing for firms today. There is a widespread feeling among some marketing scholars that many senior business professionals are losing faith in the *idea* of marketing as something that firms need to take seriously. Verhoef and Leeflang (2009: 14) list several worrying consequences, including:

- The marketing function has dropped lower on the corporate hierarchy.
- Marketing and management issues are receiving less attention in the boardroom (McGovern et al., 2004).
- Marketing is now perceived as a cost, not an investment.
- Marketers are being marginalised, in the sense that many strategically important aspects of marketing have moved to other functions in the organisation (Sheth and Sisodia, 2005).
- The synergies that result from mixing marketing decisions have disappeared.
- The roles of the general manager, chief financial officers (CFOs), and 'other penny pinchers and number crunchers' have become more important than the role of chief marketing officers (CMOs) (Nath and Mahajan, 2008).

If these observations are true, then it is clear all the different communities of marketers (practitioners, academics, students, professional associations) need to work much harder at promoting the idea of marketing as something that is progressive, strategically important, and relevant to modern business.

To think about the issue in opposite terms, let us imagine an organisation that has no marketing department or marketing managers, and had never even heard of the term 'marketing'. For most of us in the twenty-first century this requires quite a bit of imagination, but we would only need to go back 100 years or so to find ourselves in a period when marketing, as a term, was relatively obscure and unknown. Many early marketing scholars and practitioners referred instead to the study of the 'distributive industries'; or more generally 'commerce', 'trade' or 'Mercantile Institutions' rather than marketing *per se* (as noted in Chapter 1).

Now, if we were to analyse the types of activities and practices that our *organisation-without-marketing* regularly undertakes we would expect to find evidence of all kinds of activities that were, at the very least, marketing-related. Contemporary marketing writers have often tended to overlook the fact that organisations and producers of all varieties have sought to promote their goods and services to potential customers and also recognised the importance of developing and improving their product ranges to keep buyers interested. To illustrate this point, we only need to turn to the writings of the eighteenth-century novelist Daniel Defoe. Before writing novels like *Robinson Crusoe* and *Moll Flanders*, Defoe was a prominent commentator on business activities (despite being a failed entrepreneur himself!). In a work published in 1727, Defoe made a compelling case for recognising the value of a customer orientation, as well as documenting the importance of positive word-of-mouth for the small tradesperson. Specifically with regard to customer orientation Defoe said:

> The sum of the matter is this: it is necessary for a tradesman to subject himself, by all the ways possible, to his business; his customers are to be his idols: so far as he may worship idols by allowance, he is to bow down to them and worship them; at least, he is not in any way to displease them, or to show any disgust or distaste at anything they say or do. The bottom of all this is, that he is intending to get money by them; and it is not for him that gets money to offer the least inconvenience to them by whom gets it; but he is to consider, that, as Solomon says, 'The borrower is always servant to the lender,' so the seller is always the servant to the buyer. (Defoe, 1727/1987: 71)

The point here, then, is to recognise that functional aspects of promotion, customer satisfaction, distribution, and even segmentation are undertaken by most, if not all organisations, irrespective of whether they are market-orientated or prioritise marketing.

4.5 A Marketing Revolution

The difference between the ideology of marketing and the practice of marketing is a subtle but vital one. An ideological belief in marketing is based on the assumption and expectation that marketing *as an idea* is an important one. The more fundamentalist one is about an ideology the more its ideas are thought of as being influential, if not absolutely essential. Some writers have argued that marketing is such a fundamental and basic system that marketing science *can* and *should* be applied to understand not only commercial activity but many, and potentially all human and economic processes (e.g. Kotler, 1976).

Marketing ideologues, that is, an advocate or official exponent of the marketing ideology, have, for example, argued that marketing values and ideas can be used to improve education, penal and health systems. This is perhaps most clearly evidenced in initiatives which attempt to promote the idea that the interaction between individual and organisation should treat the individual like a customer and the organisation as a service provider. The *idea* that prisoners, or students, or medical patients are 'customers' and that penal officers, teachers and doctors are correspondingly 'service providers' is one of the powerful consequences of marketing ideology (see Box below).

A key difference here is between a definition of marketing as a progressive and transformative ideology on the one hand, and an understanding of various administrative and functional processes which involve marketing related processes, on the other. Although the basic principles of this marketing ideology can be found throughout the history of economic thought (e.g. Tosdal, 1933), it was most clearly articulated by North American business and management academics in the post Second World War period in what came to be termed 'the marketing concept'. At least this is what we are usually led to believe. It is not an overstatement to suggest that many people concur with Kelley (2007: 53) who asserts that: 'It is generally accepted that the modern marketing era began in 1954'. This was the point at which Peter Drucker would popularise the marketing concept in a widely cited quote:

> Marketing is not only much broader than selling, it is not a specialized activity at all. It encompasses the entire business. It is the whole business seen from the point of view of the final result, that is, from the customer's point of view. Concern and responsibility for marketing must therefore permeate all areas of the enterprise. There is only one valid definition of business purpose: to create a customer. (Drucker, 1954: 39)

When marketers talk about the marketing concept they are typically referring to a series of interrelated arguments regarding the purpose of business and the value of maintaining customer loyalty. While there are many views and opinions about how to define organisational success, as well as the possible factors that might be said to either promote or inhibit it, the marketing concept is, at its core, based on a belief that an understanding of consumer needs and wants is fundamental to all successful organisations.

One of the aims of this chapter is to help you to reflect critically on the ideological basis that the practice of marketing is founded upon. While we might describe the marketing concept as a kind of corporate 'religion' for the 1950s and 1960s (and beyond) we should take care not to over-generalise these types of views. Nonetheless, some practitioners went so far as to liken the so-called 'marketing revolution' – essentially the enshrinement of the marketing concept as a philosophy of business at the Pillsbury Company – to the Copernican revolution of the sixteenth century (Keith, 1960).

Are Students Consumers?

There has been a massive increase in the number of people entering higher education over the last few decades. Higher education changed from an opportunity that was only available to the few to one that was accessible to a mass public. Many social commentators view this as a positive and progressive social development, opening up opportunities to people that would have previously been closed to them. But some writers are concerned that the growth in the student numbers has been accompanied by the increasing marketisation of education and that this has led to some less positive outcomes. For example, Svensson and Wood (2007: 18) state, 'Students are seen as customers of knowledge at many universities. Likewise, universities regard themselves as suppliers of knowledge to these customers. In extension, many universities go a step further and regard their students as collaborators in the quest for knowledge. It is apparent that these universities have been strongly influenced by marketing metaphors.' One of the potential problems, Svensson and Wood (2007: 27) argue, is that once students are seen as consumers the nature of the learning experience is undermined. They go on to state: 'This focus on the marketing paradigm, we contend, has led some students to perceive that admission to the degree and the payment of the attendant fees are equal to the conferral of the degree. They have "bought" the product and so assume that they have "ownership" of it from the first days of their degree studies.' Others would argue that a marketing ideology is not problematic to a context like education and may in fact be highly appropriate. After all, education can be seen as a service, and students pay for that service. Universities actively promote their 'products' and operate as a business. Questions about whether or not students can and should be thought of as consumers is related more broadly to an ideological debate about the legitimate scope of marketing. This debate has been an on-going one ever since modern marketing ideas were formulated in the 1950s and 1960s (see Luck, 1969). If you are a student reading this book, do you consider yourself to be a consumer, and if so, what ideas underpin this view?

Whether religion or scientific revolution, we should not assume that marketing management and business organisations 'suddenly' came to realise the benefits of a customer orientation at this point. Again, the comment from Defoe 1727/1987 above should be enough to disabuse us of this idea. More recently scholars such as Percival White (1927) or Lee Bristol (1932) clearly enunciated the idea that, in White's (1927) case, all organisational activities should be oriented around the consumer – with production only beginning after the consumer had been consulted regarding their needs, wants and desires.

Bristol (1932) and White (1927) both make a vigorous argument for the careful evaluation of all marketing and distributive activities, sketching a role for a 'Director of Distribution' – essentially an early version of the marketing manager and quite similar to the extended role of the sales manager that Tosdal (1925) talks about (Strong and Hawes, 1990). Stressing the importance of focusing attention on consumer requirements through a variety of quantitative and qualitative market research methods, Bristol explains that

... it is my sincere belief that the developments of the future will start from a market analysis and a discovery of needs and requirements in that market before the products are created to supply those needs. Does this not seem a more logical and orderly procedure and one that gives promise of fewer business tragedies in the future? (Bristol, 1932: 116)

Many scholars and practitioners of marketing would agree with Bristol on this point. But there are key differences that should be borne in mind – Bristol is talking about a fairly ambiguously defined 'market', not target market or market segment. We will come back to this issue again. But for the moment, recognition that Bristol (1932) and White (1927) are both pushing marketing towards the centre of an organisational agenda, and thereby undermining the centrality of a production emphasis that had, until then, prevailed in organisations is enough. The shift in emphasis will become more politically fraught as we shall see and this will have implications for the ideological function of marketing. Certainly, while some companies such as Procter and Gamble and General Electric appear to have situated marketing activities as central to their business operations early in the twentieth century (see Dyer et al., 2004), such views were not diffused to a wide audience until the 1950s. Registering this, we will now turn to the debates surrounding this idea in the 1950s and 1960s, in order to link this work with more recent attempts to measure the market orientation of any given company.

4.6 Moving Towards a Definition of the Marketing Concept

As Drucker (1954) noted, marketing is supposed to be broader than selling. Selling suggests that firms 'push' goods on to consumers without first attempting to understand their requirements. This is sometimes referred to as a sales orientation. A marketing orientation, by contrast, was meant to encourage organisations to produce those goods and services that customers desired. Importantly, marketing as a business activity was not, for Drucker (1954), an activity that one department should be involved in, but rather a marketing ethos should permeate the whole organisation.

This is a powerful statement for anyone interested in marketing. In many respects this statement outlines the foundations of marketing as an ideology. Drucker argued that we need to stop thinking about marketing in narrow, functional terms. Marketing should be understood as a general business philosophy that 'encompasses the entire business' and 'permeates all areas of the enterprise'. This would have been music to the ears of marketing professionals at the time. Interestingly enough, these ideas were promoted by practitioners involved with marketing. There are a number of reasons why this might have been the case.

By the 1950s, the US economic system was massively stimulated by consumer demand which had been largely curtailed during the Second World War as armament production was a governmental objective, which meant that consumer goods production was severely restricted and demand unfulfilled. With the conclusion of the Second World War consumers were understandably interested in regaining their pre-eminent status in the marketplace. And there were a number of key factors that encouraged business practitioners – not academics (Benton, 1987) – to call for attention to the marketing concept, as well as to marketing management.

Companies were operating in a turbulent business environment. Disposable income levels were rising among consumers, as had standards of living. Industry and production facilities had undergone massive expansion during the War. In short, North American consumers had more money, and there were greater numbers of producers chasing the consumer's dollar, and this made consumer purchasing behaviour difficult to predict.

In this climate we see management and marketing practitioners developing new ideas which would radically shift the place of marketing in the business enterprise. Marketing was represented as one strategy to help organisations understand, predict and to some extent control, the level of risk that they faced when producing products and services. Marketing was rapidly becoming the intellectual and practical axis for all organisational activities. As McKay (1954) pointed out:

> The modern marketing concept calls for an integrated company and distribution organisation, designed to carry out ... [the] marketing plan, and all the required marketing functions, effectively, economically, and on time. (McKay, 1954: 4)

Taking this one step further, Barwell (1965) defined the marketing concept as a 'philosophy' and this remains one of the most ideological, and at least for marketing institutions, influential definitions of marketing. Barwell writes:

> This customer focused philosophy is known as the 'marketing concept'. The marketing concept is a philosophy, not a system of marketing or an organisational structure. It is founded on the belief that profitable sales and satisfactory returns on investment can only be achieved by identifying, anticipating and satisfying customer needs and desires.

Likewise, Borch explains that 'In our company, we feel that marketing is a fundamental business philosophy' (Borch, 1958: 18). What is particularly striking about Barwell's (1965) and Borch's (1958) statements is the type of language and terminology they employed. Marketing is discussed here as a *belief* and a *philosophy*. Barwell (1965), in particular, tells us that returns on investment can *only* be achieved through the marketing concept. This is quite different from stating that a market focus is one among several ways to achieve corporate success.

4.7 The Practical Implications of the Marketing Concept

One of the problems with many ideologically inspired projects is that conditions on the ground and practical 'realities' often mean that many intentions and aspirations fail to materialise. An enduring criticism of the marketing concept when it is defined in these kinds of ideological terms is that while it sounds all well and good in theory, in practice it is virtually impossible to implement. Kotler explains why:

> Just as marketing stresses the customer's point of view, other departments must stress efficiency. This results in a large number of conflicts with marketing … Marketing, in trying to mobilize the company's resources to develop satisfactions, often causes other departments to do a poorer job *on their terms*. (Kotler, 1967: 138; emphasis in original)

Even in the most market oriented organisations marketers must work together with other organisational groups and interests. Marketing ideology is only one aspect of business practice and other parts of the organisation are guided by different, often competing, sets of ideas (see Table 4.1).

Each department has a core set of beliefs and is charged with accomplishing certain activities and so each will attempt to do this vigorously in the face of other departments' activities. Thus we get the potential for ideological conflict within the same organisation, with each using their own beliefs as justification for their activities and norms. This issue is compounded by the fact that as an ideological principle, the effectiveness or validity of the marketing concept cannot be demonstrated conclusively in the face of opposing ideological beliefs either in scientific terms (i.e. is the marketing concept true) or business terms (i.e. does adopting the marketing concept lead to return on investment). This may also go some way to explain one of the popular criticisms of marketing management from non-marketers who see marketing as unaccountable, untouchable, expensive and slippery (Shultz, 2003).

Table 4.1   Summary of organisational conflicts between marketing and other departments

Other Departments	Their Emphasis	Marketing Emphasis
Engineering	Prefer long design lead time	Short design lead time
	Emphasis on functional features	Sales features
	Few models	Many models
	Standard components	Custom components
Purchasing	Prefer standardised parts	Non-standard parts
	Price of material important	Quality of material
	Economical lot sizes	Large lot sizes to avoid
	Purchasing at infrequent	stock-outs
	intervals	Immediate purchasing for
		customer needs
Production	Long production lead time	Short production lead time
	Long runs with few models	Short runs with many models
	No model changes	Frequent model changes
	Standard orders	Custom orders
	Ease of fabrication	Aesthetic appearance
	Average quality control	Tight quality control
Inventory	Fast moving items	Broad product line
	Narrow product line	Large range of stock
	Economical levels of stock	
Finance	Strict rationales for spending	Intuitive arguments for spending
	Hard and fast budgets	Flexible budgets to meet changing
	Pricing to cover costs	needs
		Pricing to further market
		development
Accounting	Standard transactions	Special terms and discounts
	Few reports	Many reports
Credit	Full financial disclosures by	Minimum credit examination of
	clients	customers
	Low credit risks	Medium credit risks
	Tough credit terms	Easy credit terms
	Tough collection procedures	Easy collection procedures

Source: Kotler, Philip. Marketing Management: Analysis, Planning and Control (2nd edn) © 1972. Printed and electronically reproduced by permission of Pearson Education inc., Upper Saddle River, New Jersey.

Does Marketing Cost Too Much?

Marketers, it seems, have always felt the need to defend their activities against the criticism that marketing costs too much, and that any benefits of marketing are hard, if not impossible to measure. In 1939 Stewart and Dewhurst wrote, 'The idea that is costs too much to distribute goods and that modern methods of distribution are wasteful and inefficient has taken root in the public mind' (Stewart and Dewhurst, 1939: 3). A decade or so later, James Culliton (1948) asked a similar question in his book on *The Management of Marketing Costs*. In the first edition of McCarthy's (1960) *Basic Marketing*, probably the first modern marketing management textbook he begins 'Does marketing cost too much? ... If a referendum were held next week to decide on whether to outlaw marketing (...) the American people would most likely vote a resounding yes' (McCarthy, 1960: 1). More recently Professor John Quelch of the Harvard Business School writes (2009: 3), 'Many chief financial officers might still agree with John Wanamaker's famous adage: "Half my advertising is wasted. I just don't know which half." But our understanding of what works in marketing, how and why, has advanced greatly in the last twenty years.' These criticisms are commonplace today and seriously question the credibility of the marketing concept and of marketing more generally.

Marketing writers have responded to some of the problems with the marketing concept ideology by attempting to ground it in more realistic and more accountable terms. By the late 1960s, early 1970s leading marketing writers such as Philip Kotler were incorporating aspects of marketing concept ideology into a strategic planning approach and this placed much greater emphasis on factors such as internal departmental conflict, current and potential competitors and other external environmental factors. In his genre defining text, *Marketing Management: Analysis, Planning and Control*, first published in 1967, Philip Kotler defines the marketing concept in slightly different terms to Drucker:

The *marketing concept* is a management orientation that holds that the key task of the organisation is to determine the needs, wants and values of a target market and to adapt the organisation to delivering the desired satisfactions more effectively and efficiently than competitors. (Kotler, 1976: 14)

In many respects Kotler's definition of the marketing concept is consistent with the other definitions we have looked at in that it reaffirms a belief that organisational goals can be achieved by focusing efforts on determining the needs of customers. It differs from the more idealistic expressions of the marketing concept in a number of significant ways. Although Kotler claims that the marketing concept is key to organisational success, he does not imply that it is the only factor or necessarily the most important one and reference to individual customer needs have been replaced with the aggregated concept of the target market. Perhaps most tellingly, the marketing concept is expressed as a relative measure rather than as an ideal state. More generally he argues that top management should attempt to reduce political infighting between departments in order to ensure the satisfaction of company objectives. This is important. Kotler does not assert that customer satisfaction is the overriding objective of all organisational activities irrespective of organisational objectives, nor does he return to a production or sales orientation. He writes,

The ultimate standard is neither cost control nor customer satisfaction at any price. Just as production, engineering, finance, and the other departments should show more concern for keeping and cultivating the customer, marketing has to show more *restraint* in interrupting production schedules and multiplying product-design and material costs. (Kotler, 1967: 139)

So instead of defining the marketing concept as an organisational quality, Kotler describes it in competitive terms. This shift towards a more grounded and less idealistic marketing concept was seen by many writers as a necessary and productive development.

For example, in a review of Kotler's *Marketing Management* Thomas (1967: 346) welcomes this less 'idealistic' approach, writing, 'Kotler has made marketing management into a respectably analytical subject matter.'

By the end of the 1970s, the marketing concept as an ideological position had become almost entirely subsumed into a managerialist perspective (see Dixon, 1992). One of the tensions that this produced was between the ideals of the marketing concept which granted a certain priority to consumer needs and wants, and the practice of management which sought to control, predict and manage consumers. Marketers often claim that consumers are central to their decision-making and that organisations seek to be consumer driven, but in terms of management practice they often treat consumers as a group to whom something is done *to*, or as a *select* constituency that is acted *upon*. Marketing, in this revised view, is not simply concerned with catering to customer requirements, with customers being active decision makers regarding their consumption choices. Kotler and Levy (1971) are far more overt in stressing that 'marketing functions to regulate the level and shape of demand so that it conforms to the organisation's current supply situation and to its long-run objectives' (Kotler and Levy, 1971: 8). More specifically, the marketing manager is tasked with, 'regulating the level, timing, and character of demand for one or more products of an organisation' (Kotler, 1973: 42).

4.7.1 Selective Demarketing

The idea of the independence and choice of the consumer seems to have been excised to some extent from these discussions of marketing and marketing management. Nowhere is this more clear than in the discussions of 'demarketing'. Before we continue, we should emphasise that Kotler and Levy explicitly point out that they do not support some of the demarketing practices that they document, for reasons that will become clear. Demarketing for Kotler and Levy is *'that aspect of marketing that deals with discouraging customers in general or a certain class of customers in particular on either a temporary or permanent basis'* (Kotler and Levy, 1971: 75). Our focus here will be on the examples that Kotler and Levy use to illustrate 'selective demarketing', that is, where a specific group of consumers are discouraged.

Customers could be being treated in this way because they are unprofitable and therefore an organisation seeks to divest them. On the other hand, the company could try to avoid dealing with them at all. Alternatively, the consumption of a product by one group of consumers could have a direct impact on the products desirability (i.e. I won't buy that because so-and-so has bought it) and consequently the company seeks to restrict access to the product or structure and delimit where the product is available from. The example we provide here is relatively innocuous. Those provided by Kotler and Levy are not in that they could raise legal and ethical objections. Let us repeat two of them in full:

> A luxury hotel catering to middle-aged, conservative people has recently attracted rich hippies who come wearing long hair and odd clothes, and who sit on the lobby floor making a good deal of noise. This has turned off the hotel's main clientele and the management must rapidly take steps to discourage further reservation by hippies.

And the next one:

> An automobile manufacturer of a luxury car purchased mainly by affluent whites as a status symbol has discovered that an increasing number of sales are going to newly rich members of the black community. As a result, affluent whites are switching to

another well-known luxury automobile. The automobile manufacturer has to decide whether to let the market take its natural course, attempt to market to both groups, or to demarket to the new customer class. (Kotler and Levy, 1971: 78)

So, where the marketing ideology defines the consumer as an active and desiring agent, when we look at some of the examples of marketing management practice that Kotler and Levy discuss, it would appear that marketing practice treats consumers as *relatively* passive receivers of organisational initiatives.

4.8 Against the Marketing Concept: Bringing Sales Back In?

The marketing concept sets up a clear distinction between organisations and consumers and then defines how these two entities should relate to one another. If interpreted in certain ways this means that firms should gather together the expressed needs and wants of consumers as the starting point from which to begin organisational planning. Critics of the marketing concept argue that while this type of language may please consumers and reflect well on organisations as caring, attentive and responsive, it does not, and should not, follow through into actual marketing practice. Opponents of this consumer-centric view of marketing point out that in reality consumers are very poor sources of information about their own future needs and desires. Consumers do not know what they might want in the future, partly because they lack knowledge. Decisions about innovation and product development can only be made by experts who understand the potential of new technology. Indeed, Stephen Brown (2006) views consumers as essentially 'conservative' and somewhat 'stuck-in-the-mud' when it comes to their consumption habits.

Consumers, Brown tells us (2006), lack imagination about what could be produced. And Kotler et al. (2005) rhetorically highlight this in a particularly stark manner. Twenty years ago they write, 'how many of us were asking for mobile phones, fax machines and copiers at home, cars with on-board navigation systems, hand-held global satellite positioning receivers, cyber-cafés or interactive television shopping networks?' (Kotler et al., 2005: 17). Not many of us at all, most probably.

Nor is it simply the case that if we were firm adherents of the marketing concept and vigorously engaged in market research that we could have established the popularity of such items. Consumers' responses to market research are notoriously unreliable. Examples of products where market research indicated little or no consumer interest include the hugely popular BMW designed Mini (Brown, 2004), the Chrysler Minivan, the Sony Walkman, even Boeing's 747 (Brown, 2006).

So, as well as focusing on those needs and wants that consumers can discuss with a market researcher, 'we in marketing must focus our businesses on the customer's needs and desires, including those needs and desires of which the customer is *not* aware, as well as those that he knows only too well' (Borch, 1958: 20). This is why Borch talks about a dual-core marketing concept. Marketing is not simply concerned with meeting explicit customer desires, but also with creating them – with managing demand, with influencing the customer. Thus, Borch maintains that a sales orientation is a very important marketing function.

In contrast to Keith (1960) who saw the gradual excision of a sales orientation from the history of his company, and Kotler (1976: 15) who argued that the 'marketing concept replaces and reverses the logic of the selling concept', a sales orientation still remains very much part of marketing's identity whether we like it or not (it is, after all, reminiscent of the old snake oil salesman) (Brown, 2001,

2007). Marketers, Borch argued, need not only to cater to customer demands, but also to 'persuade the prospective customer, through all the arts of selling and advertising, to purchase the products and services that have been developed' (Borch, 1958: 20).

In other words, marketers must not necessarily defer to the customer – marketers should not necessarily be the voice of the customer in the organisation. In some cases it is up to marketers to take innovations to the market and to show consumers how they can be used to satisfy needs and wants. The late head of Sony, Akio Morita, argued just this point. Sony was not an organisation led by market research or the consumer. As he put it: 'Our plan is to lead the public with new products rather than ask them what kinds of products they want. The public does not know what is possible, but we do. So, instead of doing a lot of market research, we refine our thinking on a product and its use and try to create a market for it by educating and communicating with the public' (Akio Morita in Kotler et al., 2005: 17). And Houston (1986: 86) uses the extreme example of the doctor–patient relationship to illustrate this issue:

> The patient does not specify the treatment; it is the doctor's task to assess the specific product needs of the patient. Yet, this does not mean that the doctor is not addressing the needs and wants of the patient; the doctor's unique offering is that special capability to identify and satisfy the patient's needs.

Others argue that adoption of the marketing concept may seem like a viable and sustainable strategic direction for individual organisations, but over the medium to long-term it will have a damaging effect on markets as a whole, as well as the ability for individual firms to compete with one another. By focusing efforts on consumer research and designing strategies as responses to supposed market wants organisations can end up falling into the trap of producing more and more 'me-too' products with little or no substantial differentiation from competitor offerings.

Torment Your Customers?

Professor Stephen Brown makes a humorous assault on the idea that marketing should be consumer focused and consumer centric. In an article in the *Harvard Business Review*, Brown (2001: 83) comments:

> I have nothing against customers. Some of my best friends are customers … Customers are a good thing, by and large, provided they're kept well downwind. My problem is with the concept of – and I shudder to write the term – 'customer centricity'. Everyone in business today seems to take it as a God-given truth that companies were put on this earth for one purpose alone: to pander to customers. Marketers spend all their time slavishly tracking the needs of buyers, then meticulously crafting products and pitches to satisfy them … My friends, it's gone too far. The truth is, customers don't know what they want. They never have. They never will. The wretches don't even know what they don't want, as the success of countless rejected-by-focus-groups products, from the Chrysler minivan to the Sony Walkman, readily attests. A mindless devotion to customers means me-too products, copycat advertising campaigns, and marketplace stagnation.

So, rather than investing in true product and service innovations firms are drawn into a cycle in which they end up providing products that are very similar to the competitors offerings, but with endless minor variations and superficial differences, which are developed for the purposes of marketing and promotion. Rather than being empowered and having their needs met, consumers end up with having to make relatively arbitrary choices in a marketplace of virtually identical products and services. Marketing success becomes increasingly reliant on effective advertising and sales efforts rather than delivering genuine consumer value. In this scenario the marketing concept actually ends up having a negative effect on the consumer. It is ironic that this ideology that was conceived to encourage organisations to focus on consumer needs and wants can end up failing consumers and organisations, if it is not tempered by the recognition of the continued need for product and service innovation and good salesmanship.

4.9 Defending the Marketing Concept

In a short article 'The marketing concept: What it is and what it is not' Houston (1986) summarises the debate between supporters and critics of the marketing concept. He concludes that many criticisms are based upon misunderstandings of the marketing concept which have emerged over several decades of discussion and that a revised and more modest marketing concept remains valuable. Houston makes it clear that in his view the marketing concept does not suggest that firms should design products based on the expressed needs of customers or that new product development should be conditional on marketing and consumer research insights alone. Houston's (1986: 85) revised definition reads:

> The marketing concept states that an entity achieves its own exchange determined goals most efficiently through a thorough understanding of potential exchange partners and their needs and wants, through a thorough understanding of the costs associated with satisfying those needs and wants, and then designing, producing and offering products in light of this understanding.

This revision addresses most of the main criticisms of the marketing concept expressed in ideological and/or ideal terms. In this definition the success of the firm (or 'entity') is not reliant on some kind of slavish adherence to the whims of consumers but on a 'thorough understanding' of 'exchange partners'. Rather than the needs of consumers being considered paramount, Houston acknowledges that it is in fact the needs of the firm which should always take priority. Consumer needs are not, for most firms, an end, but rather a means to an end. Put more simply organisations exist to 'maximise returns to shareholders by developing relationships with valued customers and creating competitive advantage' (Doyle, 2000: 300). Thus companies should not exist to cater to all the needs and wants of all customers, but only to those that will enable a company to satisfy their own organisational objectives, whatever they may be.

4.10 Evidence for the Marketing Concept

Houston's defence and conceptual re-visitation of earlier work, and subsequent redefinition, forms an essential part of the history of the marketing concept.

Other researchers have approached questions about the relevance and validity of the marketing concept by seeking to measure it in empirical terms. This body of research sets out to test whether adherence to the ideological principles of the marketing concept can be shown to produce observable and measurable organisational benefits. Kohli and Jaworski (1990), for example, attempted to further understand how the marketing concept could be implemented in terms of actual organisational practice. Moving away from talking about the marketing concept, Kohli and Jaworski (1990: 1) prefer to discuss *market orientation*, stating: 'We use the term "market orientation" to mean the implementation of the marketing concept. Hence, a market-orientated company is one whose actions are consistent with the marketing concept.' They set out to identify and define specific processes and activities that create a market orientated organisation. To achieve this they interviewed practising managers asking them to describe what market orientation meant to them in their roles as managers, the organisational factors which they believed promoted or discouraged a market orientation, and to identify business situations where a marketing orientation might be relevant or not. They conclude that while a marketing orientation might be desirable in some cases, it may be not be desirable in others:

> Under conditions of limited competition, stable market preferences, technologically turbulent industries and booming economies, a marketing orientation may not be strongly related to business performance. (Kohli and Jaworski, 1990: 16)

As well as identifying some of the organisational systems that help to create a market orientation, such as promoting interdepartmental communication, having less rigid departmental divisions and divides, and implementing market-based reward systems, they also point out that implementing a true market orientation brings with it a number of significant resource implications. Before deciding to implement the marketing concept into actual organisation practices it is vital to evaluate whether these costs are justifiable.

In a later study Jaworski and Kohli (1993) attempted to further formalise their findings from focus group interviews by empirically testing a range of hypotheses about the marketing concept and market orientation. While their findings did show that market orientation is an important determinant of business performance, they were unable to demonstrate a clear relationship between market orientation and market share. For many practising managers this finding is probably quite understandable. Achieving market share gains is dependent on a wide range of factors, some of which are specific to particular industries and markets. No matter how important one believes marketing to be in achieving favourable business outcomes it can never provide a complete account, at least not empirically. A final point to note from Kohli and Jaworski's studies is the finding that a market orientation appears to be facilitated by the extent to which top managers placed an emphasis on market orientation in the first place. In essence, this shows that the success of the marketing concept in practical terms, is to a large degree dependent upon senior managers believing in it in the first place, and then being able to instil a certain kind of organisational responsiveness in others (Hult et al., 2005). Although significant advances have been made in measuring the marketing concept and therefore identifying its causes, it seems that its potential power is, if only in part, derived from the belief that decision makers place in its core ideas and values.

4.11 Conclusion

Houston (1986) and others have put forward a strong case in support of a marketing concept, albeit one that is refined, more limited in scope and arguably less ideological. The outstanding issue for marketing is the extent to which these revisions help to maintain and enhance the perceived value of marketing, not only for marketers themselves, but for others in organisations tasked with making decisions about marketing functions. A refined and less ambitious marketing concept is likely to be far less controversial and more compatible with other organisational systems than a marketing concept expressed in more ideological terms. But without a general belief in a strong ideologically informed marketing concept one could argue that marketers are more easily compromised and marginalised as other organisational ideologies become more embedded in everyday practice. Without a strong marketing concept, and a *strong belief in the idea* of the marketing concept, there is less reason to include marketers in high-level decision-making processes and as a result, the status and value of marketing, and the marketing profession, are likely to be diminished.

4.12 Learning Activities

The premise and promise of a customer orientation is explored within this chapter and it seeks to ask how marketing legitimates itself as an ideology and practice. The learning activities below require you to look again at some of the assumptions of marketing and the rhetoric of customer orientation. Before you begin the learning activities remind yourself of the learning aims for the chapter so that your time and efforts are focused.

Learning Activity One: Legitimating Marketing

In this activity you are encouraged to reflect on what types of resources and evidence would be useful to a marketing manager who is attempting to convince a sceptical Chief Executive of the value of marketing. A Chief Executive of a medium-sized consumer goods manufacturing organisation is looking at the composition of the board of directors. The CEO is sceptical about the need for a marketing representative on the board, taking the view that the marketing function should be represented by an existing board member. You have been asked to deliver a short presentation to the CEO and the board outlining the reasons why marketing activities need to be represented at a senior level.

　　Prepare your presentation for the board along with a short written statement outlining the reasons for your recommendation. What ideas are useful for your justification, and to what extent is your argument based on a underlying marketing ideology?

Learning Activity Two: Harming the Customer?

You have been commissioned by HLACM (The Humane League Against Cruel Marketing) to assist them in their latest campaign. The group petition marketing practitioners who are perceived to be selling socially acceptable goods that are much sought by customers but which ultimately cause harm to the customer, their friends or their relatives. Examples of recent campaigns include protests against alcohol, cigarettes, gambling and pornography. The latest campaign is against retailers and manufacturers of 'ready meals'. The group have identified over 1000 marketing professionals involved in the production or sale of 'ready meals' and they are looking for a creative and effective way of reminding the marketer of the harm that they are doing.

Your role is to come up with a concept that will meet this brief. You should research the health, social, cultural, environmental and economic problems associated with 'ready meals' and consider how you will overcome the marketer's response that they are merely providing solutions to customer problems.

You may wish to read the following articles: Bell and Emery (1971); Feldman (1971).

4.13 Further Reading

Dixon, D.F. (1992) 'Consumer sovereignty, democracy, and the marketing concept: A macromarketing perspective', *Canadian Journal of Administrative Science*, 9 (2): 116–25.

This article argues that the ideology of the marketing concept (which is analysed as a particular type of modern myth or a story) actually undermines the credibility and status of marketing knowledge. It calls for marketers to base their ideas on more realistic assumptions about markets and individual behaviour.

Houston, F.S. (1986) 'The marketing concept: What it is and what it is not', *Journal of Marketing*, 50 (2): 81–7.

This article argues that the marketing concept has become widely misunderstood and misused. Houston attempts to correct these misunderstandings to show how we should and should not use the marketing concept. His arguments can help us to further understand some of the conceptual limits of the idea.

Jaworski, B.J and Kohli, A. (1993) 'Market orientation: Antecedents and consequences', *Journal of Marketing*, 57 (3): 53–60.

One of the most persistent criticisms of the marketing concept is that it has become little more than an appealing *idea*. Jaworski and Kohli's work is part of an influential movement in marketing theory that seeks to understand how the marketing concept can be implemented in terms of actual marketing practice. For an idea to be useful it should be able to be applied to real situations and contexts. Rather than focusing on the idea of the philosophy of the marketing concept we should instead examine how it is reflected in the actual behaviours, practices and activities within organisations.

4.14 References

Adorno, T. W. (1989) 'The culture industry revisited', in S.E. Bronner and D.M. Kellner (eds), *Critical Theory and Society: A Reader*, pp. 128–35. New York: Routledge.

Alderson, W. (1957) *Marketing Behavior and Executive Action*. Homewood: Richard D. Irwin.

Barwell, C. (1965) 'The marketing concept', in A. Wilson (ed.), *The Marketing of Industrial Products*. London: Hutchison.

Bell, M.L. and Emery, C.W. (1971) 'The faltering marketing concept', *Journal of Marketing*, (October): 37–42.

Benton, R. (1987) 'The practical domain of marketing: The notion of a "free" enterprise economy as a guise for institutionalized marketing power', *American Journal of Economies and Sociology*, 46 (4): 415–30.

Borch, F.J. (1958) 'The marketing philosophy as a way of business life', in E.J. Kelley and W. Lazer (eds), *Managerial Marketing: Perspectives and Viewpoints A Source Book*, pp. 18–24. Homewood: Richard D. Irwin.

Bristol, L. (1932) *Profits in Advance*. New York: Harper.

Brown, S. (2001) 'Torment your customers (they'll love it)', *Harvard Business Review*, 26 (1): 74–88.

Brown, S. (2001) *Marketing – The Retro Revolution*. London: Sage.

Brown, S. (2004) 'O customer, where art thou?', *Business Horizons*, 47 (4): 61–70.

Brown, S. (2006) 'Fail better! Samuel Beckett's secrets of business and branding success', *Business Horizons*, 49: 161–9.

Brown, S. (2007) 'The failgood factor: Playing hopscotch in the marketing minefield', *The Marketing Review*, 7 (2): 125–38.

Culliton, J.W. (1948) 'The management challenge of marketing costs', *Harvard Business Review*, 26 (1): 74–88.

Defoe, D. (1727/1987) *The Complete English Tradesman*. Gloucester: Sutton.

Dobscha, S. and Ozanna, J.L. (2001) 'An ecofeminist analysis of environmentally sensitive women using qualitative methodology: The emancipatory potential of an ecological life', *Journal of Public Policy and Marketing*, 20 (2): 201–14.

Dixon, D.F. (1992) 'Consumer sovereignty, democracy and the marketing concept: A macromarketing perspective', *Canadian Journal of Administrative Science*, 9 (2): 116–25.

Doyle, P. (2000) 'Value-based marketing', *Journal of Strategic Marketing*, 8 (4): 299–311.

Drucker, P. (1954) *The Practice of Management*. New York, NY; Harper Collins.

Dyer, D., Dalzell, F. and Olegario, R. (2004) *Rising Tide: Lessons from 165 Years of Brand Building at Proctor and Gamble*. Boston: Harvard Business School Press.

Feldman, L. P. (1971) 'Societal adaptation: a new challenge for marketing', *Journal of Marketing*, (July): 54–60.

Fromm, E. (1976/2007) *To Have or to Be?* New York: Continuum.

Fromm, E. (1942/2001) *The Fear of Freedom*. London: Routledge.

Houston, F.S. (1986) 'The marketing concept: What it is and what it is not', *Journal of Marketing*, 50 (2): 81–7.

Hult, G., Tomas, M., Ketchen, D.J. Jr. and Slater, S.F. (2005) 'Market orientation and performance: An integration of disparate approaches', *Strategic Management Journal*, 26 (12): 1173–81.

Jaworski, B. and Kohli, A. (1993) 'Market orientation: Antecedents and consequences', *Journal of Marketing*, 57 (3): 53–60.

Keith, R.J. (1960) 'The marketing revolution', *Journal of Marketing*, 24 (3): 35–8.

Kelley, D. (2007) 'I bet you look good on the salesfloor', *Journal of Strategic Marketing*, 15 (February): 53–63.

Kohli, A. and Jaworski, B. (1990) 'Market orientation: The construct, research propositions, and managerial application', *Journal of Marketing*, 54 (2): 1–18.

Kotler, P. (1967) *Marketing Management: Analysis, Planning, and Control*. Englewood Cliffs: Prentice-Hall.

Kotler, P. (1973) 'The major tasks of marketing management', *Journal of Marketing*, 37 (October): 42–9.

Kotler, P. (1976) *Marketing Management: Analysis, Planning, and Control*, 3rd edn. Englewood Cliffs: Prentice-Hall.

Kotler, P. and Levy, S.J. (1971) 'Demarketing, yes, demarketing', *Harvard Business Review*, (November/December): 74–80.

Kotler, P., Wong, V., Saunders, J. and Armstrong, G. (2005) *Principles of Marketing*, 4th European edn. Harlow: Pearson.

Luck, D.J. (1969) 'Broadening the concept of marketing too far', *Journal of Marketing*, 32: 53–63.

McCarthy, E.J. (1960) *Basic Marketing: A Managerial Approach*. Homewood: Richard D. Irwin.

McKay, E.S. (1954) 'How to plan and set up your marketing program', in (no author) *Blueprint for an Effective Marketing Program*, Marketing Series Number 91. New York: American Management Association.

McGovern, G.J., Court, D., Quelch, J.A., Crawford, B. (2004) 'Bringing customers into the boardroom', *Harvard Business Review*, 82 (11): 70–80.

Marion, G. (2006) 'Research note: Marketing ideology and criticism: Legitimacy and legitimization', *Marketing Theory*, 6 (4): 245–62.

Nath, P. and Mahajan, V. (2008) 'Chief marketing officers: A study of their presence in firms' top management teams', *Journal of Marketing*, 72 (January): 65–81.

Quelch, J. (2009) 'In praise of marketing', *Harvard Business School: Working Knowledge Series*, February 5, 2009, http://hbswk.hbs.edu/item/6015.html

Schor, J.B. (2007) 'In defence of consumer critique: revisiting the consumption debates of the twentieth century', *The Annals of the American Academy of Political and Social Science*, 611: 16–30.

Schudson, M. (2007) 'Citizens, consumers, and the good society', *The Annals of the American Academy of Political and Social Science*, 611 (1): 236–49.

Shultz, D. (2003) 'Marketing gets no respect in the boardroom', *Marketing News*, 37(24): 9.

Strong, J.T. and Hawes, J.M. (1990) 'Harry R. Tosdal', *Journal of Personal Selling and Sales Management*, 10 (Spring): 73–6.

Sheth, J.N. and Sisodia, R.S. (2005) 'Does marketing need reform', *Journal of Marketing*, 69 (October): 1–25.

Stewart, P.W. and Dewhurst, J.F. (with the assistance of Louise Field) (1939) *Does Distribution Cost Too Much?* New York: The Twentieth Century Fund.

Svensson, G. and Wood, G. (2007) 'Are university students really customers? When illusion may lead to delusion for all!', *International Journal of Educational Management*, 21 (1): 17–28.

Thomas, M. (1967) 'Book review: Marketing management: Analysis, planning and control', *Journal of Business*, 40 (3): 345–7.

Tosdal, H. R. (1925) *Principles of Personal Selling*. Chicago: A.W. Shaw.

Tosdal, H.R. (1933) 'Some recent changes in the marketing of consumer goods', *Harvard Business Review*, 11 (2): 156–64.

Verhoef, P.C. and Leeflang, P.S.H. (2009) 'Understanding the marketing department's influence within the firm', *Journal of Marketing*, 73 (2): 14–37.

White, P. (1927) *Scientific Marketing Management: Its Principles and Methods*. New York: Harper.

The Management of Marketing

5

5.1 Introduction

The field of marketing is not principally defined by the study of markets, but by the actions and behaviour of people and organisations in markets. The goal of most marketing students is to not simply study and understand marketing but to one day practise marketing as a marketing professional. Marketing is something that is performed by, to and for these people and organisations. Marketers have long sought to have their activities recognised as a profession and have established institutes, associations and other bodies to try and promote their status as professionals. It is important for us to consider how some of the debates and discussions about marketing which have been expanded upon in earlier chapters might translate and impact on the kinds of activities and practices that one might reasonably expect to be undertaken when practising marketing.

These questions are not as straightforward as they may first appear. What marketers do in terms of actual practices and actions is important, but it is also necessary to consider how marketers see themselves and how others see them. There is an interesting dynamic between what marketers actually do, what they think they should be doing, and how they account for the activities and processes for which they are responsible. In short, the chapter asks two questions: What do marketers do? and What is the role of discourse in the way marketers account for what they do?

Given the amount of theoretical writing on marketing that exists (see Chapters 3 and 4), and the ever-growing historical perspective on the subject (see Chapters 1 and 2), these may come as surprising questions. After all, with all the texts on marketing at their disposal, you'd think people would know for sure! But a lot of people are uncertain about how marketing is managed. A big part of the problem is that, as Carson and Brown (1994) note, marketing 'seems to be held together by the sometimes divergent, often overlapping, belief systems of those that consider themselves marketers. Marketing ... is not what marketers do; marketing is what marketers perceive it to be' (cited in Baker, 2000: 306).

If this is the case, perhaps it is appropriate to turn to marketing managers themselves to shed some light on marketing practice. This involves leaving 'space for many voices' since there is 'much to be learned from letting ... managers speak for themselves' (Brownlie et al., 1999: 10). An important part of the approach in this chapter is therefore to try to give 'voice' to the individuals trying to cope with the management of marketing. Exploring the world of the marketing manager entails looking at several elements of marketing work: the practices of marketers in their attempts to 'manage' the market; the management of those marketers by the organisations they represent and are hired by; and the control of the knowledge that supposedly defines the marketing profession and thus the identities of individual marketers. As you will see, a key part of this work is to do with constructing (and crossing) social boundaries – boundaries around markets, professions and people.

To help you understand what is meant by 'practice' in relation to the arguments contained in this chapter, it is worth turning to the anthropologist, Marianne Lien, who has studied marketing managers closely. Lien (1997: 11) sees marketing as both a 'practice' and a 'discipline'. The former she defines as 'whatever people in the marketing department do that they refer to as marketing'. The latter is 'a vocation, a profession, and an institutional discipline', which can be seen as an 'expert system' (Giddens, 1991). The idea of expert systems will be pursued in Section 5.4. For now, you are encouraged to explore claims of 'doing' marketing in more detail.

5.2 What *Does* a Marketer Do?

Even the business men and women who are supposedly working in the 'front line' far from the 'ivory towers' of marketing academia do not always agree on this issue, or on whom should be allowed to call themselves a marketer. You will encounter many opinions on marketing practice as the chapter progresses, but to set the scene, consider this internet thread from the interactive 'Work and Money' part of the website *Ask MetaFilter* (2008). The original question from Subscriber S1 was headlined 'What does a marketing director do?' The debate that followed, seemingly between a number of managers (although only S4 makes their position as a marketer clear), is shown in the box below.

What Does a Marketing Director Do?

Here is the opening question:

> My firm is trying to decide whether to hire a marketing/sales director. I have been tasked with gathering information. So, what are the key responsibilities and duties of a marketing/sales director? My firm provides environmental consulting services. Currently, our technical project managers develop clients, and most people within the firm are wary of hiring non-technical people in marketing because they are afraid of the stereotypical phony used-car salesman types. (S1, 8 January 2008)

Here are three of the responses:

> It sounds like your company needs a marketing director, not a marketing/sales director. The marketing director would create and manage a marketing program that usually would consist of advertising in multiple forms, along with other ways of increasing the presence of your company... (S2)

> The most important thing a marketing director is supposed to do is keep in touch with what your customers want, and help you figure out if you're really providing that ... Understanding the market is job number one. Sales is just selling

whatever you've got. Often sales-folks are too focused on making numbers to be truly thoughtful about what the company does. (S3)

Your company sounds a lot like mine ... I am a marketing director, and I am anything but a phony used-car salesman type ... I'm responsible for setting marketing strategy for the company, and, because it's a relatively small firm, usually implementing it as well. That means I influence the company's branding/positioning, determine our marketing goals, identify where/how/what we will be advertising, create and send out marketing emails, sales materials, etc ... My role also includes things like market and client research. In a small firm like yours, if you are going to hire a marketing director, s/he needs to be knowledgeable and comfortable with actually doing the marketing.(S4)

It is interesting to look at the different perceptions each subscriber has of the role of the marketer. For instance, despite their opening question, S1's firm appears to have managed quite well so far without employing anyone called a 'marketing director'. They do not see any differences between the roles of marketing and selling, and are actually mistrustful of marketing people. S2 believes it is definitely a marketer that S1 needs, and feels that managing a programme of advertising is a key function for this person. S3 stresses the primary need for the marketers to understand the market, and dismisses the sales function as insufficiently 'thoughtful'. This theme is taken up by S4 who stresses the knowledge that a marketer needs, along with an extensive list of quite high level strategies (e.g. branding) and more tactical activities (e.g. emails) that they should have responsibility for and, indeed, actually do. Moreover, he is at pains to reassure S1 that he is not a 'phony'.

As these voices show, the practice and discipline of marketing are a little tricky to pin down. For some people, things like the 'marketing concept' allow them to talk of marketing as a unified entity with a widely agreed-upon remit in the organisation. While for others, the different activities that a marketer can be asked to carry out, combined with the varying levels of status afforded to marketers, mean that marketing is always going to be fragmented. As this chapter unfolds you will see that the ways in which marketers themselves describe their work contributes to this confusion.

The lack of clarity over what constitutes marketing practice stems in part from the fact that, in addition to facing accusations of exploiting consumers/customers (see Chapter 4), marketers have to defend their positions inside the firm. Indeed, it has been claimed that 'around 85% of marketers have to fight against internal politics before they start working on their actual job' (Young, 2006: 23). Thus, 'as contracted workers, marketers are required to present their ideas and results in an arena where their expertise is open to the whims and preferences of major company managers ... To put it more simply, marketing is now a market in itself' (Edwards, 2000: 58). In this rather strange market, marketers are involved in much of what might be called 'boundary work', even if many of these boundaries are imaginary. The role of marketers typically entails attempting to span boundaries, like those between the organisation and its environment, including the market, yet at the same time marketers are busy erecting boundaries around themselves in order to mark out their areas of expertise; for instance, by comparing the importance of their work to other functional departments like finance or sales, or by contrasting marketing management with marketing-related activities like advertising or market research.

The situation is further complicated since, as Alvesson and Willmott (1992: 7) note, those who occupy management positions are not 'just doing their job'. They cannot be adequately studied as 'robots' who simply serve the predetermined needs of some higher institution (e.g. capitalism or a professional association) or as individuals who merely act selfishly in accordance with their own personal interests. Instead, 'caught between contradictory demands and pressures ... they run the risk of dismissal, they are 'victims' as well as perpetrators of discourses and practices that unnecessarily constrain their ways of thinking and acting'. Once again, therefore, you can see the importance of discourse in the management of marketing (see also Chapter 3). A discursive perspective on marketing work will be returned to later in the chapter, but for now, let's consider the notion of practice more closely.

5.3 Why Study Marketing Practice?

This is an important area to explore because of the role of marketing practice in the social construction (or shaping) of markets. In this section it will be argued that marketing involves activities that both shape individual economic exchanges (for example, by manipulating the marketing mix), and also shape the rules and norms (like markets) for such exchanges. Kjellberg and Helgesson (2006: 842) suggest that the large number of theories encountered by marketers, such as those originating in marketing itself as well as in strategy, economics, etc. 'can be expected to influence practice and hence participate in shaping markets'.

But what is meant by the claim that marketing practice shapes markets? Lien (1997: 22) believes that the various theories in use (which can be seen as marketing discourses – see Chapter 3) by marketers have 'performative consequences', i.e. they make something happen. To understand these performances, Callon (1998) employs notions of 'framing' to unpack what he calls 'the construction' of the market. Framing demarcates those elements which are taken into account and those which are ignored in a person's worldview. Callon (1998: 17) argues: 'it is owing to this framing that the market can exist and that distinct agents and distinct goods can be brought into play', for instance in strategic decisions made by managers over which products to sell to which markets, and against whom to compete. Indeed, some scholars define the entire function of marketing as 'the redefinition of market structures and relations (above all competitive relations) through the substantive, cultural redefinition of goods' (Slater, 1997: 45).

Such redefinitions matter because they are thought to influence people's actions. Vickers (1995: 87) claims that market actions 'are based, not on discoverable and therefore objectively existing economic knowledge, but on ... what can be referred to as imaginative constructions'. Note, for example, how the executives of this multinational corporation (see box below) imagine the world. Think of the impact these views might have on, respectively, the firm's distributors, their customers and their employees as Coca-Cola's senior managers seek to make such marketing dreams into reality.

Coca-Cola

Hays (2005) describes how senior executives at Coca-Cola view the world. Consider the far-reaching market shaping potential of these grandiose exhortations. She claims that CEO Woodruff preaches of putting Coke 'within an arm's reach of desire' (2005: 6). His successor, Ivester, endorses concepts like 'a 360-degree landscape of Coke' (2005: 6), while the CEO of Coca-Cola's bottling arm, Schimberg, maintains 'I expect all our people to live in the marketplace. That's the culture of this company' (2005: 276).

In shaping these sorts of constructions, Lien (1997: 90) believes that marketers' 'discursive elaboration of an imagined "market" serves, simultaneously, as a key factor in the reproduction of the locality itself'. In other words, markets are not necessarily naturally occurring entities; instead they are effectively shaped by the very act of defining groups of people as customers. In marketing managers' struggle for some sort of market control, marketing practice communicates difference between one customer segment and another. Thus for managers the concept of the market performs two functions: it serves as a model 'of' the world as it is (e.g. viewing a market as comprising certain researchable and ultimately accessible customers), and as a model 'for' appropriate action (e.g. embarking on the segmentation, targeting and positioning process).

Marketers are not all-powerful in making their plans, of course. Kjellberg and Helgesson (2006) are sceptical towards narratives that portray business practice as fully coherent and integrated. They believe that narratives seem more truthful when they tell of different organisations or individuals maintaining differing views on a product's position in the market. Thus the realisation of any single coherent 'market' becomes almost impossible. They illustrate this argument by noting the combined marketing activities (e.g. market research, segmentation, distribution, advertising, point of display management, media consumption, coupon handling) of a firm like Procter & Gamble and its intermediaries and customers to create a multi-segment shampoo market. The market model thus generated is likely to vary according to the beholder: P&G may view 'their' customers rather differently to the way in which their market research agency assessed the market, which may differ in turn from the broader customer market targeted by the retailers (who of course stock rival shampoos), and be perceived quite differently again by consumers as they construct their identities partly through what they buy. Nevertheless, marketing seems to 'work' here since simultaneously performed different versions of the same market can happily co-exist.

Now it is time to consider marketing theory in the form of the body of knowledge that comprises the 'discipline' of marketing, beginning with the idea of expert systems and how they have spread around the world, thus influencing practice across international boundaries.

5.4 Expert Systems in Marketing

This section shows how the globalisation of some of the 'big' discourses identified in Chapter 3 can affect management practices. In modern society individuals often have to make choices about how to live their lives in areas that hitherto may have been taken for granted, such as how to conduct personal or trading relationships in an apparently global economy (Giddens, 1990). As resources to guide their thinking about these activities, people are dependent on 'expert systems' which comprise macro discourses (such as 'the sovereign customer') they can draw upon to socially construct themselves and others, while taking account of pre-existing local discourses. Expert systems are propagated by TV programmes, magazine articles, and management 'guru' books like the best-selling marketing textbooks by authors like Phillip Kotler discussed in Chapters 3 and 4. In this way, a discourse like 'marketing management' can become incorporated into the sense-making practices of individuals embedded in many different cultures.

It appears that marketing and other managers internationally are increasingly socialised as a (high status) group called 'managers', thanks to the popularity of expert systems such as US-centred MBA programmes (Westwood, 2001). Globalisation is typically evoked in management texts to promote to these would-be 'American' managers the opportunities of marketing products to other cultures. For instance, in their popular management book, tellingly entitled *Managing Cultural Differences*, Harris and Moran (1991: 24) state 'culture knowledge provides insights into people, so both managers and other professionals benefit ...'. This approach affirms the power of the Western observer's discursive classification systems (Westwood, 2001). These expert systems have the potential to exert considerable influence on how managers throughout the world make sense of themselves.

The market model can become a dominant discourse by 'the repeated verbal expression among the populace at large that a particular social pattern is in general practice within society' (Salzman, 1981: 237). Sets of established practices, both locally generated and originating from further afield, are drawn upon by practitioners as they 'do' marketing. For example, look how these Indian managers in the box below, all with some responsibility for marketing, talk about their work to a team of researchers (Ellis et al., 2009).

Voices – Indian Managers

First, note how these managers describe their companies' management approaches:

> One of the things about Indian companies is pretty much we are becoming international in the way we look at things. Professional management, respect of law, respect of the environment .... Like we are a family controlled business but once we reach a particular size then professionalism becomes quite common. (*Company Director & Advisor, Trade Enterprise Council*)

> We are the leader in the market and it is a challenging task for us to retain the leadership ... We want to continuously improve all business processes product range and services, take the initiative. Focus on the use of resources and global volumes in select products because then you can get the scale of production that we want. (*General Manager, Strategic Planning, Engineering/IT sector*)

And note how these marketers describe their role and personal background:

> My background is basically sales and marketing generally and I have most of my education in India, worked mostly with Cadbury's in India and in the US for a short while. Thereafter I was marketing director for Diageo. (*Head of Dairy Business, Food Manufacturer*)

> I did my MBA in Bombay and from university I worked for an advertising company in the US called J Walter Thompson which is one of the largest companies in the world, yes. So I worked there for about two years and then I got this idea to come back to India ... and two of my friends joined me who were doing their MBAs.
> (*Company Director, Ticketing Systems Supplier*)
>
> I did quite a few things for export somewhere around 1998 and somehow it has not got out of me so far... I have a strong capacity as an agent for, say, somebody who is just getting market information so [I] sell business information, market managing... There is no proper information about what I have been doing really.
> (*Export Manager, Timber Sector*)

In these accounts there seems to be an acceptance and internalisation of both Indian and Western values in Indian management practices (Fusilier and Durlabhji, 2001). This may be the result of managers having a childhood spent in an Indian cultural context and subsequent training in Western management techniques, as well as exposure to the regulatory changes in the country since India opened its markets more readily to the global economy in 1991. Moreover, while it is clear these marketers are proud of their background and draw easily upon marketing management vocabulary and Western corporate names to frame their roles and careers, you can also see some vagueness about what they actually do. This supports the observations made earlier in the chapter about the difficulties in defining the practice of marketing.

It is not just in recently 'Westernised' cultures that the spread of expert systems has occurred. Perhaps surprisingly, Wu (2008: 147) shows how advertising was 'a powerful part of public discourse' in 1920s China. In this period it is possible to determine an interweaving of local political discourses with more Western market-based ones. For instance, Glosser (2003) describes how an entrepreneur-owned magazine *Jiating xinqi* (Family Week) promoted the habit of drinking milk in the 1920s. The magazine encouraged small family size as a vehicle to rationalise urban Chinese consumption habits, such that 'the small family ideal itself became a "product" that entrepreneurs tried to sell' (Wu, 2008: 151). This is a striking instance of how the social composition of the market can potentially be shaped by marketing practice. Another example is found in the 1921 advertisement by the Nanyang Brothers Tobacco Company which used the discourse of 'the good citizen' to promote cigarettes. The advertisement's wording included lines such as, 'The citizens of the Republic of China should use national goods. When you buy Chinese cigarettes ... the colour and taste are better than those of imported ones' (2008: 157). Again, you can see how marketing practice here appears to have been influenced both by existing local discourses and by the broader management discourse of market positioning.

However, even given the apparent globalisation of expert systems, a belief in the need for organisations to employ marketers is not universal. Holden et al. (2008) encounter considerable ambivalence about the perceived value of Western marketing knowledge in Russia. They plot recent Soviet attitudes to marketing, noting that in the 1970s/80s, any interest in marketing was largely intellectual. After 1991, Russia faced an onslaught of Western products, marketing educators and consultants that 'swept in a language that reflected for the citizens of the former Soviet Union completely unknown modes of existence and economic life' (2008: 5). Yet, even after several years of transition to a market economy, marketing terminology is still a complex issue for translators: 'For a start, the very word marketing ... still appears to connote Russian perceptions of the Western way of doing business rather than a general principle of business which places the customer at the centre of business activity' (Holden et al., 2008: 6). They conclude that understanding marketing in this context requires the recognition that many Russians have a long-held distrust of the marketplace.

A marketing manager may therefore have his/her work cut out trying to persuade sceptical Russians of their status in society. Perhaps they need to tell some better stories about how marketing 'works'?

5.5 More Stories about Marketing Managers

Let's pause at this point and listen to more voices. After all, maybe you are still contemplating a career in marketing? A considerable proportion of the readers of this book are probably doing just that, especially if some recent statistics are to be believed. The BBC News website (2009) reports that, while investment banking had fallen in popularity amongst final year UK undergraduates from second to nineth place since the previous year in a list of potential careers, marketing was in third place, up from fourth. Some 12.6 per cent of all final year students said that they had made applications for marketing jobs. A career in marketing thus continues to hold its attractions. So, to add to the clamour that you have heard so far in this chapter, here are some more descriptions about what you might be letting yourself in for. They come from a number of different sources, all with a 'stake' in the management of marketing.

First, the education system: If you are thinking about pursuing a study-based route to your 'dream' job in marketing, you might still be pondering what course you should take. Websites like the independent Braintrack (2009) contain information about university and college courses worldwide. In its discussion of marketing careers, it advises that 'a company's success relies heavily on the effectiveness of its marketing ... Employers look for marketing managers with a bachelor's or master's degree ... in business administration, advertising or journalism with an emphasis on marketing'. You are thus being encouraged by such sites to pursue a formal education in the discipline of marketing as it will serve you well in your future career.

Second, organisations that employ marketers: Here is what the job description of a marketing vacancy says about your potential role. The Brand Republic Jobs (2009) website contains a 'Marketing Manager' position with 'a leading FMCG organisation whose portfolio includes a number of well-known household brands'. They are seeking someone who will report to the Commercial Director and who will 'prepare marketing strategies' for brand management. The ad states 'This is an exciting and challenging role where you will be involved with market insight to identify competitor markets, and propose new opportunities for consumer market research and product development. You will also manage corporate PR strategies and coordinate media briefing'. Sounds good, doesn't it? (For more such descriptions, turn to the learning activities at the end of this chapter.)

Third, a professional association: Let's see what the UK's leading professional body, and one responsible for world-wide training of marketers, the Chartered Institute of Marketing (CIM) has to say about its *raison d'être* in its mission statement: 'To be the pre-eminent body on marketing practice, standards and associated knowledge on an international basis and for this to be acknowledged by governments, marketers, business, education and others' (CIM, 2006). This statement reveals much about the desired status of the marketing profession, but it is still somehow incomplete. What about explaining how this credibility is going to be achieved?

Fourth, the authors of marketing textbooks: You will no doubt have seen on bookstore shelves plenty of what Brown (1995) has termed 'Big Fat' books about marketing. In possibly the best known of these, Kotler (1988: 35) quotes a marketer to claim:

> the marketing manager is the most significant functional contributor to the strategic planning process, with leadership roles in defining the business mission; analysis of the environmental, competitive, and business situations; developing objectives, goals and strategies; and defining product, market, distribution and quality plans, to implement the business strategies.

In other words, due to its boundary spanning function, connecting the firm to customers and markets, and engaging with a host of other internal and external stakeholders, marketing is effectively 'sold' in these books as an area of work that is core to organisational success. This sort of mainstream marketing writing employs rhetoric that often positions marketing as a locus of order and control in a 'complex and changing world'. Thus marketing is evoked as some sort of driving force of organisational success against the inconsistencies of a dynamic, often hostile, environment (Hackley, 2003).

Fifth, we find some scholars who beg to differ from the common claims made for marketing's authority: They believe that the way in which marketing managers have been represented in most marketing textbooks can be described as 'one dimensional' (Brownlie and Saren, 1997). This is because such representations seem to be naive about the realities of trying to manage external and internal relations in the host of different contexts that marketers find themselves embedded. The recommendations of textbooks can lose sight of the day-to-day pressures on marketing managers of intrusive emails, report deadlines, impatient bosses, unreasonable customers, work fatigue, and even limited competence. Thus so called 'best-practice' in marketing, however articulate the theoretical claims that underpin it, may never be achieved. Ultimately, much of marketing management is 'conducted amongst all the pressures and privations of contemporary managerial practices, with limited resources and conflicting priorities, by hard-worked individuals' (Wilson, 1999: 104).

Finally, people working in contemporary marketing-related contexts still make self-deprecating comments: Here is what the PR practitioner Mark Borkowski, who has been described as a 'PR guru' by the BBC, told an interviewer (*The Word*, 2009: 58 emphasis in original): 'I love the craft of publicity. I'm not sure if I love the *profession* I'm in. Publicity and spin are widely despised, yes, but luckily paedophilia and bankers have shot up the hate charts. It goes: paedophiles, bankers, estate agents and then us, the publicists in fourth place'. Despite the 'craft' that goes with the job, it seems that Borkowski thinks the general public do not trust marketers very much.

As scholars, how can we make sense of these different stories of marketing management?

5.6 Legitimising the Marketing Profession

One of the most powerful stories told by marketers is of the status that they deserve when they assert themselves as 'professionals'. It is to this notion that the chapter now turns, as it explores how marketers have tried to build boundaries around their work as a 'professional' undertaking. We take a particular sociological perspective in analysing professions in which, instead of trying to confirm the 'body of knowledge' held by marketers, the fundamental issue becomes one of discovering the circumstances in which people in this occupation attempt to turn it into a profession and themselves into 'expert', professional people.

In order to unpack the status of marketers, this section draws upon the idea of 'the professional project' (Larson, 1977). This is an approach that acknowledges:

- professions are interest groups;
- such groups may consciously pursue economic interests but may well have other motives such as a pursuit of social status;
- professions' opportunities for income derive from their knowledge and qualifications;
- the actions of members of professional groups can be seen as a strategy of 'social closure'.

This involves erecting a boundary that effectively excludes non-experts from becoming marketers. A lot of this boundary work is down to impression management. Ellis (1999: 338) lists a number of practices that the UK legal, accountancy and marketing professions have adopted in their attempts to gain credibility by making 'the right impression'. These include 'cultivating historical roots, producing the producers (e.g. the CIM's training of marketers), passing examinations, ... gaining Royal Charters, appropriating bits of knowledge from other disciplines (e.g. psychology, economics), undertaking academic research, political lobbying'. All these practices can be seen as part of an overall strategy of social closure.

The marketing discipline has thus long attempted to build its credibility, setting itself apart from, but still central to, the functioning of the marketplace. More recently however, Firat and Dholakia (2006: 136) suggest that taking a postmodern orientation (see Chapter 2) to marketing necessitates managers and consumers becoming 'partner-players' in constructing needs and wants. In this partnership, marketing should not be distanced from the consumer: 'it is no longer a somewhat occult art accessible only to marketing professionals'. Thus, they maintain, 'organisations will have to become not providers but co-constructors – in 'business with' the post-consumers' (2006: 194). Thus marketing has moved beyond the remit of designated 'marketers' and there has been a shift from managed to collaborative marketing, as you can see in the way in which websites like e-bay or Amazon work.

Firat and Dholakia conclude that postmodern thinking views the notion of 'professionally managed marketing acts as illusory...' (2006: 150) and that 'we can expect a de-professionalisation of marketing; in the sense that everyone becomes a marketing professional, everyone is required or expected to become informed in marketing know-how' (2006: 152). This is similar to Gummesson's (1997) notion of everyone in the organisation being 'part-time marketers', but goes even further: a key difference in marketing de-professionalisation from the contemporary idea of marketing management is that practitioners would be responsible to the external stakeholders they term 'their communities', and not merely to the organisation that the practitioner represents.

Nevertheless, marketers have struggled for decades to gain legitimacy for their profession. So, while acknowledging the potential for de-professionalisation, it is perhaps more useful to study how the discourse of marketing continues to exert a significant influence over the practices of those workers designated as 'marketing managers'.

5.7 Talking About 'Doing' Marketing

Some marketing scholars have attempted to plot the practices of marketers, most notably in what have been termed the Contemporary Marketing Practice (CMP) studies (e.g. Coviello et al., 2002). Using a series of cross-national surveys, CMP work investigates how marketing in practice may differ from the academic literature, in particular as managers juggle transactional and relational approaches (see Chapter 6). This work has provided valuable insights into global marketing practices, for instance in comparing practitioners' views of the most appropriate marketing strategy for emerging economies like those of West Africa and South America with those used in more 'developed' nations (Dadzie et al., 2008). However, the questionnaire-based, measurement approach that characterises the CMP methodology means that it can only really scratch the surface of how marketers 'do' marketing. Some complementary approaches to making sense of marketing practice are needed.

This section explores how managers come to see themselves in terms of what they call 'marketing'. As Morgan asks, 'What difference does this make to their way of working? What difference does it make to their sense of identity?' (1992: 154). To understand, we need to pay attention to the language that marketers use.

Svensson (2004: 21) argues that 'marketing work should first and foremost be understood as language *use*, or more specifically as discourse' where 'discourse' is seen as language use as a social practice or form of action. Moreover, as Iedema (2003) notes, workers are not only having to 'do' their work but to 'talk about it' too. Workers are increasingly required to 'self-present' to various stakeholders, for instance as marketers attempt to justify their spending plans to CEOs (cf. Edwards, 2000). Self presenting is what you might do in order to convince your peers of your suitability to carry on leading a project, for instance. This sort of language use creates what Svensson (2004) terms the 'marketing scene', a form of social order in which 'reality' is organised, categorised and made sense of. It is important to understand that what takes place in managerial marketing events such as meetings cannot be separated from the rest of society. Instead, the use of various discourses by managers can be seen in part as 'a reflection (*and* a reproduction)' of a fragmented socio-cultural environment 'within, and in relation to the boundaries of, which marketing work operates' (Svensson, 2004: 195) (as noted in Chapter 3). Note how such boundaries, around marketing and the market, and between consultant and client, are constructed in the Box below.

Discourse at Work in a Meeting

Svensson et al. (2008) analyse how the discourse of 'marketing orientation' (a variant of the 'marketing concept' discourse discussed in Chapter 4) is drawn upon in a meeting between a Danish marketing management consultancy firm (B&B) and a potential new client (DigitalTV). The consultant Anders explained that B&B had conducted a study of consumer behaviour on the internet because 'the Internet companies had ... constructed their Internet solutions without asking whether this was really what the consumers really wanted.' Anders went on to summarise some of the study's findings. 'This is what you wished to know', he said. 'I will help you somewhat on the way there. The study is

(Cont'd)

very broad, deals with buying behaviour in general, and I would never make use of the conclusions from this study on your specific customer.' A DigitalTV manager asked, 'Did the study deal with what the consumers were lacking?' Anders hesitated: 'Hmm, you know, we as consumers are very complex ... You as a consumer behave differently. That is why it is important to companies to find out what precisely *your* customers want. You should not be interested in everybody.'

Svensson et al. (2008) interpret Anders' talk in this meeting as a representation of marketing orientated activities. This is indicated not only in the way the consumer study is talked about, and in Anders' promise to provide knowledge, but also in his frequent references to the complexity of consumer behaviour. Arguably, in order to transform a potential client into an actual one, some kind of professional competence must be displayed. Drawing upon the rhetorical resource of market orientation is one mode of accomplishing this. In doing so, the consultant displays a sort of marketing virtue; marketing should be guided by the principle of responding to consumers' demands, he says, but he is also keen to stress that this is far from simple.

The case above illustrates how marketing work often betrays a host of tensions. For example, the grand narrative of 'instrumental reason' appears to call for adherence to the managerial imperatives of marketing work (i.e. to control the market), whereas the discourse of 'neo-liberalism' calls for acceptance of the need to adapt the marketing mix to consumer needs (Svensson, 2004). The identity of the marketing practitioner is constructed by a range of such simultaneously occurring discourses. The former portrays the marketer mainly as some sort of 'tamer of the market wilderness', while the latter supports the view of the marketer as a 'mediator' between producer and consumer (cf. Callon, 1998). The evocation of 'the market' in these discourses can provide a sense of empowerment for the marketer, although the market model can equally be used to portray actors (both marketer and customer) as passive victims of market mechanisms.

A discursive view of practitioners' talk remains alert to the fact that, thanks to the status of the marketing management discourse, the 'conceptual tool-kit' of elements of strategic planning are easily available for readers of management texts (i.e. managers) in 'their re-presentation of marketing practice' (Brownlie, 1997: 275). Brownlie notes how participants are typically adept at using their conceptual vocabulary to provide interviewers with persuasive accounts (or 'micro-stories') of their activities as marketing managers. This vocabulary may well be drawn from mainstream marketing writing, especially given the ubiquity of Culliton's (1948) description of the marketing manager as a 'mixer of ingredients' in this writing (again, see Chapter 3).

The voices you have heard throughout this chapter have suggested that constructing or 'shaping' is an important process within the world of marketing management. This shaping is being both 'done to' and 'performed by' the following 'things': marketing practitioners, marketing practice, the marketing discipline and markets. In other words, you can see shaping as an adjective and a verb, such that these entities are both enacted and acting upon each other recursively in a process that is manifested through the discourses of marketing.

If we return to the idea of the marketing discipline and its relationship with practice, marketing textbooks can be argued to both create chaos and bring into being the 'controller' of that chaos: the manager (Hackley, 2003; Harding, 2003). The discourses of managers appear to reflect an awareness of this. Managers' talk often reveals their vulnerability as actors in a market-based society (which, of course, they have helped to create) as well as their heroic attempts to battle market forces. Seemingly resisting the de-professionalisation of marketing predicted by Firat and Dholakia (2006), managers position themselves as marketing experts and members of 'marketing departments', legitimately able to divide up the market and effectively control relationships. Yet at the same time, market participants (i.e. marketers) are constructed as individuals under attack from calculating competitors and struggling to master the complexity of relations with the sovereign customer. The (mis)fortunes of the market offer managers a means of coming to terms with changing everyday experience, as well as providing an explanatory device for their supposed failures and successes, no matter how flawed the 'big' market discourse might be. Marketing managers are thus caught in a 'swirl of reality complexes' (Vickers, 1995), the ebbs and flows of which they help to generate. Well, we did warn you that marketing was difficult to pin down ...

5.8 Conclusion

So what can you conclude about the management of marketing? This chapter illustrates that it is far less simple to define marketing practice than many of marketing's stakeholders would have us believe. The role of what is generally accepted as the 'marketing manager' may have to be re-defined or, better still, closed definitions of marketing management resisted. Such resistance would acknowledge the irresolution between the boundaries and interrelationships that, perforce, exist between marketing viewed as, *inter alia,* both:

- a practice and a discipline
- a global and a local discourse
- a profession and a de-professionalised occupation
- shaping and being shaped, and
- powerful and vulnerable.

It is these tensions that seem to better capture the ambiguities of the management of marketing than the reductionist definitions offered in so many contemporary marketing textbooks.

5.9 Learning Activities

In leafing through most marketing textbooks you experience an overwhelming sense that the role of the Marketing Manager is fairly well defined. In this chapter the stability of the role unravels and the idea of the marketing profession is thrown open to question. Working through the plurality of perspectives on the role of the marketer, the learning activities encourage you to look at how marketing presents itself and how marketers speak of their profession. Before you begin the learning activities remind yourself of the learning aims for the chapter so that your time and efforts are focused.

Learning Activity One: Recruit a Marketer

For two more examples of how the marketing industry tends to view what marketers do, take a look at some recent recruitment advertisements. As you read and compare them,

a Try to search for any patterns of consistency over the presence of key terms describing the vacant roles, and the skills needed to occupy them.
b At another level of analysis, think what is missing from these descriptions.
c How is the world of 'marketing management' represented in these portrayals? Does it differ between the different contexts and hierarchies shown in the ads?

In a B2C context, we find this on the Brand Republic Jobs (2009) website:

> **Product Marketing Executive** [for] a company with over 60 years of heritage in developing and marketing consumer durable day to day products … Working within a small team, you will assist a senior Product/Retail marketing manager to handle all product and trade marketing related activities to the UK grocery convenience and wholesale trade. You will assist with managing new product introductions, NPD, packaging and branding, through to all trade and consumer based activity in store, including advertising. You will also work in a market in-sights team as well as having an input into sales and field marketing strategy … You will ideally be degree qualified in a business or marketing area.

Compare this with the following B2B job in *Marketing Week* (2007):

> **VP Marketing, Software Solutions** [for] a global leader in software and processing solutions for financial services and the public sector. [The VP Marketing is to be responsible for providing] market understanding by e.g. industry analyst reports, competitor analysis, industry association news, positioning primary brands in the relevant market and creating sales tools, … [overseeing] client communication, through interactive marketing, newsletter, user groups, conferences and meeting clients, … [developing] business partnerships with consultants, hardware providers, industry bodies and other software vendors … [and being] capable of working collaboratively with other areas of the business … [Applicants need to have] the ability to craft messages for a range of contact types including technical audiences.

Learning Activity Two: Marketing Speak

You have encountered the idea of managers helping to 'construct' markets through their words and actions. This can occur, for instance, when organisations announce the launch of new products or the targeting of new market segments. To try and make a little more sense of such pronouncements, you are encouraged to analyse the legiti-misation and market shaping practices contained in the write-ups found in the trade press or typical company press releases regarding new marking initiatives.

a In some announcements of your choice, see if you can plot how the language used by marketing managers can effectively structure the markets which they claim to serve.
b How are various social actors such as 'the customer' or 'the competition', or indeed 'the firm' itself, characterised in these texts?
c Where is the locus of control in these portrayals of the marketplace?

5.10 Further Reading

Alvesson, M. (1998) 'Gender relations and identity at work: A case study of masculinities and femininities in an advertising agency', *Human Relations*, 51 (8): 969–1005.

This paper explores gender relations and gender identity, based upon an ethnography of a Swedish advertising agency. The discussion problematises ideas of masculinity and femininity within management and argues for a rethinking of their roles in non-bureaucratic organisations.

Ellis, N. (2008) '"What the hell is that?": Representations of professional services markets in *The Simpsons*', *Organisation,* 15 (5): 705–23.

This article uses a cartoon to contextualise tensions faced by managers embedded in contemporary markets. It demonstrates how, on one hand, *The Simpsons* TV show reflects critical thinking about professions, yet on the other, offers some more ambivalent, even sympathetic notions of professional identity.

Ellis, N. and Ybema, S. (2010) 'Marketing identities: Shifting circles of identification in inter-organizational relationships', *Organisation Studies*, 31 (3): 279–305.

This study shows marketing managers to be 'boundary bricoleurs' who discursively mark different self/other boundaries that constantly shift as they position themselves, and their colleagues, competitors, customers and suppliers, as 'inside' or 'outside' the organisation, the market, the relationship or their field of expertise.

Svensson, P. (2007) 'Producing marketing: Towards a socio-phenomenology of marketing work', *Marketing Theory*, 7 (3): 271–90.

In this article, a meeting between an ad agency and a client is interpreted by drawing upon a discursive understanding of the productive nature of language. The author argues that marketing work (practice) is contingent upon as well as generative of the social and discursive accomplishment of a notion of 'marketing work'.

Walker, I., Tsarenko, Y., Wagstaff, P., Powell, I., Steel, M. and Brace-Govern, Y. (2009) 'The development of competent marketing professionals', *Journal of Marketing Education*, 31 (3): 253–63.

Here, the authors examine both graduate and employer perspectives on the essential skills and knowledge needed by marketing professionals. They believe their findings have implications for the development of curricula to produce 'employable' graduates and to assist universities in retaining a 'competitive advantage'.

5.11 References

Alvesson, M. and Willmott, H. (eds) (1992) *Critical Management Studies*. London: Sage.
Ask MetaFilter (2008) 'What does a marketing director do?', available online at http://ask.metafilter.com/80497, accessed April 2009.
Baker, M.J. (ed.) (2000) *Marketing Theory: A Student Text*. London: Thomson Learning.
BBC News (2009) 'Students fear harsh job market', available online at http://news.bbc.co.uk/l/hi/education, accessed May 2009.
Braintrack (2009) 'Marketing manager job description', available online at http://braintrack.com/businessdegrees, accessed April 2009.
Brand Republic Jobs (2009) 'Marketing manager', available online at http://jobs.brandrepublic.con/job/351695/marketing manager, accessed April 2009.

Brown, S. (1995) *Postmodern Marketing*. London: International Thompson Business Press.

Brownlie, D. (1997) 'Beyond Ethnography – towards writerly accounts of organizing in marketing', *European Journal of Marketing*, 31 (3/4): 264–84.

Brownlie, D. and Saren, M. (1997) 'Beyond the one-dimensional marketing manager: The discourse of theory, practice and relevance', *International Journal of Research in Marketing*, 14: 147–61.

Brownlie, D., Saren, M., Wensley, R. and Whittington, R. (eds) (1999) *Rethinking Marketing: Towards Critical Marketing Accountings*. London: Sage Publications.

Callon, M. (ed.) (1998) *The Laws of the Markets*. Oxford: Blackwell Publishers/The Sociological Review.

Carson, D. and Brown, S. (1994) 'Editorial', *Journal of Marketing Management*, 10(9): 549–52.

Chartered Institute of Marketing (2006) 'About us: The CIM's Mission Statement', available online at http://www.cim.co.uk/cim/abo/html/abo.cfm, accessed 9 November 2007.

Coviello, N.E., Brodie, R.J., Danaher, P.J. and Johnston, W.J. (2002) 'How firms relate to their markets: An empirical examination of contemporary marketing practices', *Journal of Marketing*, 66 (July) 33–46.

Culliton, J. (1948) *The Management of Marketing Costs*. Boston: Harvard University Press.

Dadzie, K.Q., Johnston, W.Y. and Pels, J. (2008) 'Business-to-business marketing practices in West Africa, Argentina and the United States', *Journal of Business & Industrial Marketing*, 23 (2): 115–23.

Edwards, T. (2000) *Contradictions of Consumption: Concepts, Practices and Politics in Consumer Society*. Buckingham: Open University Press.

Ellis, N. (1999) 'A disco(urse) inferno: The pitfalls of professionalism', *Marketing Intelligence & Planning*, 17 (7): 333–43.

Ellis, N., Rod, M., Beal, T. and Lindsay, V. (2009) 'Doing business in Asia: Discursive constructions of managerial practices in relationships between Indian and New Zealand organizations', 4th IMP Asia Conference, Kuala Lumpur, 6–10 December.

Firat, A.F. and Dholakia, N. (2006) 'Theoretical and philosophical implications of postmodern debates: Some challenges to modern marketing', *Marketing Theory*, 6 (2): 123–62.

Fusilier, M. and Durlabhji, S. (2001) 'Cultural values of Indian managers: An exploration through unstructured interviews', *International Journal of Value-Based Management*, 14: 223–36.

Giddens, A. (1990) *The Consequences of Modernity*. Cambridge: Polity Press.

Giddens, A. (1991) *Modernity and Self-Identity*. Cambridge: Polity Press.

Glosser, S.L. (2003) *Chinese Vision of Family and State, 1915–1953*. Berkeley: University of California Press.

Gummesson, E. (1997) 'Relationship marketing as a paradigm shift: Some conclusions from the 30R approach', *Management Decision*, 35: 267–73.

Hackley, C. (2003) '"We are all customers now…" – Rhetorical strategy and ideological control in marketing management texts', *Journal of Management Studies*, 40 (5): 1325–52.

Harding, N. (2003) *The Social Construction of Management: Texts and Identities*. London: Routledge.

Harris, P.R. and Moran, R.T. (1991) *Managing Cultural Differences*, 3rd edn. Houston: Gulf.

Hays, C.L. (2005) *Pop: Truth and Power at the Coca-Cola Company*. London: Arrow Books.

Holden, N., Kuznetsov, A. and Whitelock, J. (2008) 'Russia's struggle with the language of marketing in the communist and post-communist eras', *Business History*, 50 (4): 474–88.

Iedema, R. (2003) *Discourses of Post-Bureaucratic Organization*. Amsterdam: John Benjamins.

Kjellberg, H. and Helgesson, C.-F. (2006) 'Multiple versions of markets: Multiplicity and performativity in market practice', *Industrial Marketing Management*, 35: 839–55.

Kotler, P. (1988) *Marketing Management: Analysis, Planning, Implementation & Control*, 6th edn. Englewood Cliffs, NJ: Prentice Hall.

Larson, M.S. (1977) *The Rise of Professionalism: A Sociological Analysis*. London: University of California Press.

Lien, M. E. (1997) *Marketing and Modernity*. Oxford: Berg.

Marketing Week (2007) 'Job search', August, online at http://www.marketingweek.co.uk, accessed August 2007.

Morgan, G. (1992) 'Marketing discourse and practice: Towards a critical analysis', in M. Alvesson and H. Willmott. (eds), *Critical Management Studies,* pp.136–58. London: Sage.

Salzman, P.C. (1981) 'Culture as enhabilmentis', in L. Holy and M. Stuchlik (eds), *The Structure of Folk Models*, pp. 175–95. London: Academic Press.

Slater, D. (1997) *Consumer Culture & Modernity*. Cambridge: Polity Press.

Svensson, P. (2004) *Setting the Marketing Scene: Reality Production in Everyday Marketing Work*. Lund: Lund Business Press.

Svensson, P., Ellis, N. and Saren, M. (2008) 'Taking a discursive approach to market orientation', 8th International Conference on Organisational Discourse, Queen Mary, University of London, 23–5 July.

The Word (2009) 'Every crowd has a silver lining', May: 58.

Vickers, D. (1995) *The Tyranny of the Market*. Ann Arbor: University of Michigan Press.

Westwood, R. (2001) 'Appropriating the Other in the discourses of comparative management' in R. Westwood and S. Linstead (eds), *The Language of Organisation*, pp. 310–28. London: Sage.

Wilson, D. (1999) *Organisational Marketing*. London: International Thompson Business Press.

Wu, H. (2008) 'The construction of a consumer population in advertising in 1920s China', *Discourse & Society*, 20 (1): 147–71.

Young, L. (2006) 'Look and learn', *The Marketer*, (November): 22–3.

Taking a Different Look at Business-to-Business Marketing

6

6.1 Introduction

Popular debates about marketing have tended to prioritise consumer markets. One of the reasons for this is that we are all familiar with the experience of being a consumer. The marketing literature has tended to reflect this popular experience by focusing on the interactions between firms and end consumers. While understanding consumers is of course important to marketers it is also necessary to recognise that most marketing activities take place between (and within) organisations. Most businesses sell their products and services to other businesses, not to end consumers, and the characteristics of 'business to business' (B2B) interactions are not the same as those in 'business to consumer' (B2C) interactions.

For most of its history B2B marketing has been the more under-represented and less visible side of the marketing discipline. It is interesting to note, however, that many recent innovations and new ideas in marketing have emerged from B2B settings which have then been translated into B2C contexts. One of the most important recent developments in marketing theory has been the trend to move away from examining single transactions and purchases and to instead consider the on-going relationships that exist between sellers and buyers. Many if not most transactions that we undertake either as consumers or businesses are only a single event in an on-going series of interconnected interactions. In some cases these interactions and relationships may last for many years. This raises a number of important issues and themes: how do firms build relationships with other firms, and how do these relationships play out over the medium to long term? It also requires us to consider the power differences between businesses of different sizes, influence and status, and the broader consequences that this may have on the operation and function of marketing.

This focus on long-term B2B relationships is discussed in this chapter in terms of what are called 'inter-organisational relationships' (IORs). It is important to understand how IORs work because individual companies such as General Motors spend billions of dollars annually on goods and services. Indeed, it is estimated that in emerging areas like e-commerce, B2B activity is 10–15 times greater than B2C (LaPlaca and Katrichis, 2009).

Although much B2B marketing and purchasing is hidden 'behind the scenes' for the average consumer transaction, it is fair to say that business markets are generally larger than consumer markets; organisations trade in more products and services than consumers; and the B2B transactions that occur between organisations have a greater impact on the lives of people than B2C transactions. For instance, the majority of the world's manufacturing labour force is now situated in export-processing zones located in some of the most heavily populated regions of the globe. This means that millions of people work for organisations in Mexico and Central America, as well as the Philippines, Indonesia and China, through to India, Pakistan and Morocco, organisations which are dependent on the success of their B2B marketing efforts to other manufacturers and retailers worldwide.

As well as providing an outline of some key elements of B2B marketing, we ask: how have researchers typically studied IORs; what have these approaches meant for how the topic is discussed in the marketing literature; and can we suggest alternative approaches? In answering these questions, we argue for more attention to the discourses used by people in accounting for and describing IORs.

The structure of the chapter is as follows. We outline the key concepts of the Supply Chain and Relationship Marketing (RM) and explain how the two are related. We then explore two major issues which permeate all IORs, i.e. power and fairness. Next we introduce the industrial network approach, explaining how this adds to an RM-based understanding of IORs. We then critique certain aspects of these theories, highlighting assumptions that restrict our understanding of IORs. We conclude by suggesting some future directions for research by drawing on studies of organisational collaboration and the more discursively orientated marketing literature.

6.2 The Supply Chain and its Complexities

The significance of B2B marketing can be shown by considering that for every consumer (or 'end-user') market there are typically several 'upstream' organisations which must exchange products and services before anything is ultimately consumed. The trade between supplying and buying organisations makes up what is commonly called 'the supply chain' (see Figure 6.1).

This metaphorical concept connects the marketplace, distribution network, manufacturing process and suppliers of components and raw materials. It represents the physical flow of goods between linked firms 'downstream' to the customer. Instead of just focusing on the consumer, you should recognise the role in the chain of customer organisations, or at least the managers who represent them. Ultimately, all organisations buy and sell goods and/or services in order to create their own offerings. Firms then sell these products to other businesses which use them to create other products (as in the case of car manufacturers) or to resell to corporate buyers or consumers as finished goods (as in the case of car dealerships). B2B marketing is about understanding and managing the complex set of buying and selling IORs between these organisations. At their most basic, IORs can be seen as the links in the chain.

But supply chains are not quite as straightforward as they may seem. In order to facilitate the core supplier–customer relationship, other organisations often have to be involved, such as providers of finance, advertising agencies and logistics companies. Moreover, it is rare for a firm to function simply as a member of a linear supply chain like the one illustrated in Figure 6.1. After all, how many companies just rely on a single supplier for their parts or materials, and how many companies just sell to one customer?

Relationships are much more likely to occur between more than two firms at any one point in the chain, especially upstream with several suppliers for the manufacture of a complex product, or downstream with a range of distributors serving mass markets. In this way, what we term 'industrial networks' are formed by patterns of IORs between collaborating and sometimes competing firms. Our understanding of IORs

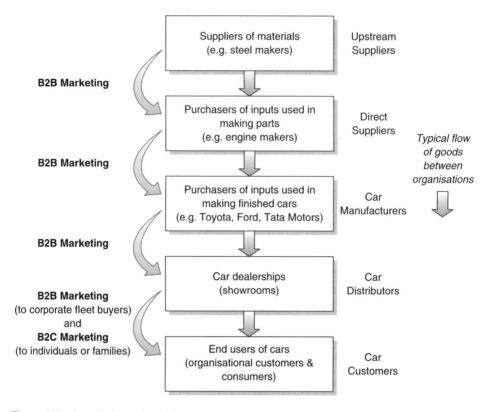

Figure 6.1   A typical supply chain

must therefore extend from links in single, linear chains to interlocking chains in the form of networks. The metaphor of a 'net' seeks to capture the many links that form up, down and 'across' an industrial sector as different organisations strive together to reach the end user.

It is common to find something called 'relationship marketing' (RM) being proclaimed as the managerial solution to handling these links or IORs (e.g. Kotler, 1992). RM embodies the following elements:

- it involves a shift in perspective from purely economic transactions to the 'fuzzier' boundaries of socio-economic exchange (i.e. recognising that relationships involve people);
- it understands the economics of customer retention, as opposed to just attracting customers;
- it recognises the need for relationships to be 'win–win' situations;
- and, in its network form, it extends the principles of relationship management to a range of other parties or stakeholders (Christopher et al., 2002).

While you will often find a chapter on RM in introductory books, here we aim to make you think about relational issues differently by questioning the theoretical approaches to relationships, chains and networks prevalent in conventional strategic marketing texts. In order to set you thinking a little more about why IORs are so important (in particular to stakeholders further 'up' the chain, such as producers of raw materials like textiles or food) the next section presents a discussion of problems with the links in FMCG supply chains and the growth of so-called 'fair trade' initiatives.

6.3 Weak Links in the Chain?

To extend our discussion of supply chains, and to set the scene for our discussion of inter-firm relations, this section looks at two major issues that permeate all IORs: those of power and equity (or fairness). Despite the large number of scholars heralding RM as some sort of panacea for marketing's ills, the fact is that many IORs do not 'work' in accordance with RM's idealistic worldview. Basically, the links in the chain are not as strong as it is thought they should be. This is especially noticeable in the global food supply chain, a fascinating context in which to examine the changing relationships between producers (farmers), FMCG manufacturers and retail intermediaries. Historically, manufacturers attempted to attract consumers 'over the heads' of the retailer, whereas now retail chains have the most power (Egan, 2001), power which they exert on all upstream members. The legacy of these changes has been one of often adversarial, and arguably unethical, relationships within the retail supply chain (see Box below).

Is Wal-Mart too Powerful?

Some retailers are very powerful actors in the supply chain. The classic example is Wal-Mart (WM). Bianco and Zellner (2003) report that it is the largest company in the world, with $245billion in sales in 2002. McKinsey estimates that an eighth of the US productivity gains in the 1990s came from WM's drive for efficiency. The firm's $12 billion in imports from China in 2002 accounted for a tenth of total US imports from that nation and, moreover, its tough line on costs has forced many factories to move overseas. WM's labour costs are 20 per cent less than those at unionised supermarkets, and perhaps not unconnectedly, in 2001 its sales staff made less than, on average, the federal poverty level. For every WM 'super-centre' that opens in the next five years, two other supermarkets will close. In its relentless drive for lower prices, WM's relationships with its suppliers are subject to great scrutiny, including 'which products get developed, what they're made of, how to price them … No wonder one consultant says the second-worst thing a manufacturer can do is sign a contract with Wal-Mart. The worst? Not sign one' (Bianco and Zellner, 2003: 49).

As we see in the Wal-Mart example above, a key measure of supply chain performance is that of 'efficiency'. However, as Parker (2002: 204) notes, this begs the question of 'efficient for whom?' The term appears to be conflated with shareholder value, yet 'if this involves transporting a product away from where it was grown or made, packing and labelling it somewhere else, sending it to distribution centres somewhere else again, and then sending it to be sold at a gigantic warehouse that has destroyed many small businesses', we might ponder the term more carefully. Crane (2000: 13) agrees, commenting that as modern marketing has outsourced and globalised, the distance between consumers and producers has widened: 'This has increasingly left customers (perhaps wilfully) unaware of the social and ecological cost of their purchases, be it rainforest destruction in Brazil, the erosion of traditional community lifestyle in Papua New Guinea or the growth in child labour in the sweatshops of Manila'.

Some observers of the food sector have begun to question the growing power of the supermarkets and the potentially damaging consequences of this power imbalance for grocery manufacturers and food producers, as well as for consumers (Lawrence, 2004). There are claims, for instance, that supermarket produce buyers are 'laughing at' the codes of practice drawn up, supposedly in partnership, by retailers and farmers (Beddall, 2002) to help 'manage' supply chain relations. Suppliers allege that pressured buyers from the multiple retailers have increased the unreasonable use of their powers: there are allegations of buyer bullying and thousands of pounds of unexpected demands. In fact, there is a perception that, in some retailers, public expressions of support for the code by senior executives are not being passed down to the buyers. Blythman (2004: 168) notes how 'the big supermarkets love to tell their customers about their "partnerships" with suppliers. The word "partnership" has a nice warm quality to it. It projects the right image to customers'. However, IORs do not always work that way, and she cites one supplier as complaining that supermarkets 'ruthlessly erode suppliers' margins with no consideration of the damage they are doing to the company or its employees'.

What Voice does the Farmer Have?

Blythman (2004: 137) describes how supermarkets can punish farmers who appear to be disloyal. She cites the experience of Devon beef farmer Richard Haddock, who tells her, 'I went to a supermarket producers' meeting where ... I stood up and talked about my negative experiences with the supermarket. Shortly afterwards I was told by a fieldsman working on behalf of the supermarket ... that he was sorry, but he could no longer come to look at my cattle. Because I had spoken out publicly, they couldn't take my meat anymore'.

Global food suppliers have even more reason to speak out, if they dare. Blythman (2004: 255) reports that in 2003, Banana Link (an organisation that campaigns to improve the conditions of banana producers) undertook some penetrating analysis. Specifically, they examined the distribution of profit along the supply chain of every £1 spent by UK consumers on loose Ecuadorian bananas. They found: 'plantation workers got 1.5 pence, plantation owners got 10 pence, the international trading company got 31 pence (which included a 5 pence EU tariff), the ripener/distributor got 17 pence, while the retailer took 40 pence'.

Maybe the concept of 'Fair Trade' provides a solution? The last few years have witnessed attempts to shift the prevailing marketing discourse from 'free' to 'fair' trade (McDonagh, 2002). Fair Trade aims to guarantee fair prices to producers plus some adherence to principles of 'ethical purchasing' (we will return to this theme in Chapter 8). It also aims for long-term business relationships that are transparent throughout the supply chain. Fair Trade initiatives seek to create positive social change by altering what occurs at each end of the supply chain while shortening the social distance between producers and consumers (Shreck, 2002). As O'Driscoll et al. (2000: 192) comment, a network perspective on marketing exchange suggests a focus on issues of 'trust, mutuality and fairness in relationships', a focus that would seem to be highly concordant with notions of Fair Trade.

The Growth of Fair Trade

The *New Internationalist* (2006: 19) reports that 'Fair Trade (FT) business is booming', citing some statistics:

Internationally, all FT product lines expanded their markets in 2005, especially for FT coffee in the US (+71%), bananas in Austria (+46%) and sugar in France (+ 125%) … 40% of UK households bought FT products in 2005, and FT brands now account for 20% of the UK roast and ground coffee market… FT goods can be bought in 55,000 supermarkets across Europe…

The box above suggests Fair Trade is growing, but is it necessarily the answer to repairing links in the chain? There are some dissenting voices. For instance, Worth (2006: 4) claims that Fair Trade is increasingly driven not by the needs of poor producers, but the demands of large corporations. Apparently the Fair Trade labelling organisations were put under so much pressure to deliver new Fair Trade products such as cotton and roses, compromises were made. Worth alleges that these organisations began to certify large, privately owned plantations rather than small cooperatives, thereby 'allowing the shocking possibility that, further down the supply chain, a garment made from FT cotton could be put together in a sweatshop and still marketed as "Fair Trade" to oblivious consumers' (ibid.). Thus, from the perspective of the stakeholders who are further upstream and relatively powerless in the supply chain, such as individual farmers, IORs in the global network for FT goods have arguably offered little in the way of progress. These stakeholders, who make up a significant number of the world's population, have been largely forgotten in our management textbooks (Ghoshal and Westney, 1993).

So why does RM not appear to be working here? Buttle (1996: 195) notes that while the 'partnership' model of IORs is gaining acceptance, there is little evidence that profit is being equitably redistributed amongst supply chain 'partners'. We can thus observe two schools of RM thought: one for which RM truly represents a 'new paradigm', and another, later tendency which broadly values RM but views it as inadequate to cope with relationships in 'the real world'. For instance, Egan (2001: 291) concludes 'marketers must learn that, if we are to prevent the premature death of RM, we must separate the rhetoric from the reality'. This is an interesting idea and one to which we shall return later in this chapter. Before we do this, we will look at some of the 'rhetoric' that has characterised marketing scholars' writing on IORs. To work out why many strategic marketing texts seem to pay the relational issues raised in this section scant attention, we need to understand how marketing scholars have commonly depicted IORs, supply chains and networks. To begin this journey, we now turn to the idea of RM in more detail.

6.4 What is Relationship Marketing?

According to the American Marketing Association website (2006), relationship marketing (RM) is 'marketing with the conscious aim to develop and manage long-term and/or trusting relationships with customers, distributors, suppliers, or other parties in the marketing environment'. Within the RM concept, exchange partners are thought to consciously pursue the goal of IOR longevity for mutual benefit. This often represents a response to the commonplace notion that a sale from a new customer will cost more to secure than one from an existing, loyal buyer. A plethora of academics have proclaimed RM as a genuine 'paradigm shift' (e.g. Grönroos, 1994; Gummesson, 1996; Morgan and Hunt, 1994) in marketing theory. Moreover, as Blois (1998) has pointed out, with influential authors like Kotler (1992) stating that companies 'must' adopt long-term relationship-building goals, RM has entered into the 'rhetoric' of management. Indeed, 'closer' relations between organisations are claimed to be increasingly common, and there is a growing recognition that competitive advantages may reside in the boundaries of a firm via its relationships with 'outside' organisations (Jap, 2001). RM thus appears to have become an important element of contemporary strategic thinking.

Although a number of marketing writers were expounding the benefits of relationship management in the 1920s and 30s (see Tadajewski and Saren, 2009), broadly speaking it is only really from the 1980s that we started to see a greater focus amongst B2B (or 'industrial') marketing scholars on the conceptualisation of a 'relationship', rather than solely on organisational buying decisions. For instance, Wilson and Mummalaneni (1986: 44) commented that for some scholars, 'relationships constitute the very essence of industrial marketing'. Such was the impact of RM on the academy, within a few years Webster (1992: 10) was able to conclude that the focus of research in B2B marketing had shifted 'from products and firms as units to people, organisations, and the social processes that bind actors together in ongoing relationships'. Later, in an article central to the mainstream conceptual development of RM, Morgan and Hunt (1994) drew upon a variety of literatures to argue, 'the presence of relationship commitment and trust is central to successful RM, not power and its ability to 'condition others" (ibid:22). They claimed that power merely 'helps us to understand RM failures' (ibid.: 34).

Morgan and Hunt's claim typifies assertions in the literature that suggest that RM is somehow morally superior to earlier approaches to B2B relationship management, resulting in the language of stakeholder relationships becoming embedded within the RM discourse. In this way, as Fitchett and McDonagh (2000: 213) comment, RM 'seemingly offers a great deal to all'. Thus the RM concept is commonly viewed as 'a philosophy of doing business successfully' or some sort of organisational 'culture' that puts the buyer–seller IOR at the centre of the firm's 'strategic thinking' (Tse et al., 2004: 1159). But are these scholars reflecting adequately on the pros and cons of relationships (see box below)?

Are Close Relationships Always a Good Thing?

Potential disadvantages of building relationships (Håkansson and Snehota, 1998) include: loss of control (managers used to being 'in-charge' now have to work with their opposite numbers in partner firms); difficulty in predicting partner behaviour (especially within cross-cultural alliances); preclusion from other opportunities (such as trading with a new supplier offering cheaper goods); and potentially unexpected demands (perhaps where a partner has different expectations of your firm's ability to respond rapidly to an important order). Moreover, close relationships may not be required for all types of product (Ford, 1990). For example, while it is typically critical from whom a component part is purchased, the sourcing of office stationery is a lot less important.

Interestingly, the many claims made about the economic justifications for RM are beginning to be questioned. Recent research findings indicate that companies will have to re-evaluate the manner in which they manage customer loyalty initiatives and try to find better ways to measure the relationship between loyalty and profitability (Reinartz and Kumar, 2002). All of which confirms that a firm simply can't afford to maintain close relationships with everyone in a marketplace. Some customers (usually those that are highly demanding and expensive to serve) must be 'let go'.

We should also not forget that satisfaction does not necessarily lead to loyalty (Varey, 2002). So-called 'loyalty' may sometimes be due to no more than convenience or lethargy on the part of the customer, for example in most consumers' tendency not to change the location of their bank accounts. Similarly, dependency is not loyalty. A customer who is 'locked in' may just feel that there are too may costs associated with changing suppliers.

We can extend our discussion of RM to the idea of IORs as key connections in supply chains. Whilst the term 'chain' may be an insufficient metaphor given the complexity of such systems, this does not invalidate discussion of supply relationships nor reduce the importance of trying to identify an inter-organisational context for them (Lamming et al., 2004). Supply chain management (SCM) has now become an area of academic study in its own right. A relatively recent phenomenon is that of so-called 'supply chain partnering', which occurs when organisations at related points in the supply chain agree to work in a cooperative rather than an adversarial manner (Boddy et al., 2000). In effect, suppliers are being encouraged to practise RM in their dealings with their organisational customers. Such thinking is concordant with the notion of 'supply networks' consisting of a set of interconnected supply chains, and involving the 'management' of both upstream and downstream relations (Harland et al., 2004).

6.5 The Contribution of IMP Network Approaches

In this section we are heeding the call of Gummesson et al. (1997) for researchers to use more IMP concepts as an input to RM research. 'IMP' refers to the Industrial Marketing and Purchasing (IMP) Group of scholars whose work is motivated more by an interest in understanding and explaining IORs than by calculating the extent to which they are cost effective (Shaw, 2003). Researchers in this approach explore how actors attempt to manage relationships and try to create a strong position (not always successfully) in a network.

Key to IMP studies is the 'interaction approach' (Håkansson, 1982) where buyers and sellers are seen as active participants in any transactions. Relationships can be broken down into a series of episodes (incorporating elements of exchange) which, over time, can lead to the interaction becoming institutionalised (or routinised). An outcome of the relationship is the 'atmosphere' which will both affect and be affected by interactional practices. For Håkansson (1982: 16), 'the detailed interaction process is subject to the perceptions of both parties of the overall state of relations between them'. Atmosphere is thus a dynamic construct and it is unrealistic to see relationships as developing along a single continuum between 'good' and 'bad', or 'distant' and 'close': all IORs 'simultaneously exhibit conflict and co-operation, with guile and self-seeking' (Ford et al., 1996: 159). Such insights offer us a more holistic view of some of the food supply chain relationships outlined in Section 6.3 than a simple RM-based perspective.

It can be argued that no relationship exists in isolation but forms part of a connected and interdependent set of relationships. The study of these sets of IORs is termed the 'industrial network' approach (Axelsson and Easton, 1992). The embedded nature of individual relationships, and of networks of interconnected actors, is only treated to a limited extent in RM research. As a result, unlike the network view, RM has major problems in recognising that, for instance, a firm will be pursuing a RM strategy while at the same time other network actors are involved in similar relationship strategies (Mattsson, 1997).

A network worldview can help to reveal much, but it can make things fairly complicated, as shown below.

Networks in the Arms Trade

Mysteriously, Curtis (2006) reports that since 2002 the UK Government has approved 199 export licences for defence exports such as small arms and chemical filters to the British Virgin Islands, the Cayman Islands and the Channel Islands – all territories with no armies! As he puts it, rather disturbingly, in terms of the networks of firms and nations 'behind' these purchases, 'it is anyone's guess where this equipment is destined'. Less opaque, but still somewhat worrying, is the revelation that in the past three years, arms have been exported by British firms to 19 of the 20 countries identified by the Foreign Office as 'countries of concern' over human rights. Despite an EU embargo on arms sales to China, Britain has managed to export '£500m worth of military and dual-use equipment – nominally "non-lethal" items' (Curtis, 2006: 32). The networks that enable such transactions to take place are facilitated by the massive influence that large arms manufacturers have at Government level. This is reflected in what Curtis terms the 'revolving door' between corporations and the Ministry of Defence: 'At least 19 senior MoD officials have taken jobs with arms companies since 1997, while 38 out of 79 personnel secondees to the MoD between 1997 and 2003 came from arms companies' – a closely woven network indeed.

As the arms trade shows, underpinning most industrial network studies is the notion that each actor (typically an organisation, but potentially individuals too) in a network controls certain activities and resources directly, but due to inter-dependencies, actors may have an indirect control over their counterparts' activities and resources. Håkansson and Johanson (1993: 37) posit that the activity structures underpinning IORs are 'formed by the views of the involved actors as to how the activities should be delimited and how they are related to each other. The structures are, in other words, constructed by the actors'. This constructionist view of networks is also adopted by Håkansson and Snehota (2000: 85) who state that choices over activity links, actor bonds and resource ties are dependent on how the emerging situations are "framed and made sense of".

In an attempt to build on these perspectives, Welch and Wilkinson (2002: 29) posit that a focus on 'ideas' (e.g. meanings or knowledge systems) can contribute to our understanding of network development. As they put it: 'Ideas encompass the perceptions individuals and organisations have about self and others, their beliefs or "theories" about how the world functions, norms about appropriate behaviour, attitudes towards particular issues as well as values concerning what is desirable' (see Box below). We believe that an approach to the study of networks that adopts such a focus on perceptions and meanings may offer a valuable extension to IMP thinking, and will develop this argument later in this chapter.

Observing British CEO networks

In the last edition of his seminal work, tellingly entitled *Who Runs This Place?*, Anthony Sampson (2004: 318) notes the complaint of a Swedish CEO who, with reference to the uniformity of the CEOs of London-based companies he encounters, states, 'I keep on meeting exactly the same people at the same kind of gatherings'. As Sampson puts it, 'Anyone looking at the chief executives and chairmen of the biggest twenty companies – and others of the top hundred – must be struck by the smallness of the pool from which they come, and the repeating interlocks, as they keep popping up in boardrooms of the others, with the same names recurring in corporations, banks or insurance companies as if they were really one immense organisation with separate subsidiaries'.

The IMP/network literature thus has much to offer us in the study of IORs, and certainly provides a less restrictive view of relationships than most B2B RM studies. There are a few concerns with this body of work, however, which also afflict the more conventional RM literature. Recall some of the problems raised earlier in this chapter over how power is wielded in supply chains, and how misleading claims over fairness are made, and disputed. Recall, too, how RM theorising did not really seem able to explain these problems. We suggest that addressing these issues demands a more nuanced understanding of IORs.

6.6 Critical Perspectives on the IOR literature

The purpose of this section is to identify methodological weaknesses within IOR research and to begin to suggest an alternative approach to the study of the subject. These weaknesses are interrelated, but we have tried to present them under five separate headings for greater clarity. First we highlight two concerns that have been raised with the main methods used in RM and SCM studies: biases towards positivism and quantification. This is followed with observations on ways in which marketing scholars have undertaken industrial network research. We shall argue that while IMP studies may provide us with a better understanding of IORs than RM-based approaches, they are not without their own limitations. Three of these limitations are, in ascending order of significance: ontological in terms of a broadly realist worldview (defined earlier in Chapter 2) (something that also dominates RM and SCM work); methodological in terms of an analytical neglect of the subjective interpretations of individual managerial actors; and epistemological in terms of a failure to acknowledge the role of language in processes of social construction.

Please note that some of our methodological discussions will get quite philosophical here. You may need to consult the glossary to understand the fairly complex arguments put forward.

6.6.1 Over-Reliance on Positivistic Relational Constructs

Moller (1994: 361) notes that much B2B research 'suffers from its strong ties to the explanatory "independent–dependent variables" type of research setting' and describes researchers as being captured by the search for 'law-like' generalisations. In contrast to this prevailing positivism, Moller and Wilson (1995) note how a 'sociological view' suggests that the key RM concept of trust is a socially constructed reality that exists at the relational level. Bagozzi (1995) makes similar observations regarding the construction of identities both of the 'self' and 'the other' amongst relationship partners. As Haytko (2004) argues, this results in too many researchers limiting themselves to testing pre-existing notions from the RM literature rather than taking an interpretive approach to analysis that tries to accommodate the 'meaning categories' of research participants. Following on from the adherence within the literature to the positivist paradigm, we also find attendant problems with data gathering methods.

6.6.2 Obsession with Quantification and Measurement

It would appear that concerns about the 'respectability' of the marketing discipline (see Chapter 5) have resulted in an entrenchment of notions of 'rigour' and 'quantification' in much marketing research (Easton and Araujo, 1994). Unfortunately, quantitative research often represents a fundamentalist and narrow view of science: typically, 'trivial' details are tested and what cannot be captured through a set of statistical techniques is then at risk of 'not existing' (Gummesson, 1997: 271). This is most obviously evidenced in the widespread use of measurement scales for RM elements. Blois (1999) takes a particularly critical view of such 'measurement' attempts. He observes that IOR studies frequently ask survey respondents to rate statements on Likert scales (e.g. 'To what extent do you feel your customer has confidence and trust in you?') which do not show much sensitivity to the complexity of relational concepts.

6.6.3 Prevalence of Realist Assumptions

As reflected in the common use of simplistic survey methods, a belief in some sort of objective 'reality' dominates B2B marketing and SCM thought (Saunders, 1995). This typically results in a view that an IOR exists as one 'true' object that researchers should try to accurately measure (e.g. Selnes and Sallis, 2003). This is a naïve assumption when, as Wilkinson (2001: 36) notes, 'there is not necessarily one "real" relationship to be discovered ... so much as many realities that shape interactions within the relationship and within the participant organisations'. The dominance of a realist perspective has also led some IMP scholars to regard the organisation as the only 'thing' that acts in an IOR, often to the exclusion of other levels of network actor, as we shall now see.

6.6.4 Focus on Organisational Actors

As Blois (1997: 369) reminds us, 'organisations do not make decisions – people do in the name of organisations'. However, the role of boundary-spanning individuals (such as marketing managers) in most management theories of business relationships is 'virtually unexplored' (Osborn and Hagedoorn, 1997: 271). As Gronhaug et al. (1999: 179) note, boundary spanners' 'interpretations of events and constructions of explanations are largely overlooked in research on business relationships'. This is a key point since, if future research is to help us understand more about IORs, it must engage with those social actors that, in effect, 'do the constructing', thereby structuring the network system via the relationships that bind the actors together. This means engaging more closely with managers themselves, but not just managers; also the way they construct meaning (as noted in Chapter 5).

6.6.5 Insufficient Sensitivity to Language

This leads us to our final and, from the point of view of this chapter, arguably our most important criticism. If, as Brennan and Turnbull (2002: 596), claim 'the entire IMP purpose (is) to try and understand the patterns of meanings and the beliefs which guide managers in their interactions with others', then we are forced to ask the following question: Why does the network literature pay such selective attention to these 'meanings'?

Researchers who take respondents' language literally and uncritically can be found throughout the IMP literature. For example, the work of Biemans (1997: 538) draws upon interviews where 'results were written down in comprehensive reports and reviewed with the persons interviewed, thus inviting them to correct errors of fact...'. Such perspectives seem to be focusing unproblematically on 'fact' or 'reality' construction. They treat what are, after all, effectively managers' 'stories' (or accounts) as factual reports (Hopkinson and Hogarth-Scott, 2001). Similar naiveté is also hinted at in the research design of Håkansson et al. (1999: 446) where managers' accounts are apparently taken as reports from which the researchers 'learn' something, but something taken at face value. Clearly, depending on the aims of any given study, this is not necessarily a flaw, but it does indicate that more subtle analyses of managers' language may reveal more (or at least something different) about IORs.

Thus, when managers use language in interviews or corporate literature to discursively construct other network stakeholders as, for instance, 'untrustworthy partners' with 'adversarial cultures', and legitimate themselves as 'market orientated' firms that adopt 'relationship marketing strategies' and 'ethical supply chain practices' in a 'competitive global environment', it would be valuable to deconstruct the discursive entities inherent in such descriptions of how social systems appear to 'work'. In other words, we would like to be able to ask how and why these linguistic claims are attempted, and to consider their possible consequences. But how can we do this? The final two sections of this chapter try to make some suggestions for alternative research directions into IORs.

6.7 Interpretive Research into Partnerships and Collaborations

Researchers exploring IORs that are predominantly not embedded in conventional supply chains (such as not-for-profit agencies working with governments) often embrace more interpretive approaches (Gray, 2004). Such studies have addressed fundamental power differences among collaborators and provided insight into how the use of language and concepts can create legitimacy (e.g. using discourse to justify one's actions in an IOR). As Phillips et al. (2004: 638) remind us, although actions may form the basis of IOR processes, 'in being observed and interpreted, written or talked about, or depicted in some other way, actions generate text'. In a business context, these texts might be spoken accounts, emails, company manuals or publicity material. Phillips et al. thus argue that institutions like inter-organisational collaborations and supply chains are constituted by the collections of texts that exist in a particular field, 'and that produce the social categories and norms that shape the understandings and behaviours of actors' (2004: 638).

Understanding peoples' language use in creating texts then becomes important since, as Hardy et al. (1998: 65) assert, the literature on IORs 'tends to focus on surface dynamics and to ignore the fact that power can be hidden behind a façade of "trust" and a rhetoric of "collaboration" and can be used to promote vested interests through the manipulation and capitulation of weaker partners'. People can thus achieve effective coordination within an IOR, not just through the management of exchanges, but also 'through the management and negotiation of meaning' (Phillips and Maguire, 2000: 4). For instance, note how we have observed supermarket bosses drawing upon the discourse of RM in claiming to build partnerships with farmers, partnerships that will supposedly benefit all stakeholders in the supply chain, and thus deflect criticism from network members. We can deconstruct other such claims, as shown below.

Transparency in Supply Chains?

A key part of collaboration in the supply chain is the supposed 'open-book' arrangements between organisations. Rhetorical claims about 'transparency' are interesting to explore. You might think that a little more transparency in supply chains would be welcomed, and given the possibilities opened up by electronic information exchange, reasonably simple to operationalise. It is certainly something promised by many of the key players in supply chain activities. For instance Blythman (2004: 284) reports that in a recent press release Sainsbury's claims to be entering 'a new era of transparency and traceability in the organic food chain'.

Some commentators question these claims, however. As Blythman asks, 'what about transparency in the *non*-organic food chain? Why should it be more opaque?' When she asked Sainsbury's press office to answer some questions about such issues, perhaps unsurprisingly, they were not forthcoming. This view is echoed by academics Lang et al. (*Guardian*, 2006: 23) who observe in a letter to the Editor that 'the City is outraged that businesses may have to publish details of their approach to the environment, employees, communities and (horror!) their suppliers … They might even have to tell us how much they pay dairy farmers for a litre of milk, or shed more light on the demands they make of suppliers … We are told this unwelcome transparency could "impede the good relationship between companies and their shareholders"'.

So much for the 'reality versus rhetoric' issue in RM. Maybe we should not be surprised at any disparities over perceptions of transparency, fairness and partnership in the field of IORs. For some observers, talk does not seem to reflect action: what people say they are doing is not what actually happens. This is undoubtedly sometimes the case; however, as we have seen in the collaboration literature, the picture *is* not so simple. More intriguingly, therefore, what about taking the view that the rhetoric *is* sometimes the reality? The more reflective collaboration scholars acknowledge that 'actions generate text', but point out the influence is not just one-way. They also see the language in those texts as exerting an important influence on peoples' worldviews and thus their behaviours. Let us explore further the significance of these ideas about discourse for B2B marketing studies.

6.8 B2B Marketing Research and Discourse Analysis

As the preceding sections have indicated, we believe it is important to bring a critical perspective to the fields of RM, networks and supply chain research. We now outline some ways forward that may help us to make better (or at least different) sense of these phenomena.

As Hirschman and Holbrook (1992) suggest, we cannot afford to lose sight of the taken-for-granted social and cultural practices that guide the linguistic constructions by means of which we make marketing reality 'real'. One important discursive feature that draws heavily on cultural norms is the use of metaphors – see below.

Metaphors Used to Describe IORs

The metaphor of 'marketing as relationship' is now widely used in descriptions of supply chains, leaving us with a number of issues that are rarely questioned. As values are also appropriated when employing metaphors, the notion of close, long-term, commercial relationships has come to represent the ideal (O'Malley, 2003). In many cultures the archetypal 'marriage' metaphor given for RM suggests a notion of a successful, monogamous relationship, freely entered into, but as Tynan (1997: 695) points out, 'the metaphor fails to deliver' on a number of issues, despite its convenience. She calls for research that examines buyer/seller relations 'without the blinkers of metaphors imported from other human relationships, and without the preconceptions of their nature, of even of their existence' (1997: 702).

As long as such metaphors are in common use, we must question their impact on the search for some sort of 'truth' in IORs. If we accept that decisions to buy and sell within chains are in fact made by individuals on behalf of organisations then we should surely note the language that these individuals themselves use in describing market practices. We should also be conscious of the language we researchers use in our marketing discourse, and of the influence the power of that discourse may have on marketing professionals *and* on our own discipline. Researchers seem to wish to confer social attributes to the relationships between customers and organisations, so that 'the language of strategy, tactics, power and intelligence gathering co-exist (somewhat uncomfortably) with that of trust, harmony and commitment' (O'Malley and Tynan, 1999: 595, brackets in original).

You will have noted that the notion of 'discourse' has become increasingly salient throughout this chapter. We now turn to the small number of studies that have begun to bring a discursive approach to the exploration of supply chains and IORs.

Faria and Wensley (2002: 606) show how Brazilian managers reproduce in their talk the difficulty of balancing two criteria posed for supply chain intermediaries: those of economic growth and of social integration. These actors use language as a resource which 'enables them to pretend that both criteria can be met and not to recognise that the economic end or condition corrupts the other criterion'. Managers' discourse enables them to cope with the tensions of SCM in this context. Hopkinson (2003) examines how the talk of managers in a distribution network constructs the focal firm in different ways. In doing so, she questions the correspondence between these participants' and theorists' constructions of organising in industrial markets. She shows how 'front-line' managerial understandings can affect how people approach their role in handling IORs.

Ellis et al. (2005) deploy interview and documentary evidence to analyse market(ing) discourses within the agri-food sector. They problematise the assumption that 'the market' for animal feeds is an objective, and self-producing social fact. Their study shows how the discursive production of supply chain positions plays a part in structuring the world of agri-food IORs and establishes some of the 'facts' about the world(s) into which marketing managers act. Through an examination of a purchasing code of practice produced by a UK manufacturer and a series of managerial interviews, Ellis and Higgins (2006) explore how codes may (or may not) assist in shaping the identity and positioning of stakeholders within the supply chain. They argue that a more subtle understanding of social constructions of managerial identities and 'the other' within the language of supply chain ethics may facilitate moves towards strategies of fairer trade.

The application of discursive approaches in inter-organisational contexts would thus appear to be a possible way to restore the voices of individual managers representing selling and buying firms in IOR research. This is important since developing academic knowledge is considerably enhanced through taking the participants' view of how network patterns emerge (Ellis et al., 2006). Attempts at theorising and explaining causalities through an etic language do not fully reflect how the actors imagine the network, creating misunderstandings and possibly missing important concepts entirely. In contrast, we argue for an epistemology that seeks to interpret locally occurring discourses rather than produce law-like models that ignore the complexity of the IOR context in which decisions are made. This requires a subtle exploration of what managers claim to 'do' in their accounts as they attempt to 'manage' within networks. To facilitate such exploration, we propose that network researchers 'approach the social phenomenon of "organisation" as a (discursive) process – organizing' (Keenoy and Oswick, 2003: 141). As such, discourse analysis holds great promise for re-interpreting IORs.

6.9 Conclusion

This chapter emphasises the key role of language in B2B marketing. A discourse analytic approach views RM as a rhetorical construct which both managers and academics utilise to make sense of marketing activities and in pursuing their own interests. This does not mean however that there are no realities outside of 'RM talk'. Rather, a critical perspective on RM discourse enables us to interpret the various processes within IORs. Those seeking to understand IORs must therefore study words as well as practices; and indeed to see discourse as a form of practice.

6.10 Learning Activities

In previous chapters, the role of marketing has been linked to the idea of boundary spanning between and within organisations. In this chapter, these inter and intra organisational relationships are seen as central to an appreciation of marketing and marketers. The question of how to conceptualise and research these relationships is put under the spotlight. Before you begin the learning activities, remind yourself of the learning aims for the chapter so that your time and efforts are focused.

Learning Activity One: Relationship Management

There are many different viewpoints on how managers should embrace notions of relationship management. For a broad perspective, the Association for the Advancement of Relationship Marketing, a partnership of organisations that aims to promote the concept of RM, can be found online at www.aarm.org. In terms of B2C relationship management, you can find out more about customer relationship management (CRM) technology by comparing the offerings of contributors to www.crm-forum.com. Note that many of these contributors are not exactly dis-interested participants in the debate. Moving to B2B markets, it is often argued that supply chain relationships can be enhanced through appropriate use of ERP (enterprise resource planning) information systems. For a view on this, visit www.pwcglobal.com/ca/eng/about/svcs/techs-erp. html. This is a website owned by consultants Price-Waterhouse Coopers.

a What sort of vision of RM do these different groups seem to be propagating?
b Are they all 'singing from the same hymn sheet'? And if not, why not?
c Are there ideas from one sector that may be applicable in others?

Learning Activity Two: Healthy Relationships

In 2003, the UK government claimed to be acting as an ally to businesses in World Trade Organisation negotiations on services. The then Trade Minister, Baroness Symons explained that for the UK, trading services internationally is of far greater importance than it is to a number of countries. One sector in which Britain has been pushing for global change is the health care market. The EU has already approved the means by which the World Health Organisation could be used to enforce privatisation in markets worldwide. The complexity of managing the relationships which underpin the delivery of global health care thus looks set to increase. This will be one of the most significant challenges for managers claiming to be practising RM as they juggle the interests of the public and private sectors, plus of course, the end recipients of that care. To find out more about the UK government's policies on partnerships in the global health care market, look for statements by ministers on these sites: www.dfid. gov.uk and www.fco.gov.uk.

a Do you agree with these politicians' arguments?
b What sort of partnerships might a drug manufacturer have to forge with non-profit making organisations?
c What tensions could there be in such relationships?

6.11 Further Reading

Araujo, L. (2007) 'Markets, market-making and marketing', *Marketing Theory*, 7(3): 211–26.

The author, a leading IMP scholar, argues that marketing practices (and not just discursive practices) have a performative role in helping to create the phenomena they purportedly describe.

Blois, K. (2003) 'B2B relationships – a social construction of reality? A study of Marks and Spencer and one of its major suppliers', *Marketing Theory*, 3(1): 79–95.

This study describes Marks and Spencer's links with one of its major suppliers. It questions whether or not 'a relationship' in the B2B context is a social construction of reality.

Ellis, N. and Higgins, M. (2006) 'Recatechizing codes of practice in supply chain relationships: Discourse, identity and otherness', *Journal of Strategic Marketing*, 14: 327–50.

This paper offers an in-depth discussion of ethics in fair trade and food supply chains, as well as an example of how discourse analysis can be applied to the B2B marketing context.

Tadajewski, M. (2009) 'The foundations of relationship marketing: Reciprocity and trade relations', *Marketing Theory*, 9(1): 9–38.

The author takes an historical perspective to note the extent to which the practice and study of reciprocity, as a predominantly industrial marketing strategy, was from the 1920s to 1950s largely RM- orientated in nature.

6.12 References

American Marketing Association (2006) 'Dictionary of marketing terms', available online at http://marketingpower.com/mg-dictionary-view2592.php, accessed 17 October 2006.

Axelsson, B. and Easton, G. (eds) (1992) *Industrial Networks: A New View of Reality*. London: Routledge.

Bagozzi, R.P. (1995) 'Reflections on relationship marketing in consumer markets', *Journal of the Academy of Marketing Science*, 23 (4): 272–7.

Beddall, C. (2002) 'The Saturday Essay', *The Grocer*, 19 October: 32.

Bianco, A. and Zellner, W. (2003) 'Is Wal-Mart too powerful?', *Business Week*, 6 October: 46–53.

Biemans, W. G. (1997) 'The managerial implications of networking', in D. Ford, (ed.), *Understanding Business Markets*, 2nd edn, pp. 537–56. London: The Dryden Press.

Blois, K.J. (1997) 'Are Business-to-Business relationships inherently unstable?', *Journal of Marketing Management*, 13: 367–82.

Blois, K. J. (1998) 'Don't all firms have relationships?', *Journal of Business and industrial Marketing*, 13 (3): 1–11.

Blois, K. J. (1999) 'Trust in business-to-business relationships: an evaluation of its status', *Journal of Management Studies*, 36 (2): 197–215.

Blythman, J. (2004) *Shopped: The Shocking Power of British Supermarkets*. London: Fourth Estate.

Boddy, D., Macbeth, D. and Wagner, B. (2000) 'Implementing collaboration between organisations: An empirical study of supply chain manufacturing', *Journal of Management Studies*, 37 (7): 1003–17.

Brennan, R. and Turnbull, P. W. (2002) 'Sophistry, relevance and technology transfer in management research: an IMP perspective', *Journal of Business Research*, 55: 595–602.

Buttle, F. (ed.) (1996) *Relationship Marketing: Theory and Practice*. London: Paul Chapman.

Christopher, M., Payne, A. and Ballantyne, D. (2002) *Relationship Marketing: Creating Stakeholder Value*. Oxford: Butterworth-Heinemann.

Crane, A. (2000) *Marketing, Morality and the Natural Environment*. London: Routledge.

Curtis, M. (2006) 'It's thriving but legal', *The Guardian*, 22 May: 32.

Easton, G. and Araujo, L. (1994) 'Market exchange, social structures and time', *European Journal of Marketing*, 28 (3): 72–84.

Egan, J. (2001) *Relationship Marketing: Exploring Relational Strategies in Marketing*. Harlow: Financial Times Prentice Hall.

Ellis, N. and Higgins, M. (2006) 'Recatechizing codes of practice in supply chain relationships: Discourse, identity and otherness', *Journal of Strategic Marketing*, 14: 327–50.

Ellis, N., Higgins, M. and Jack, G. (2005) '(De)constructing the market for animal feeds: A discursive study', *Journal of Marketing Management*, 21: 117–46.

Ellis, N., Lowe, S. and Purchase, S. (2006) 'Towards a re-interpretation of industrial networks: A discursive view of culture', *The IMP Journal*, 1 (2): 29–59.

Faria, A. and Wensley, R. (2002) 'In search of 'inter-firm management' in supply chains: Recognising contradictions of language and power by listening', *Journal of Business Research*, 55: 603–10.

Fitchett, J. and McDonagh, P. (2000) 'A citizen's critique of relationship marketing in risk society', *Journal of Strategic Marketing*, 8 (2): 209–22.

Ford, D. (ed.) (1990) *Understanding Business Markets: Interaction, Relationships and Networks*. London: Academic Press.

Ford, D., McDowell, R. and Tomkins, C. (1996) 'Relationship strategy, investments and decision making', in D. Iacobucci (ed.), *Networks in Marketing*, pp. 144–76. London: Sage.

Ghoshal, S. and Westney, E. (1993) *Organization Theory and the Multinational Corporation*. Basingstoke: Macmillan.

Gray, B. (2004) 'Complementarities and tensions in theorizing about interorganizational collaboration', Paper presented at the *Workshop of the Special Interest Group on Interorganizational Relations*, British Academy of Management, London, June.

Gronhaug, K., Henjesand, I. J. and Koveland, A. (1999) 'Fading relationships in business markets: an exploratory study', *Journal of Strategic Marketing*, 7: 175–90.

Grönroos, C. (1994) 'Quo vadis, marketing?: Towards a relationship marketing paradigm', *Journal of Marketing Management*, 10 (4): 347–60.

Guardian (The) (2006) 'Letters', 20 October: 34.

Gummesson, E. (1996) 'Relationship marketing and imaginary organizations: A synthesis', *European Journal of Marketing*, 30 (2): 31–44.

Gummesson, E. (1997) 'Relationship marketing as a paradigm shift: Some conclusions from the 30R approach', *Management Decision*, 35 (4): 267–72.

Gummesson, E., Lehtinen, U. and Grönroos, C. (1997) 'Comment on "Nordic perspectives on relationship marketing"', *European Journal of Marketing*, 31 (1): 10–16.

Håkansson, H. (ed.) (1982) *International Marketing & Purchasing of Industrial Goods: An Interaction Approach*. Chichester: John Wiley.

Håkansson, H. and Johanson, J. (1993) 'The network as a governance structure: Interfirm cooperation beyond markets and hierarchies', in G. Grabher (ed.), *The Embedded Firm: On the Socioeconomics of Industrial Networks*. pp. 35–51. London: Routledge.

Håkansson, H. and Snehota, I. (1998) 'The burden of relationships or who's next', in P. Naude and P. Turnbull, (eds), *Network Dynamics in International Marketing*, p. 16–25. Oxford: Pergamon.

Håkansson, H. and Snehota, I. (2000) 'The IMP perspective: Assets and liabilities of business relationships', in J.N. Sheth and A. Parvatiyar (eds), *Handbook of Relationship Marketing* pp. 69–43. Thousand Oaks: Sage.

Håkansson, H., Havila, V. and Pederson, A-C. (1999) 'Learning in networks', *Industrial Marketing Management*, 28 (5): 443–52.

Hardy, C., Phillips, N. and Lawrence, T. B. (1998) 'Distinguishing trust and power in interorganizational relations: Forms and facades of trust', in C. Lane and R. Bachmann (eds), *Trust Within and Between Organizations*, pp. 64–87. Oxford: Oxford University Press.

Harland, C., Zheng, J., Johnsen, T. and Lamming, R. (2004) 'A conceptual model for researching the creation and operation of supply networks', *British Journal of Management*, 15: 1–21.

Haytko, D. L. (2004) 'Firm-to-firm and interpersonal relationships: Perspectives from advertising agency account managers', *Journal of the Academy of Marketing Science*, 32 (3): 312–28.

Hirschman, E. and Holbrook, M. (1992) *Postmodern Consumer Research : The Study of Consumption as Text*. London: Sage.

Hopkinson, G. C. (2003) 'Stories from the front-line: How they construct the organization', *Journal of Management Studies*, 40 (8): 1943–69.

Hopkinson, G. C. and Hogarth-Scott, S. (2001) "What happened was ..." Broadening the agenda for storied research', *Journal of Marketing Management*, 17 (1–2): 27–47.

Jap, S. (2001) 'Perspectives on joint competitive advantages in buyer-supplier relationships', *International Journal of Research in Marketing*, 18: 19–35.

Keenoy, T. and Oswick, C. (2003) 'Organising textscapes', *Organization Studies*, 25 (1): 135–42.

Kotler, P. (1992) 'It's time for total marketing', *Business Week* ADVANCE Executive Brief, 2.

Lamming, R., Caldwell, N. and Harrison, D. (2004) 'Developing the concept of transparency for use in supply relationships', *British Journal of Management*, 15: 291–302.

LaPlaca, P.J. and Katrichis, J.M. (2009) `Relative presence of business-to-business research in the marketing literature', *Journal of Business-to-Business Marketing*, 16 (1–2): 1–22.

Lawrence, F. (2004) *Not On the Label: What Really Goes into the Food on Your Plate,* London: Penguin.

Mattsson, L. G. (1997) '"Relationship marketing" and the "markets-as-networks approach" – A comparative analysis of two evolving streams of research', *Journal of Marketing Management*, 13: 447–61.

McDonagh, P. (2002) 'Communicative campaigns to effect anti-slavery and fair trade', *European Journal of Marketing*, 36 (5/6): 642–66.

Moller, K. (1994) 'Interorganizational marketing exchange: Metatheoretical analysis of current research approaches', in G. Laurent, G. Lilien and B. Pras (eds), *Research Traditions in Marketing*, pp. 347–72. Boston: Kluwer.

Moller, K. and Wilson, D. T. (eds) (1995) *Business Marketing: An Interaction and Network Perspective*. Boston: Kluwer Academic.

Morgan, R.M. and Hunt, S.D. (1994) 'The commitment-trust theory of relationship marketing', *Journal of Marketing*, 58: 20–38.

New Internationalist (2006) 'Ethical consumption', November: 19.

O'Driscoll, A., Carson, D. and Gilmore, A. (2000) 'Developing marketing competence and managing in networks: a strategic perspective', *Journal of Strategic Marketing*, 8 (2): 183–96.

O'Malley, L. (2003) 'Understanding the relationship metaphor'. Presentation at *ESRC Research Seminar on Relationship Marketing*, University of East Anglia, 12 December.

O'Malley, L. and Tynan, C. (1999) 'The utility of the relationship metaphor in consumer markets: A critical evaluation', *Journal of Marketing Management*, 15: 587–602.

Osborn, R. N. and Hagedoorn, J. (1997) 'The institutionalisation and evolutionary dynamics of interorganizational alliances and networks', *Academy of Management Review*, 40 (2): 261–78.

Parker, M. (2002) *Against Management*. Oxford: Polity Press.

Phillips, N. and Maguire, S. (2000) 'The dynamics of trust and identity in intra-organizational relations: A discursive perspective', Paper presented at *Word Views, Work Views and World Views Conference,* King's College, London, July 26–8.

Phillips, N., Lawrence, T. B. and Hardy, C. (2004), 'Discourse and institutions', *Academy of Management Review,* 29 (4): 635–52.

Reinartz, W. and Kumar, V. (2002) 'The Mismanagement of Customer Loyalty', *Harvard Business Review,* 80 (7): 79–86.

Sampson, A. (2004) *Who Runs This Place?: The Anatomy of Britain in the 21st Century.* London: John Murray Publishers.

Saunders, M. J. (1995) 'Chains, pipelines and value streams', in R.A. Kemp and R.C. Lamming (eds), *Proceedings of First Worldwide Research Symposium on Purchasing and Supply Chain Management,* Arizona State University, March 23–5.

Selnes, F. and Sallis, J. (2003) 'Promoting relationship learning', *Journal of Marketing,* 67: 80–95.

Shaw, E. (2003) 'Marketing through alliances and networks', in S. Hart (ed.), *Marketing Changes,* pp. 147–70. London: Thompson Learning.

Shreck, A. (2002) 'Just bananas? Fair trade production in the Dominican Republic', *International Journal of Sociology of Agriculture and Food,* 10 (2): 11–21.

Tadajewski, M. and Saren, M. (2009) 'Rethinking the emergence of relationship marketing', *Journal of Macromarketing,* 29 (2): 193–206.

Tse, A.C.B, Sin, L.Y.M, Yau, O.H.M, Lee, J.S.Y. and Chow, R. (2004) 'A firm's role in the marketplace and the relative importance of market orientation and relationship marketing orientation', *European Journal of Marketing,* 38 (9–10): 1158–72.

Tynan, C. (1997) 'A review of the marriage analogy in relationship marketing', *Journal of Marketing Management,* 13: 695–703.

Varey, R.J. (2002) *Relationship Marketing: Dialogue and Networks in the E-Commerce Era.* Chichester: John Wiley.

Webster, F. E. (1992) 'The changing role of marketing in the corporation', *Journal of Marketing,* 56 (October): 1–17.

Welch, C. and Wilkinson, I. (2002) 'Idea logics and network theory in business marketing', *Journal of Business to Business Marketing,* 8 (3): 27–48.

Wilkinson, I. F. (2001) 'A history of network and channels thinking in marketing in the 20th century', *Australasian Journal of Marketing,* 9 (2): 23–53.

Wilson, D.T. and Mummalaneni, V. (1986) 'Bonding and commitment in buyer-seller relationships: A preliminary conceptualisation', *Industrial Marketing & Purchasing,* 1 (3): 44–58.

Worth, J. (2006) 'Buy now, pay later', *New Internationalist,* November: 2–5.

Consumer Surveillance and Marketing Research

7

7.1 Introduction

The idea that organisations should seek to find out what their customers really feel and want in order to be able to meet those needs is a powerful one, and it is a fundamental argument for the importance of marketing. After all, how can firms hope to ever know anything about their customers and the marketplace more generally without gathering information from them? The marketing research industry evolved rapidly over the last century as new technologies and techniques were developed to help researchers capture important market intelligence. As consumers we are all now probably quite familiar with the process of completing surveys and providing feedback to the organisations we interact with. We may have even been involved in other types of research programmes such as focus groups and interviews.

But marketing research does much more than simply provide firms with information about consumers. Research raises consumer expectations. If firms are prepared to spend the time, effort and money collecting this type of information it would suggest that they feel that those views and opinions are important. In Western societies at least we have all become used to the idea of being 'watched', with our activities and behaviours being recorded routinely often without our direct knowledge or consent. When we surf the web we know that the sites we visit and the activities we undertake are capable of being recorded, and we also know that the loyalty card we use at the supermarket provides firms with all kinds of data about the things we buy and when we buy them. Marketing research is an important part of the broader 'society of surveillance', and this has some important implications for consumers, firms and society more generally.

The chapter begins with a brief overview of the development of the marketing research industry from its origins a century ago, in political straw polls (Section 7.2 The Early Development of the Market Research Industry). Section 7.3 (Market Research Post 1945 – Technology and Internationalisation) explores how the development of market research was influenced by new technologies and its role in the internationalisation of trade.

As we shall discuss here, the basic argument for marketing research is an absolutely crucial element of the general justification for marketing in the organisation. At a time when the strategic value of marketing is being questioned, it is important to have a clear understanding of the purpose of research before, and in addition to, knowledge of particular techniques and approaches. Section 7.4 (Marketing Research and the Marketing Concept) to Section 7.8 (The Demands on Commercial Marketing Research) consider various different perspectives on organising marketing research. Most descriptions of marketing research that you will find represented in marketing research textbooks describe a highly formalised, mechanistic process (e.g. Malhotra and Birks, 2006). This is, however only one way to think about marketing research. The value, purpose and approach to marketing research are, like all types of organisational conduct, partly dependent on cultural and social factors.

There are more and more debates surfacing about privacy and protection of data, the rights of governments and corporations to 'snoop in' on aspects of citizens' everyday lives, and the potential abuses that can occur if these activities are not controlled (Ball and Webster, 2003). At the same time many cultures are turning techniques borrowed from marketing research into a mass entertainment form. The popularity of reality television, including shows like Big Brother and Loft Story, demonstrate just how sophisticated the research industry has become, as well as how conditioned we are as a society about the use of intense, continuous surveillance and monitoring in our everyday lives.

The final part of the chapter (Section 7.9 Surveillance Culture and Section 7.10 The Emergence of Market Information Systems) discusses the relationship between marketing research, surveillance and intelligence systems. Many theorists (Arvidsson, 2004; Lyon, 2001; Zwick and Denegri-Knott, 2009) suggest that twenty-first century societies are rapidly becoming 'surveillance societies'. This means that surveillance is increasingly both desirable and necessary in order for many of the systems and processes that we rely on everyday to function properly. Marketing research is an integral part of the surveillance society because the data that is collected about consumers is used to protect, control and monitor them as well as attempting to find out details of their behaviour, thoughts and values.

7.2 The Early Development of the Market Research Industry

Almost every kind and form of organisation conducts some sort of marketing research. This includes commercial organisations involved with the supply of products, services and experiences to end consumers and business buyers. But this list also extends to public sector organisations, political parties and charities. It would appear that nowadays all organisations have an insatiable need for market information of one kind or another. The marketing research industry has responded to this demand by supplying an ever-greater variety of research methods, techniques and styles. New research techniques are promoted to organisations on the expectation that they can be employed to discover aspects of consumer behaviour that were previously obscured. Alongside traditional methods of research based on questionnaires and focus groups, researchers now deploy video surveillance and participant observation techniques (e.g. Bonsu and Darmody, 2008; Pace, 2008).

The Body and Research

We tend to concentrate on the spoken and written word in marketing research, whether this is through the completion of a questionnaire or the recording of an interview. Developments in medical science however have allowed marketing research firms to explore sensory responses to marketing phenomena. These have included a range of hardware tools for example:

(Cont'd)

- A psychogalvanometer (also known as a lie detector) which measures the electrical skin resistance. It can be used to measure the emotional response to marketing stimuli (e.g. advertisements). The eye camera and pupil dilator allows marketers to follow the path taken by the eye as it scans an image or text. The pupil dilator examines the emotional response to the stimuli.
- Functional magnetic resonance imaging allows the marketer to monitor activity in the brain when the individual is subjected to marketing stimuli.

Early market research was closely associated with the development of North American capitalism in the late 1800s (Ward, 2009a). Industrialisation, mass production and urbanisation were radically altering trade and social relations. The preliminary research studies initially drew inspiration and focus from economics with researchers focusing on the institutional dynamics of market systems rather than individual consumers (Bartels, 1988). At the beginning of the 1900s, the study of economics was approached with optimism. New technology had improved production facilities and governments sought to promote competition between individuals within the populace, scaling back on welfare programmes for the poor and needy. The demands of the rational consumer were being seen to be catered for by a market mechanism and thus the system became the subject of the research. The first market researchers were schooled in scientific management (echoing the points made in Chapter 1, Section 1.6) and the ideas of using information to monitor and control systems. This is apparent in the work of Charles Coolidge Parlin in 1911 and his focus on the agricultural industry, believed to be the first piece of market research (Alderson, 1956).

Interest in the consumer arose less out of curiosity and more out of economic necessity and opportunity. Magazine and newspaper publishers in the United States were keen to acquire information on their readership to be able to present a demographic to sell to advertisers (Ward, 2009b). The greater the information on their readership in terms of buying habits the easier it became to sell the audience to the potential advertisers. Basic typographies were drawn up to identify the different readerships. These were often based upon social class distinctions and were crude in construction due to the limited range of information available on the readers (Squire, 1988). Market research was accordingly a means by which the audience could be commodified (Arvidsson, 2004).

Many of the original market research organisations and market research methods were developed by or in collaboration with universities. Paul Lazarsfeld and Robert Merton of Columbia University for example are closely associated with the development of focus groups within market research (Jeřábek, 2001). Lazarsfeld and Merton occupied a sphere which placed them in close proximity to George Gallup and Elmo Roper, both of whom were developing careers out of the growing interest in sociology, politics and statistics (Abrams, 1977). Gallup and Roper were employing social science methods to transform the original 'straw polls', where newspapers undertook impromptu interviews as people left the polling booths. Gallup, with a PhD in psychology set up the American Institute of Public Opinion in 1935 and saw opinion polls as a means of supporting democracy. This was a particularly difficult time for the United States, when the future of democracy was in question with the rise of communism in Russia and fascism in Europe. Gallup drew from the ideas of statistical science to compile an approach to straw polls that drew from quasi probability sampling (Robinson, 1999). The sample would be drawn from locations around the country with interviewers sent out to find and interview individuals from a particular demographic. The aim was to achieve a representative sample. Gallup was able to balance the demands of scientific rigour, commerce and journalism (Gallup, 1966) which offered significant commercial opportunities. The polls were pitched to the media to provide content and editorial material for newspapers and magazines (Berinsky, 2006).

7.3 Market Research Post 1945 – Technology and Internationalisation

Following the Second World War and the emerging consumer society in the United States, the crude class-based typology opinion polls were increasingly found to be unsuited to the new environment. Companies were looking for more detailed insights in to consumer thoughts and behaviour (Bourdieu, 1984). The market research industry grew rapidly during the 1950s and 1960s with an increasing number of social scientists joining commercial organisations (Arvidsson, 2004). Motivational research, pioneered by Ernest Dichter employed an adaptation of Freudian psychoanalysis to explore how consumer decisions were motivated by the unconscious (as described in Chapter 1). Through depth interviews researchers sought to uncover how 'hidden' motives informed an individual's decision-making process (Packard, 1960). These new insights were used to identify new product opportunities and to inform creative work for advertisements. There were weaknesses connected to the Motivational Research approach concerning reliability and validity which limited its applicability for broader commercial use (Rothwell, 1955). Increasingly however, following motivational research's lead, consumer preferences were being divorced from social class and psychographic variables were increasingly used to examine AOI (Attitudes, Opinions and Interests). Like the Research Bureau, collaboration between social scientists and commerce introduced innovative research techniques to incorporate greater numbers of variables through which to devise clusters or 'lifestyles'. Perhaps one of the best-known lifestyle methodology was the VALS system devised by Stanford Research Institute in the 1970s (Winters, 1989).

Over the next 30 years, the disaggregation of the individual from rigid classifications intensified, provoking a greater willingness to consider both quantitative and qualitative methods to devise representations of the identities amongst consumers. Developments in information technology and communications also radically altered the methodologies and methods used, with telephones and the internet reducing the cost of undertaking surveys and offering new opportunities to represent and be representative of the real.

The applicability of approaches across cultures has also increasingly come under the spotlight as the larger research firms explore new markets for research in Africa and the Far East (Tan and Liu, 2002). The Western-devised techniques commonly employed in the United States and Europe rely upon culturally shaped ideas of truth, the individual and society. These assumptions may not hold fast when these techniques are exported or deployed to people and places far removed from the origins of these techniques (Nancarrow et al., 2005).

Firms wishing to export their goods and services overseas are dependent upon reliable and accurate information on the distant markets and people they wish to sell to. This symbiotic relationship between market research and the export of goods has, according to Maxwell (1996), meant that market research has been central to the growth of transnational trade. The function performed by market research is not simply to gather information to enable the international seller to open the doors of the local market for the export of goods. Market research performs a far more intricate task and is complicit in the codification of consumer desire and transformation of the product to fit local tastes.

The purchase and consumption of goods is a means by which individuals support representations of their identity (to be discussed to a greater extent in Chapter 9). The goods through which identity is constructed are purchased locally but they are part of the global exchange of products and services. For Maxwell (1996), this disjuncture between the local consumption and global exchange is the focus of attention for market research. He argues that individuals place greater trust on goods which are familiar or near, this accordingly requires marketers to appreciate these local values. The values and desires held by a consumer are diverse and they are neither stable nor predictable. It is the role of research to try to capture and translate these into a language that the sellers can use for product development. The purpose of this research is to narrow down the possible meanings for the consumer and suppress the foreignness of the goods being produced and marketed by the firms located some distance from the point of consumption.

Global trade has been facilitated through technology. This has enabled the development of trademarked research techniques but the same technologies have also been significant in democratising the market research process. Cool hunting is the activity of spotting and forecasting cultural trends. Its approach often rests on interviews, ethnography and covert observation (Bulik, 2005). Although there are a number of 'Cool hunting' research and consultancy firms, cool hunting has also witnessed a move to 'open source research' where individuals from around the world collaborate online to produce information on the latest trends and fashions without charging a fee (see for example http://www.trendguide.com/). Typically with such a move online, there has been a series of counter movements such as Uncool hunters which examine those elements of culture which are surreal, forgotten, kitsch or trash. This democratisation of marketing research, with individuals collaborating to offer stories about their consuming experiences may perhaps be a limited blurring of the boundaries between commercially produced market research and consumer narratives, however it gives recognition and support to the growing ideas of pluralism within market research.

7.4 Marketing Research and the Marketing Concept

The basic argument for marketing research is an absolutely crucial element of the general justification for marketing in the organisation (Vecchio, 1991). At a time when the strategic value of marketing is being questioned (Swinburn, 2005) it is important to have a clear understanding of the purpose of research before, and in addition to, knowledge of particular techniques and approaches.

It is uncontroversial to suggest that all firms must seek to innovate in order to remain competitive. Innovation may involve the introduction of new products and services, the improvement or adaptation of existing offerings, or attempts to move into emerging markets. There is however a longstanding debate concerning how organisations should go about identifying which innovations it should and should not pursue. The strategic decision to move in one direction necessarily excludes the opportunity to take other directions simply because organisations have limited resources and can only exist within certain risk parameters.

The marketing literature often presents a simplified dichotomy on how organisations can, and have historically, approached this problem (Tadajewski, 2009). Firms can either choose to take an inside-out approach to innovation and change, often termed a production or sales orientation, or they can adopt an outside-in approach, often termed a marketing orientation. The first of these approaches is based on the premise that resources within the firm are in the best position to foresee, predict and respond to the market. After all, research and development personnel have the expertise to come up with new viable product ideas, operations personnel have the expertise to come up with new methods for generating greater efficiencies, and organisational personnel have the expertise to attract, retain and better utilise scarce human resource expertise. There is an argument to suggest that any one or a combination of these organisational constituencies is best suited to the tasks of formulating strategy (Chaston et al., 2000). The need for marketing and consumer research under these circumstances is limited. Consumers are expected to adopt new innovations in favour of obsolete offerings and respond to greater efficiencies. The need for marketing is equally limited, confined to a simple set of functional and administrative processes (see Chapter 5). An active and aggressive sales force rather than a complex system of research is the main requirement of marketing to promote, advocate and raise awareness of organisational activities.

The marketing concept proposes an alternative ideology to this firm-based principle. A market orientation, it is argued, is the only way to deliver strategic direction to the organisation by grounding decisions in an understanding of the market and the consumer (Sørensen, 2009). Innovations are only viable if they can be incorporated into an identifiable and viable consumer segment. Rather than approaching innovation on the basis of what can be delivered, a marketing orientation proposes that it should be defined by what consumers would like to be delivered (Webster, 1994).

The controversies surrounding this debate are discussed extensively in Chapter 4. What is of primary importance here is that at least some commitment to a market orientation is necessary before marketing research becomes viable or worthwhile to consider in anything like a strategic capacity. The commercial marketing research industry is the direct product of the success of the marketing concept over the last half century. This is because the products that this industry promises to deliver to organisations, i.e. in-depth intelligence and insights into market trends and consumer behaviour only have value if organisations continue to operate on the expectation that these insights will provide strategic direction and help guide future marketplace success.

This point shows that the marketing research industry is necessary to validate the basic idea of marketing in the first place, as well as providing specific information or insights. It is also important to recognise the implicit as well as the explicit uses of marketing research information. Of course there are many instances where marketers use research data to find out things that they otherwise would have not known but marketing research can also be used in a 'political' capacity within the organisation (Hanson, 2001). Managers might for example commission, use and even distort marketing research to justify a set of strategies, programmes and decisions which have already been agreed (Lavidge, 1990). Research data can also be used to demonstrate to various stakeholders that a firm listens and responds to their public, regardless of the further use made of the data (Cooper and Owen, 2007).

In addition to a consumer research function, market research processes underpin many other core marketing techniques. The process of segmenting, targeting and positioning for instance is heavily reliant on increasingly sophisticated methods for classifying and categorising consumers in terms of expected commonalities (MacLachlan and Johansson, 1981). For many consumer markets a mixture of demographic and behavioural techniques is commonly used alongside lifestyle and psychographic measures (Tynan and Drayton, 1987) (See below). New product and brand development strategies often draw on a range of research based activities such as focus groups to pre-test products and services (Janssen and Dankbaar, 2008).

Web 2.0

Traditional market research is usually limited to one exchange between the researcher and the respondent at a particular time. This is typified by the use of depth interviews or the questionnaire where the researcher intervenes in an individual's life for a brief time and through a given method entreats the respondent to divulge information and in so doing allows the researcher the opportunity to extract data. The development of the internet and the popularity of applications such as blogs, social networking sites, twitter, Second Life etc sometimes labelled Web 2.0 offers the potential for the dynamics of research to be transformed. Web 2.0 promotes greater social interaction via web-based applications, allowing individuals to participate, liaise, coordinate, collaborate and communicate more easily and with greater functionality in their exchanges. Market researchers are finding that individuals that participate in blogs, discussion forums and social networking sites are often highly informed about products and technology and are willing to divulge a considerable amount of personal information and opinion. Rather than intervene, researchers are looking to connect with the participants and to benefit from the social dynamics afforded by the developments in technology. Famously, President Barack Obama used Web 2.. technology in his election campaign, using social networking as a means of keeping in touch with the ideas of his supporters and encouraging political donations.

In addition to its immediate or explicit findings, the process of research itself continues to provide marketers with a powerful set of symbolic values which can then be incorporated into all kinds of marketing communications. There is now an entire genre of advertising that incorporates a discourse of the research scientist in which a recently discovered formula or a latest piece of expert analysis is used to explain the benefits of particular products and services, and public relations activities often keenly point out the research-informed credentials of their responsible and forward-looking clients.

Research techniques are also important for measuring marketing effectiveness which is an important aspect of the legitimisation and justification for marketing. Publishers routinely research their readerships, both in terms of population characteristics and size in order to attract advertisers. Other uses of research in marketing include research into the perception and value of brands right down to the size of market share gains. All rely heavily on a comprehensive system of research and intelligence.

7.5 The Marketing Research Process

The prevailing representation of most marketing research instruction, whether it is applied and practice orientated or academic in nature, generally describes a *process* that is linear, sequential, progressive, objective and task orientated. In this view marketing research can be understood as a series of discrete activities (such as defining research questions, collecting data and reporting findings) which should be undertaken in a particular order so that the desired intelligence is achieved in an efficient and timely manner. This systematic and rigorous approach to organising the marketing research process is typically contrasted with *ad hoc*, informal or organic approaches to research gathering.

To illustrate the difference between these approaches let us consider a hypothetical organisation that is considering a series of brand extensions for its main brand. One of its current products has a large but stagnant market share and the marketing manager is proposing that a range of new products be developed to target a different segment of consumers. Before the manager is prepared to authorise further product development it is necessary to establish whether there is likely to be a viable segment for the proposed brand extensions, and whether any proposed new products are likely to cannibalise the existing product range.

An *ad hoc* approach to this problem might be to ask some of the sales representatives for their views on the proposals on the understanding that their everyday experiences and informal knowledge about consumer preferences and reactions are likely to provide sufficient knowledge and intelligence to be able to make an informed decision. Another approach would be for the marketing manager to look back at previous new product initiatives as well as recent activities of competitors and then make an expert judgment about the most appropriate way to proceed. The alternative to this *ad hoc* approach would be to commission a systematic study of the research problem involving the design of a programme of market research where the two issues of segment viability and likeliness of cannibalisation come to form the main research questions. A questionnaire might be developed, or a series of focus group interviews planned to provide some insights into the core issues.

Despite the various possible approaches outlined in the example, marketing research texts tend to promote a systematic and formal approach. For example, one of the most popular texts in this area, *Marketing Research: An Applied Approach* (2006) by Naresh Malhotra and David Birks, presents a schema of the research process based on this representation on page one of the first chapter and then goes on to use this to structure the rest of the text. Their schema presents marketing research as involving six stages, beginning with (1) Problem Definition, and then followed by (2) Research Approach, (3) Research Design Development, (4) Fieldwork or Data Collection, (5) Data Preparation and Analysis, and finally (6) Report Preparation and Presentation.

A formal and systematic approach to marketing research promises to supply credible, scientific data which marketing managers can use to make objective decisions to inform strategy. In practical terms it is also important for marketing professionals to be able to represent their activities and proposals as being based on reliable and sound research in order for it to appear credible and viable to others in the organisation. It is important to take into account that recommendations made by marketing managers often commit the organisation to long term investments as well as exposing it to new risks. A decision to undertake brand extension for example will probably commit an organisation to long term and substantial investment in branding activities, communications, and product development and expose it to the risks associated with new product failure, dilution of brand equity and loss of market share. For decision makers in the organisation to accept these types of investments and risks it is absolutely essential that marketing professionals are able to supply a credible justification for their proposals. For many organisations marketing research data that is thought to be systematic, scientific and objective is crucial in this regard.

It is perhaps unsurprising therefore that there is a prevailing common-sense expectation that a highly formalised approach to marketing research is preferable to *ad hoc* and informal approaches. Proponents of the systematic research method argue that it is better able to deliver objective, scientifically valid and generalisable findings and overcomes the problem of subjective, context-specific, value laden and biased research outputs which are more likely from informal and *ad hoc* approaches. The view that all good marketing research is formal marketing research is, however, open to criticism. These criticisms are based on alternative cultural values as well as arguments developed by philosophers of science.

7.6 Cultural Values and Marketing Research

This dominant approach to marketing research as a linear and systematic process has much in common with many of the other models and schemas that one might expect to find in any conventional marketing textbook. It is part of the tradition of scientific management that became very influential in North American business schools throughout the second half of the twentieth century and which has defined most approaches to marketing and marketing management up to the present day (Brown, 1995). In his cultural analysis of marketing management, Usunier (1996/7) argues that this way of thinking and representing marketing owes its origins, at least in part, to a particular cultural outlook on management. Anglo-American cultural values have tended to privilege scientific management styles which are formulaic, non-subjective and process orientated. These cultural values about marketing can, like all values, be contested because they are relative to particular cultures and spaces. To illustrate the culturally specific character of these values, Taylor et al. quote comments from three French marketing research professionals:

> I respect research but generally it's experience that tells you if it will work in France. I would say that 80% of the time we do not need tests. When I look at the ways American people approach planning – they investigate 10 ways of doing it, 'evaluating' and they enjoy it. In France we would rather say 'We think this is the way to do it, and we try it.' (Taylor et al., 1996: 6)

From a formal marketing research process perspective (an 'American' perspective) these kinds of comments are highly problematic. Such an approach to planning marketing research could be considered *ad hoc*, impressionistic, unsystematic, subjective and ill-informed. It also contradicts certain approaches to the Marketing Concept which are based on the expectation that organisations should base their strategies on a close understanding of customer needs based of careful research rather than the hunches, desires and wishes of people in organisations.

On the other hand however, those advocating the kinds of approach to research illustrated in this quote might be equally critical of the Anglo-American view which prioritises systematic styles of research. It could be argued that the need to rely on information gained via formal marketing research programmes to make decisions is indicative of a lack of necessary experience, intelligence and strategic maturity in marketing professionals. Formal systems of research can equally be criticised for being long-winded, slow, non-responsive, bureaucratic and expensive as opposed to the wisdom of an experienced marketing manager (Johansson and Nonaka, 1987). One might suggest, for example, that the very fact that an organisation insists on marketing managers commissioning research to inform their strategic decision making shows a general lack of confidence in marketing as a profession.

The point here is not to suggest that more formal systems of marketing research are necessarily any better or worse than more informal ones, but rather to acknowledge that the way alternative approaches to research are valued is heavily influenced by our cultural values about, among other things, the value of science, the status of the professional, attitudes towards formal systems of management bureaucracy, beliefs about leadership, and attitudes about consumers and markets.

7.7 Alternatives to Systematic and Formal Approaches to Marketing Research

Certain aspects of the research process must logically fall into a particular sequence. It is clearly not possible to analyse data before it has been collected or to attempt to answer research objectives before research questions have been prepared. Research conducted according to the principles of hypothetico-deduction, that is where one or a series of research hypotheses are presented and subsequently tested, demands a formal, linear and uni-directional approach to the research process.

There is, however, a strong argument to suggest that this particular view of marketing research as a formal, linear process has been overstated. In Chapter 2, we discussed the emergence of interpretive research as a response to the principles of empirical science (often termed positivism). Interpretivism should not however be thought of as a single research philosophy as such but rather as a collection of approaches to research practice. One of the practical differences between interpretivism and positivism is the way in which the research process is conceived and how this impacts on research design decisions. Some approaches to interpretive research such as Grounded Theory require researchers to enter the research field with as little prior knowledge as possible. Clearly, it is impossible to enter into research with a completely blank canvas or to bundle away prior learning. A researcher using a Grounded Theory approach sets out to loosen the connection between a predefined body of literature and the decisions on research questions, method and analysis (Glaser and Strauss, 1967). The idea behind this approach is that by having few or no specific expectations it is possible to generate theories out of the research phase itself rather than seeking to reaffirm or reject a set of pre-determined research statements or hypotheses. The goal is to follow an inductive interpretive research approach that seeks to analyse 'the actual production of meanings and concepts used by social actors in real settings' (Gephart, 2004: 457).

The research process is therefore often cyclical rather than linear. The carefully planned and prescriptive process usually found with positivist research is replaced by an experience of research that may be best described as 'emergent' (Price, 2009: 410). Decisions on the sampling and even direction of the questioning are subject to how the researcher interprets the data. Through continuous comparison of data from the various sources, the researcher codes the data to devise themes that assist in the development of provisional conceptualisations of theory (Goulding, 2002). Data collection may therefore take place before any research questions are prepared and in some extreme cases no formal questions may be produced. The researcher may move from and between data collection phases to analysis and back to data collection over a prolonged period of time. The findings from one stage of analysis may be used to re-inform the conceptual basis for the research which may then be used to structure subsequent phases of research design. The end point of the research is only reached when the process of data comparison does not generate new themes or directions and the researcher is satisfied that a robust account is offered of the context with connections between theories which will withstand the rigours of questioning (Suddaby, 2006).

There are a number of difficultles associated with this style of research. Interviewees, research ethics committees and senior management involved with a Grounded Theory research project often require considerable support from the research team. The length of time the project can take, the absence of a carefully organised schedule and clearly articulated boundaries for the research can provoke confusion and frustration for the participants (Price, 2009). The inductive approach associated with Grounded Theory can also be difficult to present using a conventional structure. Most research products take a written and printed form appearing in academic journals or as reports. The conventions of this medium tend to require that research is delivered in a linear fashion, that is, beginning with an introduction, proceeding to data and finishing with findings. But while many interpretivist styles of research projects finally appear in this format they often are not conducted in this way.

7.8 The Demands on Commercial Marketing Research

Many of the issues discussed in relation to interpetivism can appear academic and esoteric and as such it can often be difficult to see how they make any practical contribution to the business of commercial marketing research. On the surface at least it can seem that the principles of positivist/scientific research, especially the search for objective truths and non-biased results, are closer to the needs of practising marketers than the types of research produced by interpretivists. There are of course many instances where organisations continue to draw heavily on large, quantitative research programmes conducted in accordance with the priorities of a scientific method but the reality of commercial marketing research is that these types of research programmes are not sufficient in and of themselves (Catterall, 1998).

The pressures on those responsible for commissioning, selling, producing and disseminating commercial marketing research data are in many important respects not primarily concerned with issues regarding method. Commercial marketing research is generally understood in most business environments to constitute a cost, often a considerable one, and it is therefore essential that those seeking to commission research, as well as those charged with delivering the findings, are able to justify and convince the buyers of research that it is a necessary, worthwhile and beneficial course of action. One of the reasons why scientific and quantitative research became the dominant technique for approaching commercial marketing research projects is because there is a prevailing assumption among both the buyers and producers of research that this constituted the most valuable, objective and credible form of research data. Whether or not this perception is valid is difficult to assess, but what is important is that research techniques that are *believed* to be valuable and able to provide insight are likely to become more widely practised than other approaches.

Successful commercial marketing research is not only about method and technique. Researchers need to carefully gauge how their research will be received by the client organisation (Latta and Schwartz, 2004). Findings need to be presented in a convincing and understandable format which often requires the use of short executive summaries and interim reports. Inexperienced researchers can feel frustrated when they eventually come to present their findings, often after a period of careful and meticulous collection and analysis conducted under the pressure of approaching deadlines, to find that the client either fails to understand or disagrees with the conclusions and therefore dismisses the report. Poor positioning of research data has no doubt led to many expensive and lengthy marketing research reports ending up gathering dust somewhere in the marketing department or being consigned to an unopened file in the corner of a hard-drive. Marketing researchers need to always focus on delivering findings that are valuable to the client. Other issues of objectivity, methodological practice and technique are of secondary importance.

Over the last decade many marketers have become much more tolerant of nonquantitative and non-formal methods of research. There are many reasons for this. Advances in information technology have made commercial access to quantitative data far easier. Organisations find it easier and cheaper to collect or purchase off-the-shelf data than ever before, and the management of this data has become virtually automatic in many important respects thanks to innovations in computeraided analysis. One might expect that these factors would make quantitatively based approaches to research more rather than less appealing to businesses and it is clear that marketers are now able to take this type of marketing intelligence almost for granted. But as with all commodities that were once scarce and then become more commonplace, this type of research has become less valuable simply because all firms are able to access it relatively cheaply and easily. The competitive advantage that such data affords is therefore diminished and as a result marketers have looked to different ways to gather marketing research in order to gain relevant, cutting edge insights into market trends and consumer behaviour.

During the same period a range of concepts emerged and became important that demanded different types of marketing intelligence and research techniques. Marketers became increasingly aware of lifestyle as a crucial consumer behaviour variable and attention to experiential factors, especially with regard to the perception of brands and brand equity, became priorities for marketing managers (Sprott et al., 2009). Instead of being able to base research around an understanding of what consumers did or didn't do (i.e. their behaviour) or around their thoughts and feelings (i.e. their attitudes and values) marketers became increasingly interested in how consumers experienced brands, and how they incorporated products and services into their own social and cultural experiences.

It is at this point that the intentions of academic interpretivist consumer researchers and commercial marketing researchers became much more closely aligned. Intepretivists were able to argue that their methods, such as the use of in-depth interviewing, observation studies and ethnography, were better suited to these emerging questions and issues than highly formalised quantitative approaches. Interpretivism was no longer confined to a set of esoteric arguments among a small group of social science philosophers in academic marketing departments but emerged as a new, commercially valuable set of techniques that promised to give leading brand managers the edge they desperately needed to retain market position in an increasingly competitive environment (Elliott and Jankel-Elliott, 2003).

7.9 Surveillance Culture

The search for insights into human attitudes and behaviour does however need to be considered in light of concerns over the legal and moral issues surrounding privacy. The advent of the computer and digital imaging has enabled an increasing prevalence of systems which identify and capture behaviour, transform it to data and communicate these data to a series of information assemblers. Clearly, it should not be suggested that the market research industry is solely responsible for these concerns; however, when situated within broader discussions about the state, culture and surveillance, the data captured, stored and manipulated by marketers significantly contributes to a perceived sense of a 'surveillance culture' (Kershaw, 2008).

Following the terrorist attacks in the United States on 11 September 2001, many Western governments have revisited issues of national security. Within the UK the Labour Government (2005–2010) began to introduce a national identity card containing biometric data on the individual. The identity card was perceived to make the performance of the state security services slightly easier as they tackled contemporary problems of terrorism, immigration and organised crime. Media discussion of the identity cards seized upon issues of cost and the potential for identity fraud. Within many of these headlines was a questioning of how the introduction of a bio-metric identity card will impact on an individual's liberty and privacy. The UK Information Commissioner, Richard Thomas argued that the country could 'sleepwalk into a surveillance society' (Ford, 2004).

Whilst it is quite easy to slip into analogies with George Orwell's totalitarian society depicted in *1984*, it is essential that any consideration of market research is undertaken with an appreciation of how it contributes to the debates on individual privacy and the cultural context in which we live. The role of technology in infringing on privacy is usually central to debates on surveillance. In common parlance, surveillance is a sense of watching, being watched, an act of monitoring. Thus we tend to think about CCTV images in our streets and shops and in the process we become preoccupied with what might be described as a voyeuristic aspect of surveillance. As Lyon notes, this is a partial understanding. To remedy this, Lyon offers the following definition of surveillance as: 'any collection and processing of personal data, whether identifiable or not, for the purposes of influencing or managing those whose data have been garnered' (Lyon, 2001: 2).

Lyon's definition encourages a fuller appreciation of surveillance, in which it becomes necessary to view both the means by which data is gathered but also how this data is used to influence behaviour. Thus, data gathered for market research purposes, whether it is through a questionnaire, focus group or hidden camera is not collected to simply fill space on a hard drive. It is collated, processed and distributed for the purposes of influencing the behaviour of those being monitored. Within discussions of 'surveillance theory' (Brocklehurst, 2001: 446), the perception of being under surveillance produces affects on behaviour as individuals seek to respond to the sense of being watched. This idea is neatly demonstrated by discussions of the Panopticon.

The Panopticon or the inspection house was proposed by the legal reformer Jeremy Bentham in 1787. It was an idea manifested through architectural design allowing the building to become an inspection machine (Bentham, 1995). This was to be applied to public buildings such as prisons, hospitals and schools where those subject to inspection could be seen at all times by an inspector without those being inspected being able to see the inspector. This was achieved through a radial design in which the inspected were located in cells surrounding the circumference whilst the inspector was located in the centre. For Foucault writing nearly 200 years later, the panopticon illuminated the centrality of power within architecture. He writes:

> Hence the major effect of the Panopticon: to induce in the inmate a state of conscious and permanent visibility that assures the automatic functioning of power. So to arrange things that the surveillance is permanent in its effects, even if it is discontinuous in its action; that the perfection of power should tend to render its actual exercise unnecessary; that this architectural apparatus should be a machine for creating and sustaining a power relation independent of the person who exercises it; in short, that the inmates should be caught up in a power situation of which they are themselves the bearers. (Foucault, 1991: 201)

Foucault usefully identifies the relationship between surveillance and power – rather than power being exerted by the inspector, the exercise of power results in self-disciplining behaviours where individuals change their behaviour to respond to a perceived sense that they are being watched.

Surveillance can be of performance (for instance the speed and pattern of a shopping exercise in a retail outlet), it can be of behaviour, the products an individual purchases over time or personal characteristics (a person's height, weight or preferences). Technology has provided far greater possibilities for surveillance. The means by which this surveillance is undertaken can be through some quite novel tools. In Japan, Toto, Japan's largest toilet company have introduced the 'Intelligence Toilet' [*sic*] system (Howell, 2009), which provides information on a person's health, such as sugar levels in urine, blood pressure, body fat and weight. Supermarkets are experimenting with retina and thumb scans in store to identify shoppers, link their behaviour from past purchases and manipulate this data to provide suitable promotional offers to the individual's mobile phones whilst they shop. The astute reader will have spotted that the body is the site of surveillance here rather than loyalty cards. Unlike loyalty cards which can be shared between people, forgotten or lost, the body provides a useful surface through which identity can be constructed. Researchers searching for insights into the consumer's true views on products and promotions are using magnetic resonance imaging (mri) to examine how the consumer's brain chemically experiences the engagement with marketing (Hedgcock and Rao, 2009).

Not all surveillance is focused on the body and instead relies upon constructing an identity based upon where we are resident, information on incomes and household composition or behaviour. A useful example of this can be seen with the use of the internet. When shopping online we frequently disclose information about ourselves without realising (Charters, 2002). This information can include our IP address so website owners can see the location of the computer, its operating system, the recent pages the visitor has visited, the pages visited on the site, the order visited and time spent. When this data is linked to login or membership information, the behaviour can be tied to an individual and webpages customised to appeal to the representation of the individual. Amazon the online retailer for example provides information on what other visitors are currently looking at, whilst providing personalised recommendations based upon past purchase behaviour and profile information. Amazon can collate these user statistics to monitor their website and generate user profiles whilst the visitor may wish to manage their behaviour to represent themselves in a positive light.

7.10 The Emergence of Market Information Systems

The preceding sections have highlighted the vast quantities of information available to the modern marketer. Although the single market research programme remains an important part of the marketing research industry, it is increasingly overshadowed by the advent of what are broadly termed Marketing Information Systems (MIS). On-going developments in computer storage and processing capacity have meant that organisations could retain much larger quantities of information about markets and consumers. Over time these data could be used to identify trends and base forecasts. As capacity continued to improve, organisations were able to respond to competitive pressures by looking to integrate different types of intelligence and research. An integrated MIS allows organisations to use research for a variety of different marketing related purposes.

EPOS technology was originally used to help retailers improve distribution and inventory efficiencies but as the technology developed it was possible to link this to a system of sales promotion. Loyalty schemes provide marketers with valuable data about consumer behaviour but the data from these schemes can also be used as the basis for customer relationship management initiatives (Rigby and Ledingham, 2004). The extension of EPOS to incorporate consumer behaviour relating to sales promotion is just one example of how consumer information has been provided beyond conventional market research tools. The tools of surveillance which were present to monitor the goods in the distribution chain are increasingly being extended to incorporate the monitoring of consumers. Radio Tags (RFID) were originally designed to monitor the movement of goods between manufacturer and retailer. Increasingly marketers are exploring how RFID can be extended to incorporate consumer use of the product (Kelly and Erickson, 2005).

RFID however is just one way in which the producer can monitor product use. Increasingly products are being designed to link the user to the producer electronically and so provide producers with information on their users. Firms such as Microsoft incorporate monitoring devices into its software to enable validation and software updates whilst discouraging piracy. This has required the development of extensive privacy guidelines for programmers and users to offset claims that an individual's privacy is being eroded. Like Microsoft, many producers suggest that the collection of user information enables them to customise the product to the user's behaviour. The trade off between user information release and user benefits is perhaps most marked in the field of motor insurance. Insurance companies such as Norwich Union have trialled motor insurance policies that incorporate global positioning satellite information in the calculation of the premium (Osborne, 2006). Occasionally referred to as a 'Pay as you Drive' scheme (Anonymous, 2004), the policyholder only pays for the frequency, location and timing of when they drive. The GPS device is located in the vehicle relaying information on the movement of the car to the insurer.

The development of technology and its employment for marketing purposes has enabled the generation, collection and retrieval of copious quantities of information, often inadvertently. If we recall Foucault, the power of surveillance lies in the way the individual self-regulates their behaviour to conform to the required condition. This may be for instance in policing their own online behaviour, driving to the speed limit or consuming items to satisfy their desired representation of their identity. Whilst appreciating the role of surveillance in generating compliance, the willingness of individuals to perhaps resist or refashion their self in opposition to such surveillance practices is also significant. Acts of resistance can include providing incorrect data on loyalty card applications, deliberately swapping loyalty cards amongst friends to confuse the data algorithms or blocking the transfer of data from the product to the producer (Terdiman, 2003).

Consumer Fightback

The use of the internet has become a popular means by which those aggrieved by corporate behaviour can showcase this behaviour and encourage collective action. There are numerous examples of such websites, several of which are listed below. Perhaps the most famous and longest running example is McDonald's protest. http://www. mcspotlight.org/

http://www.virginaircrewlies.com/
http://www.aviation-uk.com/index.html
http://www.webgripesites.com/

The power relationship is not necessarily in one direction (as will be discussed in greater length in Chapter 8). Whilst the organisation may use techniques of surveillance with consumers, employees and members of the supply chain as a means of control, those subject to the surveillance regime are able to use these methods against the organisation through hacking, whistleblowing or disinformation. Many international companies are subject to consumer-devised blogs and websites where individuals share information on their experience with that company. This is sometimes referred to as consumer-generated media (Trufelman, 2005) and provides a popular forum for word-of-mouth exchanges on such issues as customer service, product quality and the latest promotional deals.

Market researchers can clearly tap into this information and participate in discussion forums either overtly or covertly to generate debate on key research questions (see for example http://www.trendsspotting.com/blog/). The sharing of information by consumers however is not always about producers or retailers. The ability for consumers to monitor the behaviour of other consumers is also a noticeable trend. A blog offers the writer an opportunity to offer stories on their experience of their life. Accordingly, blogs will often report on the behaviour of neighbours, fellow shoppers or partners.

The role of marketing, marketing information and market research in the construction of a 'surveillance society' is usually overlooked by writers of textbooks. There is a moral issue here that marketers will increasingly need to address, namely for what purpose are the technologies and practices used, to what end, on whom and for who's benefit? The last 20 years has seen a proliferation in the type, quality and quantity of information available on consuming behaviour. Market research rests ultimately on the willingness of consumers to divulge information on their behaviour for the overall benefit of more effective and efficient products and services.

This level of trust is increasingly challenged, with many consumers being reluctant to take part in focus groups and surveys. A number of individuals are seeing the value that organisations place on information, some of these individuals are performing as professional respondents and participating in research activities for personal gain (Gillin and Sheppard, 2003). One thing is quite clear, in many developed countries the individual subject of research is fully aware of the value of their involvement and is expecting to accrue some benefit from the research process, whether that is status, entertainment or financial – the days of blindly filling in a customer survey for the benefit of the marketer are coming to an end.

7.11 Conclusion

In this chapter we have sought to provide the reader with an account of how marketing research has developed as a practice and as an industry. The ideological role of marketing research in the support of the marketing concept has been presented with an explanation of how the development of the marketing discipline has been influential in the techniques and philosophy of research.

The marketer is seemingly faced with a sisyphean responsibility. This is a continuous task of data accumulation involving the shifting through data sets for insights to help hone promotions, products and services. This both serves to fulfil the demand of a market orientation but also offers moral support and justification for the collection and generation of data about individuals. New technologies have greatly assisted marketers in the speed, variety and quality of the collection, collation and analysis of the data. This has enabled marketing researchers to obtain a wider range of more detailed data on consumers and their habits. This we suggest raises important social and cultural issues for the performance of marketing research.

The scale of the information accumulated on individual and aggregated behaviour provokes concern about individual privacy. Within this chapter we have framed this concern through the idea of a 'surveillance culture'. The surveillance can be presented as a means to spot and address deviant behaviour, however fewer aspects of everyday mundane life are free from observation and recording (Lyon, 2002). This can lead to new product opportunities such as the case of 'pay as you drive' motor insurance, which we highlighted in the chapter. It has also however enabled the development of an industry driven by databases in which consumer data is digitised and traded. Subjected to statistical packages, this data offers simulations of a market allowing marketing managers to predict and profile the customer that may desire the product or conversely, in the case of banking, the level of risk associated with the customer (Zwick and Denegri-Knott, 2009).

The commoditisation of customer information has been an aspect throughout the history of the development of market research. With the quantity and quality of customer information becoming more apparent to customers and citizens, the questions surrounding power and trust, qualities integral in the relationship between researchers and the researched, perhaps take on a new immediacy.

7.12 Learning Activities

Discussions of marketing research within marketing textbooks tend to concentrate on the benefits that the technologies of research offer marketers and consumers in tailoring product offerings to meet customer needs. This is only a partial appreciation of marketing research. In this chapter we examine the origins of marketing research and how these origins have helped shape the industry. We also explore the role that marketing research plays in shaping the norms and values within a society. The Learning Activities below provide you with an opportunity to both apply methodologies and methods of marketing research whilst also looking at how information can be used by organisations to model behaviour. Before you begin the learning activities remind yourself of the learning aims for the chapter so that your time and efforts are focused.

Learning Activity One: Reconstructing Loyal Customers

Many firms in both the business to consumer and business to business sectors offer loyalty cards to reward repeat purchasing amongst their customers. You will have read in the chapter how the capture of data from loyal customers is also subject to concerns about privacy. In this learning activity we want you to establish just what data the organisation can capture from the consumer who uses a reward card. To do this you will need to identify a loyalty card system. Most loyalty card systems require the individual to 'sign up' or 'apply'. You are required to review the data collected during the application process and then consider how through the use of this loyalty card the organisation can combine the personal data with the behavioural data to produce a longtitudinal snapshot of the person and their behaviour. To what extent does this collection of data provide a full representation of the individual?

Learning Activity Two: Creative but Effective Research Wanted

If you talk to many market research executives, part of the pleasure of working in this role is the ability to develop creative but effective approaches to research that will help mangers to make an important decision. This can often involve conceiving of a problem in novel and multifaceted ways. In this Learning Activity we want to give you the opportunity to consider how you might construct a research project when confronted with a managerial problem.

Your brief is to produce a plan of research which helps managers at a leading automotive manufacturer to decide upon the range of engines it will offer to its customers in its new version of a sports utility vehicle (SUV). The current vehicle has a strong brand following and it is renowned in this category for the quality of its handling and its sporting drive. The vehicle is to be relaunched in the near future, and in line with the manufacturer's broader concerns with the environment, the manufacturer wishes to focus on the vehicles minimal impact on the environment (CO_2), low fuel consumption (MPG) whilst retaining the appeal of the sportiness of its drive and handling.

The managers want a plan of research which examines how customers would feel and behave should the manufacturer replace the high powered diesel and petrol engines with a range of lower powered hybrid engines for this vehicle. When developing your plan consider what the problem is that the managers wish to address, what information they need to inform their decision and how you will collect this information.

7.13 Further Reading

On the History of Market Research

Schwarzkopf, S. (2009) 'Discovering the consumer: Market research, product innovation, and the creation of brand loyalty in Britain and the United States in the interwar years', *Journal of Macromarketing*, 29 (1): 8–20.

In this article, Schwarzkopf explores whether the practices of market research and the concern with lifestyle emerged earlier than the academic literature in marketing suggests. The paper focuses on the relationship between Lever conglomerate and its international advertising agency J. Walter Thompson (JWT). In the process it provides a rich and compelling account of how the market research industry emerged and its role as an innovation in management thinking.

On Global Market Research

Douglas, S. P. and Craig, C. (2006) 'On improving the conceptual foundations of international marketing research', *Journal of International Marketing*, 14 (1): 1–22.

Within this section we introduce the idea that undertaking research internationally poses issues which are distinct from domestic market research. In this article Douglas and Craig outline how the ideas of emic and etic expose questions on the assumptions being carried into cross cultural research. The authors discuss the idea of 'decentering the research perspective' to remove the dominant culture or philosophy which underlies the research design.

On the Research Process

Shaw, E. (1999) 'A guide to the qualitative research process: evidence from a small firm study', *Qualitative Market Research: An International Journal*, 2 (2): 59–70.

The process of market research is often presented in a formal and linear manner in textbooks and there is an assumption that all organisations will adopt this approach. Shaw, in the article above, questions the applicability and appropriateness of this approach when undertaking research in small business enterprises.

On Interpretive Research

Cova, B. and Elliott, R. (2008) 'Everything you always wanted to know about interpretive consumer research but were afraid to ask', *Qualitative Market Research: An International Journal*, 11 (2): 121–9.

This is the introduction to a guest edited issue of *Qualitative Market Research: An International Journal*. The introduction provides students with an outline of the development of interpretive research in marketing and outlines some of the debates surrounding the origins, development and applicability of interpretive consumer research.

On Marketing Information Systems

Brady, M., Saren, M. and Tzokas, N. (2002) 'Integrating information technology into marketing practice – the IT reality of contemporary marketing practice', *Journal of Marketing Management*, 18 (5/6 July): 555–78.

Technology is central to marketing practice and in this article by Brady et al., the need to view technology through a holistic lens, above and beyond merely research is espoused. The need for marketers to appreciate how technology is not merely a tool but is fundamental to the very conceptualisation of marketing is discussed. In outlining the stages and assimilation of IT in marketing, the authors consider the implications for the marketer and the industry.

On Surveillance and Research

Smith, A. and Sparks, L. (2004) 'All about Eve?', *Journal of Marketing Management*, 20: 363–85.

Within this section we discuss at some length the tensions of loyalty and privacy that are entwined in the retailer reward card systems. In this article by Smith and Sparks, the authors pick one individual from a record of loyalty card records and analyse her 1,551 product purchase transactions over a two year period. Having labelled this individual 'Eve' the authors proceed to ask what a retailer (and academics) can learn from this behavioural data and the tensions between aggregate data and individual data analysis.

7.14 References

Abrams, M. (1977) 'Social research and market research: The case of Paul Lazarsfeld', *Journal of the Market Research Society*, 19 (1): 12–17.

Alderson, W. (1956) 'Charles Coolidge Parlin', *Journal of Marketing*, 21 (1): 1–2.

Anonymous (2004) 'Could pay-as-you-drive insurance work?', available online at http://news.bbc.co.uk/1/hi/magazine/3574010.stm, accessed 27 March 2008.

Arvidsson, A. (2004) 'On the 'pre-history of the panoptic sort': Mobility in market research', *Surveillance & Society*, 1 (4): 456–74.

Ball, K. and Webster, F. (eds) (2003) *The Intensification of Surveillance: Crime, Terrorism and Warfare in the Information Era*. London: Pluto Press.

Bartels, R. (1988) *The History of Marketing Thought*, 3rd edn. Columbus: Publishing Horizons.

Bentham, J. (1995) 'Panopticon or the Inspection House', in M. Bozovic (ed.) '*The Panopticon Writings*, pp. 29–95. London: Verso.

Berinsky, A. J. (2006) 'American public opinion in the 1930s and 1940s', *Public Opinion Quarterly*, 70 (4): 499–529.

Bonsu, S.K and Darmody, A. (2008) 'Co-creating second life: Market-consumer cooperation in contemporary economy', *Journal of Macromarketing*, 28 (4): 355–68.

Bourdieu, P. (1984). *Distinction*. London: Routledge.

Brockkhurst, M. (2001) 'Power, identify and new technology homework: Implications for "new forms" of organizing', *Organization studies*, 22 (3): 445–66.

Brown, S. (1995) *Postmodern Marketing*. London: Routledge.

Bulik, B.S., (2005) 'Cool hunting goes corporate', *Advertising Age*, 76 (31): 3–26.

Catterall, M. (1998) 'Academics, practitioners and qualitative market research', *Qualitative Market Research: An International Journal*, 1 (2): 69–76.

Charters, D. (2002) 'Electronic monitoring and privacy issues in business-marketing: The ethics of the doubleclick experience', *Journal of Business Ethics*, 35: 243–54.

Chaston, I., Badger, B. and Sadler-Smith, E. (2000) 'Organizational learning style and competences', *European Journal of Marketing*, 34 (5/6): 625–42.

Cooper, S., and Owen, D. (2007) 'Corporate social reporting and stakeholder accountability: The missing link', *Accounting, Organizations & Society*, 32 (7/8): 649–67.

Elliott, R. and Jankel-Elliott, N. (2003) 'Using ethnography in strategic consumer research', *Qualitative Market Research: An International Journal*, 6 (4): 215–23.

Ford, R. (2004) 'Beware rise of Big Brother state, warns data watchdog', available online at http://www.timesonline.co.uk/tol/news/uk/article470264.ece, accessed/January 2010.

Foucault, M. (1991) *Discipline and Punish*. Harmondsworth: Penguin.

Gallup, G. (1966) 'Polls and the political process – past, present, and future', *Public Opinion Quarterly*, 29 (4): 544–50.

Gephart, R. P. (2004) 'Qualitative research and the Academy of Management Journal', *Academy of Management Journal*, 47 (4): 454–62.

Gillin, D.L. and Sheppard, J. (2003) 'The fallacy of "getting paid for your opinions"', *Marketing Research*, 15 (3): 8.

Glaser, B. G. and Strauss, A.L. (1967) *The Discovery of Grounded Theory: Strategies for Qualitative Research*. New York: Aldine.

Goulding, C. (2002). *Grounded Theory: A Practical Guide for Management, Business and Market Researchers*. London: Sage.

Hanson, J.H. (2001) 'Breaking the cycle of marketing disinvestment: Using market research to build organisational alliances', *International Journal of Nonprofit and Voluntary Sector Marketing*, 6(1): 33–49.

Hedgcock, W. and Rao, A.R. (2009) 'Trade-off aversion as an explanation for the attraction effect: A functional Magnetic Resonance Imaging study', *Journal of Marketing Research*, 46 (1): 1–13.

Howell, D.D. (2009) 'The riddle of the smart machines', *TechTrends*, 54 (1): 33–7.

Janssen, K.L. and Dankbaar, B. (2008) 'Proactive involvement in innovation: Selecting appropriate techniques', *International Journal of Innovation Management*, 12 (3): 511–41.

Jeřábek, H. (2001) 'Paul Lazarsfeld – the founder of modern empirical sociology: A research biography', *International Journal of Public Opinion Research*, 13 (3): 229–58.

Johansson, J.K. and Nonaka, I. (1987) 'Market research the Japanese way', *Harvard Business Review*, 65(3): 16–19.

Kelly, E.P. and Erickson, G.S. (2005) 'RFID tags: commercial applications v. privacy rights', *Industrial Management & Data Systems*, 105 (6): 703–13.

Kershaw, S. (2008) 'Culture of surveillance may contribute to delusional condition', available online at http://www.iht.com/articles/2008/08/30/arts/truman.php, accessed 26 March 2009.

Latta, M. and Schwartz, B. (2004) 'Creating satisfied clients', *Marketing Research*, 16 (2): 26–31.

Lavidge, R.J. (1990) 'Seven tested ways to abuse and misuse strategic advertising research', *Marketing Research*, 2 (1): 41–8.

Lyon, D. (2001) *Surveillance Society: Monitoring Everyday Life*. Buckingham and Phildelphia, PA: Open University Press.

Lyon, D. (2002) 'Everyday surveillance: Personal data and social classifications', *Information, Communication and Society*, 5 (2): 242–57.

MacLachlan, D.L. and Johansson, J.K. (1981) 'Market segmentation with multivariate aid', *Journal of Marketing*, 45 (1): 74–84.

Malhotra, N. K. and Birks, D. (2006) *Marketing Research: An Applied Approach*, 3rd edn. London: FT Prentice Hall.

Maxwell, R. (1996) 'Out of kindness and into difference: the value of global market research', *Media Culture and Society,* 18: 105–26.

Nancarrow, C., Vir, J. and Barker, A. (2005) 'Ritzer's McDonaldization and applied qualitative marketing research', *Qualitative Market Research: An International Journal*, 8 (3): 296–311.

Osborne, H. (2006) 'Norwich Union offers 'pay as you drive' insurance', available online at http://www.guardian.co.uk/money/2006/oct/05/business.motorinsurance, accessed 27 March 2009.

Pace, S. (2008) 'YouTube: An opportunity for consumer narrative analysis?', *Qualitative Market Research: An International Journal*, 11 (2): 213–26.

Packard, V. (1960) *The Hidden Persuaders*. London: Penguin.

Price, D. (2009) 'Grounded theory', in S. Cameron and D. Price (eds), *Business Research Methods: A Practical Approach*, pp. 409–25. London: McGraw Hill.

Rigby, D.K. and Ledingham, D. (2004) 'CRM done right', *Harvard Business Review*, 82 (11): 118–29.

Robinson, D.J (1999) *The Measure of Democracy: Polling, Market Research, and Public Life, 1930–1945*. Toronto: University of Toronto Press.

Rothwell, N.D (1955) Motivational Research Revisited. *Journal of Marketing*, 20 (2), 150–154.

Sørensen, H.E. (2009) 'Why competitors matter for market orientation', *European Journal of Marketing*, 43 (5/6): 735–61.

Sprott, D. Czellar, S. and Spangenberg, E. (2009) 'The importance of a general measure of brand engagement on market behavior: Development and validation of a scale', *Journal of Marketing Research*, 46 (1): 92–104.

Squire, P. (1988) 'Why the 1936 Literary Digest Poll failed', *Public Opinion Quarterly*, 52 (1): 125–33.

Suddaby, R. (2006) 'From the editors: What grounded theory is not', *Academy of Management Journal*, 40 (4): 633–42.

Swinburn, A. (2005) 'CEOs continue to be unimpressed by marketers' skills', *B&T Weekly*, 54 (2530): 4.

Tadajewski, M. (2009) 'Eventalizing the marketing concept', *Journal of Marketing Management*, 25 (1/2): 191–217.

Tan, T.T.W. and Lui, T.J. (2002) 'Globalization and trends in international marketing research in Asia', *Journal of Business Research*, 55 (10): 799–804.

Taylor, R.B., Hoy, M.G. and Haley, E. (1996) 'How French advertising professionals develop creative strategy', *Journal of Advertising*, 25 (1): 1–14.

Terdiman, D. (2003) 'Gaming the Safeway Club Card', available online at http://www.wired.com/techbiz/media/news/2003/07/59589, accessed 26 March 2009.

Trufelman, L.P. (2005) 'Consumer-generated media – challenges and opportunities for public relations', *Public Relations Tactics*, 12 (5): 17–27.

Tynan, A.C. and Drayton, J. (1987) 'Market segmentation', *Journal of Marketing Management*, 2 (3): 301–35.

Usunier, J.-C. (1996/7) 'Atomistic versus organic approaches', *International Studies of Management & Organization*, 26 (4): 90–112.

Vecchio, D. E. (1991) 'Market research as a continuous process', *Journal of Consumer Marketing*, 8 (1): 53–9.

Ward, D.B. (2009a) 'Capitalism, early market research, and the creation of the American consumer', *Journal of Historical Research in Marketing*, 1 (2): 200–23.

Ward, D.B. (2009b) *A New Brand of Business: Curtis Publishing Company and the Origins of Market Research*, 1911–1930. Philadelphia, PA: Temple University Press.

Webster Jr., F. E. (1994) 'Executing the new marketing concept', *Marketing Management*, 3 (1): 8–16.

Winters, L. C. (1989) 'SRI announces VALS 2', *Marketing Research*, 1 (2): 67–9.

Zwick, D. and Denegri-Knott, J.D. (2009) 'Manufacturing customers', *Journal of Consumer Culture*, 9 (2): 221–47.

Consumer Rights and Resistance

8

8.1 Introduction

Many writers argue that the philosophy of the market is in itself a good way to promote and achieve fairness and freedom for individuals. If consumers don't like the products or services offered by one firm they are free to switch to what they see as a better option. Over time, the market mechanism will mean that better firms will survive and weaker, less efficient ones will fail. By making choices in line with their own interests and preferences, consumers unknowingly work together to make the marketplace efficient and free. Even the biggest and most powerful organisations much obey this 'invisible hand' and in this context, marketing performs an important role in achieving social equality and democracy. For many consumers however, this philosophy does not always seem to work in practice. Critics of the free market have shown that markets often produce undesirable outcomes for consumers, arguing that there is an essential requirement for markets to be regulated and controlled. Individual consumers can often appear relatively weak compared to the power of large global organisations and need other ways of representing and protecting their rights than that offered by the principles of the free market alone. As markets and marketing have developed and become more influential so too have movements which try to limit this influence in some way. Some of these movements are organised to help consumers 'resist' the market or to try and develop alternatives to market based society and its powerful corporations.

The statistics below illustrate the magnitude of corporate influence with a small number of them not only responsible for more economic activity than a large number of nation states, but also growing and thus increasing their power notably in relation to national governments.

The Power of Corporations

1 Of the 100 largest economies in the world, 51 are corporations; only 49 are countries (based on a comparison of corporate sales and country GDPs).
2 The Top 200 corporations' sales are growing at a faster rate than overall global economic activity. Between 1983 and 1999, their combined sales grew from the equivalent of 25.0 per cent to 27.5 per cent of World GDP.
3 The Top 200 corporations' combined sales are bigger than the combined economies of all countries minus the biggest 10.

4   The Top 200s' combined sales are 18 times the size of the combined annual income of the 1.2 billion people (24 per cent of the total world population) living in 'severe' poverty.
5   While the sales of the Top 200 are the equivalent of 27.5 per cent of world economic activity, they employ only 0.78 per cent of the world's workforce.
6   Between 1983 and 1999, the profits of the Top 200 firms grew 362.4 per cent, while the number of people they employ grew by only 14.4 per cent.

Go to the website below and view the remainder of the statistics presented.

Source: http://www.globalissues.org/article/59/corporate-power-facts-and-stats

Such growing corporate influence can be viewed as having a number of problematic consequences. Naomi Klein's (2000) *No Logo*, for instance, has charged corporations and specifically their marketing and branding activities with the casualisation of workforces in post-industrial economies, the erosion of public space by private interest, and more broadly the undermining of civic rights. These contemporary charges against corporate power are just the latest episode in a wider history of criticism of capitalism and industry. As noted in Chapters 1 and 2, the history of marketing and advertising has been accompanied by a parallel history of academic criticism (associated for instance with Critical Theory) and popular anti-corporate protest across the globe.

Such issues of corporate power and protest bring with them important questions about consumers. First, to what extent are corporations, and their marketing, branding and advertising activities, all-powerful and pernicious societal institutions? And, more importantly in this chapter, to what extent are consumers powerless victims of the market, as suggested by so-called 'deterministic' accounts of social relations? Second, what are the possibilities for consumers to 'escape' corporations and the market, and to resist some of its more negative outcomes? Our goal in unpacking these questions through the course of this chapter is to present you with more 'active' views of the consumer that include ideas of resistance, escape or freedom from the market. Or, to use more academic language, our interest is in understanding consumer agency in the context of the structural constraints presented by markets and corporate activities.

8.2 Structure, Agency and Consumption

We begin by outlining a framework you can use to address these questions about the relationship between producers (that is, corporations, marketers and so on) and consumers. The framework consists of two key elements. The first element comprises theoretical material from the work of Karl Marx and from the Frankfurt School of Critical Theory (already described in Chapter 2) which provide different accounts of what we might mean by 'structural constraints'. The second element is drawn from the work of British sociologist Alan Aldridge who presents us with different images of the consumer. We select two of the four images he describes to outline and discuss 'consumer agency', and its relationship to the market. Let's begin with Marx.

In thinking about the relationship between producers and consumers, one view is that consumption is a direct and dependent outcome of production. In other words, all our choices as consumers, and the meaning of the objects and services we consume, are determined by the actions and activities of marketers, advertisers, corporations and other types of 'producer'. From this viewpoint, consumption is determined by production – and consuming behaviour is a function of the structural constraints fabricated by producers. There are at least two ways to think about what these structural constraints are, and why they might be a problem.

Karl Marx's description and criticism of the nature of the British economy in the nineteenth century remains highly relevant for understanding capitalist economies. He argued in Volume 1 of his famous text *Capital* that the manner in which production processes were organised (that is, how key factors of production, notably land and labour, were brought together to serve the interests of the capitalist) in the industrialising economy of the nineteenth century involved an inequitable relationship between the capitalist and the labourer. For Marx, as products are made for the market – and thus accrue exchange value rather than simply use value (see Box below) – the worker becomes alienated from the fruits of their labour. That is to say, whilst pre-capitalist modes of production involved individuals making things for their own and immediate use at home, and perhaps exchanging them for goods made by others at local markets, the capitalist system creates a vast market where money provides a measure of equivalence between objects that allows them to be valued in terms of each other and then exchanged. In the process, the person that owns the thing you have produced is not known to you.

What is Really Meant by 'Market Value'?

Karl Marx explains in *Capital* (1976, first published in German as *Das Kapital* in 1867) that the 'market' through which goods and services are sold at a price is not a natural and permanent state of things but the outcome of changing social dynamics. There is a range of different systems through which human needs can be satiated, however for Marx, it is the transformation of the commodity which helps to define the socio-economic environment. Marx explains this transformation in terms of the change from use value to exchange value.

For Marx, all commodities are products of social relations, outputs of an individual's labour. Use value concerns the properties of the commodity and the need or desire that the commodity fulfils – it is the *value in use* of the commodity. Through the preconditions of trade, private property rights and market demand, the commodity is imbued with exchange value that enables it to be traded for other commodities. Exchange value manifests itself as wholly independent from use value – thus the value of the commodity is determined less by what it can do and who made it and more by the value it can accrue relative to other commodities. For Marx, the replacement of use value by exchange value changes the nature of the relationship between the individual and the broader society due to the centrality of the commodity in structural constraints.

The worker and the consumer are key subjects in Marx's account of structural relations, tied together in the figure of the commodity (the product or service) and to the owner of the resources necessary for the production of that commodity. As workers, our social position is determined by the fact that we are forced to sell our labour in order to acquire money and resources to support ourselves and our dependents. The *value* of the labour is not determined by the skills and energies of the worker, but by the demand and market rate for the skills offered by the worker. The worker thereby loses control of the value of their labour to the market but in return receives a weekly wage or monthly salary. This compensation moves workers into the role of consumers, as they look for leisure and entertainment outside work, but here again the commodity plays a debilitating role.

Marx talks about 'commodity fetishism' to point to the manner in which commodities place a veil over the source and origins of their production. As Fine and Saad-Filho (2004: 25–6) explain, Marx:

> draws the brilliant parallel between commodity fetishism and feudal religious devotion. God is humanity's own creation. Under feudalism, human relationships with God conceal and justify the actual relationship to fellow beings, an absurd bond of exploitation as it appears to the bourgeois (capitalist) mind. Capitalism, however, has its own God and bible. The relationship of exchange between things is also created by people, concealing the true relationship of exploitation and justifying this by the doctrine of freedom of exchange.

Commodities take on a life of their own; they confront the individual without recognition of the toil of the labourer but as goods of themselves and for themselves. The result is to conceal the inequitable social relationships of production that made their manufacture possible in the first place. Consumers are thus involved in the reproduction of a system which not only exploits their own productive capacities, according to Marx, but in their role as consumers, exploits and facilitates the alienation of other labourers who are producing commodities for them. All the while, the capitalist – the producer – is benefiting from individuals who first sell their labour time and then use their wages to buy things that perpetuate an asymmetrical system. Consumers might be considered as ideological victims of the system, seemingly blind to their exploitation of self and others.

Whilst Marx's ideas can provide us with an understanding of structural constraints rooted in the capitalist economic system, and associated with the exploitative relationship between capital and labour, Critical Theory (CT) can be said to offer a more *culturally driven* account (though one still sympathetic to a Marxist position). A CT perspective can be viewed to emphasise how structural constraints are reproduced in the realm of culture, especially popular culture. A particular concern for CT is how the logic of commodification, typically associated with goods and physical objects, had been progressively extended to incorporate the arts and leisure industries by the early twentieth century in Western Europe and the USA. The exploitative realities and ideological role performed by consumer culture noted by Marx came to be played out now in the cultural realm, especially through the emergence of producers of culture, such as music companies. The goal of CT is to present a systematic critique of these social conditions and to overcome the cultural domination it involves. As a producer of 'culture', marketing can also be subjected to CT analysis, as noted in earlier chapters.

For theorists such as Marcuse (1968) and Packard (1960), the goal of marketing is to set out to understand the cause/effect relationships that can be employed to produce emotional commitment to goods and services. In other words, to create a psychological and emotional dependence between the consumer and the commodity, and to encourage consumers to act in ways that they realise might well fly in the face of their own best interests. Marketing's dominant methodology is the reduction of individuals to 'consumers' characterised purely through standardised character traits. But we do not build up individual personalities through consumer durables – at best we can only say that we are producing self-images that are pseudo-individualistic. Adorno and Horkheimer (1947: 123) spoke specifically of this process:

> Marked differentiations such as those of A and B Films, or of stories in magazines in different price ranges, depend not so much on subject matter as on classifying, organizing and labelling consumers. Something is provided for all so that no one can escape; the distinctions are emphasised and extended. The public is catered for with a hierarchical range of mass produced products of varying quality, thus advancing the rule of complete quantification. Everybody must behave (as if spontaneously) in accordance with his previously determined and indexed level, and choose the category of mass product turned out for his type. Consumers appear as statistics on research organization charts, and are divided by income groups into red, green and blue area; the technique that is used for any type of propaganda. (Adorno and Horkheimer, 1947: 123)

For writers such as Adorno and Horkheimer, the structural dynamics of capitalism resulted in a representation of the consumer's attitudes and behaviour largely shaped by the demands of capitalism. They suggested that the proliferation of sites for leisure and consumption activities increased the capacity for the ideological control, domination and manipulation of consumers by producers. As with Marx, consumption became an outcome of production, and consumers' behaviour was aligned and determined by capitalists' activities with problematic consequences. The increasing uptake of commodified social relations results in a separation of the population from alternative and more 'authentic' social relations as well as a distortion of the authentic nature and meaning of objects. Culture, in the form of art or music, was being produced in increasingly standardised ways, 'manufactured' in the same manner as other commodities. The resultant creation of a 'mass' and debased culture was, for Adorno and Horkheimer, accompanied by passive, superficial, distracted and 'vulgar' modes of consumption.

When we talk about 'structural constraints' on consumption, then, we can imagine them either in terms of relations of production or the nature and impact of culture industries. In more recent times, a collection of disparate social cause groups have focused their attention on issues of globalisation, transnational capitalism and consumerism (Starr, 2000), opposing many of the dark sides of capitalism forewarned by Marx and CT. The globalisation of capital and the power of corporations are deemed by these groups to have negative consequences for democracy, social welfare and the environment. Within these concerns is an emphasis on the transitional nature of capitalism and the necessity for action to place checks and balances on corporate behaviour. Monbiot (2000) argues that the fight for power in the twenty-first century is between people and the corporations; at stake within this power struggle is liberal democracy. Protestors fearing the limited power of the state to balance corporate power are encouraging a notion of civic responsibility and civil disobedience as a means to bring attention to the power struggle. Against this context, how might we begin to talk about the consumer? Are we still, if we ever were, passive 'victims of the system' in the manner imagined by Marx and others?

Aldridge (2003) created a 2 x 2 matrix with which to compare and contrast different images or, as we shall call it in this chapter, *discourses* of the consumer. This means that rather than examining actual consumers, or their patterns of behavior, Aldridge is interested in how consumers are represented or portrayed by others. His matrix is based on two different dimensions that pertain to fundamental aspects for understanding consumption.

1 Is the consumer sovereign and responsible for generating demand? Or are consumers subject to powers that encourage them to consume? These contrasting discourses offer different views about where power lies in the relationship between production and consumption. Is it with producers, or with consumers? Are consumers dominant or dominated? In answering this question, we can think back to the Marxist and CT insights from earlier.

2 Is consumption a purely functional or a largely symbolic activity? Is it instrumental or expressive? Here we are in familiar territory for marketing students in talking about whether utility maximisation and rational behaviour, or symbolic expression and various forms of 'irrational' behaviour, drive consumption.

Taking together these two axes – consumers as dominant or dominated, consumption as instrumental or expressive – Aldridge creates a matrix populated by four representations of the consumer:

- The Victim (instrumental/dominated) – these consumers have made poor decisions or have been subject to scams. They are victims of the 'system' in the sense that they have suffered loss or disadvantage through the process of consuming.
- The Dupe (expressive/dominated) – this characterisation of the consumer suggests that he/she is subject to control and surveillance through the mode of consuming.
- The Rational Actor (instrumental/dominant) – with its origins in economics, the rational actor combines an ordered approach to the decision-making process and self-interested motivation.
- Communicator (expressive/dominant) – this characterisation has its origins in sociology and anthropology, as here the consumer is represented as using consumption as a means of achieving symbolic exchange. The rational actor and the communicator prioritise the actions and interests of consumers (rather than the producer) in understanding consumption.

In the remainder of this chapter, we wish to focus on two of these four images – the consumer as rational actor, and consumer as communicator – because they present a more 'active' view of the consumer, and enable us to form competing understandings of consumer agency. To augment Aldridge's two images, we will present you with a further two discourses: the 'discourse' of consumer rights, which maps onto the image of the consumer as rational actor; and the 'discourse' of consumer 'resistance', which we map onto the image of the consumer as communicator. Each of these discourses provides a different understanding of the nature of consumer agency, and the ways in which consumers can behave and create meanings from marketing and advertising activities not necessarily aligned with or determined by producers. Whilst the discourse of rights is articulated in quasi-legalistic terms and part of the fabric of market ideology, the discourse of resistance can be said to be more broadly about identity and the expression of in-group membership. We turn first to the rational actor and ask: what kinds of consumer agency are assumed in this portrayal?

8.3 The Rational Actor

The 'rational actor' is a characterisation of the consumer as motivated by self-interest. Here, consumption is pursued through a measured, calculated and reasoned approach to decision making premised on the desire for maximisation of satisfaction. In Chapter 4 we outlined in more depth the various elements of this 'rational' discourse about the consumer. This characterisation however carries into the discussion some subtle assumptions about the morality of forms of consuming and consumption and the individual's engagement with the marketplace. We begin to identify these assumptions by analysing a 'campaigner' for consumer rights in the UK: *Which?* magazine.

8.3.1 Which?

Which? magazine was originally published in the UK by the Consumers Association in 1957. Today the consumer group has taken the name of the magazine and *Which?* is a registered charity. It employs in excess of 500 members of staff and is the largest consumer body in the UK with over half a million members. *Which?* presents itself as imparting independent expert advice on consumer matters. The monthly magazine and special interest reports remain central to *Which?* though these have been complemented by consumer affairs, legal advice and a comparison/switching service for utilities. In addition, it offers social networking opportunities for registered members to share information on service providers in their local area. None of this is particularly new. The internet is awash with price comparison (e.g. www.pricerunner.co.uk) and product review websites (e.g. www.dooyoo.co.uk). See the Box below for a number of other websites by national associations or campaign groups for consumer rights. It is the position that *Which?* takes on its role as an advocate for consumer rights that distinguishes it from these competing sites.

Conventionally price comparison and product review websites allow the consumer to compare different products and check their prospective purchase price prior to buying. Due to advertising, commission or sponsorship, most of these websites are free to use and do not require registration. This is in stark contrast to *Which?* reports and magazines that require subscription. There is very little on the *Which?* website that is free to users who are not also subscribers. *Which?* seeks to present itself as an independent body, free from interference by business or government. Its website carries no advertising. *Which?* offers 'authoritative' consumer advice from a panel of 'experts' who are vetted to prevent bias or the promotion of self interest. Its website promotes itself as 'No advertising, no bias, no hidden agenda' (www.which.co.uk). The reviews are undertaken under laboratory conditions. The process of reviewing is thus treated as though it were a science, seeking legitimacy through the robustness associated with scientific endeavour.

All products tested are purchased at full price to avoid any accusation that the manufacturer has subsidised the testing or provided a non-standard product. The products are assessed by the 'independent experts' and using a five star ranking system they are rated against set criteria which are deemed relevant for the product category. This ranking system provides the team with a means of comparison and allows them to select which of the products are deemed 'Best Buys' and those that the reader is encouraged to avoid. The criteria used are of importance here. *Which?* is not concerned with the style and image associated with brand names, thus the symbolic value of the product is not incorporated within the review process. Instead, *Which?* reviewers are solely concerned with the functionality of the product – the use value.

Some Representatives of Consumer Rights

A selection of resources and groups concerned with consumer rights and the provision of consumer information:

http://www.consumer-voice.org/index.asp
http://www.consumer.org.nz/
http://www.consumerassociation.ie/choice.html

It is of course quite possible to question the independence of *Which?* from commercial influence. *Which?* is not free from market forces and the selection of products and product categories will be influenced by demand for its advice and reviews. More significantly for this chapter, its positioning as an expert and unbiased source of product information does construct the consumer in a very specific way. In this regard, *Which?* presents the consumer as a labourer in the realm of consumption. In contrast to conventional critiques of consumer society that trivialise consumer-based issues, the act of shopping for *Which?* is treated seriously. Buying is presented as an activity not dissimilar to that of a worker, with duties and responsibilities that must be fulfilled. Indeed Aldridge suggests that *Which?* 'reduces the labour involved in consumer calculations' (1994: 905). In reducing the time involved for the consumer to search and appraise products, the consumer is offered the means to make 'the right choice'. The consumer is expected to take responsibility for their consumption choices and bad consumption decisions are deemed to be the fault of the consumer. Their failure lies in not incorporating the information within their decision-making.

The analogy of the consumer as a worker is supplemented in this discourse by the analogy of the consumer as a responsible citizen. Aldridge (1994) suggests that the duty of the consumer is to make the right choice. Here *Which?* blurs the boundaries between the consumer and the idea of the responsible citizen. To be a citizen places a responsibility on the individual to be a good consumer and likewise when consuming, a good consumer will be a good citizen. This should not be too surprising considering the fact that *Which?* is grounded in the historical 'consumer rights' movement. Consumer rights – the right to safety, to be informed, to choose, to be heard etc. – offers a challenge to the idea of the self-correcting abilities of the market. Economic theory, such as the theory of market regulation offered by the Chicago School, posits that the market mechanism is at its most efficient when competition alone is used to control errant behaviour within the market. The actors within the market are seen to pursue self-interest by maximising their satisfaction through the market. The consumer rights movement has been successful in a number of economies in having legislation passed that protects consumers, and provides consumer groups with a legal means for pursuing negligent companies. Consumer rights thus make the organisation accountable to the law/judiciary/government rather than/in addition to the market.

For Tiemstra (1992), the consumerist movement performed a valuable service for business when its legitimacy was questioned. The consumerist movement identified means by which business could address issues of legitimacy and come to be held accountable. Far from being a form of consumer resistance, the consumerist movement has actually embraced the consumption opportunities offered by the capitalist system. As such, the *Which?* example demonstrates how consumer activity is treated by consumer movements as a civil and political responsibility. In representing the consumer and consumption activity in this way, attempts to generate borders between the political sphere and the marketplace become difficult to sustain. The act of consuming thus takes on a quasi political role and in consequence political issues are addressed through market solutions. This issue will be developed further through examination of Cause-related Marketing (CRM) and Fair Trade.

8.3.2 Cause-related Marketing

For the majority of the 1980s and 1990s, right-wing economic and social policies dominated government agendas in the US and UK. These were the times for privatisation, deregulation, liberation of markets under Reagan and Thatcher, times in which the relationship between the state and the market became more intimately linked. In the UK, the policies and ideological outlook of the Conservative Government between 1979 and 1997 had begun to encourage a greater confidence in the ability of the market to provide certain social services. For Gabriel and Lang (1995: 180) the resultant privatisation programme undermined the concept of citizens having rights and obligations; instead the idea of citizenship was conflated with that of the *consumer*. In the spaces left by the so-called 'rolling back of the State', businesses became increasingly incorporated in questions of social responsibility.

Although the later years of the 1990s in the UK are often simplistically portrayed as a New Labour-led move away from Thatcherite policies, the Labour government remained preoccupied with working through the tensions created between the 'citizen' and the 'consumer'. Opinion polls were claiming that corporations in the UK were second only to the government for responsibility for social ills (Gray, 1997). The calls from environmental, social welfare and consumer groups for business to undertake social responsibility intensified. The well-publicised corporate scandals and debacles such as Enron, Bhopal and the Exxon Valdez oil disaster added weight to the pressure for business to demonstrate their social values. In this context, Cause-related Marketing emerged as an important practice in the UK.

In a pioneering article that sought to introduce academia to the prominence of CRM, Varadarajan and Menon (1988: 60) defined it as:

> the process of formulating and implementing marketing activities that are characterised by an offer from the firm to contribute a specified amount to a designated cause when customers engage in revenue-providing exchanges that satisfy organisational and individual objectives.

The dominant characteristic of CRM is the link between consumer purchase and a firm's donation to a charitable cause (Singh et al., 2009). CRM allows the brand manager to enhance company image and increase sales by building the brand through association with a moral dimension. The brand manager uses consumer concern for business responsibility as a means of securing competitive advantage. At the same time, a charitable cause receives substantial financial benefits. It is argued that CRM creates a 'win–win' situation for all concerned, the 'feel-good marketing' of the last two decades (Berglind and Nakata, 2005). Indeed, CRM is frequently instigated by charities themselves as a means by which to offset the decline in the frequency and amount of individual direct donations (Henley Centre, 1998).

The term 'cause-related marketing' originated in the early 1980s in the United States (Barnes and Fitzgibbons, 1992). The Travel Related Services Unit of American

Express is credited with the pioneering use of the term. The initial growth of CRM was phenomenal, dispelling suggestions that it was merely a fad. By 1988, Schiller (1988) estimated that CRM campaigns in the US were providing yearly donations of $100m to not-for-profit organisations. In 1998, the IEG cause-related marketing survey estimated spending had grown to $545 million; by 2005 it rose to an estimated $1.08 billion (Keene, 2009). Such new forms of philanthropy are, according to Ceasar (1987), related to the blurring of the divisions between the public, private and non-profit sectors. The shifts in giving patterns have been brought about by the withdrawal or reduction of public funds from the non-profit sector, and the encouragement of the private sector to replace the aid provided by the State (Nickel and Eikenberry, 2009).

The demands of the state and the consuming citizen for corporations to demonstrate a greater social responsibility have, according to Cordtz (1990), encouraged business to alter the manner in which it assists non-profit organisations. A balance is being sought between the pressure of consumers for corporations to demonstrate social responsibility, and the needs of the marketplace to show 'added value' from the corporation's activities. Mullen (1997) argues that there has been a changing expectation within corporations regarding 'giving' to non-profit organisations. There is a desire to link the donation of corporations' resources to the attainment of measurable results. Mullen writes: 'Corporations increasingly want added value for their charitable giving activities with creative strategies that produce tangible results' (1997: 42). Corporations are becoming more selective about the causes they support, limiting objectives and establishing targets more carefully. They are subjecting their philanthropic acts to the rigours of accounting, requiring a return on investment.

The development of CRM has not been without its critics. First, and perhaps unsurprisingly, the terminology surrounding philanthropy has changed to coalesce with the new environment. The words generally associated with philanthropy, words such as caring, benevolence, benignity, charitableness and humanitarianism, words which carry gentler, more humble, connotations have been succeeded by notions of 'strategic giving' (Mullen, 1997), 'pragmatic altruism' (Buhl, 1996: 127) and even the derogatively termed 'phoney philanthropy' (Wagner and Thompson, 1994: 9). In addition to the shifts in language, it is necessary to consider the format in which the CRM exchange takes place. By linking charitable donations to, (probably) pre-existing, consumption decisions, it could be argued that the adoption of CRM means that social commitments are made without requiring any additional activity. If we accept that questions of moral commitment cannot be completely divorced from the financial benefits that are produced by strategies like CRM, it might become necessary to consider how our engagement as consumers with these campaigns is constructed.

One principal criticism of CRM could be to suggest that it removes individual responsibility from an important arena for moral consideration. The moral aspect of the exchange is wedded to the commercial exchange and in the process, the moral decision making is subject to the regimes of the market. Authors such as Zygmunt Bauman have expressed dismay that all perceptions and expectations, as well as life-rhythm, qualities of memory, attention, motivational and topical relevances are moulded inside the new foundational institutions – that of the market (Bauman, 1987: 166). Thus the rights of the citizen become defined as those of the consumer.

In this discourse, the citizen is characterised not as someone able to assume responsibilities, but as a consumer of supplied services. They have 'rights', but these are simply the right to be satisfied and the right to complain. In this way they are denied the opportunity of questioning the fundamental principles of corporate organisation (see Ozanne and Murray, 1995 in the further reading recommendations for an extension of this theme). Following this line of argument, CRM is perceived to represent an extension of this marketisation thesis. The mechanisms of CRM remove many of the decisions that were previously discharged by the individual and subsume them within a commercial exchange. Despite first appearances, then, perhaps CRM does not fit comfortably with the original desire of this chapter to present an image of a consumer who is able to exercise choice independent of the will of the market in the activity of consumption (as giving to charity in this case).

8.3.3 Fair Trade

CRM presents one element in the re-consideration of the relationship between consumption, business and society. Over the last couple of decades a range of 'moral' aspects of consumption have become pronounced. These moral aspects have incorporated 'ethical' investment (the Co-operative Bank), environmentally 'friendly' packaging (Biopac), action against animal cruelty (line-caught tuna) and healthy eating (reduction of salt and saturated fats). Each of these aspects seeks to adjust the political, cultural and social aspects of consumption through the marketplace, providing the consumer with a choice to allay particular aspects of their ethical preferences through decisions concerning their purchase behaviours. As noted in Chapter 6, retailers, distributors and manufacturers are under increasing pressure to be transparent in the sourcing and processing of materials within the supply chain. This pressure extends beyond providing product and country of origin information – it entails a wider view of how members of the supply chain are treated and the environmental and social impact of the product and producer.

In Chapter 6 we noted that fair trade has been proposed as a potential mode for addressing problem issues in the supply chain. It is important at this point to clarify possible complications with the terminology. Fair trade is generally used to refer to the wider issues of economic power and justice associated with trading relations between developed and developing countries. This usage of the term encompasses the campaigning bodies for fairer trade, as well as the organisations and networks associated with enabling fair trade. However, Fairtrade© is a copyrighted term with a more specific meaning, referring to the certification and labelling process associated with the Fairtrade Labelling Organisation (FLO) International. The FLO is the umbrella body that oversees Fairtrade© accreditation.

Fairtrade© emerged from a fragmented and supply-focused activity which was predominantly concerned with the sale of non-branded goods offered for sale by not-for-profit alternative trading organisations. In the UK, this is best illustrated by the fact that fair trade was initially associated with charity shops and alternative retailers, most notably in the link between the Oxfam charity shop and Traidcraft. From this fragmented system, a niche industry was transformed by the development of a Fairtrade© certification system to oversee and audit fair trade practices. Since the mid-1990s, this legitimacy has seen a growth in companies trading solely on and through fair trade principles as well as for-profit organisations that extend existing product lines through Fairtrade© branding but which do not adopt the ideology of fair trade in the other areas of their business (Davies, 2007).

In Chapter 6 we also noted the significant growth in the fair trade market. Fairtrade© claim that globally the fair trade market was valued at 3.2 billion Euros in 2007, an increase of 47 per cent on sales in 2006. The largest markets for fair trade produce are the US and UK, with growth being seen in Scandinavian countries. The range of products offered via fair trade is predominantly agricultural and horticultural goods, including flowers, fruit, coffee and cotton. Increasingly manufactured goods, for example towels and jeans, are supplementing commodity items.

Fair trade offers a 'linking mechanism' between the product, the place of production, the members of the supply chain and the consumer. More specifically, the linking mechanism addresses the inequality of power between the consumers and supply chain members of the developed world with the producers and processors of goods found in the developing world. To facilitate this linking, a system of audits and certification processes is needed to guarantee the fairness of the system. Fairness is sought by guaranteeing fair prices to producers plus some adherence to principles of ethical purchasing. There is also a requirement for a 'producer narrative' (Alexander and Nicholls, 2006) whereby the provenance of the product and the story of the producers are accessible and made meaningful to consumers. The transparency also necessitates an opening up of the conventional supply chain so that consumers can compare 'standards' evident within the chain promoting fair trade and non fair trade principles. Like CRM, fair trade suggests that the marketplace is a legitimate channel for consumers to address social concerns. Whilst CRM uses the emotional association with the charitable brand in the actual purchase, fair trade works on the principle of fairness and the assumption that consumers will pay extra for products that have been produced according to certified standards.

Both CRM and fair trade, however, position the consumer as a rational actor whose responsibility is to incorporate the moral dimension in their purchasing activities. Far from resisting or subverting the marketplace, the participation in CRM and fair trade affirms the centrality of consumption and the market as the means by which social and economic inequity is addressed. The moral question is incorporated into the consumer's decision-making criteria; it is subsumed within a technical–rational package that enables the consumer to select or not to select whether they wish to support workers' rights, minimum wage policies or the welfare of animals in their weekly shop.

However, the value of the fair trade market has attracted larger firms that possess far greater power which they can wield with accrediting bodies. We noted in Chapter 6 a number of dissenting voices regarding the extent to which fair trade can restore the links in the supply chain. We described Worth's (2006) point that Fairtrade© is increasingly driven not by the needs of poor producers, but the demands of large corporations. Worth describes the compromises reached by Fairtrade© labelling organisations in their dealings with large corporations in relation to roses and cotton products. Worth alleged that labelling organisations had begun to certify large, privately owned flower plantations rather than small cooperatives. This compromise can be interpreted as an outcome of the fact that the ideology of fair trade and the principles by which firms seeking Fairtrade© depend on the very market mechanism which it seeks to employ to avoid charitable aid. In so doing it arguably subjects itself to the commercial pressures of the marketplace.

The initial solidarity and shared political ideology which characterised the fair trade movement in its early stages can be said to have been transformed by the arrival of large corporations and a far more market-oriented approach to fair trade. Fairtrade itself has become a significant consumer brand, as well as a political ideology. As a brand it competes with alternative fair trade systems, alternative environmental/social/political campaigns as well as non-Fairtrade branded goods. As firms are increasingly seeking to respond to CSR pressures and more brands adopt fair trade principles, the ability of Fairtrade© to differentiate itself may become more difficult.

This would assume that the fair trade movement has succeeded in changing the market. It might also however mean that the fair trade agenda becomes less prominent and the value of accreditation becomes less important for brands.

Which?, CRM or fair trade can be presented as responses to failures in the market. These responses are premised on the ability of the market to possess the means to resolve problems caused by tensions within the marketplace. The consumer is portrayed as possessing sufficient distance and free will from the persuasions of marketing and advertising to be able to incorporate these elements of moral sentiment and social responsibility within their cognitive decision making. In so doing, consumers exercise political intentions through the market and the act of consuming. It is worth noting here that this characterisation of the consumer relies heavily upon prioritising the mental processing of the consumer, at the expense of other aspects of the consumer and consuming. This perhaps offers only a partial appreciation of the consumer. It might also offer a reason for why authors such as Miller (1995) have sought to move the debate away from why consumers buy to what shapes the meanings associated with moral consumption practices. In this sense, we now turn to look at a different notion of consumer 'agency' – that consumers are active meaning-makers who shape the message of any given commodity in ways that are not wholly dependent on the intentions or activities of producers.

8.4 The Communicator

In contrast to the Rational Actor, where consumption is approached in a reasoned fashion, and viewed instrumentally as a means to accomplish an end, the Communicator is seen to approach consumption in a more playful and rebellious manner. The role of consumption becomes a communicative act between people engaged in social interaction – in short, we are expressing something, and are often *aware* that we are expressing something, through consumption. Consumers' self-awareness and reflexivity about their consumption means that consumption is engaged with in a 'knowing' manner. This knowingness can take a number of different forms, including the consumer distancing themselves and resisting the market through alternative expressions of consumption.

In this section we will explore the nature of this playfulness and rebellion by exploring three examples of how consumers seek to 'fight back' against what they perceive to be the lure and negative consequences of the market. The examples used include Adbusters Media Foundation (AMF) and their call to 'Buy Nothing', the politics of food consumption and the Slow Food movement's campaign to resist the industrialisation of food, and finally the existence of new consumption communities that attempt to usurp the market. All three, in slightly different ways, provide grounds for consumers to seek, resist or escape from 'the market' and perceived changes in the way in which consumption is organised.

8.4.1 Adbusting

The AMF is a Canadian organisation that effectively utilises marketing to support its anti-marketing and anti-corporate activities. Based on the Canadian Pacific coast, AMF has achieved worldwide acclaim and has become a symbol of the new pro-civic, anti-corporate culture. Founded by Kalle Lasn, AMF promotes and reports on 'culture jamming', the 'game' of unsettling the dominant corporate culture. It is a:

> loose global network of artists, writers, environmentalists, ecological economists, media-literacy teachers, reborn lefties, ecofeminists, down-shifters, high school shit disturbers, campus rabble rousers, incorrigible, malcontents and green entrepreneurs. (quoted in Campbell, 2000: 8)

One aspect of the AMF agenda is to persuade people to question the dominant ideology that informs and is displayed in advertising. Through parody of established commercial adverts, AMF undertakes a system of subvertising that seeks to expose the tensions between the product and the image. These anti-corporate protestors are media and marketing savvy. Utilising the principle of détournement (Debord, 1967), protestors seek to challenge the basic assumptions of consumer society. Détournement involves turning around the desired corporate meaning and in the process bringing into question that which was assumed to be stable.

The annual Buy Nothing Day (BND) has developed into an international informal event supported by the AMF and a range of environmental, fair trade, anarchist and anti-capitalist groups. BND is a day in which consumers are encouraged not to consume, to purchase nothing and to 'reclaim their lives' by using the time they would normally spend shopping on other activities. The event is organised by local activists and coordinated through social networking sites. It aims to raise awareness of the social, economic and environmental problems associated with consumer society. Through abstinence for 24 hours, BND hopes that consumers will consider the environmental and social impact of their activities throughout the remainder of the year. Through stunts and parties anti-corporate protestors seek to expose the nature of corporate capitalist society. This is not a wholesale rejection of consumption or capitalism. Rather, it is a criticism of the excesses of consumption and the particular organisational structures that provide for a specific form of consumption. This is an important point to develop, since it leads to an understanding of criticisms of AMF.

The 'subvertising' that AMF employs is designed to expose the 'reality' behind the advertisements. By mocking an original advertisement, as illustrated by the example below, AMF is engaging in satire, taking inspiration from the advertising and advertisers that they seek to critique. For the satire to work effectively, the satirist needs to maintain a comfortable distance from that which they are satirising. It also requires audiences to comprehend the message within the satire, i.e. the critique of advertising. This requires viewers to be knowledgeable of debates on consumer culture, a pre-requisite that has led some critics to suggest that AMF is primarily a movement for educated, western, middle class individuals (Rumbo, 2002).

The form of activism that AMF promotes relies upon maintaining a nuanced distinction between a criticism of advertising *per se* and the criticism of a particular form of advertising. AMF could be construed to be part of the very 'advertising and consumer culture' that it protests against. The AMF offers its services to organisations as an advertising agency, plus visitors to the site can purchase 'fashion clothing' and 'coffee table' books. These goods are sourced from ethical suppliers and their advertising does not promote what are perceived to be negative social values (such as greed, self doubt, addiction). AMF is embedded in the

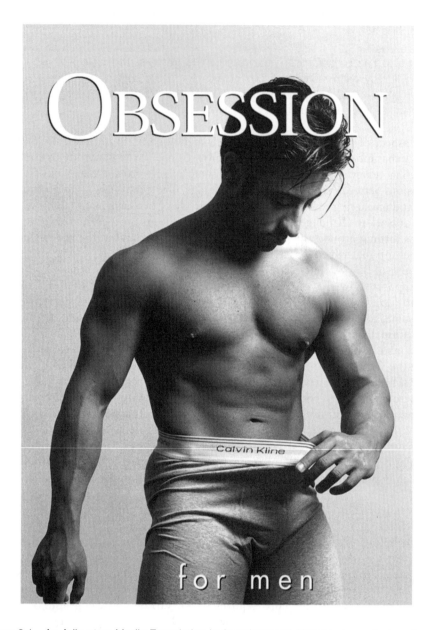

Figure 8.1   An Adbusters Media Foundation 'subvertisement'. With kind permission of Adbusters Media Foundation.

advertising industry and the high production value advertising arguably removes that comforting distance that the satire depends upon. By the same token the quality of the goods that they sell offers consumers (that are able to afford the 'alternative' goods), a means to wear something different and so be distinct from the 'mainstream'.

Accordingly, AMF is argued to be merely another option in the consumer market place and like the counter-culture of the 1960s, the movement reinforces rather than challenges the status quo (Frank, 1998). As Wickens notes in regard to BND:

> the whole point about Buy Nothing Day and other initiatives of its type is that it's simply another way of people expressing themselves through their buying behaviour; in this case satisfying an emotional need to reject consumerism. In this respect Buy Nothing Day is a brand in itself, albeit a non-profit one. It has a strong emotional message. (Wickens, 2007: 31).

Wickens proceeds to suggest that rather than an attack on brands, AMF and BND are supporting quality brands at the expense of mass produced and cheap disposable commodities. This criticism does not however address the psychological aspect of the BND and AMF campaigns which intimates that consuming has become an addiction of which the (mass) consumer is blissfully unaware. Through 'subvertising', a process of 're-education' is attempted to awaken consumers to the problematic nature of consuming.

8.4.2 The Cultural Politics of Food

The rejection of a particular manifestation of consumer society and industrial organisation is also evidenced in the Slow Food movement. Like AMF the Slow Food movement is premised on the work and ideas of one individual from which a myriad of local interest groups, based all around the world, have sought to form networks to promote both a response and an alternative approach to contemporary consumption. The origins of the Slow Food movement are usually traced back to Carlo Petrini, who founded the Slow Food movement in Italy in 1986 allegedly in response to the opening of a McDonald's outlet in Rome (Jones et al., 2003). Slow Food is an international non-profit making organisation based on democratic principles and individual voluntary membership. Its logo is a snail, reinforcing the relaxed approach to life and is a comical riposte to the speed of food production associated with the fast food industry.

The philosophy of the Slow Food movement is developed from a manifesto produced by a founding member – Folco Portinari. The manifesto (http://www.slowfood. org.uk/manifesto.html) adopts a polemic style and bemoans how human beings have become subject to the creature it created during the Industrial Revolution, namely the machine. The machine offers efficiency and speed in production and these traits have extended to human lives and consumption activities. The consequence is that we:

> are enslaved by speed and have all succumbed to the same insidious virus: Fast Life, which disrupts our habits, pervades the privacy of our homes and forces us to eat Fast Foods. (http://www.slowfood.org.uk/manifesto.html)

Incorporating both nostalgia for a quieter, more refined time with a romanticism of fine food and local production, Slow Food is a response to the fast food associated with McDonald's and the processes of McDonaldisation where industrialisation in the food sector promotes standardisation, efficiency, predictability and replacement of humans by machines in the production process (Ritzer, 1997). The method of production and materials incorporated within the production have been the source of sustained and high profile criticism from authors such as Eric Schlosser and his best selling book, *Fast Food Nation* (2002) and the film maker Morgan Spurlock's *Supersize Me* (2004). Whilst fast food was once celebrated as a means of producing affordable, convenient and readily available food, increasingly questions are being raised about how this approach to food production impacts on human health (e.g. obesity and heart disease), the environment and social relations.

Industrialisation has provided for an increasing distance between the source of production and the consumption of food. Regional foods are now produced and consumed outside of their ethnic, social and geographical origins. In opposition to this trend, the Slow Food movement promotes regional food and fair trade whilst seeking to incorporate environmental considerations in the production of food. The Slow Food movement argues that the industrialisation of food production has removed the communal aspect of food consumption and with it the social mores of eating together.

In a similar vein to AMF, then, the Slow Food movement is arguing that the pace and scale of change associated with globalisation and consumer society makes necessary the identification and defence of spaces for humans to remove themselves from the pressures associated with these changes. Within the relative tranquility of these spaces, individuals are deemed to be able to pause and reflect on their existence and their relationship with the environment, other people and the speed and nature of change.

The Slow Food movement is not anti-market or anti-consumption. Jones et al. (2003: 303) usefully remind us that:

> While it would be both wrong and misleading to see debates about eating habits and behaviours polarised into a 'Slow Food–fast food' debate it is important to recognise that both clearly have important, if broadly defined, marketing orientations in that they can be seen to be powerful reflections of consumer needs and demands.

The Slow Food movement is however playing on concerns within advanced capitalist countries that corporations have become too powerful and that the individual is divorced from the means of production (echoing Marx's concern). The remedy being offered is an alternative positioning strategy to fast food. Wonderfully romanticised images of distant times in local places are offered where conviviality is asserted against the mechanised, mass production and industrialised reality of contemporary food production. Slow Food is able to offer those individuals with the time and money the means of accruing social distinction through association with a discerning palette and 'educated eating habits'. In short, the Slow Food movement is resisting the disenchantment associated with consuming industrially produced food by re-enchanting food production and consumption. The extent to which it is simply a bourgeois, market-based response that creates social status for a certain sector of society to the exclusion of others is a point for debate.

We should also note, in contradistinction to some of the romantic and elitist images of the Slow Food Movement, that academic work from anthropology and consumer research illustrates that it would be unwise to assume that local food patterns and preferences are being replaced wholesale by the mass culinary offerings of industrial production. This is perhaps best illustrated in the context of the globalisation of food, and the spread of global brands. The point here is not so much that, say, McDonald's makes small adaptations to its product offerings in order to speak to local food tastes and preferences. It is more that research which studies how it has been 'consumed' by local populations illustrates processes of creolisation and hybridisation.

In these processes, an interaction occurs between two cultures – the original culture of the brand or product, and the culture that receives or is the target for that brand or product. During this interaction, the original cultural meaning of the brand or product is changed, as members of the target culture come to make sense of it through their own cultural lenses. This is not to say that the target culture is unchanged – the local culture will accommodate the 'outside' brand or product, and changes will ensue in its referent system. As such, there is a reciprocal interaction between the global brand and the local food culture which involves changes to both entities, rather than a wholesale replacement of the latter by the former. This is the outcome of so-called processes of creolisation or hybridisation (Howes, 1996).

Caldwell's (2004) ethnographic study of McDonald's in Russia illustrates how Muscovites re-invented and changed the meanings of McDonald's to fit in with existing Russian food culture. Indeed, her research found that some younger consumers thought that McDonald's was an authentic Russian product, such was the extent to which it had been 'domesticated' into the local culture by consumers. The organisation too came to understand that it required to transform the meaning of its products and service offerings beyond tinkering with its menu. As such it engaged in a process of so-called 'Nashification', associating its brand with the Russian concept of Nash (trust or home), and making it speak to the local culture in its own voice. Consumer agency is expressed in such processes of re-signification (changing the meaning of something), and appropriation of the brand.

8.4.3 The Burning Man Project

Apart from organisations like AMF, or the Slow Food movement, or indeed the everyday processes of re-signification noted above, there are other ways and sites in which consumers have attempted to resist the vagaries of the market. One of these is the formation by consumers of so-called New Consumption Communities (NCCs) which are purposively created to organise different modes for production and consumption. Such communities are typically created in a reactive mode to markets, seeking to offer an alternative to the perceived injustices of capitalist arrangements for production and consumption. In particular such NCCs can be said to set out to reconnect individual consumers and inculcate a community basis for consumption against the abstracting and atomising tendencies of market mechanisms. NCCs could take the form of local trading schemes, organic vegetable growing, online swapping and alternative exchange schemes. They could also take the form of festivals or events, such as the Burning Man Project in Nevada, USA.

The marketing academic Robert Kozinets undertook an ethnographic study of the Burning Man project over a number of years in the late 1990s and early 2000s. Burning Man seeks to promote itself as the antithesis of Disneyland. It is a gift-based, community oriented festival event which seeks to distance itself from the perceived negative and passive elements of consumer society. Attendees at the festival are expected to co-create the event and accordingly there is a strict 'no spectator' rule. Commercial selling is not permitted on the festival site and brand names cannot be visible. In contrast to the controlled, de-personalised, efficient and structured nature of the experience found at Disneyland, the Burning Man promotes the development of personal bonds, hedonism, creative expression, excess and flamboyance. The festival reaches its climax with the burning of the effigy of a man, with participants encouraged to concentrate on what aspects of their consumer lifestyle they wish to lose in the fire.

The Burning Man event is of course dependent on the market for meaning and whilst it presents itself as distant to the market, Kozinets notes that the boundaries between the market and Burning Man are fairly porous, which makes a simple dichotomous relationship between them difficult to sustain. Indeed he notes that:

> Burning Man's community, with its gift economy, suggests that we need not conceptualise an emancipatory community in terms of the absence of markets per se or of opposition to capitalism. (2002: 33)

Instead Burning Man, like AMF, fair trade and Slow Food seeks to re-instil creativity and community, to seek agency against a particular market logic that is characterised as being dominated by large, distant and unaccountable corporations.

Perhaps we need to remind ourselves, however, that markets themselves are traditionally the source of spectacle and subversion. In an insight into the spectacle and carnivalesque of the market, Buttimer and Kavanagh (1996) argue that historically the market and the carnivalesque have been interlinked. The market was a place where traditional social mores were suspended and over-turned. The market was a place where excessive consumption of food and drink was allowed, displays of the diseased and deformed, noise and music, dissimulation, inversions, profanity, prostitution, cheating, stalking, fighting and gaming were all permissible. Kozinets notes that Burning Man was an important place for art and radical self-expressiveness. Like the carnival, consumption is a paradox. It offers choice, whilst controlling what choice is available. It alienates those who consume as it brings communities together.

8.5 Conclusion

In conclusion, then, we have seen that the Rational Actor and Communicator may share a similar oppositional position on the Aldridge matrix. However the assumptions underpinning these two representations are very different. Both the Rational Actor and Communicator can be seen to share unease with aspects of the marketplace. Whilst the Rational Actor seeks to introduce measures to address the 'natural' inequities in the market and thereby allow consumers to pursue their consuming activities in a structured manner, the Communicator seeks means of distancing him/herself from the marketplace that has developed. In both cases we see consumers attempting to remedy dissatisfaction with a particular model of capitalism and consumer society. However, we have also sought in this chapter to move beyond a simple oppositional characterisation of consumer rights and resistance, showing the nuances and blurrings associated with both. In this regard, we have hopefully demonstrated how these positions are dependent upon the marketplace for meaning, whilst the market we understand and experience has been shaped by ideas of rights and resistance.

8.6 Learning Activities

Presenting the consumer as a victim and so subject to the machinations of large multinational companies provides for a neat and overly simplistic account of the consumer. In this chapter, a more 'active' representation of the consumer is offered through which to develop a more nuanced examination of the relationship between the individual, corporations and the market. Before you begin the learning activities remind yourself of the learning aims for the chapter so that your time and efforts are focused.

Learning Activity One: Protest Against GM Foods

In recent years there have been numerous protests against the development of GM (genetically modified) crops by a variety of stakeholders in numerous countries across the globe. In 2008 there were mass protests against GM crops in India, in part organised by the 'Coalition for GM Free India'. Conduct some internet-based research on GM crops in India. What are consumers protesting against with regard to GM crops? What is the Coalition for GM Free India, and how does it organise protest? Do you think it is an effective organisation for consumer resistance?

Learning Activity Two: Alternative Organisations

Identify the names and goals of groups or communities (perhaps a New Consumption Community) in your local area or country that attempt to organise the exchange of goods and services 'outside of' the capitalist marketplace. What are the values of this group or community? How do they organise exchange? Who benefits from it? To what extent is 'the market' still implicated in their work? To what extent do they offer 'alternatives' to the market?

8.7 Further Reading

Gabriel, Y. and Lang, T. (2008) 'New faces and new masks of today's consumer', *Journal of Consumer Culture*, 8(3): 321–40.

The first recommended further reading by Gabriel and Lang – well-known writers on consumer culture – describes the contemporary relationship between the worlds of work/production, and that of consumption.

Ozanne, J.L. and Murray, J.B. (1995) 'Uniting critical theory and public policy to create the reflexively defiant consumer', *American Behavioral Scientist*, 38(4): 516–25.

Arnould, E. (2007) 'Should consumer citizens escape the market?', *The Annals of the American Academy of Political and Social Science*, 611: 96–111.

The article by Ozanne and Murray (1995) is described and implicitly criticised by Arnould. The structure of Arnould's article reflects well the structure of this chapter, and offers you more material from critical theory (Baudrillard and Habermas) with which to understand (in a more complex way) the points made. Read Ozanne and Murray first, and then turn to Arnould.

Diversi, M. (2006) 'Street kids in Nikes: In search of humanization through the culture of consumption', *Cultural Studies <=> Critical Methodologies*, 6(3): 370–90.

This article demonstrates the contradictions and complexities involved in talking about structure and agency in regard to consumers. This ethnographic study of streetkids in Brazil demonstrates the 'flimsiness' of seeing consumers either as completely determined by the market or able to escape it completely.

Sandlin, J.A. and Callahan, J.L. (2009) 'Deviance, dissonance, and détournement: culture jammers' use of emotion in consumer rsistance', *Journal of Consumer Culture*, 9(1): 79–115.

The final piece of recommended reading gives you an insight into so-called 'culture jammers', introduced briefly in this chapter, and the particular role of emotions in this form of consumer resistance.

8.8 References

Adorno, T. and Horkheimer, M. (1947/1972) *Dialectic of Enlightenment*. Translated by J. Cumming. New York: The Seabury Press.

Aldridge, A. (1994) 'The construction of rational consumption in *Which?* magazine: The more blobs the better?', *Sociology*, 28 (4): 899–912.

Aldridge, A. (2003) *Consumption*. London: Polity Press.

Alexander, A. and Nicholls, A. (2006) 'Rediscovering consumer-producer involvement: A network perspective on fair trade marketing', *European Journal of Marketing*, 40 (11/12): 1236–53.

Barnes, N.G. and Fitzgibbons, D.A. (1992) 'Strategic marketing for charitable organisations', *Health Marketing Quarterly*, 9 (3/4): 103–14.

Bauman, Z. (1987) *Legislators and Interpreters*. London: Polity Press.

Berglind, M. and Nakata, C. (2005) 'Cause-related marketing: More buck than bang?', *Business Horizons*, 48: 443–53.

Buhl, L. (1996) 'The ethical framework of corporate philanthropy', in D. Burlingame and D. Young (eds), *Corporate Philanthropy at the Crossroads*, pp. 165–79. University of Indiana Indiana: University Press.

Buttimer, C. and Kavanagh, D. (1996) 'Markets, exchange and the extreme', in S. Brown, J. Bell, and D. Carson, (eds), *Marketing Apocalypse: Eschatology, Escapology and the Illusion of the End*, pp. 145–70. New York: Routledge.

Caldwell, M. (2004) 'Domesticating the French fry: McDonald's and consumerism in Moscow', *Journal of Consumer Culture*, 4: 5–26.

Campbell, D. (2000) 'Subvertise, don't advertise', *The Guardian Media*, 9 October: 8–9.

Ceasar, P. (1987) 'Cause-related marketing: The new face of corporate philanthropy', *Nonprofit World*, 5 (4): 21–6.

Cordtz, D. (1990) 'Corporate citizenship: No more soft touches', *Financial World*, 159 (1): 30–6.

Davies, I.A. (2007) 'The eras and participants of fair trade: An industry structure/stakeholder perspective on the growth of the fair trade industry', *Corporate Governance*, 7 (4): 455–70.

Debord, G. (1967) 'Society of the spectacle', available online at http://www.nothingness.org/SI/debord/index.html, accessed 18 August 2009.

Fine, B. and Saad-Filho, A. (2004) Marx's *Capital*, 4th edn. London: Pluto Press.

Frank, T. (1998) *The Conquest of Cool: Business Culture, Counterculture and the Rise of Hip Consumerism*. Chicago: University of Chicago Press.

Gabriel, Y. and Lang, T. (1995) *The Unmanageable Consumer: Contemporary Consumption and its Fragmentations*. London: Sage.

Gray, R. (1997) 'Cause for thought', *Marketing*, 2 (January): 21–3.

Henley Centre (1998) 'The future of charity consumer and leisure', *Futures*: 46–51.

Howes, D. (ed.) (1996) *Cross-Cultural Consumption: Global Markets, Local Realities*. London: Routledge.

Jones, P., Shears, P., Hillier, D., Comfort, D. and Lowell, J. (2003) 'Return to traditional values? A case study of Slow Food', *British Food Journal*, 105 (4/5): 297–304.

Keene, A. (2009) 'Cause related marketing blogSpot', webblog available at http://www.blogcatalog.com/blogs/cause-related-marketing.html, accessed 20 July 2009.

Klein, N. (2000) *No Logo*. London: Flamingo.

Kozinets, R.V. (2002) 'Can consumers escape the market? Emancipatory illuminations from burning man', *Journal of Consumer Research*, 29: 20–38.

Marcuse, H. (1968) *One Dimensional Man*. London: Sphere Books.

Marx, K. (1976) *Capital: A Critique of Political Economy*, Volume One. London/New York: Penguin/Vintage.

Miller, D. (1995) *Acknowledging Consumption: A Review of New Studies*. Routledge: London.

Monbiot, G. (2000) *Captive State*. London: Macmillan.

Mullen, J. (1997) 'Performance-based corporate philanthropy: How 'giving smart' can further corporate goals', *Public Relations Quarterly*, 42 (2): 42–8.

Nickel, P.M. and Eikenberry, A.M. (2009) 'A critique of the discourse of marketized philanthropy', *Behavioral Scientist*, 52: 974–89.

Ozanne, J.L. and Murray, J. B. (1995) 'Uniting critical theory and public policy to create the reflexively defiant customer', *American Behavioural Scientist*, 38 (4): 516–25.

Packard, V. (1960) The Hidden Persuaders. London: Penguin.

Ritzer, G. (1997) *The McDonaldization Thesis: Explorations and Extensions*. London: Sage.

Rumbo, J. D. (2002) 'Consumer resistance in a world of advertising clutter: The case of Adbusters', *Psychology and Marketing*, 19 (2): 127–48.

Schiller, Z. (1988) 'Doing well by doing good', *Business Week*, 3082, 5 December: 53–57.

Schlosser, E. (2002) *Fast Food Nation: What The All-American Meal is Doing to the World*. London: Penguin.

Singh, S., Kristensen, L. and Villasenor, E. (2009) 'Overcoming skepticism towards cause related claims: The case of Norway' *International Marketing Review*, 26 (3): 312–32.

Starr, A. (2000) *Naming the Enemy*: *Anti-corporate Movements Confront Globalisation*. London: Zed Books.

Supersize Me. (2004) (Film) Written and directed by M. Spurlock, M. Kathburl Pictures. USA.

Tiemstra, J. P. (1992) 'Theories of regulation and the history of consumerism', *International Journal of Social Economics*, 19 (6): 3–25.

Varadarajan, P. R. and Menon, A. (1988) 'Cause-related marketing: A coalignment of marketing strategy and corporate philanthropy', *Journal of Marketing*, 52(July): 58–74.

Wagner, L. and Thompson, R. L. (1994) 'Cause-related marketing: Fundraising tool or phony philanthropy', *Nonprofit World*, 12 (6): 9–13.

Wickens, M. (2007) *Marketing Week*, 30 (47): 31.

Worth, J. (2006) 'Buy now, pay later', *New Internationalist*, November: 2.

Consumer Society and the Production of Identity

9

9.1 Introduction

The impact of marketing on our everyday lives extends well beyond the satisfaction of our 'core' requirements. Marketing has become important in many cultures, so much so that modern societies can be considered to be 'consumer societies'. Many of our expectations, values and experiences in life draw upon and include marketing-related features. We routinely use brands to 'say' something about ourselves and marketers use this as a way to connect mass produced goods and services to individual needs, wants and desires. In fact some writers go even further to propose that marketing ideology has actually contributed to the creation of the very idea of the self as something that is important and relevant to us. It is certainly the case that questions about identity and the self have become more and more important in the last few decades and it is not unreasonable to assume that marketing and consumption might have something to do with this. But questions about the self and identity are not clear cut or straightforward. Marketing and consumer researchers are interested in examining where we (think) we get our identities from in the first place, and how free we are to choose and change, and 'produce' and 'consume' our identities.

The idea that 'identity' is something that is produced and consumed might appear to be slightly confusing at first. Most of the time we think of identity as something that is 'ours'. It is something that defines us as who we are, and perhaps more importantly, differentiates us from others who have their own identities. It is also unusual, especially in marketing and management, to talk about people and their identities as things which are produced and consumed. We tend to limit the use of terms like production and consumption to goods, services and products. In order to appreciate this perspective, it is necessary to expand our ideas about what constitutes production and consumption.

There is certainly something individually specific about 'our' identity. But it is also true that many aspects of our identity are shaped, crafted and influenced by factors outside of ourselves. Many of us might feel that most of the time we choose to be who we are and how we want to be. We make choices about how we want to appear through our clothing, cosmetics and style. We make choices about what we believe in, in terms of religion, political preferences and support for various causes. We choose to pursue particular interests, professions and hobbies. All of these preferences and selections (as well as many others) contribute to 'our' identity. But while we certainly shape or make our own identities, it is also true that we do not make them under circumstances chosen by ourselves. The time and place where we live and work, and the cultural and social realities of everyday life, prescribe to a great extent what and who we are able to be.

Many social and cultural commentators (e.g. Featherstone, 1988; Kellner, 1988) on the 'postmodern condition' (Lyotard, 1984), point out that one of the most important features of '(post-)modern' life is that we all think a lot more about who we are, who we want to be, and how we might go about achieving particular identities than people in the past. One explanation for this greater emphasis on identity and the self in (post-)modern life is that contemporary consumer culture encourages us all to see ourselves as individuals with the autonomy to craft and design who we want to be (as noted in Chapter 3 and critiqued in Chapter 8). In consumer culture, who we are is always a kind of 'work-in-progress', and the market offers important and useful resources that we can employ to achieve the identities we aspire to.

Branding and Social Context

What, why, when, where and how we purchase is not just a question of seeking functional or psychological benefits; it is also profoundly shaped by the society and culture(s) in which we are embedded. Contemporary branding theory and practice, especially when related to fast-moving consumer goods (FMCGs), fashion and retail sectors, are illustrative. Take the Nike trainer (sneaker): its functional or tangible benefits (e.g. protection of the foot, quality of production) are typically much less relevant for consumers than the lifestyle associated with this brand's identity. Rather than physical material, brands offer cultural materials (a set of values or an idealised way of life), grafted on to the physical product through expensive, long-term investment in branding, advertising and marketing campaigns, with which consumers can construct and express their own identities. Consumers thus use brands to 'produce' an identity via purchase, display and use; our branded selves can then be 'consumed' by others as a mark of who we perceive ourselves to be and which social groups we wish to belong to.

The principal objective of this chapter is to assist you develop an understanding of how the various contextual factors associated with consumer society both facilitate, as well as limit, the kinds of identities available to us as individuals. In short, it is to address the relationship between context (historical, economic, social, cultural etc.) and the production and consumption of identities. This relationship is, of course, fairly well-studied in the consumer behaviour and consumer research literatures, often via research findings derived from questionnaire surveys, in-depth interviews with consumers or introspective methods. But we do not want to turn to this literature for this chapter. Instead, we will introduce you to a different academic tradition to marketing for inspiration – that of literary criticism and cultural studies – and analyse two different instances of literary and popular culture: a TV series and a classic American novel.

The use of literary forms like novels or poetry, and of popular culture like films and TV series, is becoming increasingly popular in management and marketing research and teaching (see, notably, Holbrook and Hirschman, 1993 and more recently, McDonagh and Brereton, 2010). Artistic reflections provide a mirror of a society to itself, and therefore give us access to portrayals of everyday life in its full complexity and, importantly, contextuality, which are very difficult to get a handle on through conventional questionnaire and interview-based research. Increasingly portrayals of marketing and consuming activities – shopping, lifestyle issues, materialism, the consuming self, critiques of consumer society – are in fact the subject themselves of certain forms of popular culture (see Box below). These are valuable resources for learning about marketing and consumption phenomena, as noted in Belk's (1986) previous analyses of the books of Henry James, Hirschman's (1993) writing on Charles Dickens's *A Christmas Carol* and Holbrook's (1991) reading of classical pieces of Western literature. To us, the artistic treatment of these subjects provides an important multidimensionality to our understandings of context and the production of identity. Before presenting an analysis of two pieces of popular and literary culture, the next section outlines conceptual materials with which to think about the relationship between context and the production and consumption of identities.

Consumption in Print and Celluloid

The following are titles of books, films and TV series where marketing and consumption issues are principal areas of concern and often critique: *Fight Club, American Beauty*, TV lifestyle programmes (such as *Location, Location, Location; 60-minute Makeover; Saturday Kitchen; A Place in the Sun; How to Look Good Naked; Jamie at Home; Grand Designs; The Dog Whisperer*), *ARENA, Clueless, Ugly Betty, Sex and the City*. We are sure you can think of many more. Read and/or watch as many of these films, programmes or novels as you can and discuss what you think they tell us about that much-used word in marketing: 'commodification'. What does commodification mean? How does it apply to people as well as objects? What is the relationship of commodification to the production of identity? And what 'kinds' of identity can we discern through such a lens? Racial, sexual, cultural, religious, professional, familial, others?

9.2 Consumer Society, Culture and Identity

In this section we provide an overview of how the relationship between context and production/consumption has been portrayed and conceptualised by scholars. These conceptualisations provide us with particular images and understandings of context and consumption, especially in relation to historical, economic, social and cultural issues. In this respect, this chapter takes a similar sort of approach as Chapter 8 in so far as it looks at *representations* of consumers, but in this chapter through popular and literary culture.

9.2.1 The Interpretive Complexities of Consumers

As noted earlier in this book (see Chapter 2), the interpretivist turn in consumer research, as well as the impact of postmodernism on marketing more broadly, has had a significant influence on our understandings of the consumer. The conventional representation of the consumer as a rational and utility-maximising creature, or as an information processor magically turning environmental inputs into behavioural outputs, has been sharply criticised as lacking theoretical sophistication. In particular, critics such as Elizabeth Hirschman (1980) (with Morris Holbrook, 1982), Russell Belk (1988), and Grant McCracken (1986) have argued that a greater appreciation of the social and cultural aspects of consumption, rather than just the psychological ones, is required for a fuller understanding of how context impacts consumer identity.

It is now acknowledged that the notion of the consumer as someone that seeks need satisfaction at all costs is unsatisfactory (Cherrier and Murray, 2004). Complex consumers are governed less by Maslovian needs than by contradictory *desires* (Cherrier and Murray, 2004; Zukin and Maguire, 2004); they are meaning-making beings whose identities rest in the symbolic systems of society and culture as reproduced in institutions like schools, the media and increasingly through marketing. Interpretive consumer research (especially those associated with Consumer Culture Theory, CCT, notably Arnould and Thompson, 2005) and social and cultural theorists (notably Baudrillard, whose work is introduced in Chapter 10) writing about postmodernism offer insights (sometimes connected, sometimes competing) into these symbolic systems.

Increasing attention is now being given in marketing textbooks to illustrating some of the complexities of consumer behaviour, and to the key role of culture in forming consumers' identities, often through the reporting of interpretive consumer research studies. For instance, you may well read about irrational or 'aberrant' consumer behaviours which defy the rational and calculative logics of much consumer psychology (see Woodruffe-Burton et al., 2002): these include addictive and compulsive consumer behaviours, experiential and hedonistic forms of consumption, forms of subcultural consumption (like fandom for instance), the conspicuous consumption of low income groups (see Box below) or the role of objects in consumers' lives. The work of Russell Belk (1988), for example, conceives of the 'self' as that which can be 'extended' by possessions of all kinds: photographs, jewellery, clothes, cars and so on. Possessions can 'reveal or conceal the extended self' (Tian and Belk, 2005: 297). Thus, possessions are meaningful in ways that are uniquely marked by our own histories and life experiences, and they simultaneously say something about us to other people. Our identities, then, come to be inscribed in objects and are meaningful to ourselves and others through shared codes of understanding.

Social Class and Consumption

It is quite common to describe consumers as members of a particular social class. Marketing research and segmentation often does this explicitly using socio-economic methods of classification and ordering. But are socio-economic measures the only and most appropriate ones for capturing the relationship between social class and consumption?

Western societies are socially stratified. This means that they are characterised by social hierarchies which place distances between different groups in society. Social hierarchies are premised on the fact that some groups have greater access to and greater availability of economic (e.g. income) and cultural (e.g. education) resources than others. These disparities are the basis of inequality between groups and they are often talked about under the rubric of social class.

Social class has objective and subjective components. Objective components of class might include wealth or income; things that can be measured and relate to our positions in capitalist relations of production. Subjective components might include our levels of education, our professional or occupational identities, and our social networks. Social class is as much a set of values, language practices, bodily comportments and emotional connections, as it is a set of monetary figures. Based on this, we can say that social class acts to produce economic and cultural differences between social groups.

(Cont'd)

Leisure and consumption activities are key sites in which class relations are acted out and inequalities between social groups produced. There is a long stream of academic work which has investigated and theorised how consumption patterns reflect and reproduce status relations between groups.

From Veblen's (1899/1994) work on the conspicuous consumption patterns of the emerging leisure classes of late nineteenth century America, through Bourdieu's (1984) claim that expressions of taste serve to classify, and to classify the classifier, to Featherstone's (1991; 2007) extension of both these writers in his work on the lifestyle patterns of the new petite bourgeoisie in a 'postmodern' consumer culture, consumption has always been an important manifestation of social stratification, and of actual and aspired movement up and down the social ladder.

9.2.2 Postmodernism, Post-Fordism and the Individualisation of Consumption

Social and cultural writers on postmodernism typically focus less on descriptions of individual or group consumption behaviours than interpretive consumer researchers, and talk more broadly about macro-level shifts in the nature of society and culture (usually through the discursive structure of the 'grand narrative'). And they would usually do so with reference to changes and transformations in the economic realm of Western capitalist societies. In this regard, a key part of recent sociological grand narratives is the idea that Western societies have undergone profound economic, social and cultural change over the course of the twenty-first century. Many label this change as a move from *modernity to postmodernity*; or as a shift from a modern to a postmodern form of society. Accounts of this change are typically related to fundamental changes in the nature of capitalism. Shifts in the organisation of production, distribution and consumption are purported to have fundamentally altered and left a deep imprint on our social lives and cultural values. As is characteristic of grand narratives, these shifts are talked about as a move from one state of affairs to another, from an 'old' to a 'new' era.

The 'old' era in Western societies was a time best described by the logic of Fordism (named after the Ford motor company). It was supposedly a time in which standardised products were mass produced, and in which mass markets of consumers emerged to buy these products. Consumer demand was propagated by a burgeoning advertising industry and the institutionalisation of credit. It was a time in the US and other Western societies which involved the consumption and increasing popularity of commodities like suburban housing, cars and labour-saving household appliances. It was a time of stability following the horrors of the Second World War when social structures (like the family, church and the state) were solid and social mores narrow and tightly regulated.

'New' times are supposedly best described under the rubric of post-Fordism. This is a time of flexible specialisation not mass production and of individualised rather than mass consumption where an increasingly important role is played by cultural intermediaries like advertisers, designers and brand consultants in society. It is a time in which a new middle class has emerged in consumer societies with specific lifestyles and cultural orientations: well-educated, cultivated and distinct tastes. It is a time of an increasing turnover of fads and symbolic content in commodified experiences of leisure, sport, tourism, entertainment or body maintenance, and of social fragmentation where the structures of the family, church and state have been dismantled and play a less significant role in people's lives.

Against this context, it is often said that many consumers in Western economies live in times of increasing risk and uncertainty. Gone are the days of stable social structures that gave relative stability of meaning to our lives. In its place, we have fragmented social structures, increasing social division and a lack of meaning and certainty in our lives (Firat and Venkatesh, 1995; Ritzer, 1993). Brands and other commodities have for many come to stand in for the social bonds previously provided by these structures. To put it bluntly: brands could be considered as new Gods, the ones we turn to for a more certain sense of self, and a more 'authentic' way of living in disorganised economic and cultural times. Brands are masks that we can take on and off at will to create a sense of ourselves to others, a kind of 'off-the-peg' identity. It is in this social and cultural context that, as noted in the chapter introduction, there is supposedly greater concern amongst consumers with their identities and a linked assumption that we are all individuals with the autonomy to craft and design who we are.

However, this idea of a 'postmodern' consumer identity as a mask that can be taken on or off at will ignores the sometimes profound economic and cultural limitations on our abilities to consume. These limitations are associated with social divisions and inequalities. For low-income groups, minority ethnic groups, non-dominant sexualities, or those in so-called developing nations, the ability to construct identities at will through the putting-on and taking-off of masks is not a luxury that many can so easily afford, either in economic or cultural terms. Indeed, perhaps this view of postmodern consumer identity is rather an elitist one, open only to a minority of the world's rich with the economic and cultural resources to enjoy play with masks. To avoid ignoring these important socio-economic issues, we would suggest that in understanding the production of consumer identity, we need to hold together an analysis of the economic, cultural and other contextual domains which make it possible. Our guiding assumption is that consumer identity is both an expression of, as well as a generator of, economic and cultural forces. Furthermore, both economic and cultural forces simultaneously enable as well as constrain expressions of consumer identity. Consumer identity is not the simple liberatory act associated with brands (Firat and Venkatesh, 1995); nor is it wholly dictated by what the market suggests.

9.2.3 Cultural Production

In order to gain an insight into how these varied social, cultural and economic contextual factors impact upon consumers' identities, we will go on shortly to present our analyses of a TV programme and an American novel. Before then, it is helpful to think about these pieces of popular and literary culture as examples of cultural production. Each of these pieces of 'culture' has been *produced* – not just by an individual author (in the case of the book), but by a range of different people and organisations (TV companies, directors, editors, marketers, distributors, presenters, actors, advertisers etc.). What is being produced in each of these cases are *representations* or *portrayals* of different kinds of issues and people that might be of interest or entertainment to a particular audience. In the two cases chosen, these are representations of contemporary gay men and of wealthy Americans at the beginning of the last century as consumers. We are analysing these pieces of culture in terms of the manner in which they represent or portray these groups, and in so doing to learn something from these portrayals about the relationship between context and consumer identity.

A key learning lesson will lie in the idea that all forms of cultural representation can be considered forms of cultural *regulation*. That is to say, as soon as we represent something, we begin to regulate how others come to understand that particular phenomenon. Scholars in cultural studies and media studies (such as Dyer, 2002) have sought to critique the forms of representation of particular social groups or social issues (we will return to this issue in Chapter 10), especially where the portrayals are negative or disparaging. The popular media is an important expression of, and outlet for, controversies which arise from time to time over how such regulation ought to operate among different sections of society. Our analysis will therefore take a particular interest in issues of representation and regulation (Du Gay et al., 1997). You should note that the analyses presented are the analyses of the authors of this book – they are not the only possible interpretations, as we note below.

9.2.4 Cultural Reception

In communication studies, there is a long tradition of so-called audience research which explores how audiences decode and understand materials. Whilst traditional communication theory often assumed that audiences passively assimilate the messages of broadcasters, marketers or TV programmes, it is now commonplace to suggest that audiences are active participants in shaping the meaning of a particular cultural form. Audiences may well understand and take up the intended meaning of the producer, but more frequently they will also appropriate that meaning in line with their own social and cultural values to create multiple understandings of the same source material. In regard to this chapter, then, the meanings that you might take from reading the texts or watching the programs we are analysing might not necessarily be the same as ours, or anyone else's.

Consumers regularly 'appropriate', or change the meaning of products or services, sometimes in ways that oppose and subvert the intended meaning of the producers. Such practices of appropriation or opposition can also be an important identity-resource for consumers. The literature on subcultural consumption, for instance, has a well-established history which shows how particular subcultural groups (ranging from gay men to bondage punks) consume particular products and brands in ways that not only create in-group membership and express common values and feelings, but also celebrate their difference and subvert the norms and values of mainstream society.

Sociologists, cultural historians, anthropologists, political scientists and social psychologists have explored how this kind of 'boundarisation' of identity and group culture creates specific patterns of behaviour and symbolic identity-formation along racial/ethnic, sexual, class and national lines of difference (Lamont and Molnàr, 2002). The application of 'boundary' concepts to a range of organisational phenomena in business can be very rich and interesting for students of marketing. Peterson and Narasimha (2004), for instance, describe how symbolic elements of culture are shaped, produced and distributed according to legal, technological, organisational, industry and market structures. Their research reveals that the production of culture can subsequently lead to 'auto-production' among loosely organised and informal communities; when marginalised groups come together, they are able to generate new and subversive meanings as they find common bonds in their marginality in a particular society.

Having set out some conceptual material to inform our analysis, the next two sections present case studies which we use to illustrate both the connection between context and consumption, and the complexity and ambiguity of identity production.

9.3 *Queer Eye for the Straight Guy*: Marketing and the Regulation of Class and Sexuality

Through a critical discussion of the American TV makeover series *Queer Eye for the Straight Guy*, we highlight the ways in which this particular media product represents gay male sexuality, and gay male consumers. First, it illustrates how production and consumption are gendered and sexualised activities, and how, therefore, marketing is centrally implicated in the reproduction of unequal relations between people of different genders and sexualities. Second, and relatedly, it demonstrates that at the heart of this production of identity is a form of cultural regulation. As we shall see, gay male sexuality is produced in highly circumscribed ways in *Queer Eye*, ways which limit the visibility and acceptance of gay men in the public sphere of television whilst on a surface level seeming to celebrate it. Many of you will not have heard of this programme, so what is it about?

Queer Eye for the Straight Guy is a popular makeover television series. Produced by US cable television network Bravo, it aired for the first time in 2003 and was cancelled in January 2007. The original concept for the programme involved a team of five openly gay men (Carson, Ted, Kyan, Jai and Thom, known collectively as the 'Fab Five') descending upon a hapless heterosexual man and transforming different aspects of his life (from his hair, clothing and fashion sense, to the layout of his apartment and knowledge of wine) in a short space of time: the quintessential premise of all TV makeover shows. Usually this 'transformation' was carried out to prepare him for an important event in his life e.g. for a marriage proposal, or to improve his relationship with his girlfriend. At the start of the third series, the programme name was abbreviated to *Queer Eye* since it moved from its initial focus on straight men, to encompass the cultural transformation of straight women and of gay men and lesbians.

Each of the five gay men possessed different areas of expertise: Ted was the 'Food and Wine Connoisseur'; Kyan the 'Grooming Guru'; Thom the 'Design Doctor'; Carson the 'Fashion Savant'; and Jai the 'Culture Vulture'. As noted in the wikipedia entry on *Queer Eye*, the aim of the show is to 'tszuj' the hapless heterosexual: tszuj is a Polari term (gay slang – part of gay code) meaning to style someone or something as follows:

> The 'Fab Five' redecorate, rewardrobe, and restyle to create a completely new 'look' for the candidate. In a typical episode, the 'Fab Five' arrive at the candidate's residence to assess his 'level of style'. The cast ransacks the home, with a running 'style' commentary on everything they find. In their investigation, each expert attempts to understand the unique preferences of the candidate in order to best advise him on how to improve. (Taken from the Wikipedia entry)

The programme was a huge hit in the USA, and was then bought up by television networks in other countries e.g. by Channel 4 in the UK. The programme won an Emmy Award in 2004, and led to a series of less successful copies in the UK, Denmark, Sweden, Finland, Norway, Australia, Spain, France, Portugal and Germany.

Queer Eye enjoyed critical acclaim for the visibility it brought to gay men, and gay lifestyles, in the public sphere. Critics however accused its producers of stereotyping gay men and of generalising that all gay men are necessarily and somehow inherently more stylish, fashionable and in possession of all forms of 'good taste' compared to heterosexual men. However, there are more complex questions, and forms of critique, that emanate from an analysis of this programme. We would certainly encourage you to watch an episode of *Queer Eye* and try to prepare your own answers to the following questions before looking at ours. Repeats are shown on a number of different cable/digital channels in the UK, USA and elsewhere.

The key question for us is: How has gay male sexuality been 'put to work' in *Queer Eye*? This involves asking: How are gay men represented in this programme? What kinds of knowledges are they supposed to possess? How do they interact with the hapless heterosexual? Does the programme reinforce stereotypes about gay men? What are the consequences of this? Finally, and more broadly, how far can 'the market' guarantee progress in lesbian, gay, bisexual and transgender (LGBT) peoples struggles for social recognition? Brewis and Jack (2006) note at least three important ways in which we can critically understand the implications of *Queer Eye*.

9.3.1 The Commodification of Minority Style

First we turn to the important role of cultural intermediaries in creating and circulating dominant cultural ideals of style, cool and beauty, and Klein's (2001) comments about 'coolhunting' as an important marketing task (see also Chapter 7). Klein notes how cultural intermediaries are always on the lookout for the latest 'undiscovered' symbolic item, and gay men seem to be it. *Queer Eye*, and the gay male sexuality upon which it draws, can be viewed as the latest in cool.

This annexing of style is a well-documented phenomenon in the discipline of cultural studies. It is typically the styles of minority groups like gay men which are tapped for the latest values and practices with which to create commodities and brand products. Klesse (2000: 24) refers to this annexing of minority style as 'an increasingly trendy aestheticization and commodification of … difference'. MacCannell and MacCannell (1993) make the point that late capitalist society appropriates marginal lifestyles, which discriminated groups have developed as coping mechanisms and protective strategies. Cultural intermediaries transform these into commodities and sell them back to the people that 'owned' them in the first place. With reference to the commodification of ethnicity, they write:

> the ghetto street habitat of gang members assuaging real pain with imaginative expressions of personal style that are immediately taken up as the code for next year's line of Guess Jeans and casual sportswear, simulacra of a hip hop urban existence, the ultimate achievement of which is to become a fad among the very groups that created the style in the first place so they must literally beg, borrow, and steal to buy back corporate copies of the life that has been taken from them. (MacCannell and MacCannell, 1993: 138)

What images and understandings does *Queer Eye* portray of gay men? What kind of mirror does this hold up to gay men? Might it be said to have similarly problematic consequences, as MacCannell and MacCannell intimate above with respect to the commodification of ghetto culture?

9.3.2 Sexuality, Taste and Class

Sender (2006) argues that *Queer Eye* is premised on the idea that the straight male consumer is a problem: straight men are reluctant to buy anything much outside the delimited spheres of 'electronics, cars, tools, and pornography' (2006: 133). It is the task of the Fab Five to 'solve' this problem and to turn straight men into 'candidates in a life of responsible and fulfilling consumption' (ibid.: 137). The Fab Five, as supposedly typical examples of gay men, bring a particular set of cultural and aesthetic knowledges to accomplish this task. They know what 'good taste' is, whether related to fashion, food or soft furnishings, and they are not frightened to use it on their straight 'clients'.

Being gay is thus associated with being 'tasteful', 'classy', 'stylish' and 'cosmopolitan'. The producers of *Queer Eye* are working, then, with the dominant understanding of gay men (as consumers) in the public sphere as affluent, savvy and brand-aware, reducing the diversity of gay men, and their consumer behaviour, to a set of cultural and aesthetic knowledges. It is not just *Queer Eye* that does this. In another piece, Sender (2001) shows how *Advocate* magazine (target market: gay consumers), has also created an ideal-type reader based on the construction of a 'dominant gay habitus' for an 'openly gay, professional-managerial class' (2001: 73).

The last part of this quotation points us in another important direction when outlining what kinds of images, roles and understandings of gay men are being offered in *Queer Eye*: that of social class. We therefore need our analysis to take shape at the intersection of sexuality *and* class. The transformation of the straight man by a 'gay aesthetic' promises him a certain kind of upward class mobility, given the association between 'gayness' and 'classiness'. Gay consumption is presented as the epitome of 'first world' citizenship and productive 'middle classness' (Brewis and Jack, 2006). The programme thereby 'embodies the neoliberal imperative to cultivate an autonomously calibrating self within a framework that privileges consumer choice over other modes of citizenship' (Miller, cited in Sender, 2006: 145). The Fab Five offer the opportunity to improve oneself as worker-citizen in its endorsement of 'the spread of self-fashioning as a requirement of personal and professional achievement through the US middle-class labor force' (Miller, cited in Sender, 2006: 145).

9.3.3 Cultural Regulation and the Market

It has been said that the success of this series is part of the increasing visibility and acceptance of gay men and women in popular culture. The 'coming out' of Ellen DeGeneres (a hugely popular and influential comedian and talk show host in the US) as a lesbian was a significant event for her fans, Hollywood as well as the American public. The success of *Will & Grace*, a TV series about a gay man (Will) and his 'faghag' (Grace), as well as films like *Brokeback Mountain* and *Milk*, and the numerous gay characters now found in films and sitcoms, suggest a new kind of visibility and, possibly, the greater acceptance and assimilation of queer people into the mainstream of Western societies. However, as Taylor suggest, this assimilation is founded on an uneasy tolerance of (male) homosexuality – such that 'respectful, consuming citizens ... can be 'just like you'; if not homosexual then definitely middle-class' (2005: 485). As Brewis and Jack (2006) note with specific regard to *Queer Eye*, Kelly (cited in Sender, 2006: 133) describes the programme as:

execrable – a catalog of homosexual stereotypes, played to a throbbing techno-disco beat, that also systematically denies its gay stars their complexity and their sexuality. From first scene to last, they trill and fuss, displaying their talents at traditionally effeminate domestic tasks.

What Kelly suggests is that the manner in which *Queer Eye* portrays gay men as sophisticated consumer helps people 'forget' that they are just that – *homo*sexual. It 'cleanses' the gay male identity of sexuality and replaces it instead with their supposedly particular aesthetic, their professional occupations and their acerbic wit. Straight society, then, we assume is able to 'handle' this version of homosexuality because it means that there is no direct confrontation with sexuality (Brewis and Jack, 2010). As such the cultural production of gay male sexuality in *Queer Eye* can actually be interpreted as homophobic. That is to say, the hidden message of the programme can be understood as follows: gay men can be visible in public culture, they can enjoy respect and celebrity, *but only under certain conditions.*

The first condition, as hinted at above, is that gay men must not be portrayed as sexual beings: sex needs to be removed from the equation to make them less threatening. Second, they must not be portrayed as having families and children: they must be individuals. Third, they must be 'middle class'. *Queer Eye* fails to acknowledge the fact that there are important socio-economic differences between gay men: the gay community, like all communities, is socially stratified according to class. It peddles the myth that all gay men enjoy an affluent status. As Badgett (1997) argues, the most frequently cited surveys upon which this claim is founded are based on 'biased samples' which produce deceptive figures. Bringing these points together, we can use Henderson (2007) to suggest that the visibility of queer people in the media is a 'class-based project' where the conditions that make gay people valuable in the public's eye are closely associated with middle-class life (bourgeois demeanour, high income and expenditure, adherence to conventional family values). In short, being gay, as illustrated in this analysis of *Queer Eye* is only acceptable in public cultural life under highly circumscribed conditions and subject to particular forms of cultural regulation.

Ultimately the answer to the question of whether the 'market', and the increasing visibility of gay lifestyles through mass media products and marketing brands, is a necessarily progressive arena for gay and lesbian people in their struggle for equality is ambiguous. On the one hand, it can be argued that market recognition constitutes an affirmation and legitimation (Peñaloza, 1996) of this historically stigmatised social group. As Kates (2004) illustrates in his empirical study of homosexual men's boycotts of corporations with dubious employment records, charitable donations and political stances, the market also provides gay consumers with brand leverage. On the other hand, the market must necessarily appropriate the oppositional ethos of the gay and lesbian community as a social movement. Celebration of gay success in the market can therefore be seen as a form of 'selling out' (Chasin, 2000), or as Ingebretsen puts it: 'Accommodation, like membership, has its privileges, but it exacts its prices as well' (1999: 135). The theme of social class, and in particular the display of social status through leisure, is the key theme in our next case.

9.4 The Great Gatsby

The Great Gatsby (1925/1950) by F. Scott Fitzgerald is widely regarded by readers and critics as a classic of American literature. Some critics have even gone as far as to argue that 'the three most distinguished American novels that have been the most unfeignedly enjoyed by intelligent readers in our time are almost certainly *Huckleberry Finn*, *The Great Gatsby* and *Catcher in the Rye*' (Fraser, 1965: 554). Furthermore, of these three, *The Great Gatsby* has the 'greatest philosophical pretensions and is the most seductive' (1965: 555). While the matter of its greatness and place in the canon of American letters may be debatable, there is little doubt that much of its magical seductiveness lies in the way in which its central characters appear to be able to play with moral constraints while, at the same time, enjoying the pleasures of the age.

The Great Gatsby was published in 1925, after the First World War. It was known as the Jazz Age, a time when Americans felt ready to let their hair down after the suffering and travails of the war and to enjoy the fun and entertainment afforded by music halls, cabaret clubs, theatre, fast cars. Most of all, it was a time of money, created by immigrants from all over the world and the creativity and energy they brought with them. It was the age when American industrialists and entrepreneurs created the wealth that marked a new spirit of philanthropy alongside relentless mercantilism. These were the dynasties founded by such famous names as John D. Rockefeller, Astor, Vanderbilt and Guggenheim.

The Great Gatsby evokes the spirit of the age marvellously well. In times of boom rather than bust, men and women are likely to be blinded by appearance rather than the more mundane, even brutal, facts of life. The novel is an ironic examination of how individuals attempt to exploit the delicately poised relationship between artifice and reality. Its central protagonist, Jay Gatsby, lives in a mansion modelled on a French villa, wears white suits with impossibly beautiful silver shirts and gold ties and drives a luxurious cream-coloured car. Daisy Buchanan, the woman he loves and for whom he makes his extravagant displays of wealth, has 'a voice full of money'. Consumerist images and fantasies drive the novel, right up to its compelling end, when the 'Great' in 'Great Gatsby' is as much a mockery of what Jay represents as it is a metaphor for the power he exerts over his friends and enemies alike through his painstaking and cunning construction of identity.

For students of marketing, therefore, *The Great Gatsby* represents an excellent way to gain a better understanding of the production and consumption of economic and social identity through wealth, leisure and class. It gives you one way of thinking through how social stratification and class relations are produced and reproduced through leisure activities. More than this, it also shows how we, and others around us, produce and reproduce who we think we are based on our and others' displays of wealth.

In the novel, F. Scott Fitzgerald portrays how individual, as well as group, identities are nebulous and hard-to-grasp because so much of what we permit others to see of us is covered over by our achievements, failures, the words we use, the style of dress we adopt, the foods we eat and the books we read – these constitute a key motif in the novel, that of 'personality'. The careful edifices we construct to show others how they should perceive us, in other words, represent the gap between artifice and reality. It is impossible, often, to distinguish between the two 'ways of being' in the world. What the novel does show clearly, however, represent that individuals can master the forces of society in order to 'make' a personality which others believe in and aspire to. In our analysis, we examine the effects of money and time, and the interrelationship between these concepts, upon personalities. Rather than simply watching the 1974 film version starring Robert Redford and Mia Farrow, do read the book before engaging with our analysis. See below for a summary of the plot.

Plot of *The Great Gatsby*

The Great Gatsby is narrated through the voice of Nick Carraway, a young man who moves from Minnesota to New York to learn about the 'bond business'. He rents a house in West Egg, a part of New York populated by the 'nouveau riche' (New Rich). While there, he hears about Jay Gatsby, a rather mysterious character who lives extravagantly and throws expensive parties. One night, Nick drives out to East Egg (where 'old money' and established social bonds live) and meets his cousin, Daisy Buchanan and her husband Tom. They introduce Nick to Jordan, a beautiful and shallow woman with whom Nick begins a romantic relationship. We find out about Tom's infidelity with a woman called Myrtle Wilson. One night, Myrtle taunts Tom about Daisy and is violently assaulted by him. As the story develops, Nick gets invited to Jay Gatsby's home and meets a man there who reveals himself to be Gatsby. Nick is surprised to find the mysterious Gatsby rather young and yet, apparently, wildly successful, having already lived a life full of fanciful adventures. We are made aware much later in the novel that Jay has made his fortune in bootlegging – the illegal activity of supplying and trading in liquor – at a time when Prohibition was in force.

Gatsby confesses to Jordan that he is madly in love with Daisy and has known her since 1917. He wants Nick to arrange a reunion between them. This Nick does and Jay and Daisy rekindle their affair. When Tom finds out, he is naturally outraged and confronts Jay about the affair at the Hotel Plaza in New York. He asserts that he and Daisy share a history which Jay can never understand. Daisy realises her real destiny lies with Tom and the affair is crushed. As Nick and Jordan drive back to West Egg, they learn that Daisy's car has hit and killed Myrtle Wilson. Nick is told by Gatsby that Daisy was driving, but that he, Gatsby, intends to take the blame for it. George, Myrtle's husband, believing this, and therefore, that Gatsby was her lover, finds him in the pool at his mansion and shoots him dead before fatally shooting himself.

Nick arranges Gatsby's funeral and leaves the East Coast for the Midwest, filled with pain and disgust at the moral decay and shallow dreams of the people he has met, 'careless people ... who smashed up things and creatures and then retreated back into their money...' The novel ends with the immortal lines of broken dreams: 'boats against the current, borne back ceaselessly into the past'.

9.4.1 Personality and The Keeping Up of Appearances

The central protagonist, Jay Gatsby, personifies both the fragility of the self and also its remarkable resilience – even denial – in the face of failure: a state Fitzgerald calls 'romantic readiness'. This paradox makes *The Great Gatsby* a particularly interesting and revealing illustration of the ways in which identity is constructed both by ideals and by the expectations of others around us. *The Great Gatsby* challenges notions of how individual personalities are shaped by cultural regulation, but in terms which aspire to escape it altogether. The narrator, Nick Carraway, through which most of the novel's events are mediated, is the slightly self-effacing outsider in the fantastically thrilling world of wealth and leisure he describes.

Very early on, we are lured into believing Nick when he speaks of Gatsby's mythical aura in mellifluous tones of wonder:

> If personality is an unbroken series of successful gestures, then there was something gorgeous about him, some heightened sensitivity to the promises of life, as if he were

related to one of those intricate machines that register earthquakes ten thousand miles away. (1950: 6)

We quickly become aware, however, that tremendous work is involved in keeping up the appearance of 'unbroken' gestures. Gatsby's life is consumed by a series of false pretences, broken promises, trails of sinister business dealings. In a telling episode, the story of his life is spun out in formulaic phrases which elicit 'incredulous laughter' from our narrator, Nick Carraway (who, like the modern reader, struggles to suspend disbelief at Gatsby's incredible stories of his exploits):

I lived like a young rajah in all the capitals of Europe – Paris, Venice, Rome – collecting jewels, chiefly rubies, hunting big game, painting a little, things for myself only, and trying to forget something very sad that had happened to me a long time ago. (1950: 62)

To Nick (and us), these 'very phrases were worn so threadbare' that they had very little significance whatsoever. But Gatsby foils Nick's scepticism. As the consumer *par excellence*, Gatsby instinctively understands the importance of winning over your sceptics by producing evidence – 'souvenirs' – of exotic adventures. He produces a medal, a decoration for his extraordinary valour during his stint as first lieutenant during the war – from the government of Montenegro, no less – and a photograph of his 'Oxford days'. How is one to react? 'Then it was all true,' concludes the dazzled and fascinated Carraway. He *consumes* Gatsby like a man who has temporarily lost his mind to a beautiful mirage: 'it was like skimming hastily through a dozen magazines'. The fact is, it is impossible to tell what is true of, and about, Gatsby. By the end, his death attracts no mourners, only his Dad, whose own proud 'souvenirs' of his son reveal the extent of Gatsby's deception of himself and others.

The extent to which we are able to transcend, or escape, our social and cultural backgrounds is also problematised in the novel. In line with sociological theory on the emergence of 'taste' (Bourdieu 1984, 1993; Mintz, 1985), marketers regard commodities, food and beverages as the outcome of social trends and the business strategies of producers, exporters and importers in a globalised world (see du Gay et al., 1997; Naylor, 2000; Roseberry, 1996). Such detailed studies posit a circuit of exchange between consumers and products in a symbiotic relationship structured by social class, age and power. Thus, 'products both reflect and transform consumers' behaviour' (Zukin and Maguire, 2004: 178).

This complex dialectic is presented in *The Great Gatsby*, again, in a paradoxical manner. While Gatsby strives to transcend place and even time, the question of whether we actually ever escape our social backgrounds remains:

I see now that this has been a story of the West, after all – Tom and Gatsby, Daisy and Jordan and I, were all Westerners, and perhaps we possessed some deficiency in common which made us subtly unadaptable to Eastern life. (1950: 64)

The reference to West Egg and East Egg – the geographical locations of the homes of the key protagonists in the novel – is clearly marked out as distinct territories inhabited by different classes of people. West Egg was where Nick comes from – toiling away as a 'bond man' while East Egg was where Gatsby and other friends of Nick, like Daisy and Tom Buchanan, lived in their fashionable white palaces of dreams. The two universes never meet, divided utterly by money.

9.4.2 Time and Money

Even time is divided by money. The structure of time in the novel has generated much discussion among critics; much less recognised, we think, is the fact that the effect of wealth, as Carraway implies, is to *slow time down*. This powerful insight is not to be underestimated in the novel because it is one of the extraordinary ways in which we are shown the difference between the rich and the less privileged. We are given to understand that even time is shaped by money. The rich, having time, are able to treat and consume it differently from the poor. Thus, they know that '*presently* dinner would be over and *a little later*, the evening too would be over and casually put away' (1950: 15). In the West, by contrast, an evening 'would be hurried from phase to phase toward its close in a continually disappointed anticipation or else in sheer nervous dread of the moment itself' (ibid.: 16).

Yet, wealth is not only a material artifact which can be displayed, admired and disposed of at one's will. It can be expressed through the ability not just to acquire objects through what Veblen (1899/1994) calls 'conspicuous consumption', but also through the capacity to waste time, to squander even that which is immaterial. If we remember that the poor and the middle classes in any society are impelled to work – that is, to exchange their (labour) time for money – then we can appreciate how much time is worth. In *The Great Gatsby*, wasting time is a way of displaying one's social status because time is the ultimate luxury and to have enough to waste speaks more loudly than money or objects ever could about how rich one is. Time, in other words, *is* money. The more leisure time one has, the wealthier one is. To display waste of time is far more powerful as an indicator of social standing than the mere waste of wealth through objects.

Used this way, time allows personalities like Tom and Daisy Buchanan (and the ethereally childlike Miss Baker) to become more inchoate, floating and disengaged from moral realities than the likes of Carraway. Ultimately, this facility the rich have generates corrosive, even murderous effects, as the novel shows, but proves difficult to resist, even for the level-headed Carraway. Although there are jarring notes of violence and racism, encapsulated by the startling outburst from rich, brutally contemptuous Tom Buchanan about the danger of the 'dominant' white race losing 'control of things' to 'other races' (ibid.: 16), the novel as a whole is intensely nationalistic in its focus on specific classes of the leisured rich in the Jazz Age.

Although it has now achieved iconic status worldwide, modern readers will, no doubt, be surprised to learn that *The Great Gatsby* was considered a relative commercial failure in F. Scott Fitzgerald's time. It sold a paltry 23, 870 copies over two printings in 1925. It was criticised for its lack of 'politics,' felt by critics at the time to be essential for 'mature persons in a mature world', as Gatsby complained in his introduction to the 1934 Modern Library reprint of the novel.

9.5 Conclusion

In this chapter, we have tried to show how identity is constructed and constrained in various ways, as particular 'selves' grapple with the 'contexts' in which they find themselves. In *The Great Gatsby*, the personality of Gatsby is revealed as an illusion to be maintained, itself a product of the time and place he lives in. And in *Queer Eye* we see how, whilst on the surface the visibility of non-dominant sexualities in the public sphere might be taken as a cause for celebration, the restrictions and regulations of the wider cultural context and its social mores should make us pause for thought. The production of identities in consumer societies as illustrated through analysis of the two artistic forms is subtly, ambiguously but also very definitely related to the social, cultural, political, historical and economic contexts in which it takes place. These contexts provide both the conditions of possibility for expressions of consumer identity, as well as a set of important restrictions on them. This is not to say that context shapes identity in some kind of deterministic fashion. But it is to say that it is tricky to know where the self ends and context starts, and vice versa.

It is also to say that consumer identities are certainly not the 'off-the-peg' masks we can put on and off at our own will. To understand postmodern identity in this way is to be complicit in the continuing reproduction of material, as well as symbolic, inequalities between consumers. We have shown that these materials are useful for conceiving of 'marketing' as inextricably linked to the forces of history, geography, politics and that 'reading' texts in this way can yield new understandings of how and why artistic products capture the popular imagination.

9.6 Learning Activities

Postmodern claims that the individual is able to dispose and reconstruct identities through the act of consumption are questioned in this chapter. The tethers of context (social class, gender and sexuality) are explored through an examination of a popular television show and literature. The learning activities for this chapter seek to develop an appreciation of identity that relates it to the social, cultural, historical and economic contexts in which it finds expression. Before you begin the learning activities remind yourself of the learning aims for the chapter so that your time and efforts are focused.

Learning Activity One: A Novel Idea

Read Brown (2005) and prepare answers to the questions that follow:

a   Why does Brown suggest that marketing practitioners might learn more from reading novels than the academic marketing literature?
b   What are the similarities and differences Brown reports between Shakar's *The Savage Girl* and Barry's *Jennifer Government*? Why does he consider Shakar's novel the better one?
c   To what ends does Brown suggest that reading novels should be put in consumer research? In this respect, what does he mean by 'novelising our findings'?

Learning Activity Two: Plasticine Beckham?

The famous soccer player David Beckham has been analysed as a cultural icon by academics. Conduct a literature search for academic publications on Beckham with particular regard to the following:

a   His role as a style icon and male role-model. In what ways might Beckham be understood as a figure in popular culture who transgresses conventional norms of gender and sexuality?
b   His role as a 'black' style icon and role model. How can Beckham be considered a black role model? Think here in terms of his tastes in music, clothing and jewellery.

c   Based on your reflections on the above, what is the role of the market and of consumer culture in promoting positive images and understandings of non-dominant identities in society?

To assist you with this task, we have provided two references to relevant material: Vincent et al. (2009) and Cashmore and Parker (2003).

9.7 Further Reading

DuGay, P., Hall, S., James, L., Mackay, H. and Negus, K. (1997) *Doing Cultural Studies: The Story of the Sony Walkman.* London: Sage.

Ideas about cultural production, representation, regulation and appropriation come from the 'circuit of culture' to be found in this book where it is applied to the Sony Walkman. This is a short, accessible and interesting book about an object you will all be familiar with which demonstrates the utility of a cultural studies approach to understanding marketing phenomena.

Roberson, J. (2005) 'Fight!! Ippatsu!! 'Genki' energy drinks and the marketing of masculine ideology in Japan', *Men and Masculinities*, 7(4): 365–84.

Roberson provides a fascinating account of the representation of masculinities within the popular media in Japan. The article illustrates how media discourse both enables and constrains the possible expressions of masculinity amongst consumers (part of the production and regulation moments in the circuit of culture above).

Veblen, T.B. (1899/1994) *The Theory of the Leisure Class.* New York: Courier Dover Publications.

Students who have read this chapter carefully will find Thorstein Veblen's study of the leisured class and the relationship between consumption and economic forces fascinating. His theory of the origins and nature of the leisured class is, of course, highly pertinent to any reading of *The Great Gatsby*. F. Scott Fitzgerald himself was certainly acutely aware of the book and its arguments.

Dwyer, R.E. (2009) 'Making a habit of it: Positional consumption, conventional action and the standard of living', *Journal of Consumer Culture*, 9(3): 328–47.

Having read Veblen, you should turn to Dwyer's article which argues for the contemporary relevance of Veblen's ideas for understanding the relationship between emulation, consumption and social stratification.

Newholm, T. and Hopkinson, G.C. (2009) 'I just tend to wear what I like: Contemporary consumption and the paradoxical construction of individuality', *Marketing Theory*, 9(4): 439–62.

Above all, this chapter sets out to illustrate the precarious nature of consumer identities. Newholm and Hopkinson present the results of a research study (funded by members of the retail industry) into the precarious and paradoxical construction of individuality amongst undergraduates and recently graduated professionals.

9.8 References

Arnould, E.J. and Thompson, C.J. (2005) 'Consumer Culture Theory (CCT): Twenty years of research', *Journal of Consumer Research*, 31 (4): 868–82.

Badgett, L.M.V. (1997) 'Beyond Biased Samples: Challenging the myths on the economic status of lesbians and gay men', in A. Gluckman and B. Reed (eds), *Homo Economics: Capitalism, Community, and Lesbian and Gay Life*, pp. 65–71. New York and London: Routledge.

Belk, R. (1986) 'Art versus science as ways of generating knowledge about materialism', in D. Brinberg and R.J. Lutz (eds), *Perspectives on Methodology in Consumer Research*, pp. 3–36. New York: Springer.

Belk, R.W. (1988) 'Possessions and the Extended Self', *Journal of Consumer Research*, 15 (September): 139–67.

Bourdieu, P. (1984) *Distinction: A Social Critique of the Judgement of Taste*. London: Routledge and Kegan Paul.

Bourdieu, P. (1993) *The Field of Cultural Production*, trans. Randal Johnson. Cambridge: Polity Press.

Brewis, J. and Jack, G. (2006) 'Consuming chavs: An analysis of ambiguous politics of chavinism on the British gay male scene', Working Paper. University of Leicester.

Brewis, J. and Jack, G. (2010) 'Consuming chavs: An analysis of the ambiguous politics of chavinism on the British gay male scene', *Sociology*, 44 (2): 1–18.

Brown, S. (2005) 'I can read you like a book: Novel thoughts on consumer behaviour,' *Qualitative Market Research: An International Journal*, 8 (2): 219–37.

Cashmore, E. and Parker, A. (2003) 'One David Beckham? Celebrity masculinity and the soccerati', *Sociology of Sport Journal*, 20 (3): 214–31.

Chasin, A. (2000) *Selling Out: The Gay and Lesbian Movement Goes to Market*. New York and Basingstoke: Palgrave.

Cherrier, H. and Murray, J.B. (2004) 'The sociology of consumption and the hidden facet of marketing', *Journal of Marketing Management*, 20 (5/6): 509–25.

Du Gay, P., Hall, S., James, L., Mackay, H. and Nagus, K. (1997) 'Designing the Walkman: Articulating production and consumption', in P. du Gay, S. Hall, L. James, H. Mackay and K. Negus, *Doing Cultural Studies: the Story of the Sony Walkman*, pp. 62–74. London: Sage.

Dyer, R. (2002) *The Culture of Queers*. London: Routledge.

Featherstone, M. (1988) 'In pursuit of the postmodern', *Theory, Culture, & Society*, 5 (2/3): 195–216.

Featherstone, M. (1991) *Consumer Culture and Postmodernism*. Newbury, CA: Sage.

Featherstone, M. (2007) *Consumer Culture and Postmodernism*, 2nd edn. Newbury, CA: Sage.

Firat, A.F. and Venkatesh, A. (1995) 'Liberatory postmodernism and the Reenchantment of Consumption', *Journal of Consumer Research*, 22 (3): 239–67.

Fitzgerald, F. Scott (1925/1950) *The Great Gatsby*. London: Penguin.

Fraser, J. (1965) 'Dust and dreams and *The Great Gatsby*', *ELH*, 32 (4): 554–64.

Henderson, L. (2007) 'Queer visibility and social class', in K.G. Barnhurst (ed.), *Media Queered: Visibility and its Discontents*, pp. 197–216. New York: Peter Lang.

Hirschman, E. (1980) 'Innovativeness, novelty seeking, and consumer creativity', *Journal of Consumer Research*, 7 (December): 283–95.

Hirschman, E.C. (1993) 'Secular and sacred consumption imagery in Charles Dickens' *A Christmas Carol*', in M.B. Holbrook and E.C. Hirschman (eds), *The Semiotics of Consumption: Interpreting Symbolic Consumer Behavior in Popular Culture and Works of Art*, pp. 286–95. Berlin: Walter de Gruyter.

Holbrook, M.B. (1991) 'Romanticism and sentimentality in consumer behavior: a literary approach to the joys and sorrows of consumption', in E.C. Hirschman (ed.), *Research in Consumer Behavior*, Volume 5, pp. 105–80. Greenwich, CT: JAI Press.

Holbrook, M.B. and Hirschman, E.C. (1982) 'The experiential aspects of consumption: Consumer fantasies, feelings and fun', *Journal of Consumer Research*, 9 (1): 132–40.

Holbrook, M.B. and Hirschman, E.C. (eds) (1993) *The Semiotics of Consumption: Interpreting Symbolic Consumer Behavior in Popular Culture and Works of Art.* Berlin: Walter de Gruyter.

Ingebretsen, E. (1999) 'Gone shopping: The commercialization of same-sex desire', *Journal of Gay, Lesbian, and Bisexual Identity,* 4 (2): 125–48.

Kates, S.M. (2004) 'The dynamics of brand legitimacy: An interpretive study in the gay men's community', *Journal of Consumer Research,* 31 (2): 455–64.

Kellner, D. (1988) 'Postmodernism as social theory: Some problems and challenges', *Theory, Culture & Society,* 5 (2/3): 239–70.

Klein, N. (2001) *No Logo.* London: Flamingo.

Klesse, C. (2000) 'Modern primitivism: Non-mainstream body modification and racialized representation', in M. Featherstone (ed.), *Body Modification,* pp. 15–38. London: Sage.

Lamont, M. and Molnàr, V. (2002) 'The study of boundaries in the social sciences', *Annual Review of Sociology,* 30: 167–95.

Lyotard, J-F. (1984) *The Postmodern Condition.* Minneapolis: University of Minnesota Press.

MacCannell, D. and MacCannell, J.F. (1993) 'Social class in postmodernity: Simulacrum or return of the real?', in C. Rojek and B.S. Turner (eds), *Forget Baudrillard?*, pp. 124–45. London and New York: Routledge.

McCracken, G. (1986) 'Culture and consumption: A theoretical account of the structure and movement of the cultural meaning of consumer goods', *Journal of Consumer Research,* 13 (1): 71–84.

McDonagh, P. and Brereton, P. (2010) 'Screening not greening: an ecological reading of the greatest business movies', *Journal of Macromarketing.*

Mintz, S. (1985) *Production, Sweetness and Power: The Place of Sugar in Modern Society.* New York: Viking.

Naylor, S. (2000) 'Spacing the can: Empire, modernity and the globalisation of food', *Environment and Planning,* 32: 1625–39.

Peñaloza, L. (1996) 'We're here, we're queer, and we're going shopping! A critical perspective on the accommodation of gays and lesbians into the US marketplace', *Journal of Homosexuality,* 31 (1/2): 9–41.

Peterson, R.A. and Narasimha, A. (2004) 'The production of culture perspective', *Annual Review of Sociology,* 30: 311–34.

Ritzer, G. (1993) *The McDonaldization of Society: An Investigation into the Changing Character of Contemporary Social Life.* Newbury Park, CA: Pine Forge Press.

Roseberry, W. (1996) 'The rise of yuppie coffees and the reimagination of class in the United States', *American Anthropologist,* 98 (4): 762–75.

Sender, K. (2001) 'Gay readers, consumers, and a dominant gay habitus: 25 years of the *Advocate* magazine', *Journal of Communication,* 51 (1): 73–99.

Sender, K. (2006) 'Queens for a day: *Queer Eye for the Straight Guy* and the Neoliberal Project', *Critical Studies in Media Communication,* 23 (2): 131–51.

Taylor, Y. (2005) 'Real politik or real politics? Working-class lesbians' political "awareness" and activism', *Women's Studies International Forum,* 28 (6): 484–94.

Tian, K. and Belk, R.W. (2005) 'Extended self and possessions in the workplace', *Journal of Consumer Research,* 32: 297–309.

Veblen, T.B. (1899/1994) *The Theory of the Leisure Class.* New York: Courier Dover Publications.

Vincent, J., Hill, J.S. and Lee, J.W. (2009) 'The multiple brand personalities of David Beckham: A case study of the Beckham brand', *Sport Marketing Quarterly,* 18 (3): 173–81.

Woodruffe-Burton, H., Eccles, S., and Elliott, R. (2002) 'Towards a theory of shopping: A holistic framework', *Journal of Consumer Behaviour,* 1 (3): 256–66.

Zukin, S. and Maguire, J.S. (2004) 'Consumers and consumption', *Annual Review of Sociology,* 30 (1): 173–97.

Marketing and the Sign

10.1 Introduction

When thinking about the value of things, it is a common assumption to see the role of the firm as one involving the transformation of expertise, capital and resources into useful and valuable products for consumers to consume. For example, a manufacturer of MP3 players transforms pieces of plastic and metal using specialist knowledge and equipment to create devices that allow consumers to listen to music in a convenient and accessible way. From this perspective, marketing is mainly thought of as an activity that takes place once the production process has finished. The marketer's role is essentially a secondary function that helps to raise awareness among potential buyers as well as adding on a number of intangible features such as brand value so that consumers can hopefully use products as part of their on-going identity projects (as noted in Chapter 9). Marketers have been understandably sceptical about this definition of the marketing function and have sought to explain how marketing is actually a much more important part of the production process. Some writers argue that marketing should be seen as a form of cultural production. In the same way that goods are manufactured in factories, values, meanings and signs are 'manufactured' by marketers as part of the culture industries. Marketers employ branding, advertising and other types of communication to achieve this by utilising a wide range of cultural capital, resources and expertise. Now look at this piece of communication.

B-A-R-B-I-E

Most of you will probably recognise this collection of six letters. Together they form a word and a sound that simultaneously make us think of one of the world's best-known toy dolls and a leading brand name that has spawned its own lucrative merchandising industry. Barbie conjures up images of a particular kind of femininity and has become a role-model of sorts for generations of young girls – beautiful, smart, glamorous and successful. Even without seeing this word or hearing the name, sight of the image below is enough for most of us to think of Barbie and the positive attributes we associate with her.

The question is, though: how do we know this? Why do so many people agree that Barbie stands for these particular things? Or, to put it more crudely perhaps: How does an essentially meaningless lump of plastic generate such strong associations, meanings which have turned Barbie's owners Mattel into a multi-billion dollar corporation? To ask these kinds of questions is to ask questions about the nature of *signs*

Figure 10.1   Do you recognise who this is?

and their relation to the activities of marketing. This relationship between marketing and signs is the focus of this chapter.

The study of signs is most commonly referred to as 'semiotics' and is associated with the disciplines of the humanities, especially linguistics, literary criticism, anthropology and cultural studies. In recent years, however, marketing scholars (notably Mick, 1986 and Umiker-Sebeok, 1987) have taken an interest in semiotics in order to think not only about what it means to do marketing work, but also to place marketing in a wider context and thus to understand how marketing and society are connected through signs.

In an obvious sense, a sign is a physical object that communicates a message (think quite literally of a signpost for instance). But in a less obvious sense, a sign refers to something other than itself. As well as being 'things-in-themselves', signs also direct our attention, or give us a message/leave a trace about something else, perhaps a past or future event, or an object or condition which does not physically present itself contemporaneously to the sign. It works like a shortcut: so, for instance, road traffic signs alert drivers to a list of dangers and hazards. And signs on toilet doors help men and women choose the correct entrance in order to avoid potential embarrassment.

In the context of marketing, signs can take many different forms primarily associated with an organisation's product, branding and promotional strategies. At a basic level, signs can add value to products, turning everyday commodities into brands and allowing marketers and producers to differentiate their products from those of competitors. Banks and IT companies, for instance, often use signs of security and dependability to convey those values to customers. Celebrity endorsements are another example of signs at work, since the association of a celebrity with the product serves to make that product desirable. Signs can thus be any part of the product, branding and promotional strategies of an organisation which set out to give a product/service/experience a particular set of meanings that will appeal to a target audience.

Moreover, signs take both textual/poetic (e.g. they can be a word) and visual forms (e.g. they can be an image or a picture). Over time, marketers work to embed these meanings, or associations, in the minds of consumers, eventually forming the basis for shared knowledge amongst consumers. As a set of social and commercial practices, marketing can be viewed as a system of signs, as well as a sign industry.

An understanding of marketing and the sign is vital in the empirical context of contemporary economy and society in advanced capitalist economies across the globe. Goldman and Papson (1996) famously commented on our societies as marked by 'cluttered landscapes of advertising'. In other words, marketing signs are everywhere in our public and private spaces, whether through billboards on roads in city centres and leading to airports, increased advertising expenditure, greater levels of corporate sponsorship in schools and civic spaces, or the prevalence of branded clothing and merchandise as consumers use these resources to create a sense of themselves as global citizens (see, in particular, Scollon and Scollon, 2003, and their concept of 'geosemiotics').

Many sign systems associated with markets and marketing are becoming increasingly global and consumers look to familiar brands to provide a cultural anchor in times of stress (as noted in Chapter 9 with reference to postmodernism). Davies et al. (2003) studied the consumer behaviour of international students who have recently arrived in a new country to study. Although many aspects of life in a new culture take time to adapt to, often causing trauma and confusion, brands and other market-related resources were often understood and recognised straightaway, providing comfort and reassurance.

In this chapter we set out to introduce you to theoretical frameworks and debates from a number of different disciplines (including linguistics, sociology and marketing) concerned with the nature of signs. By the end of this chapter, you should have a clearer understanding of some of the key debates around the economy of signs – through television, advertising and other public media – and its dominant role in our lives. Further, you should be able to appreciate how differing interpretations of the relations between signs and objects and between signs and other signs can have political effects. That is to say, how signs reproduce unequal relations between different social groups.

The chapter is structured into three key sections. In the first section (10.2), you will be introduced to semiotics through the structuralist linguistic analyses of de Saussure and Peirce. Both analyses provide differently accented accounts of how language is structured as a system of differences (Saussure) or is generative of meaning (Peirce). Both analyses have been particularly influential in examinations of marketing signs, especially in discussions of how advertising, celebrity, clothing and fashion systems work (for instance by Judith Williamson and Roland Barthes).

In 10.3, you will be introduced to the political economy of the sign as it appears in an entirely familiar area of your lives as students: the digital landscape. The question of what is 'authentic' or 'inauthentic' (and 'unethical' to view) on the internet is a source of controversy and debate not just among policy makers and consumers, but also macromarketing scholars. This section highlights debates about the nature of the sign in the twenty-first century, when the crossing of borders by people and ideas has become commonplace and apparently seamless.

Finally, you will be introduced in 10.4 to the work of an extremely influential figure in the sociology of human signs: Erving Goffman. Goffman's dramaturgical analysis of gender behaviour in commercial advertisements raises important questions not just about the depiction of men and women in ads, but theoretically about the ontological nature of gender structures. His work is a very useful segue to consider poststructuralist thinking on the sign and the ethical nature of visual representation.

10.2 Semiological and Structuralist Analyses

In certain marketing textbooks, the most common way of explaining to students how signs work is to draw upon theory from the discipline of linguistics. In this respect the semiological work of Swiss linguist Ferdinand de Saussure (1857–1913) and the semiotic work of American pragmatist philosopher Charles Sanders Peirce (1839–1914) are the most commonly deployed sources for thinking about signs. What holds both together is their attempt to theorise the relationship between signs and objects as a basis for understanding how meaning is made.

10.2.1 Ferdinand de Saussure

De Saussure offers us a framework for understanding not only how meaning is made, but also how particular words come to have unique meanings. At the heart of his framework lie two important principles:

1 The meaning of a sign (be it an object, event, person or phenomenon) is arbitrary.
2 Meaning is structured and emerges from differences within a linguistic system.

First, then, we need to understand that the meaning of words is arbitrary and not essential, i.e. contained within the thing itself. Let us take the following example. The English word 'd-o-g' refers to a furry canine; yet in other languages like French or German, a different word is used (chien and Hund, respectively). That a furry canine is called different things in different languages points, at one level, to the arbitrary nature of language. At a more complex level, however, why is it that within the English language we have chosen this particular combination of letters to stand for a furry canine and not to a fluffy feline? There is no essential reason for English-speakers to use this collection of three letters to refer to the furry creatures at all – we could just as well use the words 'cat', 'cow' or 'frog'.

To translate this point into de Saussure's terminology, the relation between the *signifier* (the word or the sound made when saying 'dog') and the *signified* (the mental concept that springs to mind when we read the word or hear it spoken) is an arbitrary one. The term *referent* is used by Saussure to refer to the physical reality of a dog rather than the word/sound or mental concept associated with it. For Saussure, meaning is not an intrinsic property of a word.

But if meaning is seemingly unnatural or arbitrary, how come in (any) language a particular word has a particular meaning? How come d-o-g is meaningful to us (English-speakers) as a smelly canine or a pampered pooch? A relatively straightforward answer is that meaning comes from social convention, i.e. from the shared codes that we learn as members of a particular community (be it a group, culture or society) to make ourselves intelligible to one another. Convention is about mutually communicative agreements between human beings that allow them to make sense of themselves, each other and the world around them. It is by being a member of an English-speaking community in which there is agreement that 'dog' relates to muts and pooches that we come to be able to generate a particular signified for this signifier. And in English, shared wisdom, or convention, tells us that the signifier 'dog' relates to something *different* to the signifier 'cat'.

Signs can float around, take on different meanings in different contexts and signify different things. You probably have a fairly fixed idea in your mind about fluffy pooches as you read this but think about 'doggy-bags' for a moment and your thought soon moves away from canine pets and onto restaurant meals we cannot finish that we decide we should get packed to take away with us. Similarly, the word 'cat' may well bring to mind the whiskered species of animals (especially given the discussion about 'dogs' here). But if you heard someone tell you they had just bought a new pair of Cats to cope with the harsh winter, you would quite rightly assume they had purchased a pair of high-priced heavy-duty designer boots rather than a couple of cats.

Taking this insight forward, the more complex answer to the question of how words generate individual meanings relates to these differences. According to de Saussure, language is structured as a system of differences and these differences provide the basis upon which any word gains its individual meaning. In an excellent introduction to the semiological tradition of de Saussure, Desmond (2003) cites the example given by famous literary theorist Jonathan Culler to explain this rather abstract-sounding idea that meaning resides in difference. Culler asks us to imagine a Martian and how we would explain to it what is meant by 'brown'. Rather than simply showing the Martian a number of brown objects, Culler suggests that the most beneficial approach would be to display objects of different colours like black, red, green or purple, as well as brown, so that the Martian could differentiate it. As Desmond suggests:

> The reason for this is that brown is not an independent concept which is defined by some essential properties, but one term in a system of colour terms defined by its relations to the other terms which delimit it ... The central point is that meaning is acquired within the context of a set of relationships of differences within a system of language, differences which are arbitrarily set by convention. (2003: 187)

To return to the d-o-g example from earlier, this insight would mean that our understanding of what dog means is structured by its difference from similar looking or sounding signifiers like god, bog or dig. According to de Saussure, and many structuralist thinkers who have developed their ideas from him, this system of differences

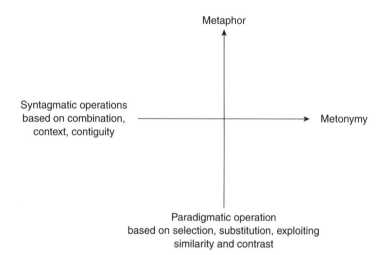

Figure 10.2   Metaphor and Metonymy along the paradigmatic and syntagmatic axes. Adapted from Dirven, R. and Pörings, R. (2004) *Metaphor and Metonymy in Comparison and Contrast*. Berlin: Mouton de Gruyter p.77. With kind permission of de Gruyter.

is organised into a series of so-called *binary oppositions* (e.g. old and young, thick and thin, black and white). He calls this organised system of binary opposition *langue* and it formed the principal focus of his academic inquiry. De Saussure contrasts the idea of langue with the idea of *parole* which refers to the individual utterances of a speaker, and the particular ways in which speakers come to use these structures competently to make themselves understood. De Saussure's analytic vocabulary extended to another set of important paired concepts:

- **Synchronic v. diachronic**: Saussure was more interested in understanding 'langue' at one point *in* time (synchronic) and how concepts or things are ascribed meaning as a result of their location within the series of signs, rather than tracing changes in the meanings *over* time (diachronic).
- **Syntagmatic v. paradigmatic**: Paradigmatic analyses focus on the individual elements of a sentence (i.e. the subject, the choice of verb, the object, a particular adjective) and examine the choice made by the speaker or the writer. By contrast, syntagmatic analyses focus on the combination or sequencing of words in any sentence, and the relations between them.
- **Metaphor and metonymy**: The concept of metaphor is often used to discuss the paradigmatic aspects of texts, as noted above. Metonymy is often used to discuss syntagmatic relations (also called contiguous relations) and the sequence of words in a sentence.

It is important to note that the correspondence of the two poles – the paradigmatic with metaphor and the syntagmatic with metonymy – was first developed, albeit rather briefly, in a brilliant paper by another structuralist, Roman Jakobson (1951/1971) called 'The metaphoric and metonymic poles'. Jakobson argued that there were two modes of structuring human behaviour. One was by 'selection' and 'substitution' (metaphor) and the other by 'combination' and 'context' (metonym). The first operates by one term substituting for another and the other by contexture or contiguity. The two poles might look like those in Figure 10.2.

There is no hard and fast distinction between metaphors and metonyms. They can often run in a continuum of meaning. An example of a metaphor using the paradigmatic operation might be an FT advertisement showing dark, stormy skies and heavy rain with the strapline: 'Where would your money take shelter in turbulent times'? Here, the inclement weather is a metaphor for economic turbulence caused by the financial crisis. Both sets of terms are similar in the effects they evoke, although they are conceptually dissimilar.

A metonym is often a small unit of a word or concept which stands in for larger units of meaning. This operation occurs in context: so, for instance the word 'tea' can stand for a range of larger units of meanings, ranging from 'tea leaves', to 'high tea' (a snack consisting of cakes, tea/coffee, scones and biscuits) as well as 'dinner' (a full meal, at least in England). In a similar fashion, the word 'crown' can refer to 'the royal family' and 'the board' refers to 'members of a board'.

When it comes to marketing, metaphor, metonymy and the paradigmatic and syntagmatic aspects of language play a crucial role as the basis for differentiating a brand in the marketplace. Marketers need to research the impact of subtle, and sometimes less than subtle, differences in the choice of metaphor on consumers when devising a promotional strategy. Desmond (2003: 191) presents the following example (see Figure 10.3) of choices that might be made in the production of advertising copy for a credit card.

Figure 10.3   Syntagmatic and paradigmatic relations for potential advertising copy
Source: Desmond, J. (2003) *Consuming Behaviour*. Palgrave Macmillan. p.191. Reproduced with permission of Palgrave Macmillan.

As you can see, the paradigmatic level of analysis presents the marketer with a number of choices of metaphor that could be used in differentiating the product's/ brand's benefits and identity from its competitors. Market research would need to be carried out amongst the target audience regarding the meanings consumers associate with ideas of convenience, freedom, flexibility, and maximum choice respectively. Desmond cites research which suggests that for farmers, as one example of a target group for credit-cards, the idea of 'choice' is viewed in a negative way. For farmers, according to Desmond, the word choice is deployed 'only when they are forced to choose between alternatives. Choice represents the time when farmers "do not have a whole lot of choice" or when something is their "only choice"' (2003: 192).

Judith Williamson's (1978) *Decoding Advertisements: Ideology and Meaning in Advertising* is perhaps the best-known and most comprehensive study of the underlying linguistic structures that give meaning to products and brands through the process of advertising. Her study combines de Saussure's analytic framework with other theories to examine: first, how adverts serve to generate meanings for products; second, how over time advertising re-organises the relationship between the signifier and the signified for a particular sign (i.e. product/brand); and finally, how advertising organises or structures consumers' desires, experiences and feelings around products and brands (and thus in line with the interests of capital). Her explanation and illustration of how advertising achieves these cultural objectives for capital is expressed in her idea of 'a currency of signs'. According to this notion, there are four stages in the relationship between a sign and a product:

- Product as signifier
- Product as signified
- Product as generator
- Product as currency

In the first stage, product as signified, Williamson explains how marketers go about creating a particular meaning for their products or brands that will differentiate it from the competition. Williamson illustrates how the process of endowing a product with value works for the perfumes Chanel No 5 and Babe. These perfumes were both made by the same manufacturer but targeted at different audiences and, therefore, in need of different images. What marketers do is to take meanings and associations from different cultural milieux e.g. from the celebrity system, the underground music scene, TV programmes like *Big Brother* or *Pop Idol*, the gay scene etc. and graft them onto the product/brand through repeated promotional tools and activities. In the case of these perfumes, Chanel borrowed from the 1970s world of modelling and film to create distinctive images for their perfumes.

Babe was a new product and they chose Margaux Hemingway (a French film star of the time associated with youth, novelty and a 'tomboy' character) to be the 'face' of the product. By contrast, Chanel No 5 was an established brand associated with 'sophistication'. To maintain this brand association over time, the manufacturers needed to keep up-to-date with whom, and what, was considered 'sophisticated' or 'chique' in any particular time period. They chose French actress and model Catherine Deneuve, famous in the 1970s, to 'stand' for their product. Williamson uses theoretical language to describe this cultural process in the following way:

> The ad is using another already existing mythological language or sign system, and appropriating a relationship that exists in that system between signifier (Catherine Deneuve) and signified (glamour, beauty) to speak of its product in terms of the same relationship; so that the perfume can be substituted for Catherine Deneuve's face and can also be made to signify glamour and beauty.

> Using the structure of one system in order to give structure to another, or to translate the structure of another, is a process which must involve an intermediate structure, a system of signs or 'meta-system' at the point where the translation takes place: this is the advertisement. Advertisements are constantly translating between systems of meaning, and therefore constitute a vast meta-system where values from different areas of our lives are made interchangeable. (1978: 25)

The basis for the differentiation of these brands lies in the significatory differences of Deneuve and Hemingway as cultural referents. If you recall from earlier, signs only have meaning as a result of a system of differences. In relation to Deneuve and Hemingway, 'it is the *difference* between their significance (taking them not as women but as signs, for this is what they are in this context) that makes them valuable in advertising. Advertisements appropriate the formal relations of pre-existing systems of differences' (Williamson, 1978: 27, italics in the original).

Over time, the link between the product and the image will become familiar, natural. In this case the product can act as a generator of meaning in its own right, i.e. without the immediate support of the actor, the model, the other sign system. Products have thus become generators of meaning and are associated with particular feelings. Products are signifiers and generators: BMW is sophistication; we therefore buy a BMW not only to communicate some perceived status to others, but also so that we can *feel* sophisticated in the process. Our desires and emotions as consumers are therefore organised by advertising and commerce in ways that connect to a product and brand, enabling companies to profit from them. As a form of currency, products are there to acquire feelings or social relations that cannot be bought.

There are two other works of note for marketing students of semiotics and structuralist analysis. First, and importantly influenced by Ferdinand de Saussure's (1974) *Course in General Linguistics,* is Roland Barthes's (1985) book *The Fashion System.* Barthes broadened the application of de Saussure's beyond the study of language and linguistic systems. Barthes believed that significatory systems, in his particular case clothing, exhibited structural features similar to that of language. As such he applied de Saussure's semiological theory of language to the study of the garment system, exploring the paradigmatic and syntagmatic elements of clothing. Barthes worked analogously with the concepts of langue and parole for instance. In relation to clothing, *langue* was the system of differences created by elite designers and photographers who wrote about and photographed clothes. *Parole* referred to the individual ways in which a piece of clothing was actually worn, and the combinations of garments that people put together in everyday life to create differences of style and meaning. The second important text is Jean-Marie Floch's (2001) *Semiotics, Marketing and Communication: Beneath the Signs, the Strategies* in which he presents a structuralist analysis of the marketing communications of various organisations in France, including the metro, pharmaceutical companies, car advertisers, IBM and Apple.

10.2.2 Charles Sanders Peirce

The American philosopher Charles Sanders Peirce has also been an important source for thinking about marketing and the sign (see Peirce, 1931/1958). In contrast to Saussure, Peirce makes the point that there are three dimensions to a sign: the sign, the object and the interpretant. A sign can be anything that stands for something (the object) to someone (the interpretant) in some context. The material sign gives rise to an 'emotional' impressiveness which he calls the interpretant. This may be another sign of something else. Peirce thus suggests that signs speak to us by referring to other signs which refer to other signs and so forth. Figure 10.4 shows the iterative nature of this process.

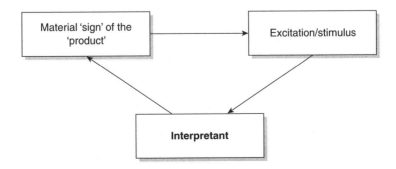

Figure 10.4   The three dimensions of the sign

If we relate these concepts to the domain of advertising, the sign (the ad) stands for the meaning of the product to someone (the interpretant). This leads to three types of relationship: in what way the ad represents the product; how well the ad communicates to the person; and whether or not the person actually buys the product.

Peirce was less interested in the relation of the sign to the interpretant. He was considerably more interested in the relationship between the sign and the object, or in marketing terms, between an advert and the object it portrays. In this respect, Peirce's distinction between three types of signs becomes important. Peirce distinguished a number of different kinds of signs, his best-known classification that of index, icon and symbol. Signs generate meaning differently depending on whether they are indexical, iconic or symbolic. Walker and Chaplin (1997) give different examples of these concepts:

- A footprint in the sand, or the trace of a pen on a flat surface. These could be examples of an *indexical* sign since 'there is a direct, causal connection between what made the mark and the mark itself' (1997: 138).
- A bronze sculpture of a cat can be considered an *iconic* sign. Iconic signs are 'those which resemble or look like what they depict in some respects if not all' (1997: 139). So whilst the sculpture might be the same shape or size as an actual cat, it might not necessarily be the same colour nor the same physical material as the live animal.
- A *symbolic* sign is 'simply an agreement amongst a group of people that such and such a mark, sound or object stands for something else' (ibid.). For instance, a rose is an almost universal symbol of love and romance.

These three forms of object–sign relationships can, of course, be found together in one ad, and are not therefore mutually exclusive. Whilst de Saussure believed that all signs were arbitrary, Peirce took the view that the symbolic relation (the last one in the list above) was the only genuinely arbitrary sign.

The *symbolic* dimension of signs as that which is generally agreed upon by societies and groups of individuals over time and space, in particular, resonates strongly with consumer researchers and marketers who seek to understand the meanings which individuals attach to the products and services they buy in various societal contexts. The implications of Peirce's theories for the student of marketing are both obvious and important. By theorising levels upon which signs can function, Peirce gives marketing theorists some key tools to explore consumers' interpretation of signs. Glen Mick, for instance, argues that Peirce's work helps researchers understand 'symbolism in the marketplace, in consumer life, and in the research arena itself' (1986: 209).

Although marketing theorists have made extensive use of semiology to explain consumer behaviour, advertising and marketing communications, there are, of course, some limitations. First, the focus on abstract sign-systems and codes of interpretation risks marginalising an understanding not only of the individual consumer's relation to the sign, but also an understanding of how meaning is dependent upon its context of production. Second, the postmodern ideas that a sign which refers endlessly to other signs and so on can deny researchers the satisfaction of uncovering the 'truth' about a certain phenomenon or context. This danger (note that it is also perceived as a strength by researchers who distrust the notion of an 'objective' or 'pre-given' truth in marketing research) can be disturbing to students and even established researchers.

10.3 Signs as Truths, Signs as Deceptions

We now consider understandings of marketing and the sign that derive from recent discussions in sociology. These discussions ask the question of whether, and how, signs tell truths about objects, or whether they are falsehoods, masking the absence of a reality or fabricating problematic realities.

It is generally acknowledged that consumers and even practitioners of marketing regard 'marketing' with some suspicion. Even enthusiastic students of marketing admit that they still think of marketing and marketers as deceitful or unethical in some way because they are trying to 'sell us something'. Marketing can be regarded as an attempt by experts to persuade us by masking, rather than revealing, the 'truth' about products and services. Marketing has been defined as the 'achievement of image and visibility goals in a cost-effective manner' (Kotler, 1986: 3). Marketing itself would appear to have an image problem. This association has led to the suspicion among scholars from other disciplines that 'marketing' hides its true purpose behind some other medium.

10.3.1 Postmodernism and the Economy of Signs

Earlier, we discussed the difficulty semiotic analysis presents for readers who want to get at the 'truth' behind signs. For many of us, the notion that there may be nothing 'behind' the sign is difficult to accept. Yet, postmodernist philosophers and writers have generated a vast body of work which promotes exactly this point of view.

For some of the seminal insights into the relationship between 'postmodernism' and 'signs,' we need to examine the controversial work of the French postmodernist, Jean Baudrillard (1972/1981; 1981/1994). Baudrillard argues that it is not signs which conceal the 'truth'; on the contrary, 'it is the truth which conceals that there is none'. In other words, signs (or what he calls 'simulations') do not refer, or imitate, or point to, something 'real'. It is important to note that earlier thinking on the sign (i.e. Saussure and Peirce, above) assumed the existence of some kind of physical reality which is representable, via word, image, sound or some other symbol. Baudrillard analyses and then rejects this distinction completely. There is no 'real', only simulations which 'threaten the distinction between "true" and "false", between the "real" and the "imaginary"':

> It is no longer a question of imitation, nor of reduplication, nor even of parody. It is rather a question of substituting signs of the real for the real itself; that is, an operation to deter every real process by its operational double, a metastable, programmatic, perfect descriptive machine which provides all the signs of the real and short-circuits all its vicissitudes. Never again will the real have to be produced. (Baudrillard, 1988: 167)

The status of the 'real' is profoundly transformed and relentlessly undermined in Baudrillard's argument. Simulations take over from the 'original and the 'authentic'. Moreover they render the 'original' and 'authentic' irrelevant. In the postmodern world there simply won't be any 'real' to copy from. In other words, simulations *generate* reality. This state of affairs is the culmination of a four-part process. According to Baudrillard, an image goes through four successive phases:

1 It first appears to reflect a 'basic reality' that is independent of the copy or image which represents it.

2 Subsequently, it conceals and perverts basic reality.
3 Following this phase, it conceals the absence of a basic reality and finally,
4 It bears no relation to 'basic reality' whatsoever.

At the final phase, the image is pure simulacrum: it refers to nothing and no one, only to itself. This is why Baudrillard calls signs 'hyperreal'. Hyperreality occurs when the image becomes pure simulation. Today, we live, according to Baudrillard, through a *hyperreality* in which signs come to refer to other signs and images rather than to anything we can identify as 'reality' (See Box below). Theme parks like Disneyworld, for instance, are pure simulacra. Their meanings derive entirely from the referents set up within those worlds and bear very little relation, if any, to anything outside them. For Baudrillard, Disneyland operates as hyperreality on at least two levels. It presents itself as imaginary, as a mask which conceals the 'true' America, but also conceals from us the fact that it *is* 'true' America. It is the classic example of what Umberto Eco (1986) calls an 'authentic fake'.

Movie Example

Avatar, the movie by James Cameron (director of the mega-blockbuster, *Titanic*), recently released, represents what its director calls a 'true hybrid' of the technological and the human. The movie, four years in the making, pushes the boundaries of 3D technology to new heights. By using a new kind of 'facial-performance-capture system,' human emotions shown on actors' faces and through their bodies are translated, second by second and captured, nuance by nuance, into CGI characters. Accordingly, 'Cameron believes ... it will be impossible for audiences to tell what is real and what is virtual' (*The Sunday Times*, 08 November 2009) and that what we will see, therefore, on digitised characters' faces is emotion purer than the 'real'.

Casinos are another example of a simulation of 'real life' which is, in fact, hyperreal. Consumers eat, drink, sit, talk, smoke and do many other things in a casino which they would probably do in 'real life', so that the act of gambling itself appears natural and normal. Yet, a casino creates a fantasy setting in which the everyday activities of eating, drinking, smoking and so on interact with the simulacra of chandeliers, sexy waitresses and staged décor to induce a state of total immersion into the artifice of its construction. Losing money itself even feels just like a game, immunising the loser from material consequences and the emotions which would normally accompany the loss of large amounts of one's money.

Baudrillard's concepts have formed part of an academic discourse and general description of twenty-first century consumerism known as 'postmodernism' (already introduced in Chapters 2 and 9). His notion of the pervasiveness of signs *as* reality 'itself' has been enthusiastically embraced by a number of marketing scholars as a way of studying production and consumption. Stephen Brown (1993), for instance, argues that postmodernism has extremely important consequences for the study of marketing phenomena (for an irreverent and provocatively reflexive 'road tour' of the subject, we highly recommend his book *Postmodern Marketing 2*). According to

Brown, postmodernism offers a fresh, critical perspective on some of marketing's established theories, such as the 'marketing concept', the 'product life cycle', 'the 4Ps' and so on. Many of these 'modern' (rather than 'postmodern') concepts rely on a homogeneous, static view of the consumer or on assumptions about the worlds they live in which are no longer accurate. In particular, he argues, the paradigms of much of marketing theory are out of touch with postmodern 'reality'. Where, for instance, does 'product' begin and 'place' end for a Starbucks customer? It can be argued that the 'price' of a Skinny Frappucino Latte probably includes the experience of being a customer as much (if not more) than the listed 'price'. If this were not so, why would anyone pay $10 for a glass of caffeinated sugary foam? In the (online) world(s) many of us inhabit today, notions of 'price', 'place' and 'promotion' have been significantly transformed.

10.3.2 The Digital Economy

One of the most obvious signs of our shift away from the material to the symbolic culture of production and consumption can be seen in the digital economy (Venkatesh, 1999). As the global economy supposedly moves towards greater integration, consumers are increasingly comfortable with moving between material and virtual worlds. Many of us spend much more time online than offline. What are the implications of this for consumers' material reality? In a postmodern framework, one could argue that cyberspace renders even our bodies incorporeal and unlocatable (Venkatesh et al., 1998: 310):

> There are no walls to bound these spaces, no physical terrain on which they can be cartographed, but they are nevertheless spaces where people move around (roam about?) without having to face each other. What characterizes the cyberspaces is the *physical location* of the subject independent of the *body*, embedded in a system of symbolic forms and information nodes.

We are possibly all familiar with the experience of being immersed in far-flung and disparate spaces, places and times online and for hours at a time without shifting in one's chair. One of the first symbols of cyberspace, the website, has morphed into highly sophisticated forms of corporate and personal identity; we now live in a global economy of signs from which we draw opinions and identify our cultural, social, religious and economic preferences. Companies today market signs and we consume them, entirely based on bits and bytes of digitally transmitted information. Because signs can be much more rapidly produced and copied than things (Baudrillard, 1983), this symbolic economy can only proliferate and grow, becoming more and more accessible and acceptable to more and more people around the world.

The desirability of this trend is a matter of debate. Postmodernists tend to regard this democratising impulse of information and communications technology as a long-overdue challenge to elitism and cultural snobbery. How many times do we hear from politicians and activists that we must link the world up to the internet, 'put a PC on every desk', give every child access to broadband and the internet, shine the 'light of technology' upon the 'dark corners' of the world? This is the rhetoric of Bill Gates, of Barack Obama, of Google. In this way, consumers are urged to engage with a certain uniform politics of desire, that of emancipating the world from ignorance through a mastery of the signs of a global economy.

10.4 Gendered Ads and Visual Ethics

In this final section of the chapter we focus on poststructuralist accounts of the sign. That is to say, we present you with discussions of the relationship between signs and objects that differ fundamentally from the views of the structuralist and semiotic thinkers presented in the first section. This account of poststructuralism is refracted through consideration of how gender relations, and gender signs, are portrayed and mediated in marketing and advertising.

10.4.1 Erving Goffman's *Gender Advertisements*

Erving Goffman (1922–1982) was a famous Canadian sociologist whose well-known book *Gender Advertisements* (1976) presents an analysis of the ways in which women and men (though more focus is placed on women), and their gender behaviours, are portrayed in a sample of commercial advertisements from selected magazines and newspapers. Goffman's interest was not so much in ascertaining how well these adverts represented 'real' gender behaviours in everyday life. Instead, he stressed the fact that adverts depict how we *think* genders behave. From this perspective, adverts present *idealised* portrayals of gender behaviour which serve two important and connected functions. First, they serve a pedagogical function in so far as they teach us what gender relations are supposed to be like, or should be like. Second, a social function in so far as they portray how we should orient ourselves to others.

Goffman organised the large number of pictures he collected for his book into sets that illustrate distinctive themes related to gender. He referred to these themes as *'genderisms'* on the basis that they revealed 'advertisers' views on how women can be profitably pictured' (1976: 25). Key genderisms included:

- *Relative size* (as judged by height): Men are portrayed as taller than women. On the few occasions where the women are taller than the men, the latter usually occupied subordinate social positions to the former (i.e. the man is the servant or the worker).
- *The feminine touch*: Women typically use hands and fingers to outline an object, cradle or caress it. They are not exhibited firmly grasping, holding or manipulating an object. Their touching of the object is not utilitarian in intent.
- *Function ranking*: Men perform the executive role (i.e. giving instructions), usually in adverts with a specific occupational context. Women (or children) in ads are shown expressing deference to instructors in a variety of forms.
- *Ritualisation of subordination*: Adverts portraying a model sitting (down) or lying on a bed are usually women or children. This can be taken as a sign of deference to another and compared to the manner in which men are often portrayed holding their body erect or holding their heads high as a sign of superiority or unashamedness.
- *Licensed withdrawal*: Women more than men are pictured engaged in involvements that remove them psychologically from social situations – as 'mentally drifting' from social interaction. They are portrayed sucking or biting their fingers, turning their gaze away from another, engaging in head/eye aversion, being spoon-fed food as if they were children.

Goffman draws our attention to two recurring and problematic themes in the portrayal of women. First, women are posed as children, acting or looking like children in ways that demean their seriousness or, as Goffman phrases it 'saved from seriousness' and 'utterly devoid of the natural sobriety which one associates with the adult mien' (Gornick, 1976 p. viii). Secondly, and compounding the first set of issues, whereas men are portrayed as 'serious' wearers of clothes, women are portrayed as only ever 'trying things on', 'as though the clothes were a costume, not the appropriate covering of a person being seriously presented' (ibid.).

Whilst Goffman's research findings are interesting in themselves, it is his theorisation of gender (the object) rather than his theorisation of portrayals of gender (the sign) which opens up a more complex understanding of the relationship between society and human behaviour beyond techniques of marketing. That is to say, the idealisation of gender behaviour, according to Goffman, does not lie in marketers' active manipulation of signs so much as it does in the institutional nature of social life which makes the reproduction of gender signs by marketers possible in the first place. To quote Goffman (1976: 23):

> The magical ability of the advertiser to use a few models and props to evoke a life-like science of his own choosing is not primarily due to the art and technology of commercial photography; it is primarily due to those institutionalized arrangements in social life which allow strangers to glimpse the lives of persons they pass, and to the readiness of all of us to switch at any moment from dealing with the real world to participating in make-believe ones.

To understand Goffman's point, we need to understand the sociological approach with which he is most associated: symbolic interactionism. Put simply, symbolic interactionists take the view that society is made up of the small and everyday interactions between humans based on the work of symbols, i.e. of signs. Symbolic interactionists take a micro-level interest in the routine social actions of everyday life (like having a conversation) through which meaning is accomplished and through which we create our identities. In common with other symbolic interactionists, Goffman takes a dramaturgical view of micro-level human behaviour: life is 'theatre' in which we all give performances, acting differently in particular accordance with the roles or expectations demanded in any social situation.

According to Goffman, social situations are of a ceremonial nature in so far as they take form through ritualistic displays that serve to present 'the divisions and hierarchies of social structure' (1976: 1). However, our displays provide us with a socially situated identity (our genders included) only if others *recognise* what our displays are intended to communicate. In order to achieve this goal, we engage in what Goffman refers to as *styling* – using a string of different verbal and non-verbal signs (e.g. style, dress, turns of phrase) to signal a particular kind of gender display and thus to become recognised as a member of a particular gender.

Goffman's dramaturgical view of (gender) signs differs in a fundamental way from both the structuralist theories outlined in the first section of this chapter, and from the 'lay theory of signs' (Goffman's own phrase) that characterise common-sensical views. The difference is an ontological one; that is to say, it pertains to our understanding of what gender is, and thereby, of the relationship between signs and objects. As you will recall, signs are often taken to be indexical: they are supposed to refer to something beyond themselves, to some deep structure and concomitant system of differences. The 'lay' theory of signs, i.e. the common-sense assumptions of people, to which Goffman refers, also shares this view. Usually, when we talk of gender, we hold in our minds the idea that our gender displays are founded either on biological grounds or are underpinned by a social structure. Gender is thus often taken as a 'natural expression' (Goffman's own phrase) of something that underpins it. Goffman fundamentally disagrees with this understanding of gender. With regard to his analysis in *Gender Advertisements*, he postulates the following:

> That a multitude of 'genderisms' point convergently in the same direction might only tell us how these signs function socially, namely, to *support belief* that there is an underlying reality to gender. Nothing dictates that should we dig and poke behind these images we can expect to find anything there – except, of course, the *inducement to entertain this expectation*. (1976: 9, italics added)

There is no biological or social-structural basis organised into a system of binary differences for gender, according to Goffman. The implication of the quote above (especially by the words in italics) is that the ideological function of gender advertisements is to sustain *speculation* and expectation that there is a structural base, or something larger than the ads themselves, when in fact there is no such thing.

> What the human nature of males and females really consists of, then, is a capacity to learn to provide and to read depictions of masculinity and femininity and a willingness to adhere to a schedule for presenting these pictures, and this capacity they have by virtue of being persons, not females or males. One might as well just say there is no gender identity. There is only a schedule for the portrayal of identity … There is only evidence of the practice between the sexes of choreographing behaviourally a portrait of relationship. (Goffman, 1976: 8)

There are, of course, some limitations with Goffman's framework. First, it is bound in time (published in 1976). Women's roles in society have changed since then, and thus the portrayal of their gender by advertisers presumably reflects such changes. Second, it is bound by culture (the ads are North American and in English). Finally, and to echo criticisms of the structuralist approaches outlined earlier, there are different ways in which the ads he presents could have been read. A reader might well have mocked or subverted the meaning apparently held in the texts/images of the adverts that portrayed the infantilisation or subjugation of women to men, for instance.

10.4.2 Ethics and Visual Representation

In this section we build upon Goffman's commentary on gender by connecting it to Schroeder and Borgerson's (2005) more recent work on the ethics of visual representation. Schroeder and Borgerson present one of the most comprehensive frameworks for analysing and evaluating the ethical dimensions of visual representations produced by marketers and advertisers. In common with Goffman, they share two starting assumptions: first, they share his poststructuralist sympathies on the nature of signs; second, they also believe that images play a pedagogical role in relations to viewers/readers. Unlike Goffman, they talk about a broader range of identity issues than just gender.

Given that images are supposed to be indexical of an object, it would follow that the identities of groups as represented in marketing imagery are supposed to be indexical of the nature of these groups. That is to say, they can be taken to say something 'true' or 'essential' about them. For subordinate groups in society, this structuring aspect of visual imagery is particularly problematic since portrayals of, for instance, gay people or ethnic minorities rarely contradict stereotypical representations of them in wider society. Schroeder and Borgerson suggest that this creates the problem of 'epistemic closure'. Epistemic closure refers to a process where images serve to close down the possible ways in which we might come to know others, and make it more likely that viewers will assume that what they see is in *fact* typical of a group. Images might make us believe that we have knowledge of someone or something we have never experienced. They might make us come to act upon this knowledge in everyday life in terms of our behaviour towards others. This knowledge can manifest itself in attitudes and behaviours that demean or diminish the dignity of other people.

Schroeder and Borgerson present a four-part framework for analysing these ethical dimensions of visual representations:

- **Face-ism:** The point of departure of this element is the consistent research finding that men's faces are more prominent in advertisements than those of women. On account of this visual prominence, men as perceived as more intelligent as well as more ambitious and attractive. They suggest an arithmetic formula for establishing the significance of face in an advert: divide the distance between the top of the subject's head and the chin by the distance between the top of the head and the lowest visible part of the model's body. This category of analysis, and the next on idealisation, are close to Goffman's work above.
- **Idealisation:** This involves studying the depiction of ideal types of groups, notably women, in advertisements – 'young, thin models, unrealistic scenarios, or unattainable goals' (2005: 588) – and the consequences for all females, but especially young girls in terms of their self-image.
- **Exoticisation:** This category deals with race, and ethnicity, rather than gender (although the two categories should not really be disconnected in analysis) and the representational conventions that stereotype and exoticise. Analyses here focus on the ways in which ethnic groups come to be portrayed as different or strange usually on the basis of their appearance (skin colour or dress).
- **Exclusion:** Who is typically left out of marketing communications? Most typically the poor or low-income groups, the disabled and certain ethnic minority groups.

These representational conventions reproduce inequalities and power asymmetries between different groups. That is to say, they point to how: certain kinds of women are subordinated to certain kinds of men; ethnic groups become stereotyped and exoticised as Other on account of their skin colour; and some groups are not even worth representing at all. In this way, we come to see how visual representations, marketing's signs, are political – they structure processes of unequal attention and valorisation between social groups. In short they produce 'unethical imagery' (Schroeder and Borgerson, 2005: 587).

10.5 Conclusion

This chapter set out to help you understand what is meant by the notion of a 'sign' and how marketing is an activity centrally concerned with the production of 'signs'. Marketing is a sign industry, and its various outputs – be they fashion or clothing, perfumes and movies, advertising copy or visual imagery – can be considered a system of signs. The chapter provided three different frameworks for analysing how signs work – a structuralist framework, a political economy framework, and finally a dramaturgical and visual ethical framework. In developing an understanding of these frameworks, and some of their shortcomings, you should be in a position to use them both as a practical professional marketing skill as well as a basis for critical academic research.

10.6 Learning Activities

This chapter has presented arguments on how signs are produced, reproduced and circulated. We have also drawn out the relevance of signs to the theory and practice of marketing. To clarify our aims, the chapter has concentrated on a number of frameworks used by various authors to help us analyse signs and how a system of signs operates. The Learning Activities for this chapter will encourage you to apply these frameworks to products with which you are familiar, bringing the ideas closer to you. Before you begin the learning activities remind yourself of the learning aims for the chapter so that your time and efforts are focused.

Learning Activity One: Meaning, Metaphor and Metonymy

Please read Stern (1988) and answer the questions below:

a What is a corporate persona?
b What is meant by the terms 'metaphor' and 'metonymy'?
c Giving examples from the article, discuss how metaphor and metonymy are used in the financial services sector to create corporate personae.

Learning Activity Two: Applying Schroeder and Borgerson

Read Schroeder and Borgerson's framework again. Then, collect a series of print and internet adverts for cosmetics (e.g. perfume) and for travel products (e.g. package holidays) and consider the following: what kinds of visual cues do the advertisements display? Do you observe instances of 'exoticisation', for instance? Apply Schroeder and Borgerson's framework to each of these adverts and examine the ethical issues that this raises.

10.7 Further Reading

Barthes, R. (1985) *The Fashion System*. London: Cape.

Barthes' book is a classic in semiotics. Not only does it represent a radical extension of de Saussure's earlier work, it offers a framework with which to analyse all sign systems including fashion. Have a read and consider how other sign systems associated with marketing and consumption could be analysed from a semiotic perspective.

Umiker-Sebeok, J. (ed.) (1987) *Marketing and Semiotics: New Directions in the Study of Signs for Sale*. Berlin: Mouton de Gruyter.

This book is a landmark publication for the marketing discipline and its interest in semiotics. Choose any chapter that interests you, and see the potential of semiotic analysis for your studies.

Prothero, A. and Fitchett, J. A. (2000) 'Greening capitalism: Opportunities for a green commodity', *Journal of Macromarketing*, 20: 46–55.

Carducci, V. (2006) 'Culture jamming: A sociological perspective', *Journal of Consumer Culture*, 6(1): 116–38.

One of the key learning outcomes of this chapter is the idea that the production of goods, or commodities, is not just a material or economic process; it is also a symbolic process that draws upon referents from cultural systems. These two pieces of further reading explore the use of images and discourses in the signification of green commodities and culture jamming. Prothero and Fitchett argue that the environmental movement needs to use the discourse of commodity culture to advance its objectives, whilst for Carducci – an article that also has significance for the arguments in Chapter 8 – the subversion of corporate representation by culture jammers fails to subvert the market system. This article also offers good insights into communication theory.

Mansfield, B. (2003) '"Imitation crab" and the material culture of commodity production', *Cultural Geographies*, 10: 176–95.

Whilst meaning is 'inscribed' in objects by marketers or producers, this is not to suggest that this meaning is fixed. Through the idea of the cultural biography of objects, this article traces the shifting meaning of 'imitation crab' (a seafood) through different processes of production and consumption.

10.8 References

Barthes, R. (1985) *The Fashion System*. London: Cape.

Baudrillard, J. (1972/1981) *For A Critique of the Political Economy of the Sign*. Trans. C. Levin. St Louis: Telos Press.

Baudrillard, J. (1981/1994) *Simulacra and Simulation*. Trans. S. Glaser. Ann Arbor: University of Michigan Press.

Baudrillard, J. (1983) *Simulations*. Trans. P. Foss, P. Pattan and P. Beitchman. Columbia University: Semiotext (e) Inc.

Baudrillard, J. (1988) *Selected Writings*. Ed. M. Poster. Stanford: Stanford University Press.

Brown, S. (1993) 'Postmodern Marketing?', *European Journal of Marketing*, 27 (4): 19–35.

Davies, A., Fitchett, J. and Shankar, A. (2003) 'An ethnoconsumerist enquiry into international consumer behaviour', in D. Turley and S. Brown (eds), *European Advances in Consumer Research*, Volume 6, pp. 102–7. Provo, UT : Association for Consumer Research.

Desmond, J. (2003) *Consuming Behaviour*. Basingstoke: Palgrave.

De Saussure, F. (1974) *Course in General Linguistics*. London: Fontana.

Dirven, R. and Pörings, R. (2004) *Metaphor and Metonymy in Comparison and Contrast*. Berlin: Mouton de Gruyter.

Eco, U. (1986) *Travels in Hyperreality*. Orlando: Hercourt Brace.

Floch, J.-M. (2001) *Semiotics, Marketing and Communication: Beneath the Signs, the Strategies*. Basingstoke: Palgrave.

Goffman, E. (1976) *Gender Advertisements*. New York: Harper.

Goldman, R. and Papson, S. (1996) *Sign Wars: The Cluttered Landscape of Advertising*. New York: Guilford Press.

Gornick, V. (1976) 'Introduction' in E. Gottman, *Gender Advertisements*. New York : Harper.

Jakobson, R. and Halle, M. (1956/1971) *Fundamentals of Language*. Volume 2. The Hague/Paris: Mouton.

Kotler, P. (1986) 'Semiotics of person and nation marketing', in J. Umiker-Sebeok, (ed.), *Marketing and Semiotics: New Directions in the Study of Signs for Sale*, pp. 3–12. Amsterdam: Walter de Gruyter.

Mick, D.G. (1986) 'Consumer research and semiotics: Exploring the morphology of signs, symbols and significance', *Journal of Consumer Research*, 13(September): 196–214.

Peirce, C.S. (1931–58) *Collected Papers of Charles Sanders Peirce*, Hartshorne, C., Weiss, P. and Burks, A.W. (eds). Cambridge, MA: Harvard University Press.

Schroeder, J.E. and Borgerson, J.L. (2005) 'An ethics of representation for international marketing communication', *International Marketing Review*, 22 (5): 578–600.

Stern, B. (1988) 'How does an ad mean?', *Journal of Advertising*, 17 (2): 3–14.

Scollon, R. and Scollon, S.W. (2003) *Discourses in Place: Language in the Material World*. London: Routledge.

Umiker-Sebeok, J. (ed.) (1987) *Marketing and Semiotics: New Directions in the Study of Signs for sale*. Berlin: Mouton de Gruyter.

Venkatesh, A. (1999) 'Postmodern perspectives for macromarketing: An inquiry into the global information and sign economy', *Journal of Macromarketing*, 19 (2): 153–69.

Venkatesh, A., Firat, A. and Meamber, L. (1998) 'Cyberspaces the next marketing frontier (?): Questions and issues', in S. Brown (ed.), *Consumer Research: Postcards from the Edge*, pp. 301–21. London: Routledge.

Walker, J.A. and Chaplin, S. (1997) *Visual Culture: An Introduction*. Manchester: Manchester University Press.

Williamson, J. (1978) *Decoding Advertisements: Ideology and Meaning in Advertising*. London and New York: Marion Boyars.

Globalisation and Ethics

11.1 Introduction

Most of the ideas that underpin classic marketing theory such as the Marketing Mix and the Marketing Concept were pioneered by North American marketers to reflect the issues and priorities of a largely US domestic market setting. This is one reason why International Marketing is often treated as a separate subject and implies that the core of marketing principles are mainly relevant within specific national contexts. Since the 1950s when most of this classic marketing theory was developed the global economy has been transformed. A wide range of factors are responsible for this process of globalisation. International agreements and treaties have reduced trade barriers and technological developments have made almost every aspect of trade more open to global markets. Academic marketing writers have struggled to adapt their core domestic principles to the new globalised marketing realities. Cultural, ethnic and racial factors that were given little if any attention are now of primary importance to marketers. While globalisation offers all kinds of potential benefits to firms and consumers, it also raises a broader range of questions about the role and impact of marketing around the world. Many of us know little, if anything, about the sources of many of the products and services we consume, and benefits to one group can and do produce exploitation of other groups. As the influence of marketing spreads around the world, marketers must face up to some of these challenges. We can no longer be content to see marketing as a largely firm-based activity directed to facilitating exchanges between buyers and sellers. Marketing is changing the world and the lives of many, if not most of its citizens. In the future, marketers will have to consider the ethical consequences of their actions in order to remain relevant, credible and legitimate.

Open any introduction to marketing text and relatively soon you will be confronted with the issue of globalisation, whether in relation to the behaviour of multinationals like Nike and HSBC, the advertising tactics of tobacco companies or the 'ethics' of global supply chains and distribution channels. But what exactly do we mean when we say globalisation? Any definition of this term is always going to be subject to critique. This said, many of the definitions of this slightly elusive term will make reference to a set of interconnected changes in society. Some pay attention to the changing role of the nation state and the increasing importance of supra-national actors in directing the flow of international trade such as the World Trade Organisation and the International Monetary Fund (Beck, 2008). Others highlight how trade between countries is now easier than it ever has been. Still other observers highlight the speed with which information travels around the world. Information in this sense can be fashion trends and knowledge about other cultures, ways of life and consumption patterns. It can also be information about environmental catastrophes which have effects that reverberate globally like the Chernobyl disaster (Held and McGrew, 2007). Equally, 24 hour news feeds, blogs and email can serve to illuminate the problematic actions of companies that would, in years gone by, have been much harder to report and inform interested consumers about.

Essentially, then, globalisation as a term indicates how social relations between people have been compressed in space and time. We have knowledge about world events almost instantly and thus can appreciate greater connections between people living in distant locations. Globalisation, as this chapter will reveal, has some benefits and raises many questions. In thinking about the globalisation of marketing, we will be asking questions about the spread of marketing and consumption practices across the globe. We will see how marketers are targeting consumers in less affluent nations, bringing them access to the types of consumer products and services that people in richer nations have long been exposed to. This, in turn, raises questions of its own – should marketers be trying to get people to buy into this consumer lifestyle at all? Are there obvious contradictions between marketing theory and practice? Marketers claim to be concerned about serving the consumer, but do they actually intend to do this at all? Are there other motives encouraging companies to globalise their market reach that do not have the consumer's best interests at heart?

11.2 The Darkside of Globalisation

The industrialisation of the world has provided some of us – a relatively small amount of us – with improved standards of living, at the same time as having serious environmental consequences, which are not limited to one country or nation (Kilbourne, 2004). But whatever issues are flagged up in relation to globalisation, there is usually one aspect that elicits stronger feelings, whether we are pro-globalisation or anti-globalisation, and that is the transnational corporation.

Indeed some allege that the discourse of globalisation was produced and disseminated as a way 'to reorder markets and trading rules to benefit corporations that were running out of markets' (Light, 2007: 234). If we were being critical, we might be tempted to say that this is one reason why recent history is characterised by the 'increasing global influence of the marketing concept' (Shultz and Holbrook, 1999: 225). Generally though, marketers are likely to focus on the benefits of consumption, especially the consumption vistas that are made available to many consumers. Again, some would argue – in line with *The Economist* magazine – itself a bastion of free trade, that the spread of consumerist values is a good thing. After all, letting consumers have access to the variety of branded goods to which affluent consumers are already accustomed is beneficial in certain respects (*The Economist*, 2001a, 2001b). It provides consumers with peace of mind; you know if you have bought a branded item that corporations tend to stand behind their product, ensuring that it is manufactured in a clean, safe way so that hopefully no harm will come to you. This is an important attribute. Chinese consumers, for example, highly value this kind of psychological reassurance (Cayla and Arnould, 2008).

Nor should we be too quick to suggest – as Naomi Klein can be interpreted as saying – that global brands are necessarily all bad, and that they contribute little to society. This said, the global reach of large corporations and the diffusion of brand values is causing a great deal of concern. Individuals who may have previously been agricultural labourers, for instance, living and working with their families on a small farm, may relocate themselves to the nearest large city, encouraged to do so by the wages paid by factory owners. To be sure, they may appreciate the financial benefits of such a move; farming often only pays a subsistence wage. But as Greenwald revealed in his recent documentary on Wal-Mart, the benefits that some experience should not be overstated. How do companies manage to price their goods such that they can claim to have 'everyday low prices', Greenwald asks?

Paying workers in developed nations poor wages is one way; employing illegal aliens is another; encouraging staff to source appropriate medical and health benefits from the state also helps. Put very simply, these products are so cheap because they are produced by workers labouring for long hours in hot, poorly ventilated factories (Greenwald, 2005).

Discipline, Consumption and Freedom?

In her book, *No Logo*, Naomi Klein (2000) presents the reader with some very graphic illustrations of what work life is like in the factories that produce the expensively branded goods that many of us have no doubt purchased at some time. Brands such as Nike, Reebok, The Gap, and a host of others, outsource their production to factories where workers are sometimes treated very badly indeed. Many of those working in these factory environments suffer from a variety of ailments, some relatively minor to some far more serious. As Mary Beth Mills says, 'Even without the strain of overtime', these workers have to change shifts frequently, moving from day to night work and 'this constant upheaval in daily routines frequently results in health problems such as disrupted menstruation, headaches and insomnia, and intestinal problems and ulcers, not to mention some of the more immediate physical threats to which women may be exposed in the workplace – toxic chemicals and gases, accidents caused by improperly maintained machinery or worker fatigue, respiratory infections from poorly ventilated work sites and so on' (Mills, 1997: 45).

This said, we should not ignore the positive benefits of working in cities like Bangkok for migrant workers. Whilst it is easy to be critical of the export processing zones that Naomi Klein condemns for their low wages, long working hours and excessive discipline, one benefit of such locations is that they enable some of the workers to attain the beauty ideal marketed to them daily: 'one of the most valued benefits for migrants is that urban employment allows them to work indoors, away from the skin-darkening effects of the sun. White skin is a crucial marker of physical beauty in both urban and rural Thai aesthetic systems' (Mills, 1997: 43).

Moreover, these workers manage to sample the sights of a cosmopolitan consumer city, 'watching television and popular movies or going to department stores, entertainment parks, and similar sites of modernity' (Mills, 1997: 45). And, for Mills, there were a variety of supplementary benefits of living in the urban environment: 'In addition to acquiring particular mass-market commodities, participation in new commodified patterns of sociality is equally attractive to many rural-urban migrants' (Mills, 1997: 46). Should these young workers accept their consumption lifestyle as a form of compensation for working in such conditions? According to Firat (1997: 82; emphasis in original) many consumers perceive the relationship between work and consumption in this way,

(Cont'd)

whether they live in developed or developing nations: 'Many young consumers in the West have come to think of the time they spend at work not to be very meaningful or important...but as a *necessity* to be able to accomplish their consumption goals'. What do you think? Do people look at their lives through the prism of consumption, rather than production, that is, the job they do? What do you think about the skin lightening benefits of factory work?

On the consumer side, securing access to the 'world of goods' (Douglas and Isherwood, 1979) pushes some to extreme behaviours. People are even killed for branded products. Are these patterns of behaviour that we can expect many to adopt? No, they are not. They are extreme cases. Nevertheless, the world is made up of a large amount of quite rightly disaffected people who will – we should not doubt that – contest the economic inequality that is not being quickly offset by the process of globalisation. Susan George (2001: 19) has framed the issue in the following way: 'studies by both UNCTAD and the United Nations University show that inequalities in most countries are inexorably rising, whether in China, Russia, Latin America or the West; 85 percent of the world's population now live in countries where inequalities are growing, not diminishing'. Pressing this point she continues: 'In any given society globalisation benefits mainly the top 20 percent, and the higher they are on the social scale, the more they benefit. In contrast, the lower they are, the more they lose of the little they have' (George, 2001: 20) (also noted at the start of Chapter 8).

In a similar way, Bauman (2007) has drawn attention to the potential for social turmoil caused by consumption inequalities. What might happen, scholars have asked, when the poor demand access to the products that have been placed in front of them through all the variety of media, but which they are still denied access? Some people might drive themselves into greater levels of debt, spending far more than they can earn. This is not just a problem that the very poor face. Schor (2008) has pointed out that the way that people evaluate their lives, that is, whether they are a 'success' or not, is not just something tied to the local community, where people try to keep up with the Jones'. As she puts it, 'the consumer norm has shifted from what one would call a "proximate", or "horizontal" norm, in which people are aspiring to lifestyles like other people in their income bracket, to one in which a high-end, affluent, media driven norm of consumption prevails' (Schor, 2008: 589). 'Vertical emulation' is now the axiological orientation they adopt. People aspire to the lifestyles of the rich and famous.

The result of this is, as noted above, that people can get into financial trouble, they may steal and thereby transgress legal boundaries (Bauman, 2007; Varman and Belk, 2008). Schor, like the Critical Theorists or Scitovsky (1992), diagnoses a further effect of rising standards of emulation: 'dissatisfaction'. This leads some people to try to limit their participation in what they perceive to be a wholly unsatisfactory way of life – they become 'conservers' rather than 'consumers' (Dobscha and Ozanne, 2008). They downshift their lifestyles, trying to get out of the 'rat race' and shift their work-life balance in a way that is more satisfying to themselves and their families.

These types of behavioural change are still, we should appreciate, a minority exercise. In response to those ready to criticise big brands or who try to restrict their participation in the marketplace, *The Economist* magazine argues that anti-brand and anti-marketing commentators fail to see the benefits of capitalism and branded products. 'Imagine', *The Economist* says,

> ... a world without brands. It existed once, and still exists, more or less, in the world's poorest places. No raucous advertising, no ugly billboards, no McDonald's. Yet, given a chance and a bit of money, people flee this Eden. They seek out Budweiser instead of their local tipple, ditch the nameless shirt for Gap, prefer Marlboros to home-grown smokes. What should we conclude? That people are pawns in the hands of giant companies with huge advertising budgets and global reach? Or that brands bring something that people think is better than what they had before? (The Economist, 2001a: 11)

These comments are almost reflective of a belief that certain forms of consumption are inevitably desired by consumers, wherever they may live, and in whatever economic circumstances they may find themselves. In short, they sound a little like comments associated with cultural imperialism.

11.3 Cultural Imperialism

By cultural imperialism, we refer to a process whereby predominantly US multinational companies export a limited range of ideas, images, products, services and brands – what we can call American mass culture – disseminating this throughout the world via whatever media channels are available. This is a process that many consider to have really grown during the 1960s and continues apace today.

Whilst global, American or Western brands do play a large role in structuring the way we look at the world, in reality US and Western cultural imperialism is far from total (Firat, 1997; Held and McGrew, 2007). For starters, it is profoundly egocentric to assume that because already developed countries bought into a particular ideal of 'middle-class' consumption, that developing nations will replicate this process (Bhattacharya and Michael, 2008).

Further tempering the egotism of large corporations, many countries such as China, Brazil, India, Russia and Indonesia do not represent markets that multinational corporations can easily enter (Bhattacharya and Michael, 2008). This is especially true when these markets possess their own vibrant industries that present stiff competition for even the best-known brands. As Bhattacharya and Michael (2008: 86) stress: 'In China, daily use of the search engine Baidu exceeds that of Google China by fourfold; QQ, from instant-message leader Tencent, is ahead of MSN Messenger; and online travel service Ctrip has held off Travelsky, Expedia's eLong.com, and Travelocity's Zuji.com'. What's more, many people, from various nations, are profoundly anti-American and continue to rally against the fact that numerous global brands are American by not buying them (Quelch, 2003).

Quelch (2003: 23) actually says that even though these tendencies are most pronounced in Islamic countries, other countries, including Germany, are well represented by 'activist websites [which] urge consumers to boycott 250 British and American products and suggest local alternatives'. Moreover, when recessionary conditions reduce disposable income, consumers shift back to locally produced products. Beyond this, it could also be argued that people do actually get bored of the big

American or European brands and desire products made locally, to the specifications of the local marketplace.

What if we are indeed about to witness a return to global brands, but global brands that come from nations other than the US or Europe? Quelch (2003) certainly seems to think this is a possibility. He predicts that China will provide brands that function as 'an alternative to US brand hegemony that will attract consumers back to the global brand marketplace' (Quelch, 2003: 23). Indeed, he claims that China will be in a similar position to that of Japan two decades ago. He hypothesises that where once consumers were reluctant to buy products that had 'made in Japan' written on them, but then slowly but surely became aware of the quality improvements, functional utility and price benefits of such products, that we will be witnessing something similar in the near future in relation to those made in China. 'Chinese brands', he suggests, 'like Legend in computers, Haier in appliances, TCL in mobile phones, and Tsingtao in beer are extending internationally. And there will be more' (Quelch, 2003: 23). Watch this space!

Realistically, Western products and aesthetic values do appear to have considerable staying power. Lindridge and Wang (2008), for instance, document how parents encourage their daughters to undergo plastic surgery to give them facial attributes associated with a more Western look: 'Participants and their mothers felt that western media exulted female beauty to be tall and white skinned, enthusiastically consuming this media as a means to learn and emulate how a modernized society acted and what its idealized citizens looked like' (Lindridge and Wang, 2008: 502). This is not simply an aesthetic value system prevalent in China, young female consumers in Thailand also think similarly (Üstüner and Holt, 2008).

So, perhaps there is some element of a global diffusion of particular ways of life, inasmuch as Western brands and images are deemed highly desirable (Mills, 1997) and certain consumption practices such as face remodelling (Lindridge and Wang, 2008) and skin lightening (Karnani, 2007) are used to re-sculpt one's appearance. Again, we should be reflexive here and appreciate that the big global brands and Western images of beauty are not the only cultural resources available for consumer appropriation. Eastern imagery could be used in a similar way (Cayla and Eckhardt, 2008).

11.4 Global Consumer Identity: Copying the Rest?

As one marketing scholar argues: 'The world is witnessing today a new form of human being called the global consumer' (Venkatesh, 1994: 22). We define ourselves as part of a global culture by virtue of the goods we consume. The benefit of this, it has been said, is that it provides us with a 'link' to groups with which we want to associate ourselves (Cova, 1996). Whereas previously we formed bonds with those from the same social class or religious denomination, such bonds no long exert the same hold they once did. In their place are the cognitive and symbolic supports provided by corporations and consumer culture. As was discussed in Chapter 2, not all consumers, wherever they may be on this planet, have the resources to engage in the symbolic construction of their desired self image. All the same, the dissemination of a global consumer culture has wider ramifications (see below).

Protecting 'Our Way of Life'?

In a paper published in the *Texas Law Review*, Sut Jhally (1993) provides an interesting and highly critical interpretation of the rationale behind the war on Iraq. You might be thinking, this seems a little odd, talking about war in a marketing textbook, but as Jhally reveals, war, consumerism and marketing can be connected, and all three have had major impacts on the world. For Jhally and many others, the likely wars and social upheavals of the future will be a result of the competition for resources – for precious fuels and desirable consumption items like diamonds. Making reference to a *New York Times* article published on 16 August 1990, when the first President Bush was referring to a possible future scenario should the now deceased Saddam Hussein, former President of Iraq, take over Saudi Arabia, Jhally describes the US President's response.

President Bush criticised the expansionist plans of Hussein, who had already entered the oil-rich country of Kuwait. If Hussein was permitted to continue along the trajectory that he had embarked upon, Bush said: 'Our jobs, our way of life, our freedom and the freedom of friendly countries around the world would all suffer if control of the world's great oil reserves fell into the hands of Saddam Hussein' (Apple, 1990). The deeply cynical among us could, at this point, gesture to the heavily dependent nature of the US economy and structures of consumption on oil and, for Jhally (1993), this was the key issue driving Bush to deploy his troops to the Middle East. As he remarked: 'An automobile- and commodity-based culture such as ours is reliant upon sources of cheap oil. In such a scenario, the peoples of the Third World will be seen as making unreasonable claims upon "our" resources. The future and the Third World can wait. Our commercial-dominated cultural discourse reminds us powerfully every day, we need *ours* and we need it *now*' (Jhally, 1993: 814; emphasis in original). Jhally is clearly making an argument that can be rebutted by reference to the possible terrorist threats posed by rulers or insurgents in countries far, far away, but what do you think: does Jhally have a point? Do you agree with his analysis? If you disagree, why?

In various places in this book so far, we have made reference to the role of consumer agency. By agency, we mean the ability of consumers to pick and choose the items they desire in crafting themselves as individuals. Here the 'global postmodern' consumer takes products from companies combining these – in hybrid fashion – with indigenous symbolic and fashion systems (Jack and Westwood, 2009). Whilst this view is appealing, surely a 'consumer culture' implies cultural homogenisation to a degree? Looking more closely at the academic literature we might even find an aspiration for cultural imperialism among marketing managers. Sounds a little like a conspiracy theory, doesn't it? Even so, it is not that far off the mark. For example, advertisers often claim that consumers are intelligent and able to critically scrutinise the claims being made, yet at the same time advertisers and marketing academics exhibit concerns about the ethics of advertising on the basis that advertising practice can 'modify...cultural beliefs' (Drumwright and Murphy, 2009: 92).

It may be useful to note that marketing journal articles utilise the language of 'core' and 'periphery' to argue that 'Because the production and control of popular culture resides in the affluent core countries of the West (especially the United States), the flow of media images is mostly from the economic centre (the West) to the periphery (the developing world), making brands that symbolize affluent Western lifestyles seem highly desirable' (Batra et al., 2000: 85).

As we alluded to earlier, similar views to those expressed by Batra et al. (2000) are articulated by some marketing practitioners. In his study of three transnational corporations, Applbaum (2000: 265) documents a 'belief in a worldwide convergence of tastes' being put forward by pracitioners. Since this is a paper that is rarely cited in the marketing literature, having been published in *American Ethnologist*, it is worth us letting Applbaum speak directly in an extended quote:

> Converging consumer tastes is both a reason firms must globalize and the instrument with which they can achieve this goal. Marketers believe that tastes converge because of the demonstration effect according to which consumers in backward markets are exposed to modern technologies, lifestyles and ways of consuming through the media. My informants spoke of the 'modern lifestyle,' which they also used as a catch-all phrase for progress … Managers saw modern lifestyles as superior, signaling [sic] this by using the terms *progress* and *evolution* in connection with the phrase. This conviction is a necessary belief for marketing managers, whose stock in trade is producing newer and better lives through consumption. By extending this logic behind consumption lifestyles to the developing world, the notions of progress and evolution are doubly implicated. (Applbaum, 2000: 265)

In the research conducted by Applbaum, his interviewees revealed that they saw themselves as encouraging the 'development' of consumers in less affluent nations, giving them access to better, higher quality branded products. They did this by 'educating' the potential consumers about the universe of items and lifestyles that are available to them thus 'further…widening [the] presence of capitalist structures and relations of consumption into which TNC [Transnational Corporation] marketers seek to draw every person on earth' (Applbaum, 2000: 274). Through consumer 'education, those residing on the geographical and monetary periphery of consumer markets are enticed to discover the modern through global lifestyle choices' (Applbaum, 2000: 274).

This said, let us recall the discussions of the marketing concept in Chapters 1 and 4. Perhaps other marketing practitioners and academics think differently to those practitioners interviewed by Applbaum? Surprising enough as it may seem, Theodore Levitt, a former Professor at the Harvard Business School who wrote an important paper on 'marketing myopia' (Levitt, 1960) in which he sketched out key ideas associated with the marketing concept, did make just such an 'homogenisation' argument. Globalisation, Levitt (1983) argued, presented an interesting set of possibilities for marketers. Enhanced technological capabilities and the cross-fertilisation of global consumer values, meant that marketers could potentially achieve quite fantastic economies of scale.

Levitt has done a complete about face from his earlier work where he agreed with the idea that marketers should tailor their products to their clients. If different cultures that previously required markedly diverse products are steadily growing together – homogenising – then organisations could benefit by producing a restricted range of products and services, actively promoting these in much the same way across the globe. This was the future for the profit-making enterprise, according to Levitt.

While there is undoubtedly resistance to the spread of consumer values which are usually associated with American values (Wernick, 1991), it remains the case that some of the world's most well-known companies can apparently market themselves in *almost* identical ways across the world. Products like Coca-Cola or McDonald's are those that make use of the economies of scale that Levitt believed could be obtained through standardised production and marketing. As Kline (1995) registers, Coca-Cola has been extremely adept at promoting its vision of Coke uniting consumers around the world, via the consumption of a sugary drink. Their 'one world' promotional campaign certainly testifies to their desire to reduce cultural difference, and stressed that we can all live in peace and harmony (see http://www.50goldenbrands. com/top-brands/1971/).

And yet, companies like McDonald's and Walt Disney, for instance, do not always hold sway with a 'standard, one-size-fits-all' package of goods and services. So 'Even though various firms have successfully planted themselves globally ... their various products continue to be consumed by different people in different ways. The key point to remember is that although the products or services being sold internationally may be "uniform" or "homogenous" in outward appearance, they can still be very different in the eyes of various customers and in the way in which they are consumed' (Asgary and Walle, 2002: 61).

Whatever the response to globalisation, be it one of acceptance and celebration, or critique and condemnation, participating in the global marketplace and consuming the goods that have been widely marketed in developed and developing nations is very appealing to many (Varman and Belk, 2008). As Arnould (2007) has suggested, there are people who *are* interested in accessing the market and all its many products, including those living in currently very poor nations like Nepal (Askegaard, 2006). Marketers have started to appreciate this, showing interest in selling to the so-called 'bottom of the pyramid' consumers, that is, to those who subsist on very low incomes. These groups, normally ignored by large multinational companies, are in fact a veritable goldmine for the attentive corporation, Prahalad and Hammond (2002) argue. Let us look more closely inside this goldmine.

11.5 Inside the Goldmine ... Marketing to the 'Bottom of the Pyramid'

'The Bottom of the Pyramid' (BOP) segment of consumers includes between 600 million and 4 billion people according to different estimates (Karnani, 2007: 91). These are amongst the poorest people in the world, often living on extremely low incomes. Despite their restricted finances, marketers are increasingly starting to target them with goods at prices they can afford. This is not to say that products are made to much cheaper specifications. They are usually offered the same branded goods of, for example, shampoo, but in much smaller sizes (e.g. individual sachets).

In line with this, it is argued that the 'aspirations' of these consumers should be shaped 'through product innovation and consumer education' (Pitta et al., 2008: 395). These groups, so the argument goes, can be provided with goods and services that enhance their everyday lives. That we should be encouraging people to view themselves as 'consumers' is relatively unproblematic, some could claim. Improving quality-of-life through consumption is praiseworthy in the eyes of a cohort of practitioners and academics (Kilbourne, 2004). The problem is that the logic underpinning the 'bottom of the pyramid' argument is in fact seriously flawed (Karnani, 2007). If these groups are spending a substantial proportion of their income on the basic necessities – 'food, clothing and fuel' which accounts for '80 per cent' of this groups spending (Karnani, 2007: 92) – then they are hardly likely to constitute a desirable market for most large companies.

Nor should we assume that these people know exactly what it is in their interest to consume, Karnani claims, contrary to Prahalad and Hammond's assertion otherwise. This is not to say that Karnani expects these people to demonstrate the rational information processing characteristics that are an ideal type of a cognitive model in consumer research (think person as a computer, evaluating products and services on the basis of their cost/price utility). As Karnani (2007: 97) explains:

> ...if for some reason, the poor consumer is deceived by marketing or is poorly informed, the BOP [Bottom of the Pyramid] initiative might even reduce his welfare. The BOP initiative could result in the poor spending money on products such as televisions and shampoo that would have been better spent on higher priority needs such as nutrition and education and health. Prahalad dismisses such arguments as patronizing and arrogant; how can anyone else decide what is best for the poor? He argues that the poor have the right to determine how they spend their limited income and are in fact value-conscious consumers; the poor themselves are the best judge of how to maximize their utility. This is free market ideology taken to an extreme, and is a potentially dangerous aspect of the BOP proposition.

The lack of literacy, little previous exposure to marketing communications, as well as a host of other 'economic, cultural and social depravations' means that we should be far more cautious about viewing the consumption choices made by those in deprived circumstances through the prism of our own experience. Of course, we should not totally dismiss the ability of the poor to reflect on their consumption decisions. What we must recognise is the extent to which corporations can manipulate the marketplace in ways that suit their purposes. In what is an incredibly contentious statement, Wilk (2001: 252) suggests that:

> At the same time it is clear that people in developing countries cannot make free choices about goods. They are not simply absorbing foreign goods into their culture, and they often do not anticipate the way their consumption will change the economy and culture. Those who have not previously been exposed to sophisticated marketing and advertising campaigns are indeed vulnerable to fraudulent and extravagant claims. Market prices are manipulated in order to lure people into dependence on foreign goods with cheap prices, to eliminate local alternatives, and [marketers] then raise prices once people have no other options ... Coercion and seduction to buy products really does take place, in the context of debt servitude, captive labor forces, and 'company stores.'

On a related point, Karnani asserts that: 'The data suggest that the poor lack self-control, yield to temptation, and spend to keep up with the neighbours. In this they are no different to people with more money, but the consequences are more severe for the poor' (Karnani, 2007: 98). The problem is that unlike those laws protecting consumers in developed countries, 'legal and social mechanisms for consumer protection are often very weak in developing countries, and even more so with regard to poor people' (ibid.). It is also relatively easy for companies from developed countries to exacerbate social problems in countries far removed from their usual operating base, by being insufficiently aware of the impact of their actions when marketing certain products.

Promoting Beauty or Affirming Racism?

Karnani (2007) describes a whole range of problems involved in marketing to those at 'the bottom of the pyramid', not least that companies might affirm social values that should otherwise be subject to critique and possible condemnation. Even though the marketing concept may indicate that we should produce products and services that cater to customers' requirements, perhaps, Karnani argues, there are some products companies should not be marketing in the 'underdeveloped' world. The most notable is one that whitens skin; whitened skin being viewed as desirable because those with such attributes are believed to command higher incomes, are more desirable as partners and more successful in life. Karnani points out that in India there still remain persistent strains of racism that are probably a remnant of the colonial period. Reflecting this is the preference for lighter skin which we mentioned at the start of the chapter. Citing Prahalad and Hammond, whose example Karnani is questioning, this product is positioned as contributing to the empowerment of female consumers because they can obtain 'an affordable consumer product formulated for...[their] needs' (Prahalad and Hammond in Karnani, 2007: 99). By contrast to this affirmative view, Karnani asserts: 'This is no empowerment. At best, it is an illusion; at worst, it serves to entrench...[their] disempowerment. Women's movements in countries from India to Malaysia to Egypt obviously do not agree with Hammond and Prahalad, and they have campaigned against these products' (Karnani, 2007: 99). What do you think? Are these consumers empowered or not? Should we be dictating what products are sold to consumers in countries such as India? Surely, if we can make informed choices about the products and services we purchase, then consumers living elsewhere can too?

In summary, whilst Karnani does see much of value in the debates surrounding marketing to those living at the 'bottom of the pyramid', he also thinks too much emphasis is being given to marketing to these groups. Rather than seeing them as a new market to be tapped, Karnani proposes the most efficient way to help them achieve a better quality-of-life is to enable them as producers. This involves providing these groups with access to relevant information and services that allow them to better navigate the marketplace and negotiate better terms for their products. In this way the poor can 'capture more of the value of their outputs' (Karnani, 2007: 109).

11.6 Global Commodity Chains: Connecting Consumers and Producers?

Now that we have begun to appreciate the increasing attention that producers and marketers in the developed world have started to devote to consumers at the 'bottom of the pyramid', it is appropriate to turn to another major change in the nature of marketing and distribution that has been witnessed over the last 20 years (or more), namely the emergence of global supply chains (see Chapter 6 on supply chains).

Countries have always engaged in trade between themselves (see McAuley, 2004). But it is only relatively recently that global trade has been made possible at the press of a switch courtesy of information technology. As a function of falling trade barriers between nations, companies outsource the production of their products to factories far away from their central offices, where the costs of production are far lower. And this has led to academics talking about the lengthening of supply chains and the emergence of 'Global Commodity Chains'. According to Gereffi (1994: 96):

> Global commodity chains have three main dimensions: (1) an input-output structure (i.e., a set of products and services linked together in a sequence of value-adding economic activities); (2) a territoriality (i.e., spatial dispersion or concentration of production and distribution networks, comprised of enterprises of different sizes and types); and (3) a governance structure (i.e., authority and power relationships that determine how financial, material, and human resources are allocated and flow within a chain).

The reason companies should be so interested in outsourcing their production is readily discernable. Corporations are aware which activities earn them price premiums (i.e. marketing and branding); the actual product itself – the trainer, for example – makes up very little of the cost that the consumer pays in the local sports retailer (Held and McGrew, 2007). Consequently, they wish to outsource manufacturing to others where it is profitable to do so. At the same time, consumers are increasingly interested in knowing more about the production relations that go into making the products they buy (Holt et al., 2004) – and some marketing academics think that there is capital to be made, by marketing goods as ethically produced (McAuley, 2004).

Since the publication of a variety of books critical of marketing and globalisation, especially *No Logo* by Naomi Klein (2000), not to mention the popularity of *Adbusters* magazine (Holt et al., 2004), companies have realised that they cannot just dismiss consumer concerns about production–consumption relations, as Nike initially did (as noted in Chapter 8). As many people now appreciate, courtesy of the internet, production and marketing activities can be deeply ethically problematic. Focusing solely on the bottom line of profits can lead to consequences that are later subject to widespread condemnation. This is not because marketers or well-known marketing companies are necessarily more likely to be unethical than other companies. Marketers, irrespective of some of the images we receive through literature and popular culture, are not all bad people. The problem is that when we start to work at a company, we focus on the job we do and perhaps not so much on the end consequences of our actions.

As Bauman (1988) highlights most vividly, in the pursuit of administrative efficiency, large bureaucratic organisations departmentalise. We have finance, marketing, production and so on, and, within reason, each may have little idea of what the others are doing. Thus marketing may decide to produce a new model of shoe. Managers are then tasked with making this as efficiently and cheaply as possible. Responding to the marketing manager's request encourages the 'rational', cost-aware manager to contract out manufacturing. The production manager may only have visited the factory once or twice, at a time known to the managers of the factory concerned. This means that the production manager only has a sanitised image of the factory. We have not seen the factory working at full production or the conditions that people ordinarily labour in (which we thereby support through the provision of contracts to the factory owner). Our ignorance can, however, be useful. To get on with our assigned organisational role, we bracket all activities beyond those that directly concern us. This means, says Bauman (1988, 1991), that sometimes the nicest people can be responsible for the most undesirable activities (i.e. sweatshop and child labour). He calls this a form of adiaphorisation: where we are morally removed from the end result of our 'small', seemingly inconsequential organisational decisions (Bauman, 1991). With the foregoing in mind, we must be careful when we feel tempted to attribute some kind of moral defect or deficiency to marketers. Rather, we should ask: 'What are the social, political, educational or organisational influences that encourage people to think about or avoid ethical responsibility'?

It seems entirely appropriate now to examine the issue of marketing and advertising ethics.

11.7 Marketing, Advertising and Ethics

When we say 'marketing ethics' or 'advertising ethics' we are invoking the definition provided by Peggy Cunningham; she defines the latter as 'what is right or good in the conduct of the advertising function. It is concerned with what ought to be done, not just with what legally must be done' (Cunningham in Drumwright and Murphy, 2004: 7). As is probably obvious by now, global marketers often bear the brunt of much criticism. As Nill (2003: 90) notes: 'international marketers are often criticized for their ethical misconduct'.

Marketers are sometimes accused of selling inappropriate products to children and adults such as foods very high in sugar and fat, at a time when people in affluent nations face rising levels of obesity (Witkowski, 2007). They are called to account for promoting alcoholic beverages to groups such as young females (Hackley, 2009), along with being condemned for promoting products in ways deemed offensive, as was the case with Benetton's 'United Colors of Benetton' campaign (Giroux, 1993–1994).

But there are counterpoints to many of these examples: does Benetton perform a consciousness raising function, by bringing important social issues to public notice? Alcohol can have a devastating effect on some people's lives, but 'alcohol use is frequently sociable' (Schudson, 2007: 238). In addition, cookies and Spyware that monitor our internet shopping habits, often without our knowledge, can also be used to provide tailored content for users; content which they value. Such research tactics can nonetheless be viewed as 'prying, intrusive and irritating' (Laczniak and Murphy, 2006: 315).

Marketers, however, can respond by citing the rationality of the consumer, stressing how intelligent and savvy most people are. Moreover, it is often remarked that people are very quick to provide huge amounts of data to market research agencies (Cronin, 2004; Hackley, 2002). When we buy many products, for example, these come with a warranty. People fill these out, providing marketers with more information than they require. This suggests, marketers say, that 'many consumers signal by their actions that they simply don't mind sharing their personal information with vendors' (Laczniak and Murphy, 2006: 317).

These issues are complicated and our interpretation of them will depend on whether we happen to work for the company producing such products, whether we enjoy receiving direct mail and spam, seeing the value in such communications techniques. There has also been much debate on the issue of whether or not advertising should be more accurately understood as a 'mirror of society', that is, whether it merely 'mirrors' existing societal norms or whether it moulds and encourages certain ways of thinking and acting (Pollay, 1986, 1987). We have reviewed a number of instances in this chapter that do suggest that marketing is a powerful force in society for both good and ill. As already discussed, there is probably some relationship here with marketing and advertising projecting images of the good life to people across the globe, which they then aspire to. The examples above about body shape and consumerism illustrate this well.

Marketing managers could be expected to rebut such arguments. Not all people, they may suggest, interpret marketing communications in exactly the same way, and so there is some plausible basis for believing that marketing messages do not define what is 'the good life'. And yet, Pollay (1987) claims, there is an element of global marketing organisations selling a particular way of looking at the world, a way that highly values the consumption of products as one of the most important paths to human happiness. Holbrook (1987: 98) disagrees:

> In this climate of jealous competitive secrecy and internecine business strategizing, one sees little of advertising as a monolithic institution in which everybody preaches the party line in perfectly synchronized unison or harmony. Rather, one sees advertisers – that is, media, agencies, and their organizational clients – as a vast particularistic assortment of atomistic elements, each engaged in a communication random walk that contributes to the informational chaos of the overall cluttered spectacle.

And surely, adds Holbrook, if advertising 'acts to oversimplify reality, distort social values, and evoke unhealthy emotions, one might expect to reply that these assertions tend to smash or at least to crack the mirror that advertising holds up to social mores, norms, and values' (Holbrook, 1987: 102). Holbrook makes a good point here. If marketing and advertising do distort the way we look at reality, presenting an ideal-image that we cannot live up to or ever achieve, then surely this will invalidate the images that are presented.

In an interesting analogy, Pollay (1987) compares the effects of advertising to rain. 'Individually', he proposes, 'raindrops are benign and have little noticeable impact. People can readily avoid most drops by their behavior and clothing, like experiencing ads with selective attention and protective cynical attitudes. Nonetheless, when raindrops abound, people are increasingly likely to get wet and are subjected to attendant risks of discomfort and disease' (Pollay, 1987: 107). Whoever we side with here – Holbrook or Pollay – what is perhaps most disconcerting when we examine the studies that have been conducted with marketing and advertising practitioners is their 'moral muteness', that is, their failure to ask ethical questions at the 'individual or organizational level' (Drumwright and Murphy, 2004: 11).

In a series of interviews with practitioners, Drumwright and Murphy have documented 'moral muteness' and 'myopia' among this group. What they mean by this is that practitioners failed to recognise ethical issues, sidelining these via a variety of strategies such as attributing consumers with a high level of sovereignty and the intellectual ability to subject marketing communications to critique (Drumwright and Murphy, 2004). Compounding this 'ethical quagmire' are financial pressures. As one advertising practitioner stated: 'Unethical things can happen when wonderful upstanding people become fixated on bottom line results' (Drumwright and Murphy, 2009: 89). Still, this fixation remains an ever present danger in a business environment that demands appropriate financial returns to shareholders.

11.8 Conclusion

This chapter has examined some of the issues surrounding the implications of globalisation for marketing and marketing ethics. We looked at examples where there are contradictions between marketing theory and the practice of multinationals. Where, for example, marketing textbooks are full of discussions about pandering to the consumer and providing them with the goods and services they require, some marketing theorists like Theodore Levitt have argued for exactly the opposite, suggesting that global marketers reduce the range of products they sell in order to achieve economies of scale. These views were not restricted to theorists alone; some marketing practitioners made similar remarks.

As we noted, marketers are extremely interested in exploiting the opportunities presented by currently 'underdeveloped' nations and markets. Marketers might target these nations because their other markets are saturated or because the legal environment is becoming less welcoming to certain types of products such as cigarettes.

As a result of globalisation, companies are now afforded the opportunity to globalise their production, moving production facilities to areas in the world where labour costs are lowest. Just as changes in technology have made this possible, it also means that consumers can monitor these corporations far more closely than was possible in the past.

What seems certain is that most consumers are unwilling to give up their current standard of living and even when they do disagree with the actions of companies in remote parts of the world that these concerns are often not enough of a motivator to encourage them to modify their own consumption behaviours. If we as consumers are not willing to 'put our money, where our belief systems are' so to speak, then we may ask, why should companies be bothered to do so?

11.9 Learning Activities

In this chapter, the role of marketing in the proliferation of trade and ideas across borders is discussed. The cultural and political implications of international trade present marketers with a myriad of ethical issues. These learning activities are designed to provide insights into the different ways in which local groups and cultures have engaged with ideas and practices associated with globalisation.

Learning Activity One: How the 'Other' Half Live

It is argued that globalisation has benefited all people and countries around the world equally. Undertake desk research on one of the following groups to examine how they are intricately involved in global trade.

a Ragpickers in India
b The Zabalee in Cairo
c E-waste processors in Guiyu, China

How has globalisation offered opportunities to these groups? What are the benefits and limitations that globalisation has offered these groups?

Learning Activity Two: Turning Japanese?

Globalisation is often seen as a recent phenomenon and it is frequently associated with the loss of local identity and the export of an American culture. It is often helpful to look to smaller-scale social trends and movements when examining this claim. Through desk research examine the development of Japanese hip-hop and consider the claims made that globalisation merely reproduces a dominant American culture. You may wish to read McAuley (2004) to review the emergence of globalisation.

11.10 Further Reading

Trentmann, F. (2009) 'Crossing divides: Consumption and globalization in history', *Journal of Consumer Culture*, 9(2): 187–220.

Trentmann documents the long history of trade between nations. He points out that we should not consider the process of international or global trade as being one of relations between a core of industrial nations and a periphery. Instead, we should attend more closely to the historical record to see how the so-called periphery has had an important role in trade networks for some considerable time.

Böhm, S. and Brei, V. (2008) 'Marketing the hegemony of development: Of pulp fictions and green deserts', *Marketing Theory*, 8(4): 339–66.

In this paper, Böhm and Brei highlight the contested nature of what constitutes 'development' for 'less developed countries'. They document the important role of marketing communications in disseminating a particular worldview which is then contested by actors in Civil Society.

Laczniak, G.R. and Murphy, P.E. (2006) 'Normative perspectives for ethical and socially responsible marketing', *Journal of Macromarketing*, 26(2): 154–77.

Taking a normative orientation, these authors outline a series of propositions about how we can improve ethical practice in marketing.

Grein, A.F. and Gould, S.J. (2007) 'Voluntary codes of ethical conduct: Group membership salience and globally integrated marketing communications perspectives', *Journal of Macromarketing*, 27(3): 289–302.

Companies have often been accused of sanitising their own activities. In other words, they produce and then refer to codes of ethics in the face of public criticism. Grein and Gould discuss some of these ideas and debates via case studies of the sports shoe manufacturer, Nike and the toy company, Mattel. The limitations of codes of conduct are outlined.

Nason, R.W. (2008) 'Structuring the global marketplace: The impact of the United Nations Global Compact', *Journal of Macromarketing*, 28(4): 418–25.

Building upon the previous paper, Nason examines the United Nations Global Compact as a means for encouraging companies to act responsibly in the world. Irrespective of the government and corporate support for this initiative, Nason is not convinced at present that it can affect any real change in the structuring of the world economy along more socially responsible lines.

11.11 References

Apple, R.W. Jr. (1990) 'Confrontation in the Gulf; Bush says Iraqi aggression threatens "our way of life"', *The New York Times*, accessed 24 March 2009.

Applbaum, K. (2000) 'Crossing borders: Globalization as myth and charter in American transnational consumer marketing', *American Ethnologist*, 27 (2): 257–82.

Arnould, E. (2007) 'Should consumer citizens escape the market?', *The Annals of the American Academy of Political and Social Science*, 611 (1): 96–111.

Asgary, A. and Walle, A.H. (2002) 'The cultural impact of globalization: Economic activity and social change', *Cross Cultural Management*, 9 (3): 58–75.

Askegaard, S. (2006) 'Brands as global ideoscape', in J.E. Schroeder and M. Salzer-Mörling (eds), *Brand Culture*, pp. 91–102. London: Routledge.

Batra, R., Ramaswamy, V., Alden, D.L., Steenkamp, J-B E.M. and Ramachander, S. (2000) 'Effects of brand local and nonlocal origin on consumer attitudes in developing countries', *Journal of Consumer Psychology*, 9 (2): 83–95.

Bauman, Z. (1988) 'Sociology after the Holocaust', *British Journal of Sociology*, 39 (4): 469–97.

Bauman, Z. (1991) 'The social manipulation of morality: Moralizing actors, adiaphorizing action', *Theory, Culture and Society*, 8: 137–51.

Bauman, Z. (2007) 'Collateral casualties of consumerism', *Journal of Consumer Culture*, 7 (1): 25–56.

Beck, U. (2008) 'Reframing power in the globalized world', *Organization Studies*, 29 (5): 793–804.

Bhattacharya, A.K. and Michael, D.C. (2008) 'How local companies keep multinationals at bay', *Harvard Business Review*, (March): 85–95.

Cayla, J. and Arnould, E.J. (2008) 'A cultural approach to branding in the global marketplace', *Journal of International Marketing*, 16 (4): 86–112.

Cayla, J. and Eckhardt, G.M. (2008) 'Asian brands and the shaping of a transnational imagined community', *Journal of Consumer Research*, 35(August): 216–30.

Cova, B. (1996) 'Community and consumption: Toward the definition of the "linking value" of products or services', *European Journal of Marketing*, 31 (3/4): 297–316.

Cronin, A.M. (2004) 'Currencies of commercial exchange: Advertising agendas and the promotional imperative', *Journal of Consumer Culture*, 4: 339–60.

Dobscha, S. and Ozanne, J.L. (2008) 'An ecofeminist analysis of environmentally sensitive women using qualitative methodology: The emancipatory potential of an ecological life', in M. Tadajewski and D. Brownlie (eds), *Critical Marketing: Issues in Contemporary Marketing*, pp. 271–301. Chichester: Wiley.

Douglas, M. and Isherwood, B. (1979) *The World of Goods: Towards An Anthropology of Consumption*. New York: Basic Books.

Drumwright, M.E. and Murphy, P.E. (2004) 'How advertising practitioners view ethics', *Journal of Advertising*, 33 (2): 7–24.

Drumwright, M.E. and Murphy, P.E. (2009) 'The current state of advertising ethics: Industry and academic perspectives', *Journal of Advertising*, 38 (1): 83–107.

Firat, A.F. (1997) 'Globalization of fragmentation – a framework for understanding contemporary global markets', *Journal of International Marketing*, 5 (2): 77–86.

George, S. (2001) 'Corporate globalisation', in E. Bircham and J. Charlton (eds), *AntiCapitalism: A Guide to the Movement*, pp. 11–24. London: Bookmarks Publications.

Gereffi, G. (1994) 'The organisation of buyer-driven global commodity chains: How U.S. retailers shape overseas production networks', in G. Gereffi and M. Korzeniewicz (eds), *Commodity Chains and Global Capitalism*, pp. 95–122. Westport: Praeger.

Giroux, H.A. (1993–1994) 'Consuming social change: The "United Colors of Benetton"', *Cultural Critique*, 26(Winter): 5–32.

Greenwald, R. (2005) *Wal-Mart: The High Cost of Low Price*. Tartan DVD.

Hackley, C. (2002) 'The panoptic role of advertising agencies', *Consumption, Markets and Culture*, 5 (3): 211–29.

Hackley, C. (2009) *Advertising and Promotion in Integrated Marketing Communication*, 2nd edn. London: Sage.

Held, D. and McGrew, A. (2007) *Globalization/Anti-Globalization: Beyond the Great Divide*. Cambridge: Polity.

Holbrook, M.B. (1987) 'Mirror, mirror, on the wall, what's unfair in the reflections on advertising?', *Journal of Marketing*, 51(July): 95–103.

Holt, D.B., Quelch, J.A. and Taylor, E.L. (2004) 'How global brands compete', *Harvard Business Review*, (September): 68–75.

Jack, G. and Westwood, R. (2009) *International and Cross-Cultural Management Studies*. Basingstoke: Palgrave Macmillan.

Jhally, S. (1993) 'Commercial culture, collective values, and the future', *Texas Law Review*, 71: 805–14.

Karnani, A. (2007) 'The mirage of marketing to the bottom of the pyramid: How the private sector can help alleviate poverty', *California Management Review*, 49 (4): 90–111.

Kilbourne, W.E. (2004) 'Globalization and development: An expanded macromarketing view', *Journal of Macromarketing*, 24 (2): 122–35.

Klein, N. (2000) *No Logo*. London: Flamingo.

Kline, S. (1995) 'The play of the market: On the internationalization of children's culture', *Theory, culture and Society*, 12: 103–29.

Laczniak, G.R. and Murphy, P.E. (2006) 'Marketing, consumers and technology: Perspectives for enhancing ethical transactions', *Business Ethics Quarterly*, 16 (3): 313–21.

Levitt, T. (1960) 'Marketing myopia', *Harvard Business Review*, 38 (4): 45–56.

Levitt, T. (1983) 'The globalization of markets', *Harvard Business Review*, May–June: 92–102.

Light, D.W. (2007) 'Globalizing restricted and segmented markets: Challenges to theory and value in economic sociology', *The Annals of the American Academy of Political and Social Science*, 610(March): 232–45.

Lindridge, A.M. and Wang, C. (2008) 'Saving "face" in China: Modernization, parental pressure, and plastic surgery', *Journal of Consumer Behaviour*, 7(December): 496–508.

McAuley, A. (2004) 'Seeking (marketing) virtue in globalisation', *The Marketing Review*, 4: 253–66.

Mills, M.B. (1997) 'Contesting the margins of modernity: Women, migration and consumption in Thailand', *American Ethnologist*, 24 (1): 37–61.

Nill, A. (2003) 'Global marketing ethics: A communicative approach', *Journal of Macromarketing*, 23(2): 90–104.

Pitta, D.A., Guesalaga, R. and Marshall, P. (2008) 'The quest for the fortune at the bottom of the pyramid: Potential and challenges', *Journal of Consumer Marketing*, 25 (7): 393–401.

Pollay, R.W. (1986) 'The distorted mirror: Reflections on the unintended consequences of advertising', *Journal of Marketing*, 50(2): 18–36.

Pollay, R.W. (1987) 'On the value of reflections on the values in "The distorted mirror"', *Journal of Marketing*, 51(July): 104–9.

Prahalad, C.K. and Hammond, A. (2002) 'Serving the world's poor, profitably', *Harvard Business Review*, (September): 48–57.

Quelch, J. (2003) 'The return of the global brand', *Harvard Business Review*, (August): 22–3.

Schor, J. (2008) 'Tackling turbo consumption', *Cultural Studies*, 22 (5): 588–98.

Schudson, M. (2007) 'Citizens, consumers, and the Good Society', *The Annals of the American Academy of Political and Social Science*, 611(May): 236–49.

Scitovsky, T. (1992) *The Joyless Economy: The Psychology of Human Satisfaction*. New York: Oxford University Press.

Shultz, C.J. and Holbrook, M.B. (1999) 'Marketing and the tragedy of the commons: A synthesis, commentary and analysis for action', *Journal of Public Policy and Marketing*, 18(2): 218–29.

The Economist (2001a) 'The case for brands', *The Economist*, 360 (8238): 11.

The Economist (2001b) 'Who's wearing the trousers?', *The Economist*, 360 (8238): 26–8.

Üstüner, T. and Holt, D.B. (2008) 'Dominated consumer acculturation: The social construction of poor migrant women's consumer identity projects in a Turkish squatter', *Journal of Consumer Research*, 34(June): 41–56.

Varman, R. and Belk, R.W. (2008) 'Weaving a web: Subaltern consumers, rising consumer culture, and television', *Marketing Theory*, 8(3): 227–52.

Venkatesh, A. (1994) 'Business beyond modernity: Some emerging themes', *Organization*, 1(1): 19–23.

Wernick, A. (1991) 'Global promo: The cultural triumph of exchange', *Theory, Culture and Society*, 8: 89–109.

Wilk, R. (2001) 'Consuming morality', *Journal of Consumer Culture*, 1 (2): 245–60.

Witkowski, T. (2007) 'Food marketing and obesity in developing countries: Analysis, ethics and public policy', *Journal of Macromarketing*, 27 (2): 126–37.

Glossary

Agency 'Agency' is derived from 'agent', or an actor who exercises some control over the world. It is a word which has become fashionable in sociology and political science in recent decades because of the decline of popular faith in big government and global business. Scholars often speak of how public citizens or the non-political elite can exercise 'agency' over democratic and non-democratic processes of government in order to effect grassroots change. The word is sometimes contrasted with 'structure', or the institutions which act either to enable or hinder 'agency'. The structure/agency debate is an ongoing one in academic circles and one can take sides depending on how one regards the balance of power between individuals and the larger, socio-economic and political structures which operate in society.

Alienation A term used by different thinkers to refer to the separation of individuals from their humanity and innate creativity. For Karl Marx, the capitalist labour process created the conditions for different forms of alienation: the separation of the worker from their work through the external ownership, control, and direction of the labour process; the separation of individuals from each other through competition in the labour market; and the inability of the individual to express their innate creativity through an eternally controlled work process.

Carnivalesque The carnivalesque – derived from 'carnival' – was made famous by Mikhail Bakhtin (1895–1975), a Russian intellectual who lived through some of the most significant events of the twentieth century, including the Russian Revolution, the excitement of the 1920s, Stalinism, the Cold War and the beginnings of the dissolution of Communism. Bakhtin first used the word in his book, *Rabelais and His World,* translated into English in 1968. For Bakhtin, the carnivalesque personifies the joyful and uninhibited acceptance of the body and of an aesthetic which celebrates affirmation and freedom, even anarchy.

Civil Society The concept of a 'civil society' has a long history. In the twenty-first century, political scientists, sociologists, politicians and journalists have taken up the term and used it to refer to societal arrangements which reflect the collective will or desire on the part of a people for a democratic, open and communal society or world. With the fall of the Berlin Wall and communism in many parts of the world, it has come to mean a radical alternative – the voice of the people or many peoples united in the vision for a fairer society -to dictatorial regimes and politicised agendas which exclude or oppress large sectors of society.

Citizenship The idea of the citizen is associated with membership of a political community. Citizenship confers a sense of identity and belonging to the individual along with rights and duties that arise with membership. The relatively free movement of economic trade and digital media across national borders has been coupled with movements of people, particularly from poorer to wealthier countries. Governments, in an attempt to control migration and also to promote a sense of national identity, have used citizenship as part of a divisive policy to judge who is allowed to belong to the political community.

Commodification This describes the process by which goods, services and, increasingly, ideas are produced for, and subsequently bought and sold in, a 'market'. This market may be a literal physical space or a much more intangible, even metaphoric, trading arena. Thus organisations like consultants, advertising agencies, professional associations and universities can be argued to be trading in various forms of commodified knowledge.

Conspicuous Consumption Thorstein Veblen (1899) coined the term 'conspicuous consumption' to refer to the purchase of objects and a kind of consumer behaviour which signals to others that one belongs to a certain privileged class. Although other scholars had written about the phenomenon before him, conspicuous consumption had not, up till then, attracted the attention of economists because it was felt that the macro-social effects of such consumption were impossible to measure. Few people today would admit to such behaviour, but Veblen noticed that its effects on society as a whole at the turn of the nineteenth century were deleterious. A key aspect of conspicuous consumption is that it should be seen as extravagant and wasteful, thus denoting extreme wealth on the part of those indulging in it.

Culture The creation and use of symbols and artefacts by people. Culture can be seen as 'a way of life' for a society, including norms of behaviour, manners, rituals, dress, language and systems of belief. People are 'acted on' by culture and act on culture: in this way they can generate new cultural forms and meanings. Cultures are thus characterised by their historical nature, relativity and diversity, and undergo change alongside the economic, political and social components of society.

Cultural Intermediaries A term often associated with French sociologist Pierre Bourdieu in his book *Distinction*. He was referring to the emergence of a 'new petite bourgeoisie' in France of marketers, designers, advertisers and public relations specialists whose task was the production and distribution of symbolic goods and services. Cultural intermediaries have a central role in the reproduction of aspirational lifestyles and associated ideas of what is cool.

Culture Jamming/Jammers Culture jammers are groups of people who want to encourage consumers to think more critically about the consumer society in which they live, and to 'de-cool' marketing and advertising. Culture jamming refers to different tactics and processes for achieving this goal including defacing billboards or online ads, or producing satirical and subversive counter ads.

Determinism The idea that all actions and events are governed by causal laws. Determinism is predicated on a belief that future events are necessitated by past and present events.

Dramaturgy An approach to sociological analysis in which the theatre is treated as an analogy for everyday life. Social action is viewed as a 'performance' in which actors (people) play parts and stage-manage their actions in an attempt to manage the impressions they make on other people. Social actors can cooperate as members of teams or organisations in order to maintain a 'front' while they hide from view the 'back-stage' processes of social relations.

Epistemology Epistemology is the branch of philosophy that examines issues relating to knowledge, that is, it is concerned with how we can ever claim to possess knowledge, what criteria we use to determine the status of knowledge and when ultimately, we would hope, our beliefs can be corroborated and certified by members of our social and academic community.

Emic An emic approach involves the consumer researcher listening to the respondent's own understanding of any given behaviour and during analysis and reporting, staying as close to the language and terminology employed by the respondent as possible.

Etic An etic approach refers to a research project that involves a consumer or marketing researcher using some theoretical perspective as a means to interpret a respondent's behaviour or actions.

False Consciousness The Marxist thesis that material and institutional processes in capitalist society mislead the proletariat, subaltern groups and other classes. These processes betray the true relations of forces between those classes, and the real state of affairs under capitalism. The resulting condition of false consciousness is essentially explained as a result of ideological control (see ideology).

Grand Narrative Regarded as characteristic of modernity, grand narratives are usually self-legitimating and purport to be a comprehensive explanation of historical experience or knowledge. The grand narrative is usually a 'totalising' ideological system (e.g. religious fundamentalism or patriarchy). The narrative is 'grand' in that it is a story *about* a story, encompassing and explaining other 'little stories' within totalising schemes.

Habitus A term introduced in the work of French sociologist Pierre Bourdieu in his book *Distinction*. It refers to a set of intellectual and emotional dispositions – values, attitudes, feelings and worldviews – that individuals acquire during primary processes of socialisation in the family and through education systems. For Bourdieu, social class is reproduced and transmitted through the habitus. It structures our subjective tastes and preferences, and enables us to make judgments about the tastes and preferences of others. The habitus is not fixed, but will adapt over our life cycle.

Homo Economicus The concept from economic theory of people as rational and broadly self-interested actors who have the ability to make judgments towards their subjectively defined ends. The term was used for the first time in the late nineteenth century by critics of John Stuart Mill's work on political economy, although it is often associated with the ideas of eighteenth century thinkers like Adam Smith and David Ricardo. The concept of Economic Man has since led to rational choice theory and taken on the specific meaning of a person who acts rationally on complete knowledge out of self-interest and the desire for material gain.

Hyperreality Hyperreality is found in branches of study like semiotics and postmodern philosophy and is closely related to words like 'simulacra'. The 'hyperreal' literally means that which is 'more than real' or 'more real than real', a state where the 'real' is indistinguishable from 'fantasy' or artifice. In a world dominated by the image, the internet and other technologies of virtual reality, scholars have argued that the hyperreal now substitutes for reality, so that many consumers today can experience feelings, emotions and events without having to undergo those actual experiences themselves.

Hypothesis A proposed explanation for an observable phenomenon. Usually based on a theory it is a tentative conjecture explaining an observation, phenomenon or scientific problem that can be tested by further observation, investigation or experimentation.

Identity An individual's sense of 'self'. Some scholars view the development of identity as a process driven by social structures and characterised by continuity and coherence; whereas others see it as much more fluid. Thus a social constructionist might argue that identity is constructed (and re-constructed) out of the many 'big' discourses culturally available to people, such as those offering a different notion of what it means to be educated, Muslim, entrepreneurial, fashionable, etc. These discourses are constantly 'at work' in helping to produce a person's identity.

Ideology A belief system or worldview. A coherent structure of thinking which obscures incongruous elements in order to uphold a particular social order.

Individualism Individualism refers to social and political ideas that emphasise the importance of the individual in our understanding and organisation of society. The promotion of individualism has been a key political objective for neo-liberal economic and social policies in recent decades. It is usually contrasted with collectivism where the concern and interests of the collective is prioritised over the interests of individual. The encouragement for individuals to enjoy the freedom to consume goods privately has led some social commentators (e.g. Zygmunt Bauman, 2007) to suggest that society and the experience of life has become increasingly fragmented.

Induction Induction is usually discussed in relation to the respective works of David Hume and Karl Popper. Essentially what Hume was concerned with was answering the question, how can we be justified in asserting that because we have observed a limited number of examples of black Ravens (the bird), that all Ravens are black. What we have here is a move from a specific number of examples to a general statement. Early marketing scholars were interested in producing generalisable knowledge. They wanted to move beyond specific examples to produce general statements about market relations that could be extrapolated to other contexts. The problem with induction is that we can never have full knowledge of all available empirical examples.

Institution A structure, organisation or process involved in the creation, maintenance and reproduction of social order. Institutions exert control and authority on individual conduct and action in society. Institutions include entities such as the law, the military, the media, and education.

Langue and parole These terms come from the field of linguistics. They distinguish between language as a socially established system of linguistic units such as words and grammatical rules (i.e. langue); and as actually produced 'everyday' speech (i.e. parole). The former term emphasises the structural relations of language, while the latter recognises that language and meaning is constantly changing as a result of language in use.

Legitimise The way that certain activities or ideas become legitimate ('legal'). It is the process of making something acceptable. Some social critics would argue that advertising legitimises certain activities that it might be best not to legitimise. For example depicting alcoholic products and consumers in a positive and normal way, and by showing that drinking alcohol is a normal and acceptable activity to undertake.

McDonaldization Refers both to a phenomenon and the title of a book, *The McDonaldization of Society* (1993)

by George Ritzer. Ritzer popularised the notion of a world where products and services conformed to a certain standard 'look and feel' in a globalised world, in the same way that a McDonald's burger looks and tastes exactly the same wherever in the world one happens to eat them. McDonaldization has, thus, become a byword for assembly-line products lacking in 'local' flavour and culture and is, therefore, used pejoratively by many academics.

Methodology The study and analysis of the principles, procedures and theories of inquiry in a discipline. It includes the analysis of particular methods as well as ontological or epistemological considerations.

Morality Morality is a concern with the question of what are considered to be good and bad forms of thinking and behaving within a society. It is an ambiguous term that overlaps with, but also informs, social etiquette, law and religion. Morality can be used descriptively to refer to the code of conduct which guides an individual or a group of individuals, or it can be used normatively to indicate what conduct ought to be followed in a given situation.

Normative Something that is based on norms. Norms are rules or standards that regulate behaviours in a social setting. They acknowledge that an ordered social life is dependent on a large number of shared expectations and obligations. It is widely thought that normative prescriptions function at all levels of society, from an individual consumer's appropriate behaviour in a retail environment, to the formation of legal systems to regulate trade between firms and indeed nations.

Ontology Ontology is concerned with being, that is, with the issue of existence and whether or not we can really understand reality.

Paradigm A paradigm provides a way of thinking about, researching and understanding the social world.

Philanthropy Philanthropy refers to the act of giving large sums of money or gifts to charitable organisations.

Positivism A term widely used in marketing and consumer research and beyond to describe research practices that seek to employ principles from the natural sciences to understand social phenomena. Positivism is closely linked to empiricism, in which the only legitimate form of knowledge is that which can be grounded in sensory experience. Positivism tends to prioritise scientific methods of data collection and analysis and seeks to establish likely truths from likely falsehoods through the use of hypothesis testing and the systematic application of statistics. In marketing and consumer research positivism tends to be contrasted with interpretivism.

Postmodernism Sometimes described as the cultural logic of late capitalism, postmodernism is not simply a stage after modernism, but rather, in the terminology of French philosopher Jean-Francois Lyotard, postmodernism is an impulse to deconstruct totalising systems of knowledge, meaning or belief such as religions, grand political theories such as capitalism or communism, or nationalisms, or humanist theories of identity (see Grand Narrative). For Lyotard, the postmodern condition is that of living without such systems or myths and for Jacques Derrida it is about celebrating this advent of an open future and the fragmentation of identities.

Poststructuralism Along with its close associate postmodernism, poststructuralism is a ubiquitous but contested term that is generally seen as an extension and critical response to the assumptions and scientific methods of structuralism. Poststructuralism has its origins in literary criticism and cultural analysis, and the term is usually employed to provide a convenient label for the diverse work of theorists such as Jacques Derrida, Roland Barthes and Michel Foucault. Poststructuralists have extended Saussure's theory of signifiers and signified to suggest that the sign does not need to be anchored to a non-linguistic referent. In the process the authority of the author and the stability of meaning within speech and the written word ('texts') become subject to debate and negotiation.

Psychoanalysis The body of ideas developed by Sigmund Freud, otherwise known as the 'father of modern psychoanalysis'. It has attracted fierce devotion and rabid criticism, in equal measure, due both to the nature of its subject matter and Freud's own unique methods. Although there are many psychoanalytic schools of thought, Freudian theories of sexuality and human behaviour remain the most famous and controversial. In psychoanalysis, the patient is encouraged to verbalise thoughts, dreams and associations which the analyst interprets as symptoms of unconscious drives – the 'death wish', 'the Oedipal complex' and so on – which can then be brought to the surface to be resolved.

Realism In the most general sense of the term refers to a philosophical claim that the physical world (objects and materials for example) exists independently of anyone perceiving it. It is often contrasted with relativism. There are many different variations of realism, including critical realism – that at least some of our sensory perception accurately represents reality, and scientific realism – that science can reveal knowledge about the real world.

Relativism A philosophical view that truths are relative rather than absolute. From a relativist perspective there is no one truthful or authoritative meaning or reading (of an advertisement for example) but rather multiple and varied meanings which might depend on a particular perspective, background and expectation.

Semiotics Simply put, it is the study of signs. More fundamentally, semiotics is the art and science of decoding sign-systems and symbolic structures which shape our view of 'reality' and how the world works, from the study of body language, for instance, to advertising, fashion, food and all other manifestations of popular culture. Some of the famous theorists with whom the word is associated include Mikhail Bakhtin, Roland Barthes, Ferdinand de Saussure, Umberto Eco and Claude Levi-Strauss. Semiotics has influenced a wide range of fields, including psychoanalysis, anthropology, media studies and consumer culture.

Sense-making Sense-making is a retrospective social process of rationally constructing reality from informational cues in order for social actors to make decisions and undertake actions. Sense-making involves the study of language, talk and communication. It is a theory usually associated with the work of Karl Weick (1995) who uses the framework of sense-making to examine the processes through which members of organisations construct meaning from the ambiguous and emergent information around them. He argues that through the interplay of bracketing, labelling and retrospection, the chaotic and complex flows of informational cues are given meaning. We literally organise reality through the spoken and written language we employ and deploy.

Simulacra Conventionally, simulation and simulacra mean 'in the likeness of (something)', that is, they are a kind of second-order reality which is dependent on an 'original' meaning or thing. The philosopher and cultural theorist, Jean Baudrillard, however, revolutionised their meanings by insisting that simulacra now stood in place of the 'real'. In his typically subversive style, he argues that 'simulacra is never that which conceals the truth – it is the truth which conceals that there is none'. In other words, the 'truth' of appearances and images can only be found in surfaces: the real is the Image.

Social constructionism A view in which social reality is seen as something that is created (constructed) within and by social groups. Rather than seeing reality as something that is fixed, external and in some way essential, constructivists tend to view reality as an emergent, fluid and socially contingent phenomenon.

Structuralism A theoretical approach which assumes that culture can be understood as a complex system of signs operating as part of a deep underlying structure. Consumer researchers might use structuralism to describe the fashion system for example, in which the meanings of different styles, colours and 'looks' operate as a complex cultural structure. Structuralists often choose to understand social practices as text or discourse. We might say that we use fashion like a kind of language, to tell a story about ourselves to others.

Structure That which makes up the social world. In marketing theory discussions about structure normally refer to social structure which describes how institutions and norms shape and determine behaviour. Structure is often contrasted with agency.

Subculture A culture within a culture. A subculture is a group of people that exhibit a particular set of values, norms and behaviours that mark them out as different from the wider culture or society they inhabit. Subcultures could be anything from youth culture, punks and rock fans, to Harley Davison owners, rave-goers and online communities.

State The state is a set of governing institutions. Modern nation states are often characterised by the presence of various forms of government, political institutions and bureaucracy. In marketing and business theory, the state is often contrasted with the free market, leading to questions such as how much state intervention in the market is legitimate, necessary or appropriate.

Truth effects Presupposes the notion of a 'general politics of truth' which Michel Foucault first proposed that each society possesses. That is, the types of discourse it accepts and makes function as true. Truth effects are normally regarded as being 'staged'. This refers to a) performative and other techniques which can be mobilised in order to generate true as opposed to false statements; b) how true and false are sanctioned and c) the status given to those who speak that which is recognised as true ('truth-tellers').

Index

Research Methods Books from SAGE

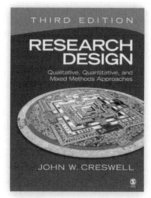

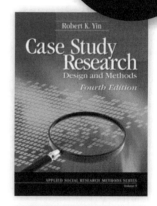

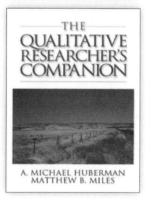

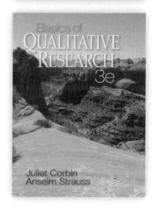

www.sagepub.co.uk

SAGE

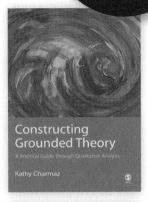

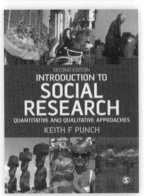
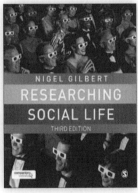

The Qualitative Research Kit

Edited by Uwe Flick

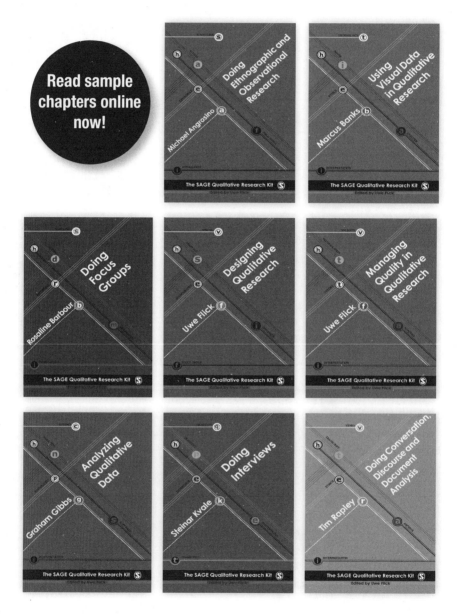

Read sample chapters online now!

Doing Ethnographic and Observational Research — Michael Angrosino — The SAGE Qualitative Research Kit — Edited by Uwe Flick

Using Visual Data in Qualitative Research — Marcus Banks — The SAGE Qualitative Research Kit — Edited by Uwe Flick

Doing Focus Groups — Rosaline Barbour — The SAGE Qualitative Research Kit

Designing Qualitative Research — Uwe Flick — The SAGE Qualitative Research Kit — Edited by Uwe Flick

Managing Quality in Qualitative Research — Uwe Flick — The SAGE Qualitative Research Kit — Edited by Uwe Flick

Analyzing Qualitative Data — Graham Gibbs — The SAGE Qualitative Research Kit — Edited by Uwe Flick

Doing Interviews — Steinar Kvale — The SAGE Qualitative Research Kit

Doing Conversation, Discourse and Document Analysis — Tim Rapley — The SAGE Qualitative Research Kit — Edited by Uwe Flick

www.sagepub.co.uk